The Joan Palevsky  Imprint in Classical Literature

In honor of beloved Virgil—

"O degli altri poeti onore e lume..."

—Dante, *Inferno*

The publisher and the University of California Press Foundation
gratefully acknowledge the generous support of the Joan
Palevsky Imprint in Classical Literature.

The Music of Tragedy

# The Music of Tragedy

*Performance and Imagination in Euripidean Theater*

Naomi A. Weiss

UNIVERSITY OF CALIFORNIA PRESS

University of California Press, one of the most distinguished university presses in the United States, enriches lives around the world by advancing scholarship in the humanities, social sciences, and natural sciences. Its activities are supported by the UC Press Foundation and by philanthropic contributions from individuals and institutions. For more information, visit www.ucpress.edu.

University of California Press
Oakland, California

© 2018 by The Regents of the University of California
First Paperback Printing 2024 | ISBN 9780520401440 (pbk)

Library of Congress Cataloging-in-Publication Data

Names: Weiss, Naomi A., author.
Title: The music of tragedy : performance and imagination in Euripidean theater / Naomi A. Weiss.
Description: Oakland, California : University of California Press, [2017] | Includes bibliographical references and index.
Identifiers: LCCN 2017029449 (print) | LCCN 2017034384 (ebook) |
    ISBN 9780520968493 () | ISBN 9780520295902 (cloth)
Subjects: LCSH: Euripides—Criticism and interpretation. | Greek drama (Tragedy)—History and criticism. | Music, Greek and Roman—History and criticism.
Classification: LCC PA3978 (ebook) | LCC PA3978 .W43 2017 (print) | DDC 882/.01—dc23
LC record available at *https://lccn.loc.gov/2017029449*

25  24
10  9  8  7  6  5  4  3  2  1

*For Nigel and Judy Weiss*

CONTENTS

Acknowledgments ix
Abbreviations xi
Note on Editions and Translations xiii

    Introduction: In Search of Tragedy's Music      1

1. Words, Music, and Dance in Archaic Lyric and Classical Tragedy      23
       Before Tragedy: Imaginative Suggestion in Archaic Choral Lyric      25
       Metamusical Play in Aeschylus, Sophocles, and Early Euripides      36

2. Chorus, Character, and Plot in *Electra*      59
       Electra and the Chorus      61
       Performed Ecphrasis      75
       Choral Anticipation and Enactment      91

3. Musical Absence in *Trojan Women*      100
       The Paradox of Absent Choreia      104
       New Songs and Past Performances      116
       Performing the Fall of Troy      130

4. Protean Singers and the Shaping of Narrative in *Helen*      140
       Birdsong and Lament      144
       New Music      167
       Travel and Epiphany      179

5. From *Choreia* to Monody in *Iphigenia in Aulis*   191
   *Spectatorship, Enactment, and Desire*   193
   *Past and Present Mousikē*   204
   *Choreia and Monody*   224

Conclusion: Euripides' Musical Innovations   233

*Works Cited*   247
*General Index*   267
*Index Locorum*   277

ACKNOWLEDGMENTS

This book would not have been possible without the support of many teachers, colleagues, friends, and family. It began as a PhD dissertation in the Department of Classics at the University of California, Berkeley, co-directed by Mark Griffith and Leslie Kurke. I owe a huge amount to that vibrant community, where I learned so much.

When I first arrived at UC Berkeley as a graduate student, I did not yet know that my interests in Greek drama would take a musical turn. It was thanks to Mark Griffith that I began to think of tragedy in terms of performance rather than just text, and it was as a result of his seminar on the Electra plays in 2009 that I became excited about the various musical images at play in Euripides' work. Mark has been incredibly generous and supportive ever since, and his extensive feedback on every part of this project has left me astonished at the depth and range of his knowledge and intellectual curiosity.

I also owe special thanks to Leslie Kurke, who has shaped how I read and think in fundamental ways. Every conversation with her has significantly improved this book and my scholarship more generally. She has been an extraordinary teacher, critic, and friend.

I have been very fortunate in my other mentors as well. As time goes by, my debt to Donald Mastronarde grows ever greater. His teaching and meticulous reading of my work has made me a better scholar. Anastasia-Erasmia Peponi allowed me to join her seminars on Greek *mousikē* and aesthetics at Stanford University, which made me think much more deeply about the musical imaginary and its relationship to live performance. Her comments on my work, both encouraging and critical, have helped me to articulate the aims and focus of this project.

I gained much from the musicologist Richard Crocker, who over tea and biscuits repeatedly opened my ears to the musical notes and narratives of Greek texts. I wish Albert Henrichs could still be here for me to tell him quite how grateful I am for his inspiration and support.

It is a pleasure to thank here some of the other friends and colleagues who have helped me at various stages in this book's life. Armand D'Angour, who was once my teacher at Oxford, has continued to give vital feedback on my work over the years. Sarah Olsen has been a wonderful reader and friend, able to discuss *choreia* and babies at the same time. Zoa Alonso Fernández, Lauren Curtis, and Sarah McCallum have helped me produce a book out of the dissertation and been lovely companions along the way. Seán Curran has been a constant source of inspiration. My colleagues in the Department of the Classics at Harvard have provided much encouragement and advice. Pauline LeVen, Sheila Murnaghan, Tim Power, and Deborah Steiner have been helpful interlocutors. Eric Csapo and Peter Wilson made it possible for me to visit them in Sydney and provided much intellectual stimulation while I was there. I have benefited from comments on various chapter drafts from Jared Hudson, David Jacobson, Rachel Lesser, Virginia Lewis, Katharina Piechocki, Nicholas Watson, and Leah Whittington. Thanks also to Nadav Asraf, Paul Johnston, and Suzanne Paszkowski for their careful proofreading and help with the bibliography, and to Roberta Engleman for preparing the index.

I am very grateful to my editor at UC Press, Eric Schmidt, for his support, advocacy, and unfailingly sensible advice. Maeve Cornell-Taylor fielded my various questions with patience and kindness. Cindy Fulton, the project editor, has carefully steered the book toward publication. Paul Psoinos has been an exemplary copyeditor, painstakingly dealing with the various mistakes of a first-time author. The thoughtful and constructive reports of the three anonymous readers, as well as that of the Editorial Committee, have much improved the manuscript.

Finally, I give heartfelt thanks to my family. Isobel was born as I was finishing the dissertation; Oliver arrived as it was nearing completion as a book. Life with them is a tiring but very happy one, and they keep me sane and grounded within my world of Greek *mousikē*. Sam has stood by me every step of the way, from Oxford to Berkeley to Harvard, and kept me afloat with his unwavering love and support. It is difficult to express quite how grateful I am to my parents, Nigel and Judy Weiss, for educating me, valuing my work, and always asking interesting questions. I dedicate this book to them.

ABBREVIATIONS

Abbreviations of authors and works follow the *Oxford Classical Dictionary*, fourth edition, ed. S. Hornblower, A. Spawforth, and E. Eidinow (Oxford, 2012). Journal titles are abbreviated according to the conventions of *L'Année Philologique*. Additional abbreviations are listed below.

Dindorf        W. Dindorf, ed., *Aristides*, 3 vols. (Leipzig, 1829).
*FGrH*         F. Jacoby, ed., *Die Fragmente der griechischen Historiker* (Leiden, 1954–69).
KA             R. Kassel and C. Austin, eds., *Poetae comici Graeci* (Berlin and New York, 1983–).
*LIMC*         *Lexicon iconographicum mythologiae classicae* (Zurich, 1981–97).
LSJ            H. G. Liddell, R. Scott, H. Stuart Jones, R. McKenzie, and P. G. W. Glare, eds., *A Greek-English Lexicon*, 9th ed., with supplement (Oxford, 1996).
*PMG*          D. L. Page, ed., *Poetae melici Graeci* (Oxford, 1962).
*PMGF*         M. Davies, ed., *Poetarum melicorum Graecorum fragmenta*, vol. 1 (Oxford, 1991).
*POxy.*        *The Oxyrhynchus Papyri* (series published by the Egypt Exploration Society under different editors, Oxford, 1898–).
Rutherford     I. Rutherford, *Pindar's Paeans: A Reading of the Fragments with a Survey of the Genre* (Oxford, 2001).
*SLG*          D. L. Page, ed., *Supplementum lyricis Graecis* (Oxford, 1974).
SM             B. Snell and H. Maehler, eds., *Bacchylidis carmina cum fragmentis*, 10th ed. (Leipzig, 1970); OR

|  |  |
|---|---|
|  | B. Snell and H. Maehler, eds., *Pindarus*, vol. 2, *Fragmenta; Indices*, 4th ed. (Leipzig, 1975). |
| *TrGF* | B. Snell, R. Kannicht, and S. Radt, eds., *Tragicorum Graecorum fragmenta*, 5 vols. (Göttingen, 1971–2004). |
| Voigt | E. M. Voigt, ed., *Sappho et Alcaeus: Fragmenta* (Amsterdam, 1971). |
| W | M. L. West, ed., *Iambi et elegi Graeci*, 2 vols., 2nd ed. (Oxford, 1989–92). |
| Wehrli | F. von Wehrli, *Die Schule des Aristoteles*, 10 vols. with 2 supplements (Basel and Stuttgart, 1969). |

# NOTE ON EDITIONS AND TRANSLATIONS

Unless otherwise stated, I generally use the most recent Oxford Classical Texts for Greek authors, with the following exceptions: Kaibel 1887 for Athenaeus; Snell and Maehler 1992 for Bacchylides; Snell and Maehler 1987 for Pindar; Hubert 1971 for Plutarch. For fragments of tragedy I follow *TrGF* (Kannicht for Euripides; Radt for Aeschylus and Sophocles).

With one exception, noted in chapter 1, all translations are my own. They tend toward accuracy rather than elegance.

# Introduction

## In Search of Tragedy's Music

*Now that the genius of music has fled from tragedy, tragedy, strictly speaking, is dead.*
—FRIEDRICH NIETZSCHE, THE BIRTH OF TRAGEDY

Each spring in fifth-century Athens, thousands gathered for the performance of tragedy, one of the main events of the City Dionysia.[1] At the Theater of Dionysus, on the southern slope of the acropolis, three playwrights each presented a tetralogy, consisting of three tragedies and a satyr play. This was not simply a theatrical event: it was a musical one. Each tragedy featured, in addition to three actors, a chorus of twelve or fifteen Athenian citizens and their instrumental accompanist, the player of a double-reed pipe called the *aulos*.[2] Between intervals of speech and dialogue, the chorus would regularly sing and dance, often at some length, in the *orchēstra*, the large space between the wooden stage building (*skēnē*) and the audience.[3] Actors could sing and dance too, sometimes sharing in the chorus's performance, sometimes singing just a few exclamatory lyrics, sometimes—especially in Euripides' later plays—performing show-stopping arias of their own.[4]

---

1. The majority of plays by Aeschylus, Sophocles, and Euripides were first produced as part of the City Dionysia (or Great Dionysia), but tragedies were performed in Attica on other occasions and at other venues too: some were produced at the Lenaea, in late January, also (at least from ca. 440 B.C.E.) at the Theater of Dionysus; some in deme theaters as part of the Rural Dionysia. Dramatic competitions at the Anthesteria probably did not begin until the late fourth century B.C.E. On dramatic festivals in Athens and Attica, see esp. Pickard-Cambridge 1968: 1–125; Csapo and Slater 1995: 103–38.

2. Sophocles apparently increased the number of choreuts from twelve to fifteen: *Vit. Soph.* 4.

3. On the shape of the *orchēstra* in the fifth century (probably rectangular or trapezoidal) and the addition of the *skēnē* (which was certainly in use by the time of Euripides), see esp. Papastamati-von Moock 2015, with further bibliography.

4. On the structure of Greek tragedy, especially its mix of lyric and dialogue, see Mastronarde 2002: 74–80.

Greek tragedy, then, was musical theater. Yet many crucial questions about the role that *mousikē* (music, song, and dance) played in a tragic performance—its connection to the plot, its ability to define the characters of the protagonists, its effect on the audience's response to the tragedy as a whole—have been mostly unanswered in modern scholarship. Left with silent texts, it has been all too easy for us to neglect tragedy's musicality, particularly since we lack a comparable contemporary dramatic tradition in which music and dance play a regular part. Opera appears to be the closest parallel (and indeed much early opera attempted to recreate the music of classical tragedy), but it remains a rather different genre.[5] Perhaps Bollywood or even musical television dramas may provide slightly better comparanda for the particular mix of speech, song, and dance found in tragedy. But we still lack, at least in contemporary Western European and North American society, a song culture comparable to that of fifth-century Athens, where choral song and dance frequently occurred both within and outside the theater, and most citizens within the audience had previously been choral performers themselves.[6] It is therefore difficult for us to appreciate the musical resonance and impact of the *mousikē* that punctuates every tragedy, even though, for the Athenian audience, such song and dance, combined with the accompanying sound of the *aulos*, must have been one of the most memorable aspects of the live performance.

Aristophanes' *Frogs*, produced in 405 B.C.E., provides clear evidence that a late fifth-century audience saw *mousikē* as a central element of tragedy. The second half of this comedy is dominated by a long and brilliant showdown in Hades between the characters of Aeschylus and Euripides, with the god Dionysus as judge. After violently disagreeing on issues of language, characters, and theme, they move on to more technical matters: the forms of their respective prologues and, finally, their music. First Euripides performs a parody of Aeschylean choral lyric, highlighting its repetitive rhythms and ponderous language, and presumably also riffing on his melodic and choreographic styles, though these are harder to

---

5. One important difference is that the libretto in opera is often secondary to the music. As in musical theater, actors in opera also tend to be the primary singers, and audience members typically do not have experience of performing such music themselves. This is not to say, however, that all operas are equally dissimilar to tragedy: some, such as Glück's *Iphigénie en Tauride*, include ballet, and modern productions often involve contemporary dance; earlier forms of opera (up to and including Mozart and Verdi) more clearly distinguish between actors' arias and recitative. On dance in opera, see esp. Albright 2006; Connery and Steichen 2015. On attempts to revive the music of Greek tragedy in early opera, see esp. Zinar 1971; Hoxby 2005; Savage 2010.

6. On ancient Greek song culture and its connection with the Athenian audience's experience of tragedy, see Herington 1985: 3–5; Bacon 1994; Revermann 2006b. Peponi 2012: 4–6 also emphasizes the cultural inclusiveness of *mousikē* in archaic and classical Greece. On the likelihood that many citizens in the audience would themselves have performed in a Dionysiac chorus (dithyrambic or dramatic), see Gagné and Hopman 2013b: 26; Peponi 2013a: 212–13.

detect in the silent script that survives.[7] In response, Aeschylus brings out the younger tragedian's "Muse," a dancer with castanets called *krotala* (he calls her "that woman who beats with the potsherds"),[8] and proceeds to parody first Euripides' choral lyric and then his solo arias. Finally Dionysus tells them both to stop; he then weighs the playwrights' respective lines on scales before deciding that instead the two tragedians should each suggest one idea for the city's salvation.[9] Aeschylus ultimately wins, and the play ends with him about to make his way back to the world of the living. Pluto, king of the Underworld, instructs the chorus to escort Aeschylus, "celebrating him with his own tunes and songs."[10]

*Frogs* gives us evidence not simply for the prominence of *mousikē* within a tragedy but for its reception in fifth-century Athens: the particular features that audiences remembered (and comedians parodied) and the corresponding reputations for particular types of music that different tragedians developed as a result. It also points to the extraordinarily significant role this type of theater could play within Athens's self-identity and sense of stability: according to Dionysus, it is through a tragic poet that "the city may be saved and keep on celebrating choruses."[11] In Plato's *Laws*, written roughly fifty years later, we find a similar idea of tragedy as central to the city's construction: the Athenian stranger calls himself and his interlocutors, as lawmakers, "composers of a tragedy" and famously describes their *politeia* as "a mimesis of the most beautiful and fine life, which we say is really the truest tragedy."[12] In this dialogue Plato views tragedy in terms of choral song and dance—a totality called *choreia*, which he presents as vital to the city's social, ethical, and physical fabric. As Anastasia-Erasmia Peponi writes, *choreia* here "emerges as a most effective vehicle of communal discipline, solidity, and stability, promoting and reproducing established ideological doctrines from and for the entire dancing and singing community."[13]

But despite the importance of tragic *choreia* within the civic imaginary and the prominence of music performed by both the chorus and actors in fifth-century theater, subsequent critics of tragedy—at least until recently—have tended to focus elsewhere.[14] Writing a few decades after Plato, Aristotle, the foremost ancient

---

7. Cf. Griffith 2013a: 137.

8. ἡ τοῖς ὀστράκοις / αὕτη κροτοῦσα, Ar. *Ran.* 1305–6.

9. μίαν γνώμην ἑκάτερος εἴπατον / περὶ τῆς πόλεως, ἥντιν' ἔχετον σωτηρίαν, Ar. *Ran.* 1435–36.

10. τοῖσιν τούτου τοῦτον μέλεσιν / καὶ μολπαῖσιν κελαδοῦντες, Ar. *Ran.* 1526–27. For an analysis of this competition, especially the musical contest, see Griffith 2013a: 115–49.

11. ἡ πόλις σωθεῖσα τοὺς χοροὺς ἄγηι, Ar. *Ran.* 1419.

12. ἡμεῖς ἐσμὲν τραγῳδίας αὐτοὶ ποιηταί . . . πᾶσα οὖν ἡμῖν ἡ πολιτεία συνέστηκε μίμησις τοῦ καλλίστου καὶ ἀρίστου βίου, ὃ δὴ φαμεν ἡμεῖς γε ὄντως εἶναι τραγῳδίαν τὴν ἀληθεστάτην, Pl. *Leg.* 817b2–5.

13. Peponi 2013b: 23; cf. Wilson 2003.

14. Important exceptions are Kranz 1933: 113–266; Pintacuda 1978; Scott 1984, 1996a; Wilson 1999–2000; Csapo 1999–2000, 2008, 2009.

scholar of tragedy, sheds frustratingly little light on what *mousikē* does within a play. Though he only briefly refers to music in the *Poetics*, he does present it as an essential element of the genre: he defines tragedy as "the mimesis of an action that is serious, complete, and has magnitude, in language seasoned in distinct forms in its sections";[15] he then explains that "seasoned" (*hēdysmenos*) refers to "language that has rhythm and melody."[16] But he goes on to rank the musical element (*melopoiia*) as the second to last in his list of tragedy's constituent parts, after plot structure (*mythos*) or "arrangement of the actions," character, diction, and thought; following *melopoiia* comes spectacle (*opsis*).[17] The relegation of *melopoiia* to fifth place here may seem surprising, especially when compared with the considerable attention that he devotes to the potent, soul-changing effects of *mousikē* within education and leisure in general in the last book of the *Politics*.[18] His focus in the *Poetics*, however, is on the more cerebral aspects of tragedy rather than its performance, perhaps as a result of his equal admiration for Homeric epic as a form of *poiēsis*.[19]

In a later section Aristotle again refers to *melopoiia* as one of tragedy's "seasonings" (*hēdysmata*), using a metaphor that is commonly interpreted to imply mere embellishment of tragedy's other, more important elements.[20] Seasonings could actually be more important than we may at first assume: for a Middle Eastern meal in particular, they are absolutely crucial for giving meat a pleasing flavor.[21] In the context of tragedy, Aristotle's culinary metaphor of *hēdysmata* applies to the elements of tragedy that produce pleasure (*hēdonē*), which would be vital for a drama's success in the theater.[22] Nonetheless, Aristotle provides no other insight into how such seasonings may work with the other elements of tragedy or what function they

---

15. μίμησις πράξεως σπουδαίας καὶ τελείας μέγεθος ἐχούσης, ἡδυσμένωι λόγωι χωρὶς ἑκάστωι τῶν εἰδῶν ἐν τοῖς μορίοις, Arist. Poet. 1449b24–26.

16. λόγον τὸν ἔχοντα ῥυθμὸν καὶ ἁρμονίαν, Arist. Poet. 1449b28.

17. Arist. Poet. 1450a8–b20. The term *melopoiia* presumably includes dance, which Aristotle primarily sees in terms of rhythm: earlier in the *Poetics* he states that dancers represent character, emotions, and actions through "rhythms put into postures" (τῶν σχηματιζομένων ῥυθμῶν, 1447a26–28). Though he does not seem concerned with its visual aspect, we may also view dance within the category of *opsis*, which he ranks in sixth place.

18. Arist. Pol. 1339a11–1342b35, esp. 1339e43–1340b19.

19. Indeed he sees the power of tragedy as independent from its performance and actors (*Poet.* 1450b17–18), and states that the *mythos* should be structured in such a way that someone who merely hears the play, without actually seeing it performed, can still experience horror and pity (1453b3–6).

20. Arist. Poet. 1450b15–16.

21. Sifakis 2001: 56–70 argues that Aristotle uses the metaphor of *hēdysmata* to refer to essential ingredients of tragedy, since music is a form of ethical characterization.

22. At Poet. 1462a15–16 Aristotle explicitly states that *mousikē* and *opsis* produce the most vivid pleasures (τὴν μουσικὴν καὶ τὰς ὄψεις, δι' ἃς αἱ ἡδοναὶ συνίστανται ἐναργέστατα), though he goes on to claim that tragedy has such vividness in reading as well as performance.

may have within a drama as a whole. As Peponi notes, "the gap between the *Politics* and the *Poetics*, then, as far as the dramatic force of *melopoiia* ... is concerned, could have been bridged by a discussion of the way in which song and music affect the audience's cognitive and emotional experience of dramatic structure."[23]

The chorus is absent from Aristotle's references to *melopoiia*, and indeed hardly appears at all in the surviving text of the *Poetics*.[24] Given his general avoidance of the chorus's role, then, his statement in chapter 18 that it should be actively involved in the drama comes as quite a surprise, at least to the modern reader:

> καὶ τὸν χορὸν δὲ ἕνα δεῖ ὑπολαμβάνειν τῶν ὑποκριτῶν, καὶ μόριον εἶναι τοῦ ὅλου καὶ συναγωνίζεσθαι μὴ ὥσπερ Εὐριπίδηι ἀλλ' ὥσπερ Σοφοκλεῖ. τοῖς δὲ λοιποῖς τὰ ἀιδόμενα οὐδὲν μᾶλλον τοῦ μύθου ἢ ἄλλης τραγωιδίας ἐστίν· διὸ ἐμβόλιμα ἄιδουσιν πρώτου ἄρξαντος Ἀγάθωνος τοῦ τοιούτου. καίτοι τί διαφέρει ἢ ἐμβόλιμα ἄιδειν ἢ εἰ ῥῆσιν ἐξ ἄλλου εἰς ἄλλο ἁρμόττοι ἢ ἐπεισόδιον ὅλον;

> And the chorus should be understood as one of the actors, and should be part of the whole and participate in the action [of the play] along with [the actors], not as in Euripides but as in Sophocles. In the other poets the sung parts no more belong to the plot [*mythos*] than to another tragedy—hence they sing interlude odes [*embolima*], a practice that Agathon first started. And yet what is the difference between singing interlude odes and if one were to attach a speech or whole episode from one [work] to another? (Arist. *Poet.* 1456a25–31)

Here Aristotle seems to wish for the chorus to have an integral role, but he does not elaborate on the extent or nature of its lyrics' contribution to the *mythos*, not even within the Sophoclean scheme that he recommends.[25] This silence regarding the chorus's role in the *Poetics*, along with the description of the chorus as an "inactive attendant" in the pseudo-Aristotelian *Problems*, led to a common view of the chorus as marginal to a tragedy's action.[26] Moreover, as Aristotle makes no

---

23. Peponi 2013b: 25. It is possible that Aristotle expanded on this subject elsewhere, since in the *Politics* he refers to "[the work] on the art of poetry" (τὰ περὶ ποιητικῆς) for a discussion of *katharsis* as one of the functions of *mousikē* (1341b40). This may have been part of the second book of the *Poetics* or a lost portion of the *Politics*: see Halliwell 1986: 190–91; Kraut 1997: 209; Sifakis 2001: 54, 166 n. 1.

24. As Peponi 2013b: 24 notes, Aristotle's division of tragedy's quantitative elements (prologue, episode, exodus, *chorikon*) in terms of choral presence at *Poet.* 1452b13–24 could be read as an acknowledgment of the chorus's key role within tragedy or alternatively as a relegation of the chorus to "a mere punctuation device in the sequence of dramatic action." Some editors regard this section of the *Poetics* to be non-Aristotelian, or at least as representing a strand of thinking altogether different from the rest of the treatise: see Halliwell 1987: 121.

25. Cf. Halliwell 1986: 242: "the *Poetics* taken as a whole supplies no compelling reason for preferring a Sophoclean chorus to no chorus at all, and the passage at the end of ch. 18 is left suspended in something of a theoretical vacuum."

26. κηδευτὴς ἄπρακτος, ps.-Arist. *Prob.* 922b26. On this view of the chorus's marginality, see Foley 2003: 15–19.

reference back to his earlier comments on *melopoiia*, we are left wondering what his prescription here regarding the chorus's role within the drama may mean for its music: if the chorus is part of the whole, how should its music be related to the *mythos*?

## *MOUSIKĒ* AND *MYTHOS*

The question of the relationship between a tragedy's *mousikē* and *mythos* lies at the heart of this book, which focuses on the integration of musical imagery and choral performance within a group of plays from the last fifteen years of Euripides' career—that is, from around 420 B.C.E. until the posthumous production of *Iphigenia in Aulis* and *Bacchae* in 405. Traditionally, however, Euripides' tragic *mousikē*—by which I mean above all the singing and dancing of his choruses, along with their instrumental accompaniment—was thought to be increasingly irrelevant to the dramatic narrative. This view can in large part be traced back to the same passage of the *Poetics* that I discussed above (1456a25–31). Aristotle's preference for the chorus to be part of the whole apparently comes as a reaction against the recent trend of *embolima*—choral songs that are just "thrown in," without any particular relevance to the dramatic context. Although he attributes this practice to the younger poets, his remark "not as in Euripides but as in Sophocles" nevertheless suggests that Euripides' choruses, unlike those of Sophocles, tend not to be immediately engaged in the action of a play, or at least not in the right way.[27] Following Aristotle's brief comment here, it was often argued in nineteenth- and twentieth-century scholarship on tragedy that the chorus becomes more and more irrelevant in Euripides' plays and that several of the choral odes in his later work are representative of the sorts of *embolima* that Aristotle criticizes.[28] Euripides' tendency to compose choral songs that begin with only an indirect connection to the previous episode and that often include extensive mythic and narrative sections also causes his choruses to seem more withdrawn from the dramatic action.[29]

---

27. Cf. Neitzel 1967: 3: "Was der Philosoph kritisiert, ist nicht, daß der Chor nicht an der Handlung teilnehme, sondern *wie* er es tut" (emphasis original).

28. On increasing choral irrelevance in Euripides and his self-contained choral odes, see, e.g., Kranz 1933: 228–62, esp. 251–54; Helg 1950: 53–57; Pohlenz 1954: 440; Lesky 1971: 454; Panagl 1971; Rode 1971: 111–13. For a discussion of this traditional view, see Neitzel 1967: 5–7; Csapo 1999–2000: 406–9; Battezzato 2005a: 161, 164.

29. On such choral distance see Mastronarde 1998: 70–72; 1999: 98–99; cf. Rode 1971: 112. See also Mastronarde 2010: 126–45 on different types of nonimmediate connections between stasima and the surrounding drama. Euripides' preference for choruses of weak or dependent status (especially women) can also add to the sense of their marginality in terms of the action of the drama: see Castellani 1989: 4, 9–11; Mastronarde 1998: 61–66; 1999: 93–98. See also Gould 1996 on the otherness of the tragic chorus in general (and, for criticisms of this argument, Goldhill 1996). The gender of choruses does not always correlate with inactivity: see Foley 2003: 17.

The argument for increasing choral irrelevance became part of a narrative of gradual decline in the chorus's role and significance toward the end of the fifth century B.C.E. and into the fourth. From the mid-420s onward, fewer lines are assigned to the chorus, the stasima tend to be shorter, and actors' song begins to be more prominent instead as they become increasingly professional and specialized, in contrast to the more amateur chorus.[30] We can clearly see such a trend if we compare, for example, Aeschylus's *Suppliants* (the date of which has been much debated, but at the latest end is in the 460s) with Euripides' *Hecuba,* produced in the 420s:[31] in the older drama the chorus is the protagonist and sings more than half the lines; in the later one *choreia* and actors' song each take up a tenth of the entire play.[32] The absurd parodies of Euripidean monody in Aristophanes' *Frogs* also demonstrate that by 405 elaborate solo songs were a well-known feature of his tragedies.[33]

But the standard narrative of choral song steadily giving way to that of the actors is misleading, in part because, compared with a play like Aeschylus's *Suppliants,* the surviving work of both Euripides and Sophocles shows a much lower percentage of lyric overall, whether choral or solo. Although there is an uneven but steady rise in the amount of actors' song in Euripides' tragedies from the late 420s onward, these plays also show a slight increase in the total number of sung lines, so that the percentage of choral song does not significantly decrease as a result. Moreover, the sharp increase in the amount of *choreia* in *Bacchae* and *Iphigenia in Aulis*, produced a year after Euripides' death, cannot be explained away simply as part of his archaizing in Macedonia, particularly as the extraordinary focus on musicality in these plays suggests a continuance of his newer, more experimental tendencies no less than a return to traditionalism. It is also unlikely that Euripides was forced to rely less on highly skilled actors in Macedon and therefore focus more on the chorus: though professional choruses were probably available, Archelaus must have drawn to his city the great actors of the day too as he transformed it into a cultural center.[34] Finally, as we have already seen in the case of Plato's *Laws,* in the fourth century tragedy continued to be understood in

---

30. On these changes, see Csapo 1999–2000: 409–12; Hall 1999, 2002. An increase in lyrics assigned to actors is evident in Sophocles' work too, though his plays contain very little unmixed actors' song and recitative (as opposed to *amoibaion*-style delivery with the chorus).

31. Almost all scholars up until the 1960s regarded *Suppliants* as a very early work of Aeschylus. For a summary of the old view and the argument that it is in fact a later play, dated perhaps to the 460s B.C.E., see Lloyd-Jones 1964; Garvie 1969.

32. For percentages of choral and solo song in Euripides' plays, see Csapo 1999–2000: 410. The percentage of choral song in *Hecuba* increases to 15% if we include recitative verse.

33. Cf. Griffith 2013a: 140.

34. Cf. Csapo 1999–2000: 414–15. On tragic performances in Macedon, see Revermann 1999–2000, esp. 254–56; Duncan 2011.

terms of *choreia*.³⁵ However much limelight actors gained during this period, then, tragedy could still be viewed as an essentially choral genre.³⁶

Despite these problems with the narrative of choral decline, more recent scholarship on the *mousikē* of Euripides' tragedies has often perpetuated the assumption that *choreia* in his later work has little to do with the dramatic narrative. As we shall see in chapter 1, the surviving plays of Aeschylus and Sophocles contain numerous moments of metamusicality—that is, references to song and dance that engage with the live musical performance. Nevertheless, we find a marked explosion of musical language and imagery in Euripides' tragedies from the end of the fifth century, above all in his choral odes. Eric Csapo drew our attention to the (meta)musicality of Euripides' later work in two seminal articles on tragic *mousikē*.³⁷ As a result, Euripides' experimentation with different forms and images of *mousikē* is frequently viewed in terms of the so-called New Music—the umbrella term used by modern scholars to encompass the changes in musical style, language, and performance through the fifth century and into the fourth.³⁸ The New Music is usually linked above all to the dithyramb and kitharodic *nomos*, and the famous fragment from Pherecrates' comedy *Chiron* demonstrates that some of the figures most associated with musical change were indeed composers of these genres: the character Music lists the musicians who have ruined her with their excessive number of strings and increased modulation, starting with the dithyrambists Melanippides and Cinesias, and then complaining about the kitharodes Phrynis and (worst of all) Timotheus.³⁹ This musical movement also, however, flourished in other dramatic genres besides the dithyramb—in tragedy, satyr play, and comedy. The many references to *mousikē* in Euripides' later tragedies (along with the jibes at his new styles in Aristophanes' plays) suggest that he was at the forefront of this cultural movement in the late 400s.⁴⁰ But while Csapo's work has been a welcome prompt in directing us toward the performative aspects of Euripidean plays, it can continue a sense of the disengagement of tragic *mousikē* from its dramatic context by linking it primarily to extradramatic trends within Athens's broader

---

35. On the chorus in fourth-century tragedy, see Jackson forthcoming.

36. On tragedy as a choral genre, see Bacon 1994; Gagné and Hopman 2013b: 19–22.

37. Csapo 1999–2000, 2004. Euripides' involvement in the New Music is also central to Kranz's discussion of "das neue Lied" (1933: 228–62); see also Panagl 1971.

38. On the origins of this term, see D'Angour 2006: 267.

39. Pherecrates fr. 155 *PCG*, quoted in ps.-Plut. 1141d–1142a. On New Music in the dithyramb and kitharodic *nomos*, see esp. D'Angour 1997, 2006, 2011: 195–206; Csapo 2004; Csapo and Wilson 2009; Power 2010: 500–516; LeVen 2011, 2014: 71–243; Franklin 2013.

40. See Csapo 1999–2000: 405–7. Following Kranz 1933, older scholarship has tended to date the beginning of Euripides' musical innovations to 415 B.C.E. as a result of the chorus's claim to "new songs" (καινῶν ὕμνων) in *Trojan Women* 512.

sociocultural landscape. The question of its *intra*dramatic significance continues to be neglected.⁴¹

Although the dithyramb was not the only site of musical experimentation and novelty in the fifth century, certain types of performance and language associated with this genre seem to have been especially prominent features of the New Music. The choral odes in Euripides' later tragedies have in particular been linked to the dithyramb, ever since Walter Kranz in 1933 labeled ten of them dithyrambic, largely because they seemed to be self-contained, independent narratives ("völlig absolut stehende balladeske Erzählung"), as dithyrambs apparently were.⁴² Csapo has shown that, like dithyrambs, these odes often include vivid descriptions of musical performance with a distinctly Dionysiac flavor, emphasizing in particular the *aulos*, circular dancing with vocabulary like *helissein* and *dineuein* (both meaning "to whirl"), and archetypal choral performers like dolphins and Nereids; the latter tend to be fifty in number, just like a dithyrambic chorus.⁴³

But, like the focus on the New Music, the tendency to connect musical discourse and performance in Euripides' work to the dithyramb continues to look for relevance beyond the plays themselves. The question then remains of how these elements may be integrated within the dramatic plot. The Dionysiac, dithyrambic character of some of his self-referential choral passages can bear witness to his experimentation with new musical trends and at the same time point to a metatheatrical engagement with his tragedies' performance context within the City Dionysia. If considered in isolation, however, this feature cannot in itself shed much light on how *mousikē* functions within a play as a whole—except perhaps in the case of *Bacchae*, in which Dionysiac *choreia* constitutes the chorus's primary activity and identity.⁴⁴ The labeling of certain Euripidean stasima as dithyrambic on account of their apparently freestanding character more explicitly continues the idea that his choral odes become increasingly divorced from the *mythos* in his later plays—"dithyrambic" becomes virtually a synonym for "*embolimon*-like." Csapo himself warns us against characterizing Euripides' *choreia* in this way, complaining that "the criterion of self-contained narration perpetuates the notion that drama's participation in the 'New Music' consisted largely in the insertion of extractable, irrelevant, and often meaningless, musical interludes which performed a purely aesthetic function at the cost of the drama's integrity."⁴⁵ Yet the

---

41. A notable exception is Peter Wilson's discussion (1999–2000) of *mousikē* in Euripides' *Heracles*.
42. Kranz 1933: 254. On the dithyrambic character of these odes, see esp. Panagl 1971; Csapo 1999–2000, 2003, 2008; Steiner 2011.
43. Csapo 1999–2000; 2003. On the dithyramb's circular formation, see D'Angour 1997.
44. On the convergence of the chorus' ritual and fictional identity in *Bacchae*, see Bierl 2013. I discuss this in more detail in the conclusion.
45. Csapo 1999–2000: 408.

focus on the New Musical and dithyrambic character of Euripides' choral odes tends to separate the plays' musicality from their dramatic context and so to strengthen the idea that the lyric element is at most a seasoning, having little connection with the dramatic structure.

The recent surge of interest in the New Music has also overshadowed both a long tradition of innovation in archaic and classical *mousikē* and the more traditional aspects of Euripides' own musical compositions. "New Music" as a term for musical change in the late fifth century is misleading, since such change occurred neither suddenly nor in a cultural vacuum. Indeed, the figure of Music in Pherecrates' *Chiron*, in her litany of complaints about various musicians, goes as far back as the dithyrambist Melanippides, who was probably active in the early fifth century, sixty or seventy years before Euripides' own period of marked musical experimentation.[46] And as we shall see in chapter 1, Euripides inherits various forms of both musical imagery and metamusical play between words and performance that are already evident in surviving archaic lyric as well as in older tragedy. Some of these effects may be deemed New Musical, but such a classification can mask one of the central characteristics of Euripidean tragedy in the last two decades of the fifth century: namely its adaptation of traditional forms and images of *choreia* for the tragic stage.

This is not to say that the presence of established lyric traditions in Euripides has previously gone unnoticed. Laura Swift has traced the influence of choral genres like *partheneion* (maidens' song), *hymenaios* (wedding song), and epinician (victory song) in a selection of tragedies by Aeschylus, Sophocles, and Euripides.[47] But she is not concerned with the musical performance of such lyric within the tragedians' works, nor does she discuss how allusions to these genres function on a dramatic level as opposed to an exclusively thematic one. This sort of focus on the vestiges of traditional types of song in Euripides' work, like scholarship on his New Music, can also lead us to underappreciate the mix of old and new—and of different lyric genres in general—in his choral odes. One of the central arguments of this book is that such a mix is crucial to the dramatic impact of much of his *mousikē* and is an important part of his musical innovation in general.

In emphasizing the dramatic relevance of *mousikē* in Euripides' later tragedies, I do not, however, overlook the undeniably aloof and often bizarrely detached character of many of these songs. When the chorus sing of Achilles traveling to

---

46. Cf. D'Angour 2006: 273–74.

47. Swift 2010. Dithyramb (not discussed by Swift) was also a traditional choral genre, but the extensive employment of dithyrambic imagery and even styles of performance in tragedy seems primarily to have been a late fifth-century phenomenon. See Battezzato 2013 on the relationship between dithyramb and tragedy. On the incorporation of traditional styles and motifs within a display of musical innovation, see LeVen 2014: she demonstrates how the New Musical poets combine old and new in constructing their position within a lyric tradition.

Troy just as Electra and Orestes are about to be reunited in *Electra,* or of the Great Mother's search for her daughter just as Helen and Menelaus are about to escape from Egypt in *Helen,* their song and dance seem to be operating on a different plane from the rest of the play.[48] Through such performances the chorus create a breach in the action, in part by looking far beyond it both temporally and geographically. Yet such apparently disconnected *choreia* can simultaneously be closely tied to the *mythos,* through both the nature of the chorus's performance and the ways it brings these far-off scenes into the theater for the audience to experience more vividly. This combination of separateness and embeddedness is another characteristic of these choral odes that makes them so remarkable compared with earlier tragic *mousikē*. My aim here is to show how Euripides was experimenting not just with *mousikē* itself, for its own sake, but with how it could be integrated within the dramatic fabric of his plays.

## THE *MOUSIKĒ* OF TRAGEDY

This book explores the dynamics of *mousikē* within four tragedies to show how it plays a vital role in directing and complementing the movement of the plot. It argues that, even in his very latest plays, Euripides produces innovative music by adapting traditional lyric styles and motifs for the tragic stage, and that this mix of old and new is a central trait of his increasing experimentation with the language and performance of *mousikē*. My focus is the chorus, the main musical element of tragedy, but I also discuss the musical performances of actors; indeed, in all four plays I analyze how the style, structure, and imagery of the chorus's song and dance are closely tied to the character and performance of the main protagonist. I use the term *mousikē* to refer to the combination of words, music, and dance more generally, and *choreia* to mean specifically choral song and dance.[49] Throughout I approach Euripides' *mousikē* through the musical imaginary—both the music, song, and dance that are vividly imagined in the lyrics of the chorus (and actors) and the conceptualizations of particular musical images within archaic and classical Greek culture more broadly.

The purpose of this book is not, then, to reconstruct these tragedies' original musical performance. It is nevertheless worth briefly reviewing what little evidence does survive for the actual melodies and forms of choreography performed on the fifth-century tragic stage.[50] Though not contemporary with Euripides

---

48. Eur. *El.* 432–86, *Hel.* 1301–68. Cf. Marshall 2014: 98 on how the chorus, in combining dramatic and theatrical identities, function both in and at a remove from the dramatic action.

49. I use the Greek *mousikē* since English lacks an equivalent term encompassing song, music, and dance. Strictly, however, tragedy is itself a type of *mousikē* rather than a genre that employs it.

50. Cf. Marshall 2014: 13–15 on categories of evidence for stagecraft and performance.

himself, the most direct evidence of his play's *mousikē* consists of two scraps of papyri surviving from the Hellenistic period that show musically notated lyrics from *Iphigenia in Aulis* and *Orestes*, respectively.[51] These are too small to give us any sense of the overall musical composition of these tragedies, but they do demonstrate Euripides' experimentation with certain melodic effects, such as melisma (the practice of extending a syllable over several different notes), which Aristophanes' parody in *Frogs* suggests was a peculiarly Euripidean trait.[52]

Vase-paintings can also provide a valuable insight into the performance, representation, and perception of different types of *mousikē*, but very few images survive of the musical performances within Athenian tragedy.[53] The most famous is an Attic red-figure column-krater dated to 500–490 B.C.E. that shows three pairs of choreuts in choreographed formation with raised arms and bent legs before a tomb or altar, and with illegible letters issuing from their mouths to show that they are singing. This used to be linked to the scene in Aeschylus's *Persians* in which the chorus summons the ghost of Darius,[54] though the vase predates the play by at least twenty years. It is possible that the bearded figure emerging from the structure on the left is instead meant to be Dionysus, witnessing a dramatic (not necessarily tragic) performance in his honor or even seeming to appear as a result of the epiphanic effect of *choreia*.[55] Another vase, an Attic calyx-krater from the mid-fifth century B.C.E., shows a group of women in a row, each in a different pose, dancing to the accompaniment of an *aulos* player.[56] If this is a representation of a tragic chorus, it demonstrates that the choreuts in a tragedy did not necessarily all strike the same pose at once (as they do on the column-krater), just as representations of dancing satyrs show that those choruses were not usually in unison formation.[57] A fragment of an Attic bell-krater from

---

51. On these papyri, see West 1992: 284–87, Pöhlmann and West 2001: 12–21.

52. Ar. *Ran.* 1314. The *Orestes* papyrus also demonstrates that melody could be divorced from the words' pitch accent in Euripidean strophic lyric. D'Angour 2006: 276–83 hypothesizes that this practice was the result of new musical experimentation in the late fifth century B.C.E., culminating in Euripides' "break[ing] free of the traditional principles of matching word pitch with musical pitch in the responsional choruses of tragic drama" (282). It is unclear whether such "traditional principles" existed for earlier choral lyric.

53. Numerous representations of tragic scenes survive on South Italian vases from the fourth century, but none includes a performance of *mousikē*: for an overview of these images, see Hart 2010: 64–83. We do, however, have numerous vases with scenes that seem to be from satyr plays, with an aulete and dancing chorus, from the early to mid-fifth century B.C.E.

54. Aesch. *Pers.* 623–80.

55. On this scene as an image of or inspired by a tragic performance, see M. Schmidt 1967; Csapo and Slater 1995: 57; M. C. Miller 2004; Taplin 2007: 29; Hart 2010: 29; Csapo 2010: 6–8; Wellenbach 2015. Green 1994: 17–18 argues that it represents a traditional motif commonly used in Athenian theater of the first quarter of the fifth century. A chorus of Persians is also depicted on a fragmentary Attic hydria dating to the first half of the fifth century: see M. C. Miller 2004; Csapo 2010: 6.

56. See Foley 2003: 10 on this image's possible association with choral performance in tragedy.

57. On dancing in satyr plays, see Seidensticker 2010; Griffith 2015: 42–43, 87.

Olbia, which shows members of a chorus wearing masks and dancing to the *aulos*, likewise demonstrates variety in their movements.[58] The way the dancers curve around the shape of the calyx-krater may also suggest circular formation rather than the rectangular one that late sources claim was the standard for tragic choruses.[59] But these images tell us little either about how the movements of the chorus and the sound of the *aulos* accompanying them may have corresponded with the words of their song or about the musical shape or dramatic relevance of an entire ode.

We are able to gain some sense of the sorts of musical effects achieved in the work of Euripides and other innovative composers from Plato's conservative criticisms of these new styles in his *Laws*. As we shall see in chapters 4 and 5, his comments on the tendency of contemporary musicians to mix together different genres and to imitate absolutely anything seem particularly illuminating for some of Euripides' late choral lyric.[60] Such complaints, however, give us little idea of the use of music and dance in the individual plays of Euripides, nor can they be treated as representative of the more mainstream reception of tragic *mousikē* in Athens. Likewise Aristotle's restrictions in his *Politics* on the types of *harmoniai*, melodies, rhythms, and instruments to be used in theatrical *mousikē*, while they indicate quite how powerfully an audience could be affected by the musical performances onstage (he claims that we change in our soul when we listen to emotionally arousing rhythms and melodies),[61] do not provide us with much insight into how tragedies were actually performed in the fifth and fourth centuries.

As we have already seen, we find more specific indications of distinctively Euripidean styles of performance in Aristophanes' comedies, especially in the competition between Aeschylus and Euripides in *Frogs*. When the two poets attack each other's lyrics, Aeschylus's criticisms (however distorted and extreme they may be) give us a sense of which musical aspects seemed most characteristic of the younger tragedian's style to his contemporary audience. When he complains, for example, that Euripides "gets [his honey] from everywhere—porn songs, Meletus's drinking songs, Carian pipe tunes, laments, and choral dances," Aeschylus implies that Euripidean lyric typically mixes together many different kinds of song and often appears foreign as a result;[62] "porn songs" alludes to the performance of his

---

58. On this fragment see Taplin 2007: 29–30; Csapo 2010: 8–9.

59. Poll. *Onom.* 2.161; Aristid. *Or.* 3.154 with scholia (Dindorf 3.535–36). Phot. *Lex.* s.vv. *tritos aristerou, aristerostatēs, laurostatai*; Hesychius s.vv. *aristerostatēs, laurostatai*. On the question of whether the chorus danced in rectangular or circular formation (or a mixture of both), see Winkler 1990; Wiles 1997: 96, 2000: 134–35; Foley 2003: 9–10; Lech 2009.

60. Pl. *Leg.* 669c3–670a3, 700d2–e1; cf. *Rep.* 397a1–b2.

61. μεταβάλλομεν γὰρ τὴν ψυχὴν ἀκροώμενοι τοιούτων, Arist. *Pol.* 1340a23. On Aristotle's discussion of affective *mousikē*, see Griffith forthcoming.

62. οὗτος δ' ἀπὸ πάντων μεταφέρει, πορνῳδιῶν, / σκολίων Μελήτου, Καρικῶν αὐλημάτων, / θρήνων, χορειῶν, Ar. *Ran.* 1301–3.

monodies by professionals rather than citizen amateurs.[63] Aeschylus's parodies in *Frogs* point to certain details of particular tragedies by Euripides as well as more general trends: as we shall see in chapter 2, his pastiche of choral lyric from *Electra*, *Hypsipyle*, and *Meleager* (1309–23) reveals the tragedian's penchant both for melodic tricks like melisma and for particular verbal styles, such as the hanging apostrophe with which the song begins, its paratactic structure, and the image of dolphins dancing to the tune of the *aulos*. Aristophanes' comedies also occasionally provide commentary on styles of choreography in the plays of Euripides and other tragedians. In the parody of Euripidean *mousikē* in *Frogs*, Aeschylus refers to dance steps, playing on the double meaning of *pous* ("foot") and *melē* ("limbs/songs"); earlier in the comedy Dionysus mentions that he had enjoyed the movements as well as the words of Aeschylus's chorus in *Persians*.[64] At the end of *Wasps* the chorus direct the sons of the tragedian Carcinus to dance crazily, whirling and kicking like his predecessor Phrynichus.[65] But, precious though these indications of tragic performances are, they allude only to particular moments of a few pieces rather than to the musical shape of an entire play.

## SONG, DANCE, AND IMAGINATIVE SUGGESTION

In general, then, we lack both the actual sounds of tragedy's music and the physical actions of its choreography. These parts of tragic *mousikē* must have had their own semantic and affective force, but since they are no longer directly audible or visible, we must instead rely on the text that has survived.[66] One way to use the text to think about the *mousikē* as a whole is to examine the meter, which can suggest the rhythmical patterns of music and dance, though it still leaves us with little sense of melody, instrumentation, timbre, or choreographic forms.[67] My approach, however, is to focus primarily on the language and imagery used in tragic lyric. The words of a tragedy are closely connected with its music and dance. Indeed, as I show in chapter 1, an ancient audience would not necessarily register a distinction between the verbal, musical, and kinetic aspects of a choral performance, since these are tied together within the ancient concept and practice of *choreia*, as well

---

63. On Aeschylus's characterization of Euripides' *mousikē* here, see Griffith 2013a: 142–43.

64. Ar. *Ran.* 1329–33, 1028–29.

65. Ar. *Vesp.* 1512–37. Three generations of tragedians are documented within the family of Carcinus: see *TrGF* 21, 33, 70.

66. The issue of music's semiotics has been discussed extensively within musicology, ethnomusicology, and philosophy: see, e.g., Agawu 2014, with additional bibliography; also Kramer 2002. On the emotive power of music, see, e.g., Kivy 1989, 1990; Bicknell 2009. I discuss the emotive force of dance, referring in particular to the concepts of kinesthetic empathy and contagion, in the conclusion.

67. For metrical approaches to the music and dance of tragedy, see esp. Pintacuda 1978; Scott 1984, 1996a; Wiles 1997: 87–113.

as *mousikē* more broadly.⁶⁸ Moreover, Euripides' late plays contain so many descriptions of *mousikē*—that is, moments when the chorus (and sometimes the actors) refer to song, dance, and instrumental music at the same time as they themselves are singing and dancing to the *aulos*—that they invite us to look for connections between the words and performance of each song. My emphasis on the metamusical aspect of his work therefore reveals how texts reflect upon and thus record something of the now-lost sounds and sights of the live performance; but it does so in a manner that remains historiographically responsible, because it finds evidence for musical practice precisely where it *has* endured through time: that is, in the words themselves. As my readings of his plays show, the metamusical passages in Euripides' work are valuable not so much for what they tell us about the actual performance as for the ways they both shape the audience's reception of that performance and together create a larger musical narrative that intersects with the dramatic one.

Those moments when choruses explicitly refer to their own musical performance have usually been called self-referential ever since Albert Henrichs identified this as a common feature of tragic choral lyric.⁶⁹ Henrichs links choral self-referentiality to what he calls "choral projection," the process whereby "choruses locate their own dancing in the past or the future, in contrast to the here and now of their immediate performance, or when choruses project their collective identity onto groups of dancers distant from the concrete space of the *orchēstra* and dancing in the allusive realm of the dramatic imagination."⁷⁰ Though Henrichs concentrates on allusions to dancing, these are often combined with descriptions of other forms of *mousikē* that can all be part of a projection. As we will see in chapter 1, vivid moments of self-referentiality occur in Aeschylean choral lyric: in the Binding Song in *Eumenides*, for example, and in the scenes of mourning in *Persians*, *Suppliants*, and *Libation Bearers*.⁷¹ Choral projection, however, is more common in the work of the younger tragedians, and above all in the later plays of Euripides.

Through the chorus's references to its own song and dance, we can tentatively reconstruct some aspects of their performance, at least insofar as it may have corresponded with their words. When they describe the *mousikē* of others with vividly performative language, we can assume some level of interaction or merging between the performance imagined in their lyrics and the one the audience see and hear in the *orchēstra*. This is not to say, however, that verbal allusions to *choreia* should be treated at face value as stage directions. Descriptions of *mousikē* need

---

68. On the importance of words to the ancient conception of *mousikē*, see esp. D'Angour 2015: 188–92.
69. Henrichs 1994–95, 1996. Cf. Heikkilä 1991.
70. Henrichs 1996: 49.
71. Aesch. *Eum.* 307–96, *Pers.* 918–1076, *Supp.* 58–133, *Cho.* 423–28.

not always have corresponded with the chorus's actual performance, and the majority of their gestures and modes of singing would not have been simultaneously referred to in the text of the play.[72] Indeed, as I demonstrate in chapter 3 in the case of *Trojan Women* in particular, performed *mousikē* can critique or undermine the denotative content of a song's words, not just enhance it.[73] I am not proposing that words were imitated by music and dance (or vice versa): we should not assume a one-to-one relationship between the language and *mousikē* of tragedy, and moreover we should understand mimesis in general—at least for this period—as representation or enactment rather than strict imitation.[74] Nonetheless, often there is a mimetic process at work through the combination of described and performed *mousikē*, and the audience's reception of the *choreia* onstage can as a result be a synthesis of what they imagine and what they actually perceive. Choral self-referentiality and projection can give us a sense of the intended impact of this musical experience on the audience, even while the music and dance themselves are lost.

The idea that there are different registers of *mousikē* is fundamental to my approach to the performance of Euripides' tragedies. It derives in part from work within Sound Studies on auditory semiotics that explores the different levels at which we perceive sound—the "polyphony of auditory experiences of the perceptual and imaginative modalities."[75] Bruce Smith has applied this conceptualization of polyphony to the sounds of Elizabethan theater.[76] When, for example, trumpets, hautboys, and drums are played at the same time as the messenger describes these sounds in one of the crowd scenes in *Coriolanus*, the audience would hear not only the physical properties of certain instrumental noises (pitch, rhythm, etc.) but the perceptual phenomena such as brightness in the trumpet or dryness in the drums, and, through the messenger's speech, also the imaginative aspect of these sounds. This latter register includes trumpet-ness or drum-ness—what Smith calls the "essence" of these auditory objects, by which he means what they represent both individually and together ("danger, anarchy, chaos").[77] This concept of different levels of auditory reception can apply to the visual aspect of performance as well: dance works on a physical and perceptual level, but also on an imaginative one, which can be shaped by the words used to describe it. In ancient Greek musical culture, the interplay of these different registers was a fundamental part of the

---

72. On the attempt to find stage directions in the words of a tragedy, see esp. Taplin 1978: 16–19. On the challenges of this approach to Greek drama, see Wiles 1997: 5; Bassi 2005.

73. Cf. Gurd 2016, who emphasizes the disconnect between language and the "materiality" of sound in Greek poetry.

74. On mimesis as (re)enactment or representation rather than precise imitation, see Keuls 1978: 9–32; Nagy 1990: 42–45, 373–75, 1996: 53–58; Halliwell 2002, esp. 118–76; Peponi 2009 (esp. 64).

75. Ihde 2003: 62. Cf. Handel 1989: 181–82 on different registers of auditory perception.

76. B. R. Smith 1999: 242–45. Cf. Johnson 2005.

77. B. R. Smith 1999: 242–43 on Shakespeare, *Coriolanus* 5.4.49–52.

experience of *choreia,* within which words, music, and dance are closely intertwined. My approach to tragedy's *mousikē* therefore depends on a basic division between two levels of *mousikē:* what is actually performed onstage and what is imagined through the words of the play.

"Choral self-referentiality" and "choral projection" refer to the imaginative plane of *mousikē* in tragedy, but neither phenomenon encapsulates it entirely. I use instead the term "imaginative suggestion" to denote the associational process whereby the verbal element of a choral performance encourages the audience to experience its music and dance in a particular way. I do not mean to suggest that such a performance must always rely on words to communicate certain images, narratives, and emotions—but since only the words have survived, we can consider the musical and choreographic elements only in relation to them. It is through the imaginative suggestion of *choreia* that the audience can see the choreuts as dolphins dancing around Helen's ship as she leaves Egypt for Sparta or hear the sound of the *aulos* accompanying them in the theater as that of Paris's syrinx as he herds cattle on Mount Ida.[78] As the latter example indicates, the tragic chorus need not merge their performances with exclusively choral *mousikē*: on the contrary, their own singing and dancing can interact with descriptions of solo performers too, such as that of the nightingale in the first stasimon of *Helen*.[79] They can even bring to life musical objects that are otherwise typically inanimate: in the third stasimon of *Heracles,* for example, the chorus call upon various Theban landmarks, including the river Ismenus and the Pythian rock, to sing and dance.[80] In doing so the chorus, through their own singing and dancing onstage, invite the audience to become immersed in the ecstatic *mousikē* that they describe, even while they complicate this experience through the incongruous disconnect between their own self-professed frailty and the ecstasy of their song. This process of merging—the simultaneity of the live performance and the imagined one—is more interactive and involves more complex interplay between the two registers of *mousikē* than the term "projection" implies. I prefer to see such references by the chorus to their own and others' *mousikē* more generally as part of the imaginary of *choreia* at work in performance.

The phenomenon of imaginative suggestion through *choreia* occurs particularly frequently in the later work of Euripides, perhaps as a result of his engagement with contemporary musical trends—a possibility that I consider more fully in the conclusion to this book. The interplay of (meta)musical language and performance, however, is by no means exclusive to Euripides' plays, nor even to fifth-century tragedy more generally. Indeed, as we shall see in chapter 1, Euripides

---

78. Eur. *Hel.* 1454–55, *IA* 573–81.
79. Eur. *Hel.* 1107–21.
80. Eur. *HF* 781–97. Cf. *Hyp.* fr. 752f, 25–28.

inherits and adapts much of his play with imaginative suggestion from archaic choral lyric: the odes of Pindar and Bacchylides, for example, frequently refer to musical performances that would merge with the chorus's own song and dance, such as the archetypal *choreia* of the Muses in *Pythian* 1 and *Nemean* 5.[81] The surviving tragedies and fragments of Aeschylus and Sophocles, as well as the earlier (pre-420) plays of Euripides, also include some highly metamusical passages that rely on the interaction of described and performed *mousikē* to achieve their full dramatic effect. As I demonstrate, however, Euripides' use of *mousikē* in his later work is nonetheless markedly different in how much he draws on traditional *choreia*, evoking the repertoire of musical figures that are frequently at work in archaic lyric and reconfiguring them within a dramatic narrative.

## THE DRAMATIC ROLE OF TRAGIC *MOUSIKĒ*

What purpose, then, do these moments of imagined *mousikē* serve within a tragedy? Henrichs sees choral self-referentiality and projection as devices primarily used to integrate the world of the drama with the ritual, Dionysiac context of its performance.[82] Anton Bierl in his work on Old Comedy similarly traces choral self-reference back to ritual, arguing that the chorus acts as an intermediary for the audience between the there and then of the myth being enacted onstage and the here and now of their own cultic performance.[83] For him, these moments of described *mousikē* have a purely ritual significance, which seems to be divorced from the plot of the surrounding drama. This approach tends to view such moments of pronounced musicality as independent not only of the *mythos* but even of the immediate performance context within the play. But when Dionysiac descriptions of *mousikē* occur within a song with a different generic frame, such as a *partheneion*, *hymenaios*, or epinician, can we explain this mix only as a merging of myth and ritual, or may it play a more integrated dramatic role? In the hymenaeal ode that the chorus sings for Iphigenia and Achilles in *Iphigenia in Aulis*, for example, it describes the *choreia* at the wedding of Peleus and Thetis with language that incorporates imagery and vocabulary often associated with Dionysiac performance. As my analysis of this song in chapter 5 demonstrates, the resulting focus on the chorus's own performance underscores with devastating irony the lack of any such wedding celebrations for Iphigenia just at the moment when Achilles has promised that he will prevent her from being sacrificed. We can

---

81. Pind. *Pyth.* 1.1–4, *Nem.* 5.22–26; cf. *Pyth.* 10.38–39, *Ol.* 4.2–4; Bacchyl. 11.112, 13.77–99. On choral projection in Bacchyl. 13, see Power 2000.

82. On the merging of myth and ritual, play and polis, in tragic *choreia*, see Kowalzig 2007a, esp. 232–42; cf. Kowalzig 2007b: 27–55. On the ritual identity of the tragic chorus, see also Winkler 1990; Nagy 1994–95; Calame 1999, 2013.

83. Bierl 2009, esp. 24–47.

understand the combination of imagined and performed *choreia* here as a way to link the story being performed onstage with the ritual context of the City Dionysia, but it is also closely connected to the dramatic fabric of the tragedy.

Henrichs does, however, link the ritual aspect of choral self-referentiality to a play's *mythos* through the phenomenon of so-called joy-before-disaster odes, whereby the chorus displays particularly exuberant ritual self-awareness just before a tragic reversal.[84] This pattern is similar to what Ian Rutherford observes in the tragic performances of joyful paeans, which are often followed by a terrible change of fortune—as, for example, when Iris and Lyssa enter following the chorus's paeanic second stasimon in Euripides' *Heracles*.[85] But only a relatively small proportion of self-referential *choreia* in Euripidean tragedy occurs just before this sort of reversal: in fact, in the four plays I discuss in this book, only the hymenaeal ode in *Iphigenia in Aulis* mentioned above comes close to following such a pattern, and this song, with its increasingly ominous images, is far from purely joyful. I show that descriptions of song and dance, combined with the chorus's actual performance, can play a much more varied and nuanced dramatic role than simply that of heralding a disastrous turn of fortune: they can drive a plot forward, shape an audience's anticipation of the central events of the *mythos* (or the lack thereof), enact offstage scenes and events that provide a crucial backdrop to the tragedy's action, and help to articulate the character of the protagonist(s).

I begin this discussion of tragic *mousikē* with a survey of musical and choreographic images and effects in archaic choral lyric and classical tragedy up until the late 420s B.C.E. in order to then show how Euripides both continues and departs from these earlier trends in the last two decades of his career. I return to this issue directly in the conclusion, where I suggest that he draws on traditional choral lyric as part of his experimentation with ever more affective forms of *mousikē*, making use of a particular mode of hearing and viewing *choreia* that requires the audience's active participation. The rest of the book is divided into four studies of individual plays. In chapter 2 I offer an analysis of *Electra*, which, with its revised dating of 420/19 B.C.E., is the first extant play to include multiple extended descriptions of *mousikē*. I argue that *choreia* both frames our understanding of Electra and has a generative power, anticipating and even enacting pivotal moments of the *mythos*. Chapter 3 is dedicated to *Trojan Women* (415 B.C.E.), in which descriptions of *choreia*, instead of generating action, underscore an overwhelming sense of loss and absence throughout the drama. Toward the end of the play, however, the chorus's

---

84. Henrichs 1994–95: 73–85. Cf. Halleran 1985: 51–67 on odes of false preparation. In Weiss forthcoming b I suggest that the overload of different lyric genres at play within such songs adds an ominous note to their performance, thus preemptively undermining the chorus's celebratory festivity.

85. Rutherford 1994–95, esp. 124–27; Eur. *HF* 636–700. On the enactment of reversal through *choreia* in Euripides' *Heracles*, see Henrichs 1996: 54–62; Wilson 1999–2000: 433–49.

musical performance also has a presencing effect, producing for the audience an auditory and visual enactment of the fall of Troy. In chapter 4 I move on to *Helen*, produced three years later, in 412, in which all allusions to *mousikē* revolve around the figure of Helen herself. This tragedy is remarkable for the series of musical figures addressed in each ode, from the Sirens in the parodos to the ship leading choral dances of dolphins in the third stasimon. I show how all these images of *mousikē* reflect Helen's own role as a choral performer at each point in the play, ultimately marking her separation from the dramatic chorus as she leaves Egypt to lead *choreia* back in Sparta. In chapter 5, I explore the dynamics of both *choreia* and monody in *Iphigenia in Aulis*, a posthumously produced tragedy. We see the presencing power of *choreia* in this play too: in the parodos the chorus brings to life a scene that is otherwise offstage—the Greek army camped at Aulis—through the merging of its own dance with the images it describes. I also explore how representations of instrumental mimesis provide a poignantly vivid impression of pastoral calm before the beginning of the Trojan War and how the hymenaeal *mousikē* in the third stasimon ironically directs us toward Iphigenia's sacrifice.

*Electra, Trojan Women, Helen,* and *Iphigenia in Aulis*, like many Euripidean dramas, all have a female protagonist and a female chorus. In all these plays, Euripides draws on the dynamics of traditional female chorality in order to present their relationship as one between a (potential) *chorēgos* and her chorus. The extent to which they fulfill these roles helps to define the character of the protagonist as well as to reflect a critical point or overarching theme of the *mythos*, such as Helen's separation from the chorus as she forms her escape plan with Menelaus in *Helen* or the complete breakdown of any civic institutions following the destruction of Troy in *Trojan Women*. The use of female choruses also means that the images of female *choreia* (Nereids, Sirens, Muses, Graces) that Euripides frequently uses in his later work create an especially effective interaction between the chorus's own performance and the *mousikē* that they describe. At the same time, female choruses add an extra mimetic layer to the process of imaginative suggestion, since the theatrical chorus was of course all male: the combination of the dramatic frame and the chorus's own costumes, masks, words, song, and dance transform them first into Argive, Trojan, Spartan, or Chalcidean women, and secondarily (and more temporarily) into various archetypal images within the Greek choral imaginary. When, as in the first two stasima of *Electra*, Euripides subverts these typically celebratory figures of female chorality, transforming them (and the chorus) into more ominous images of *mousikē*, this shift tends to mark an analogous turning point in the plot of the tragedy as a whole.

My aim is therefore to show how closely both performed and imagined *mousikē* can be tied to the *mythos* of a tragedy, even—or perhaps especially—in this group of plays from the last two decades of Euripides' career, when *choreia* is traditionally thought to have become less relevant to the drama itself. My approach opens up new ways of understanding each tragedy by viewing it in terms of its musical structure and examining the relationship between the verbal and musical parts of its performance. Sometimes my readings reinforce existing ones, demonstrating how (meta)musicality works alongside other, less neglected aspects of tragedy and how it is just as vital to a play's overall affective impact. Sometimes they complicate or oppose more traditional readings of the plays: in chapter 5, for example, I argue against the view that the final choral song in *Iphigenia in Aulis* is spurious.

More indirectly, this book demonstrates the close link between *mousikē* and the *pathos*, both pleasurable and instructive, that Aristotle identifies as being characteristic of the best arrangement of the actions.[86] It reveals the affective force of the combination of choral song, dance, and instrumental accompaniment that draws the audience into the drama and helps to direct their response to it.[87] The actions of the chorus—and so of the play as a whole—therefore include singing and dancing, the "seasonings" that are so vital to a tragedy's performance and impact.

The chronology of the plays I analyze here demonstrates that there was no steady decline in the dramatic involvement of the chorus in Euripides' plays from the 420s onward. On the contrary, in the posthumously produced *Iphigenia in Aulis*, the chorus not only sing for a high proportion of the play but become increasingly involved in Iphigenia's drama, finally singing with her as she leaves for her sacrifice. Though the emphasis on the chorus's musicality in these tragedies can add to an impression of distance from the dramatic action, it also helps to integrate it within the plot. This study demonstrates how, toward the end of the fifth century, Euripides was increasingly experimenting with the language and performance of *mousikē* and finding new roles for it to play within a tragedy as a whole.

---

86. Arist. *Poet.* 1449a33–34, 1452a2–1454a15.

87. Cf. Visvardi 2015 (esp. 1–43) on how the chorus produces and shapes emotions in the audience, which are tied to cognitive processes of understanding the drama as a whole; also Easterling 1997: 163–65.

# 1

# Words, Music, and Dance in Archaic Lyric and Classical Tragedy

Neither Euripides' experimentation with *mousikē* nor musical innovations in late fifth-century Athens in general should be viewed within a cultural vacuum, as a movement wholly divorced from previous musical trends. On the contrary, we should consider Euripides' "new music" against the backdrop of a long tradition of (meta)musical performance, both in nondramatic lyric and in earlier productions on the tragic, comic, and satyric stage. In this chapter I review this tradition, providing a selective survey of passages in archaic choral lyric and classical tragedy prior to 420 B.C.E. that draw the audience's attention to the musical and choreographic elements and effects of the live performance. This survey focuses on the workings of imaginative suggestion through *choreia*—that is, the associational process whereby the verbal component of a choral performance encourages the audience to experience the musical part in a particular way. This phenomenon is, I suggest, a natural consequence of the Greek conceptualization of *choreia* (and *mousikē* more broadly) as a totality, whereby words, rhythm, melody, and dance movements are closely intertwined. The text—which is all that remains for us now—is therefore always related in significant ways to the musicality of the original performance, even while our own ability to retrieve and reimagine that original relationship necessarily requires much additional work that the Athenian audience presumably did not need to undertake.

I begin this chapter by demonstrating how frequently imaginative suggestion is at work in archaic choral lyric. The metamusical effects I discuss here suggest a common repertoire within the Greek choral imaginary of particular animals, objects, attributes, gestures, and archetypal singers that invite not only comparison with the live chorus, but also a merging of imagined and performed *mousikē*. As we saw in the introduction, these could all be seen as forms of choral projection—moments when choruses project their identity onto other dancing groups in a different time and place. I am calling the process at work here imaginative suggestion, since I wish to emphasize both the close association of words with music and physical movement, and the participation of the audience in the chorus's assumption of different musical identities. When these choruses evoke images to which their own performance may correspond or be assimilated, they invite the audience to hear and visualize them in this way through the combination of the verbal and musical elements of their *choreia*.[1]

In the second half of this chapter I move from archaic lyric to classical tragedy. My purpose here is twofold. On the one hand, I want to show in part how the fifth-century tragedians inherit the workings of imaginative suggestion from a long tradition of nondramatic choral lyric and adapt it for the tragic stage, so that it becomes bound up with a broader dramatic narrative. By looking at the dramatic use of such metamusical interplay between imagined and performed *mousikē* in the works of Aeschylus and Sophocles, as well as in some of Euripides' earlier work, I provide a corrective to the common scholarly assumption that "later Euripidean music" constitutes a radical departure from earlier musical experimentation in tragedy and in Greek lyric more generally.[2] This corrective therefore also supports a critical approach to the phenomenon of the so-called New Music more generally that treats it not as a sudden musical revolution in the late fifth century but as "only the latest, and best documented, in a series of revolutions."[3] On the other hand, this survey still demonstrates a contrast between earlier tragedy and the plays that I discuss in the following chapters: in his later plays Euripides is indeed doing something musically different, even if the break is not so sudden as is generally assumed. But such novelty is also a form of archaizing, since it is Euripides who above all looks back to and draws from the musical motifs of archaic choral lyric, experimenting with how they can be integrated within a dramatic plot.[4]

---

1. For the many members of the audience who were or had been themselves dancers, the chorus's movements in the *orchēstra* might also trigger particular bodily responses through a process of kinesthetic empathy: see the conclusion for a discussion of this concept.
2. The term "later Euripidean music" comes from Csapo 1999–2000.
3. LeVen 2014: 83. On the tradition of musical innovation prior to the New Music see also Wallace 2003: 77–81; D'Angour 2011: 184–206; Prauscello 2012; Franklin 2013.
4. This musical trend goes hand in hand with Euripides' tendency to archaize in his later plays in other areas too, such as in reintroducing trochaic tetrameters and including a detachable prologue in which a character speaks directly to the audience: see, e.g., Wilamowitz-Moellendorff 1895: 145; Burkhardt 1906; Kranz 1933: 232–35; Michelini 1987: 101–2. Kranz notes the innovative nature of this tendency, calling it a "Neubelebung ältester Form" (1933: 232).

## BEFORE TRAGEDY: IMAGINATIVE SUGGESTION IN ARCHAIC LYRIC

*Choreia* encompasses both music and dance. It is a subset of *mousikē*, which similarly comprises song, instrumental music, and dance: Socrates in Plato's *Alcibiades* calls it the art of "playing the kithara and singing and stepping correctly."[5] But while the performance of *mousikē* can be purely instrumental or consist only in song, *choreia* always involves "an alliance of body and voice";[6] as the Athenian Stranger in Plato's *Laws* states, "*choreia* is as a whole both dance and song."[7] Within this unity of words, dance, and music, there appears to be an especially close connection between the verbal and choreographic elements: later in *Laws* he says that the whole art of dancing (which in this discussion primarily means *choral* dancing) arose as a result of the "representation of things spoken by means of gesture."[8] The phenomenon of choral self-referentiality, defined by Henrichs as "the self-description of the tragic chorus as performer of *khoreia*,"[9] is the most explicit manifestation of the close tie between the verbal and musical (choreographic, vocal, instrumental) elements of *choreia*. Any degree of metamusical commentary within a choral performance draws attention to an already existing association, guiding and enhancing (and sometimes complicating) the audience's reception of what it sees and hears.

Plutarch, writing four hundred years later than Plato, elaborates on the close association between words and dance in his dialogue *Table Talk*:

"καὶ ὅλως," ἔφη, "μεταθετέον τὸ Σιμωνίδειον ἀπὸ τῆς ζωγραφίας ἐπὶ τὴν ὄρχησιν. . . . ⟨ταύτην γὰρ ὀρθῶς ἔστι λέγειν ποίησιν⟩ σιωπῶσαν, καὶ φθεγγομένην ὄρχησιν ⟨δὲ⟩ πάλιν τὴν ποίησιν· †ὅθεν εἶπεν οὔτε γραφικὴν εἶναι ποιητικῆς οὔτε ποιητικὴν γραφ⟨ικ⟩ῆς, οὐδὲ χρῶνται τὸ παράπαν ἀλλήλαις· ὀρχηστικῆι δὲ καὶ ποιητικῆι κοινωνία πᾶσα καὶ μέθεξις ἀλλήλων ἐστί."

"And in general," he [Ammonius] said, "one should transfer Simonides' saying from painting to dancing.... ⟨For it is possible to correctly call this [dance]⟩ silent ⟨poetry⟩, and again poetry vocalized dance: †thence he said that neither does painting share in poetry, nor poetry in painting, nor do they make any use whatsoever of each other. But in the case of dance and poetry there is complete commonality and participation between each other." (Plut. *Mor.* 748a3–10)

---

5. τὸ κιθαρίζειν καὶ τὸ ἄιδειν καὶ τὸ ἐμβαίνειν ὀρθῶς, Pl. *Alc.* 108c7–8.

6. Peponi 2013b: 15. As D'Angour 2015 observes, words were an integral part of the ancient conception of *mousikē*, even though several types of musical performances (e.g., the auletic nome) involved only instrumental sound.

7. χορεία γε μὴν ὄρχησίς τε καὶ ὠιδὴ τὸ σύνολόν ἐστιν, Pl. *Leg.* 654b3–4.

8. μίμησις τῶν λεγομένων σχήμασι, Pl. *Leg.* 816a5. Cf. 795e1–2, when the Athenian Stranger categorizes one type of dancing as "representing the *lexis* [speech, word, diction] of the Muse" (Μούσης λέξιν μιμουμένων).

9. Henrichs 1994–95: 58.

Plutarch is not specifically discussing *choreia* here: though in this passage he is talking about dance (*orchēsis*) in general, the conversation as a whole is concerned with pantomime instead. But the example he gives to demonstrate this sort of communion of words and body is one of Pindar's *hyporchēmata*—choral performances in which the connection between song and dance was apparently particularly pronounced.[10] The *hyporchēma* he quotes makes this link particularly explicit through a series of choreographic instructions:

Πελασγὸν ἵππον ἢ κύνα (1)
Ἀμυκλαίαν ἀγωνίωι
ἐλελιζόμενος ποδὶ μίμεο καμπύλον μέλος διώκων,
οἷ' ἀνὰ Δώτιον ἀνθεμόεν πεδί-
ον πέταται θάνατον κεροέσσαι (5)
εὑρέμεν ματεῖσ' ἐλάφωι·
τὰν δ' ἐπ' αὐχένι στρέφοι-
σαν {ἕτερον} κάρα πάντ' ἐπ' οἶμον . . .

Represent a Pelasgian horse or Amyclaean dog, whirling with your foot in the contest, as you chase after the bending song, as she [the dog] flies over the flowery plain of Dotion, seeking to find death for the horned deer, whom, as she turns her head on her neck along every path . . . (Pind. fr. 107a SM, quoted in Plut. *Mor.* 748b)

This *hyporchēma* fragment also indicates that the relationship between song and dance, even in a type of performance in which the two are so obviously tied, is not a precisely mimetic one. The presentation of alternatives here is crucial: the chorus give themselves instructions to represent a horse *or* a dog; the song they "chase" is then conflated with a fleeing deer, whose movements (the turning of her head) may merge with the chorus's own. They thus offer different suggestions for the objects of their representation not only to themselves, as performers, but also to the audience, who can see them at one moment as horses, the next as dogs or deer.[11] The words of the song invite the audience to see certain images in the dance that is simultaneously performed, but these work almost metaphorically, encouraging equivalences between what is heard and what is seen rather than a literal, one-to-one representation.[12] There may be little change in actual choreography

---

10. Athenaeus describes the *hyporchēmatikē* as a style "in which the chorus dances while singing" (ἐν ἧι ᾄδων ὁ χορὸς ὀρχεῖται, 14.631c5). In fact the term *hyporchēma* may have been a misnomer dating from late antiquity, "understood as an antonym of stasimon on the mistaken assumption that stasimon implies a stationary chorus" (Henrichs 1994–95: 59). Cf. Dale 1969: 34–40.

11. Cf. Peponi 2015: 214: "the object of mimesis is approached from the start with an open and double possibility. The dancer, or dancers, are asked to enact either a dog *or* a horse" (emphasis original).

12. An analogous process of imaginative suggestion is evident in Japanese song-and-dance traditions such as Noh and Kabuki: "significant movement in dance is an equivalence, that is, a metaphor, for certain verbal meanings of the song . . . movement is not exclusively mimetic, not literal nor directly illustrative of the text. Rather, it is suggestive" (Hoff 1976: 1).

from one image to the next, but the association with the words of the song is sufficiently free and flexible to allow the chorus to assume multiple identities within just a few lines. The multiplicity of referents offered in these lines also, as Peponi notes, encourages an active and demanding mode of viewing on the part of the audience: the disjunctives ("or") "challenge any kind of singularity in the perception of the viewer" and so "transform comprehension from an act of simple recognition into a moment of complex contemplation."[13] This fragment thus provides a metamusical commentary on the phenomenon of imaginative suggestion and the work it requires of its audience, as it simultaneously occurs in and through the chorus's actual performance of the *hyporchēma*.

The fluidity of this associational process, whereby the chorus can flit from representing one thing to another, is also evident in Alcman's first *Partheneion*. Peponi has explored how the two choral leaders in this song, Agido and Hagesichora, are described through a series of metaphors as horses, doves, and stars.[14] She focuses on a network of deictics relating to sight, whereby the audience are invited "not to 'see' *what is really present* but instead, while looking at what *is* present, to imaginatively transform the actually visible agents and their actions into a virtual and imaginary spectacle":[15] that is, such language both draws the audience's attention to what they see and at the same time constructs it in a particular way, turning it into an imaginative visualization. This effect is especially clear when the chorus first liken Hagesichora to a prize-winning horse and then shift from this simile to picturing both her and Agido as such animals:[16]

> δοκεῖ γὰρ ἤμεν αὔτα (45)
> ἐκπρεπὴς τὼς ὥπερ αἴτις
> ἐν βοτοῖς στάσειεν ἵππον
> παγὸν ἀεθλοφόρον καναχάποδα
> τῶν ὑποπετριδίων ὀνείρων·
>
> ἦ οὐχ ὁρῇς; ὁ μὲν κέλης (50)
> Ἐνετικός· ἁ δὲ χαίτα
> τᾶς ἐμᾶς ἀνεψιᾶς
> Ἀγησιχόρας ἐπανθεῖ
> χρυσὸς [ὡ]ς ἀκήρατος·
> τό τ᾽ ἀργύριον πρόσωπον, (55)
> διαφάδαν τί τοι λέγω;
> Ἀγησιχόρα μὲν αὔτα·

13. Peponi 2015: 215.
14. Peponi 2004a.
15. Peponi 2004a: 301 (emphasis original); cf. Peponi 2015: 214.
16. In line 61 and its translation here, read either "robe" (φᾶρος, a common offering for a divinity) or "plow" (φάρος, a suitable dedication for a goddess associated with fertility and agriculture like Orthria): see Campbell 1982: 206.

ἁ δὲ δευτέρα πεδ' Ἀγιδὼ τὸ ϝεῖδος
ἵππος Ἰβηνῶι Κολαξαῖος δραμήται·
ταὶ Πεληάδες γὰρ ἅμιν (60)
ὀρθρίαι φᾶρος φεροίσαις
νύκτα δι' ἀμβροσίαν ἅτε σήριον
ἄστρον ἀυηρομέναι μάχονται.

For she seems to be preeminent, just as if one were to set among grazing herds a horse, sturdy, prize-winning, thunderous-hoofed, [one] of [those seen in] winged dreams.

Don't you see? The horse is Enetic; but the hair of my cousin Hagesichora blooms like unmixed gold; and her silver face, [but] why do I speak about what's obvious? This is Hagesichora here! And second in beauty, Agido, a Colaxaean horse next to an Ibenian one, will run. For these doves are fighting for [with?] us, as we bring a robe to Orthria through the ambrosial night, rising like the star Sirius. (Alc. fr. 1 *PMGF*, 45–63)

To effect the transformation of Agido and Hagesichora into the vehicle of the simile, the chorus ask the audience, "Don't you see?" (50). This question not only urges them to appreciate the comparison; it is a reproof for not visualizing the performers as they should. By flitting from the equine imagery to the vision of Hagesichora there in front of them, then back to the horses again, the chorus encourage a complete merging of identities. They simultaneously describe Hagesichora's hair/mane as golden and face as silver, aspects of her beauty that they claim are "obvious" (56), but that they in fact construct for the audience by positioning themselves in the role of spectator.[17] According to Peponi's reading, the chorus then refer to the two chorus leaders as *Peleades* —most likely doves, but perhaps also the Pleiades star cluster, which in later lyric poetry is often depicted as a chorus.[18] Given the flexibility of imaginative suggestion, whereby choreuts can adopt multiple identities in quick succession and the audience in turn can hold multiple images in mind, the two possible meanings of *Peleades* are not necessarily mutually exclusive.[19] Finally, the chorus compare them to the star Sirius, thus transforming "the light, airy, and spectacular running of the two women next to each other into the rising of the

---

17. See also Peponi 2012: 86 on the choral enactment of the Spartan audience here.
18. On the Pleiades as a star chorus in classical Greek literature, see Csapo 2008: 266–67. On Alcman's chorus as a star chorus, see Ferrari 2008, esp. 69–104. On the *Peleades* in Alcm. fr. 1 *PMGF* as Hagesichora and Agido rather than a rival chorus, see esp. Segal 1983; Peponi 2004a: 303. For a review and bibliography of the different interpretations of the *Peleades*, see esp. Calame 1997: 6; Stehle 1997: 79; Swift 2010: 179.
19. Cf. Peponi 2004a: 305–6 on the implicit association of doves with the Pleiades here. Athanassakis 2000 examines the link between the Peleades (doves) and Pleiades (stars) in ancient and modern Greek folk traditions. Swift 2010: 180 also stresses the fluidity of the myth of the Peleiades: originally maidens, they were transformed into doves as they fled Orion and were later catasterized.

brightest star in the heavens."[20] At the same time, throughout this song the chorus facilitate the audience's experience of their leaders as Agido and Hagesichora—a characterization that, as Gregory Nagy has argued, would be "part of a seasonally recurring institutional mimesis of authoritative role models like divinities or royal ancestors."[21] Different chorus members each year may play these roles as part of an annual rite, as well as in later reperformances. The choreography of both the chorus and these two girls may have also encouraged these multiple, overlapping layers of representation, but it is the combination of the dance and the song that brings about the transition from vision to visualization.

The interplay between the succession of choral images and the chorus's own performance in this song indicates that the phenomenon of imaginative suggestion is a very early one in Greek lyric, already extensively developed by the time Alcman was composing his poetry, in the seventh century B.C.E. Moreover, the particular images at play here demonstrate that the association of particular animals, objects, and activities with *choreia* that frequently occurs in the later plays of Euripides had long been part of the Greek choral imaginary. As we will see in chapter 5, for example, in the parodos of Euripides' *Iphigenia in Aulis* equine imagery is similarly used to affect the audience's experience of *choreia* when the chorus describe the horses racing alongside Achilles with markedly choreographic language.[22] The particular combination of equine and avian imagery that we see in Alcman's song when the chorus picture Agido and Hagesichora as doves (and perhaps stars) as well as horses is also evident in the second stasimon of *Iphigenia in Tauris,* produced probably in 414 or 413 B.C.E. The chorus begin this ode by comparing themselves to the mourning halcyon bird and swan (1089–105) and end it by wishing they could fly back home:

λαμπροὺς ἱπποδρόμους βαίην,
ἔνθ' εὐάλιον ἔρχεται πῦρ·
οἰκείων δ' ὑπὲρ θαλάμων (1140)
ἐν νώτοις ἁμοῖς πτέρυγας
λήξαιμι θοάζουσα·
χοροῖς δ' ἐνσταίην, ὅθι καὶ
†παρθένος εὐδοκίμων γάμων
παρὰ πόδ' εἰλίσσουσα φίλας (1145)
ματέρος ἡλίκων θιάσους.

If only I could step along the bright horse-courses, where the sun's fire goes; and above my house's rooms I could stop moving the wings on my back; and I could take my stand in choruses where also †as a maiden at glorious weddings, whirling my foot alongside the bands of my dear mother's companions. (Eur. *IT* 1137–46)

---

20. Peponi 2004a: 306.
21. Nagy 1990: 349.
22. For an extensive discussion of choruses' equine associations see Steiner forthcoming: chapter 4.

Choruses of birds, bird riders, horses, and knights also appear in archaic vase-painting, and these images, combined with Aristophanes' comic choruses of birds and knights, indicate that such animals had choral associations in the broader Greek cultural imaginary.[23] Euripides' chorus, however, end their wish by picturing themselves dancing as *parthenoi* back in Greece, and this image suggests that the combination of equine and avian imagery may have been especially common within the parthenaic choral imaginary. It is through such associations, as the chorus prompt the audience to visualize them first as racing horses and then as birds, that they momentarily transform themselves into the parthenaic group that they once were while they simultaneously make the audience recognize the distance between their former life in Greece and their current position in Tauris. Since the race courses along which they wish to fly are the sun's, they also evoke the image of a star chorus, just as Alcman's chorus do through the double meaning of *Pelēades*.

One animal that does not appear in Alcman's *Partheneion* but does in other contexts, especially those with some link to the dithyramb, is the dancing dolphin. A series of archaic and early classical black-figure vases that depict dolphins or dolphin-human hybrids as choral performers complements the association of these creatures with dancing in choral lyric and suggests that a chorus could be visualized by an audience as these animals and vice versa.[24] As we shall see in chapter 2, several vases show men riding dolphins and explicitly associate the scene with *choreia*: the riders on the Oltos Psykter, for example, appear to be singing, with the words *epi delphinos* ("upon a dolphin") coming out of their mouths; other such scenes include an *aulos* player, the typical accompaniment for a choral performance like a dithyramb as well as for a naval journey. As Csapo has shown, dolphin choruses are especially associated with the dithyramb.[25] But rather than being depictions of particular dithyrambic performances, these vase images—like those that depict choruses of birds and bird riders—can be understood more broadly as visual expressions of how frequently the ability to see and hear a chorus as some other dancing group was evoked within Greek *choreia*.

Dancing dolphins also appear in literary sources prior to the numerous references to them in Euripides' later tragedies. In Pindar fr. 140b the metamusical play between this choral image and the live performance is especially pronounced:[26]

---

23. Scholars have typically interpreted these images of animal choruses as representing protocomic performances: see Sifakis 1967, 1971; Green 1985; Rothwell 2007. It is possible, however, that they were (also?) linked to the dithyramb: see Csapo 2003; Rusten 2006; Hedreen 2013: 178–87.

24. On these vases see Csapo 2003; Kowalzig 2013. On dolphin choruses see also Vidali 1997.

25. Csapo 2003. Cf. Kowalzig 2013.

26. The genre of this fragment is uncertain, though it is usually classified as a paean: see esp. D'Alessio 1997: 45; Rutherford 2001: 382–87.

> ἐγὼ μ[
> παῦρα μελ[ι]ζομεν[
> [γλώ]σσαργον ἀμφέπω[ν ἐρε-
> θίζομαι πρὸς ἀϋτά[ν
> ἁλίου δελφῖνος ὑπόκρισιν, (15)
> τὸν μὲν ἀκύμονος ἐν πόντου πελάγει
> αὐλῶν ἐκίνησ' ἐρατὸν μέλος.

> I ... singing a few songs, tending to the bright-tongued ... am roused to ... in the manner of a sea-dolphin, which the lovely song of *auloi* set moving in the expanse of the waveless deep. (Pind. fr. 140b SM, 11–17)

Pindar's chorus here explicitly liken themselves to a dolphin dancing to the music of the *aulos*, just as they sing and dance to the same instrument.[27] They thus seem to merge with the animal, encouraging the audience to see and hear one as the other.

In addition to certain animals, choruses are frequently associated with archetypal choral groups like the Muses, Graces, Nereids, and Sirens in archaic Greek poetry—and, as we shall see, in Euripidean choral lyric as well. The description of the "most beautiful chorus" of Muses singing to the accompaniment of Apollo's lyre in Pindar's *Nemean* 5, for example, encourages multiple interactions between the mythic narrative and the live performance.[28] A particularly vivid scene of dancing Nereids occurs in Bacchylides 17, when the chorus sing of Theseus's journey (with dolphins) to Nereus's house and his subsequent amazement at the maidens' performance:

> τόθι κλυτὰς ἰδών
> ἔδεισε⟨ν⟩ Νηρῆος ὀλ-
> βίου κόρας· ἀπὸ γὰρ ἀγλα-
> ῶν λάμπε γυίων σέλας
> ὧτε πυρός, ἀμφὶ χαίταις (105)
> δὲ χρυσεόπλοκοι
> δίνηντο ταινίαι· χορῶι δ' ἔτερ-
> πον κέαρ ὑγροῖσι ποσσίν.

> There he was awe-struck upon seeing the glorious daughters of blessed Nereus: for from their splendid limbs shone a gleam as of fire, and around their hair gold-braided ribbons were twirled; and they were delighting their hearts by dancing on liquid feet. (Bacchyl. 17.101–8; trans. D. Campbell, adapted).

---

27. The use of the noun ὑπόκρισις here is striking: though I have translated it as "manner," this seems to be an early example of its mimetic sense of "playing a part," which is frequently found in Aristotle's work.

28. ὁ κάλλιστος χορός, Pind. *Nem.* 5.23.

Here Theseus enacts the role of the audience, prompting their own admiration for the dithyrambic chorus's dancing, which merges with that of the Nereids despite their difference in gender.[29] The audience are thus encouraged to visualize the chorus's appearance in a particular way—to "see" gleaming, fast-moving limbs and gold in their hair—and so to feel similar awe not just at their dancing but at their temporary embodiment of figures that are so far from their actual appearance and identity.

The process of imaginative suggestion can work acoustically as well as visually, guiding the audience's reception of vocal sound. References to the Sirens, maidens renowned for their devastatingly alluring voice, are especially effective in acoustically framing a chorus's song. Alcman's first *Partheneion* once again provides an early example of such an effect. Toward the end of this song, the Sirens appear to be presented as rival singers, but they function as a musical model for the performing chorus:[30]

> ἁ δὲ τᾶν Σηρην[ί]δων                                (96)
> ἀοιδοτέρα μ[ὲν οὐχί,
> σιαὶ γάρ, ἀντ[ὶ δ' ἕνδεκα
> παίδων δεκ[ὰς ἅδ' ἀείδ]ει·
>
> But she is not more songful than the Sirens, for they are goddesses, and instead of eleven this group here of ten girls sings. (Alc. fr. 1 *PMGF*, 96–99)

The repetition of song words (*aoidotera, aeidei*) makes clear that the point of comparison here is the Sirens' singing rather than their physical appearance.

In another fragment attributed to Alcman we find an explicit reference to the acoustic merging of chorus and Siren(s): "The Muse has cried out, the shrill Siren."[31] Aelius Aristides, who preserves this fragment, observes that, in shifting from Muse to Siren, Alcman is saying "the chorus itself instead of the Muse has become what he says."[32] As Peponi notes, "next to the obvious identification of the Muse with the Siren is the latent linking of the Sirens with the chorus. This means, in turn, that the chorus symbolically incarnates the archetypal choral activity of the Muses/Sirens in their ritual song."[33] The choral activity being highlighted here is specifically song: the Muse/Siren "has cried out"; the Siren is described as "shrill."

---

29. Though such imagery may support the classification of Bacchyl. 17 as a dithyramb, the invocation of Apollo at the end (130–32) seems strongly paeanic. On its genre see esp. D. A. Schmidt 1990; Zimmermann 1992: 91–93; Calame 2009; Tsagalis 2009; D'Alessio 2013: 119–22.

30. The precise meaning of these lines is much disputed, particularly since the article ἁ could refer either to the Sirens' voice or to Hagesichora: for the latter option, see esp. Hutchinson 2001: 100–101; Bowie 2011: 49. Peponi argues that ἅδ' in line 99 also refers to Hagesichora, so that she, rather than the whole chorus, is compared with the Sirens (2012: 85–86).

31. ἁ Μῶσα κέκλαγ' ἁ λίγηα Σηρήν, Alcm. fr. 30 *PMGF.*

32. τοῦτο ἐκεῖνο ⟨ὁ⟩ χορὸς αὐτὸς ἀντὶ τῆς Μούσης γεγένηται, Aristid. *Or.* 28.51.

33. Peponi 2012: 87.

Through this brief reference to the Siren, then, the chorus has momentarily *become* one, so that their sound is heard as hers. The swift transition from Muse to Siren also demonstrates the fluidity of such choral associations, whereby the chorus can be imagined as one thing, then another.

The Sirens function as an acoustic model in Pindar's poetry too, thus shaping the audience's reception of the chorus's song. In his second *Partheneion* the chorus stress the sonic element of the Sirens' *choreia* through the word *kompos*, meaning both "vaunt" and "din":[34]

πάν-
δοξον Αἰολάδα σταθμόν
υἱοῦ τε Παγώνδα                                                  (10)
ὑμνήσω στεφάνοισι θάλ-
λοισα παρθένιον κάρα,
σειρῆνα δὲ κόμπον
αὐλίσκων ὑπὸ λωτίνων
μιμήσομ' ἀοιδαῖς                                                 (15)

κεῖνον, ὃς Ζεφύρου τε σιγάζει πνοὰς
αἰψηράς.

I will sing of the all-glorious house of Aioladas and of his son Pagondas, flourishing with wreaths on my maiden head, and I shall represent in my songs, to the accompaniment of the *lōtos* pipes, the loud vaunt [*kompos*] of the Sirens, the one that silences the quick blasts of the west wind. (Pindar fr. 94b SM, 8–17)

In claiming to represent the Siren's powerful sound, the chorus elevate the musical force of their own song (and so also their praise for the Aioladai), suggesting it is able to move the audience as powerfully as the Sirens can silence the winds.[35]

Imaginative suggestion can also shape the audience's reception of instrumental sound, so that the accompaniment to a song becomes part of its narrative. In Pindar's *Pythian* 12, for example, the *aition* for the *aulos*'s "many-headed *nomos*" simultaneously recreates it, encouraging the audience to hear in the auletic accompaniment the Gorgons' dirge (*thrēnos*), Euryale's "loud-sounding wail" and Perseus's cry;[36] in this way the ode also reenacts Midas's victory in the auletic contest at Delphi.[37] The actual musical accompaniment to a song can also be manipulated through the description

---

34. *kompos* also has a connotation of praise here: see Peponi 2012: 83–84 on the mix of this semantic aspect with its meaning as loud vocal sound.

35. *Contra* Swift 2010: 183, I do not see a sense of musical rivalry here. Stehle 1997: 96 likens the Sirens in Pind. fr. 94b to the magicians who lull the winds in the Hesiodic *Catalogue of Women*: "the audience is like a wind or storm that [the *parthenoi*] 'silence' as the Siren does."

36. κεφαλᾶν πολλᾶν νόμον, Pind. *Pyth.* 12.24; ἐρικλάγκταν γόον, ibid. 21.

37. On the ode's engagement with its own musical accompaniment, see Phillips 2013; cf. Steiner 2013. On the likelihood that this ode was performed to an auletic accompaniment, see Phillips 2013: 38.

of other instruments, which then seem sonically present even if they are not there physically. We will see in chapter 5 an example of such instrumental layering in Sappho fr. 44 Voigt, when the vivid description of multiple instruments being played in celebration of the marriage of Hector and Andromache magnifies the actual accompaniment of the kithara, which thus becomes part of this mythical scene. Euripides frequently exploits this effect by building up multilayered sound pictures, exploiting the versatility of the *aulos* to create the illusion of several instruments being played at once. A particularly powerful example is the complex interplay between imagined and performed *mousikē* in the second stasimon of *Helen*, when the auletic accompaniment is combined with verbal descriptions of *krotala* (castanets), *tympana* (hand drums), *kymbala* (cymbals), *rhombos* (a spatulate blade that produced a sound by being whirled through the air on a string), and the *aulos* itself.[38]

Choruses can also assume apparently inanimate identities through the associational relationship between the verbal and musical elements of their performance. We have already seen in both Alcman's *Partheneion* and Bacchylides 17 that the visual appeal of choruses can be conveyed through their metallic sheen: Hagesichora with her golden mane and silver face; the Nereids with their gleaming limbs and golden ribbons. Leslie Kurke has demonstrated that choruses in archaic Greek poetry are frequently "assimilated to precious or top-rank objects, the products of divine or uncanny crafting" and even as sets of moving statues in perfect formation.[39] We see this same phenomenon at work in Pindar's *Paean* 8, in which the chorus picture the singing *Kēlēdones* as acroteria sculpted on the mythical third temple of Apollo at Delphi:[40]

ὦ Μοῖσαι, το⟨ῦ⟩ δὲ παντέχ[νοις
Ἁφαίστου παλάμαις καὶ Ἀθά[νας
τίς ὁ ῥυθμὸς ἐφαίνετο;
χάλκεοι μὲν τοῖχοι χάλκ[εαί                            (105)
   θ'ὑπὸ κίονες ἔστασαν,
χρύσεαι δ' ἒξ ὑπὲρ αἰετοῦ
ἄειδον Κηληδόνες.

But what pattern, O Muses, was displayed on this [temple] through the all-skillful hands of Hephaistos and Athena? Bronze were the walls, and bronze columns stood beneath, and six golden *Kēlēdones* were singing above the gable. (Pind. *Pae.* B2.102–8 Rutherford = 8.65–71 SM)

This ecphrastic image provides a both visual and acoustic model for the chorus's own dancing and singing. The pattern of the *Kēlēdones* is also their rhythm (*rhyth-*

---

38. See chapter 4, pp. 167–79, on Eur. *Hel.* 1301–68.
39. Kurke 2012: 224; cf. Kurke 2013.
40. On the interplay of chorus and crafted object here, see Power 2011; Weiss 2016.

*mos*, 104), the combination of their choreographic formation and the beat of their song. These lines emphasize their metallic appearance, as golden statues above bronze walls and columns, but the *Kēlēdones* also produce song—indeed they seem to be comparable to the Sirens or Sphinx, conceptualized as "perennial *parthenoi* whose singing threatens civilised order."[41] The chorus thus answer the question they pose to the Muse not only in the words of their song but also in its actual performance, and the combination of these elements invites the audience to see and hear them as the singing statues they describe. This fragment demonstrates how the interplay between words, music, and dance can bring an otherwise absent scene or structure—here the mythical third temple at Delphi—into the performance space.[42] In this respect it is like modern site dance, which frequently aims not just to interact with the performance setting but to physically transform it.[43]

This rich interplay between imagined and performed *mousikē* occurs in a paean; my other examples of imaginative suggestion at work in archaic lyric have included epinicians and above all *partheneia*. Scholarship concerned with the New Music, however, has tended to focus on the dithyramb as the primary site for such metamusical effects and in particular as the primary influence on Euripides' musical innovation in the late fifth century B.C.E.[44] Some of the few surviving dithyrambs display markedly musical language: in addition to Bacchylides 17 (which is traditionally categorized as a dithyramb, despite its paeanic elements), Pindar fr. 70b in particular includes a vivid depiction of Dionysiac *mousikē* that interacts with and goes beyond the chorus's own musical performance. In the opening strophe the chorus describe a vividly synaesthetic mix of movement, sound, and light that conveys the ecstasy of worship for Dionysus and the Great Mother:

σεμνᾶι μὲν κατάρχει
Ματέρι πὰρ μεγάλαι ῥόμβοι τυπάνων,
ἐν δὲ κέχλαδ[εν] κρόταλ' αἰθομένα τε            (10)
δαῒς ὑπὸ ξανθαῖσι πεύκαις·

---

41. Power 2011: 74.

42. If this paean was originally performed at Delphi, its choral architecture would interact with the physical performance space, superimposing previous versions of the temple upon the recently built Alcmaeonid one: see Weiss 2016.

43. One modern comparandum is Joanna Haigood's *Ghost Architecture* (2003): in this performance installation at the Yerba Buena Center for the Arts in San Francisco, dancers represented the movement and physical space of the four buildings that had previously occupied the site of the performance space, thereby bringing its past into the present. On this piece see Kloetzel and Pavlik 2009: 52–63.

44. Musical innovations were also evident in the kitharodic genre, as Timotheus's *Persians* makes clear: Csapo and Wilson 2009; Power 2010: 500–549; LeVen 2014: 150–220. Satyr play was another site for musical experimentation and metamusical play: see Griffith 2013b.

ἐν δὲ Ναΐδων ἐρίγδουποι στοναχαί
μανίαι τ' ἀλαλαί τ' ὀρίνεται ῥιψαύχενι
σὺν κλόνωι.

In the presence of the holy Great Mother the roarings of drums begin, and amid [these] the castanets ring out and the gleaming torch beneath the golden pines, and the loud-sounding cries of the Naiads and ecstatic cries of *alalai* are stirred up with neck-tossing clamor. (Pind. fr. 70b SM, 8–14)

Through this description of cultic song and dance, the dithyrambic chorus not only draw attention to their own performance but construct it as something beyond what the audience actually see onstage: the male choreuts momentarily become the female Naiad nymphs, shaking their heads, shouting loudly, and beating their drums.[45] They also draw on the audience's own experience as spectators and performers of various forms of cultic *mousikē* associated with Dionysus and the Great Mother, and in doing so involve them within their ecstatic performance.[46]

The focus on Dionysiac *mousikē* here, which includes references to particular choral groups like dolphins and Nereids, is a marker of the dithyrambic genre. Many of the most intensely metamusical passages in Euripidean tragedy have a similarly Dionysiac character, and verbal descriptions of multiple instruments, voices, and ecstatic dancing like this one in Pindar fr. 70b magnify the chorus's own performance in honor of the god on both the dithyrambic and the tragic stage. But as we have seen, metamusical play in general is by no means confined to the dithyramb prior to the late fifth century, and the same sort of imaginative suggestion that Pindar's dithyramb sets in motion is at work in other lyric genres as well. It is against this broader backdrop of archaic lyric that we should approach Euripides' experimentation with the dramatic effects of *mousikē*.

## METAMUSICAL PLAY IN AESCHYLUS, SOPHOCLES, AND EARLY EURIPIDES

Tragedy was first and foremost a choral genre, and the predominance of *choreia* in Aeschylus's surviving plays suggests that early tragedy was by its very nature an amalgamation of different types of choral song. We may then naturally expect tragedy to have inherited the use of the choral imaginary in performance that we have seen at work in various types of archaic lyric and to exhibit a similar associational relationship between words, dance, and music. In this half of the chapter I look at moments of metamusicality in the plays of Aeschylus and Sophocles to show how the suggestive interaction between the verbal and musical elements of

---

45. Gurd 2016: 111 notes Pindar's emphasis on timbral sounds here.
46. See the conclusion for further discussion of this process.

*choreia* that we have seen in the songs of Alcman, Pindar, and Bacchylides can operate in a performance by a dramatic chorus. I move from demonstrating the archaic precedents for various metamusical effects in the theater to seeing how such elements of *choreia* (and *mousikē* more generally) can function within the frame of a dramatic narrative.

My aim is not so much to trace a continuous tradition of metamusical play but rather to emphasize that Euripides was not the only tragedian to experiment with the dramatic effects of *mousikē* and language about it. And as I will suggest in the final section, his own experimentation in this area is not exclusively confined to the late 420s onward: *Electra* may be the first extant play in which musical discourse and performance play a central role, but we should not see this as a sudden, revelatory moment in his career. At the same time, Euripides' surviving plays, especially those from the last fifteen years of his career, do differ from those of Aeschylus and Sophocles in how they respond to and incorporate elements of the choral imaginary, exploiting the dramatic effects of imaginative suggestion—the play between imagined and performed *mousikē*—that we previously saw occurring in nondramatic lyric.

My focus here is on metamusical play in tragedy, but it is important to note that this is by no means the only dramatic genre to contain self-reflexive pointers to *mousikē*. Aristophanes' surviving comedies include frequent allusions to musical performance: in *Birds*, for example, the chorus constantly draw attention to their own birdlike singing; *Lysistrata* ends with celebratory *choreia* and "new music" performed by both the Athenian and the Spartan ambassadors;[47] several plays feature parodies of tragic or dithyrambic *mousikē*, such as Agathon's solo performance of his choral song in *Women at the Thesmophoria*, the references to the dithyrambic poets' predilection for imagery of flying in *Birds* and *Clouds*, and Aeschylus's rendition of Euripidean lyric in *Frogs*. But it is satyr play that seems to have been especially prone to self-conscious musical display:[48] the surviving part of Sophocles' *Ichneutae*, for example, is focused on the noise produced by Hermes' newly invented chelys lyre, to which the satyr chorus react with panic and excitement;[49] one of the fragments of his *Inachus* similarly includes comments on a novel musical sound, this time that of Hermes' syrinx;[50] and in the famous fragment of

---

47. Μοῦσαν... νέαν, Ar. *Lys.* 1295. *Mousa* here can also be translated as "Muse."

48. On the musicality of satyr play, see esp. Griffith 2013b: 261–76; also Seidensticker 2010; Lämmle 2013: 177–201; Griffith 2015: 31–32, 42–43, 137–38, 140–41, 144–45. Satyr drama apparently employed particular dance movements to represent the characteristic habitus of its imaginary chorus. As Griffith 2015: 42–43 shows, the *sikinnis*, its most characteristic dance form, seems to have been closely linked to the movement of young animals; verbal descriptions of satyrs behaving like animals must have had a metachoreographic effect, heightening the audience's experience of the chorus.

49. On the staging of a new type of music in this play, see Power 2018.

50. Soph. *Inachus* fr. 269c8, 16–20, 25–27. On these lines see Griffith 2013b: 271.

Pratinas's satyr play the chorus indignantly express their alarm at the *aulos*'s takeover of their *mousikē*.⁵¹ As we shall see, Euripides' "prosatyric" *Alcestis* also contains an early example of metamusical play between the language and performance of *choreia*. Musical experimentation in tragedy should therefore be understood in the light of other contemporary dramatic genres as well as against the backdrop of archaic choral lyric.

## Aeschylus

It has long been recognized that Aeschylus employs musical imagery in his tragedies and works it into the dramatic narrative.⁵² The clearest example is the motif of the *nomos anomos* in the *Oresteia*: the chorus use this oxymoron—meaning both "tuneless tune" and "lawless law"—to describe Cassandra's song of lament in *Agamemnon*, but the phrase also conveys the violation of legal and natural order in the trilogy as a whole.⁵³ At the same time, it is tied to the repeated musical juxtaposition of paean and lament, which highlights "the irony of false victory and of the prayer thwarted by the curse, and ... marks the passage of triumph into despair."⁵⁴ This unsettling paradox is resolved at the end of the trilogy with a marked change in *choreia*—a transition from both the lament that dominates *Libation Bearers* and the Erinyes' own terrifying song and dance (especially their Binding Song, which I discuss further below) to the final procession of a new chorus of Attic women raising the paeanic cry of *ololygē* with Athena herself as their leader.⁵⁵

As this example of musical resolution at the end of *Eumenides* demonstrates, musical performance, not just imagery, can be closely bound up with the plot of an Aeschylean tragedy.⁵⁶ The different forms of *choreia* performed by the different choruses of the *Oresteia*—the Argive elders, the libation bearers, the Erinyes/

---

51. *TrGF* I, 4 F 3 (Ath. 14.617).

52. On musical symbolism in Aeschylean tragedy, see esp. Haldane 1965; Fleming 1977; Pintacuda 1978: 83–125; Scott 1984; Wilson and Taplin 1993.

53. Aesch. *Ag.* 1142. On the double meaning of this phrase (referring to both musical and legal order), see Fleming 1977; cf. Pintacuda 1978: 112–13.

54. Haldane 1965: 37.

55. The trilogy ends with the line "Now raise a cry of *ololygē* to crown our song!" (ὀλολύξατε νῦν ἐπὶ μολπαῖς, *Eum.* 1047). Fleming 1977 suggests that in the final scene "the conflicting nomoi are reconciled by a final, musical allusion to the kitharodic Nomos" (233). Scott 1984: 22–151 argues for a connection between meter and theme in the trilogy: the return of the lecythion meter at the end of *Eumenides*, replacing the heavily iambic songs of the women in *Libation Bearers* and of the Erinyes in the first part of *Eumenides*, signals the end of conflict as "words of justice are sung to the meter associated with justice" (135). Wilson and Taplin 1993 argue that the transformation of the Erinyes' songs and their incorporation within the city at the end of the trilogy represent the incorporation of tragedy itself with Athens.

56. Cf. Scott 1984, who discusses the musical form of his tragedies primarily in terms of meter; also Pintacuda 1978: 83–125, who similarly focuses on rhythm in his analysis of the links between lyrical form and meaning in Aeschylus.

Eumenides, the Attic women—mark different stages of the narrative. *Mousikē* can also produce dramatic action as well as reflect it: in *Libation Bearers*, the long, elaborate *kommos* of Electra, Orestes, and the chorus generates the siblings' resolve to kill Clytemnestra and Aegisthus, demonstrating the powerful link between mourning and revenge.[57] It also generates a sense of epiphany, as they repeatedly call on Agamemnon to hear their lament. In *Persians*, the chorus succeed in raising the ghost of their king through their song and dance as they obey Atossa's instructions to "accompany these libations to the dead with auspicious songs and call up the divine Darius."[58] As we shall see, Euripides also deploys this powerful potential of *mousikē* to push a plot forward, whether through changing the form of musical performance, anticipating a crucial point of the action, or heralding the arrival of a character.

The chorus can also make use of the close relationship between the verbal and musical aspects of their performance to enact a scene that is otherwise offstage. Most choral songs in tragedy would involve some degree of associational relationship between words, music, and dance even without any explicit metamusical signposting. We may expect the correlation to be especially strong when the song is a narrative rather than dominated by gnomic judgments, and even more so when it includes a description of some sort of movement, such as Io's wanderings in *Suppliants* (540–79) or the journey of Helen, followed by the Achaeans, to Troy in *Agamemnon* (688–98). But occasionally the process of imaginative suggestion is more clearly at work, such as when the chorus of *Agamemnon*, recounting the sacrifice of Iphigenia, remember how she used to sing at her father's banquets:

ἔβαλλ' ἕκαστον θυτή- (240)
  ρων ἀπ' ὄμματος βέλει φιλοίκτωι,
πρέπουσά θ' ὡς ἐν γραφαῖς, προσεννέπειν
θέλουσ', ἐπεὶ πολλάκις
πατρὸς κατ' ἀνδρῶνας εὐτραπέζους
ἔμελψεν, ἁγνᾶι δ' ἀταύρωτος αὐδᾶι πατρὸς (245)
φίλου τριτόσπονδον εὔποτμον παι-
  ῶνα φίλως ἐτίμα.

She cast on each of her sacrificers a pitiful glance from her eyes, shining forth as if in a picture, wishing to address them, since often in her father's hospitable banqueting halls she had sung, and unwedded, with a pure voice, she lovingly used to honor her beloved father's paean for good fortune to accompany the third libation. (Aesch. *Ag.* 240–47)

---

57. On the link between lament and revenge in the Greek tradition, see Alexiou 1974; Holst-Warhaft 1992; Foley 2001: 19–56.
58. χοαῖσι ταῖσδε νερτέρων / ὕμνους ἐπευφημεῖτε, τόν τε δαίμονα / Δαρεῖον ἀνακαλεῖσθε, Aesch. *Pers.* 619–21.

Here the chorus prompt the audience to visualize this scene themselves by picturing Iphigenia "as if in a painting" while they also create a vivid acoustic image by describing the paean she used to sing. Since the chorus are themselves singing, their own performance merges with that of Iphigenia, so that this scene of the past, which contrasts so poignantly with the present of their narrative, comes to life sonically as well as visually. Yet the impression here is also distinctly *not* one of merging: the disconnect between her performance—a paean sung by a young female soloist—and the collective song of these Argive elders is also deeply unsettling. Iphigenia's voice is thus both heard and silenced, just as it is at the scene of her sacrifice, where "her pleas and cries of 'Father' ... the war-loving chieftains set at naught."[59]

The simultaneous enactment of what the chorus describe in song is especially effective in the parodos of *Seven against Thebes,* in which the terrified chorus of Theban women imagine the approaching army led by Polynices against the city. They focus on its noise—the war cries, the thud of the horses' hooves, the clash of shields—and at the same time combine these sound pictures with their own cries of lament:[60]

> †ἐλεῖ† δὲ γᾶς ἐμᾶς πεδί' ὁπλόκτυπ' ὠ-
> τὶ χρίμπτει βοάν·
> ποτᾶται, βρέμει δ' ἀμαχέτου δίκαν                    (85)
> ὕδατος ὀροτύπου.
> ἰὼ ἰὼ θεοὶ θεαί τ' ὀρόμενον
> κακὸν ἀλεύσατε.
> ὀᾶ·

The soil of my land, struck by hooves, brings the cry near to my ear! It's flying, and it's roaring like unconquerable mountain-beating water. *Iō iō* you gods and goddesses, ward off the surging evil! *Oa!* (Aesch. *Sept.* 83–89)

As J. A. Haldane observes, "reiterated aural images accumulate to create the impression of a continual, maddening cacophony, so permitting the audience to experience the terrifying reality of the siege."[61] As the chorus's song becomes increasingly frantic, their cries continue to mix with the various sounds of the army. This effect is especially pronounced at the start of the second strophe and antistrophe, when they utter the staccato cry *e e e e* and then immediately describe the noise they hear: the "rattle of chariots"; the "bombardment of stones."[62]

---

59. λιτὰς δὲ καὶ κληδόνας πατρῴους / παρ' οὐδὲν ... ἔθεντο φιλόμαχοι βραβῆς, *Ag.* 228–30. The performance by a female soloist of a paean (usually sung by a male chorus) also appears as a manifestation of her sacrifice on the army's behalf, whom she displaces as Greece's savior: as I show in chapter 5, Euripides portrays this sacrifice with a similar use of the paeanic genre at the end of *Iphigenia in Aulis.*
60. On the noise of *Seven,* see also Stanford 1983: 55–56; Porter 2013: 20–22; Gurd 2016: 74–78.
61. Haldane 1965: 36.
62. ὄτοβον ἁρμάτων, Aesch. *Sept.* 151; ἀκροβόλος ... λιθὰς, 158. Cf. Gurd 2016: 75–76.

The Theban chorus's enactment of the scene that they describe is not merely acoustic. In the middle of their song, they address the audience directly (as well as themselves and Eteocles) to draw attention to the army's noise, which they are simultaneously creating through their own song and dance:

ἀκούετ' ἢ οὐκ ἀκούετ' ἀσπίδων κτύπον;  (100)
πέπλων καὶ στεφέων πότ' εἰ μὴ νῦν †ἀμ-
φὶ λιτὰν† ἕξομεν;
κτύπον δέδορκα· πάταγος οὐχ ἑνὸς δορός.

Do you hear or don't you hear the clash of shields? When, if not now, will we be able [to throw?] robes and garlands around [the gods] as a prayer-offering? I see the clash! It isn't the clatter of [just] one spear. (Aesch. *Sept.* 100–103)

As we shall see in chapter 3, the noun *ktypos* ("clash, noise, din") and related words are often used in tragedy to refer to the percussive element of lament: in their *kommos* with Electra and Orestes the chorus of Aeschylus's *Libation Bearers* sing of how their "beaten, all-wretched head rings with noise [*ktypos*]"; Hecuba in Euripides' *Trojan Women* uses the verb *ktypeō* to refer to her striking of the ground with her hands.[63] So here too the chorus produce the noise they describe through their own gestures of lament but urge their audience to hear this as the din of the approaching army and feel their fear as a result. The synesthetic statement "I see the clash [*ktypos*]" turns the sound picture into a full visualization of the army's ominous approach and at the same time highlights the combination of sound and physical movement conveyed by *ktypos* and enacted through their own beating of their bodies and the ground.[64]

Later in the play, as the bodies of Eteocles and Polynices are brought onstage, the chorus explicitly encourage the audience to see and hear in their gestures of lament the brothers' journey to Hades:

ἀλλὰ γόων, ὦ φίλαι, κατ' οὖρον
ἐρέσσετ' ἀμφὶ κρατὶ πόμπιμον χεροῖν  (855)
πίτυλον, ὃς αἰὲν δ' Ἀχέροντ' ἀμείβεται.

But, O friends, along the wind of lamentation, row with your hands about your head the escorting stroke of oars, which is always crossing the Acheron. (Aesch. *Sept.* 854–56)

Here the double meaning of the verb *eresset'* ("row" but also "put in quick motion, ply") in line 855 links the beating of hands on the head both acoustically and visually with the beat of the oars in the water as Charon's boat brings the brothers

---

63. κτύπωι δ' ἐπερροθεῖ / κροτητὸν ἁμὸν πανάθλιον κάρα, Aesch. *Cho.* 427–28; Eur. *Tro.* 1306.
64. Cf. Porter 2013: 22 on this synesthetic statement ("the audience can see, in turn, a sound being danced on the *orchēstra* in a corresponding rhythmic pattern").

across the Acheron. Such representative movement may have been a traditional part of ritual mourning: in the antiphonal lament of Xerxes and the chorus in Aeschylus's *Persians*, the king similarly bids them to "row, row, and groan for my sake."[65] In later tragedy, however, images of rowing tend to be linked to the dithyramb instead, often through the figure of the dancing dolphin, as we shall see in chapter 4 in the case of the third stasimon of *Helen*. The "fifty-oarer" (pentoconter), a standard type of ship design in this period, shared with the dithyramb the same number of rowers/dancers and the same musical accompaniment of the *aulos*. The chorus of *Iphigenia in Tauris* draw on these associations when they imagine Iphigenia's journey back to Greece on a ship with fifty oars, to the accompaniment of Pan's syrinx and Apollo with his lyre (1123–36). The fifty oars of her imaginary vessel evoke the fifty choreuts of a dithyramb, while the instrumental accompaniment finds its analogue in the *aulos*, to which rowers would row and both tragic and dithyrambic choruses would sing and dance.[66]

The technique of imaginative suggestion, so common in archaic lyric, can therefore play an important part in linking a choral performance to the dramatic narrative, even as it extends the scope of the drama outside the spatial and temporal confines of the tragedy itself. But *mousikē* can also be integrated within a drama more simply, by being closely related to the ritual character of the chorus. The close alignment of musical performance and choral character—which we see in Euripides' *Bacchae*, with the maenads' exuberant *choreia* for Dionysus—is common in Aeschylean tragedy, particularly in dramas like *Suppliants*, *Libation Bearers*, and *Eumenides*, in which, as the titles suggest, the chorus play a dominant role; given the common Greek view of Persians as being especially prone to effeminate mourning, we can add *Persians*, in which the chorus's song is dominated by lament.[67] It is when a chorus's ritual performance in large part defines its character that we find vivid moments of choral self-referentiality, when they explicitly describe their own *mousikē* while performing it. In *Suppliants*, for example, as we shall see in chapter 4, the chorus compare their song to that of the mourning nightingale, thereby heightening the impact of their own lament and their plight as suppliants. And when the chorus of *Libation Bearers*, in the middle of their *kommos* with Orestes and Electra, vividly describe their cries and gestures of lament (423–28), they thereby assert their choral identity as mourners.

Another especially vivid example of this correlation between choral performance and identity is the Erinyes' Binding Song in *Eumenides*,[68] which they perform

---

65. ἔρεσσ' ἔρεσσε καὶ στέναζ' ἐμὰν χάριν, Aesch. *Pers.* 1046.
66. On the merging of the syrinx, lyre, and *aulos* here, see Weiss forthcoming a.
67. On this conceptualization of Persians in the Greek imagination and its dramatization in Aeschylus's play, see Hall 1989: 83–84.
68. ὕμνος... δέσμιος, Aesch. *Eum.* 344–45.

over Orestes. Beginning with the line "Come now, let us join together a choral dance," they draw attention to the nature of their performance, and in particular emphasize its violent physicality:[69]

| δόξαι δ' ἀνδρῶν καὶ μάλ' ὑπ' αἰθέρι σεμναὶ | [3rd strophe] |
|---|---|
| τακόμεναι κατὰ γᾶς μινύθουσιν ἄτιμοι | |
| ἁμετέραις ἐφόδοις μελανείμοσιν | (370) |
| ὀρχησμοῖς τ' ἐπιφθόνοις ποδός· | |
| | |
| μάλα γὰρ οὖν ἁλομένα | [3rd ephymnion] |
| ἀνάκαθεν βαρυπετῆ | |
| καταφέρω ποδὸς ἀκμάν, | |
| σφαλερὰ ⟨καὶ⟩ τανυδρόμοις | (375) |
| κῶλα, δύσφορον ἄταν. | |

Men's beliefs, even [those that are] very proud [while] beneath the bright sky, melting away [when] beneath the earth they are diminished, dishonored, as a result of our black-clothed attacks and the hostile dancing of our feet.

For leaping high from above I bring down the heavy-falling strike of my foot, legs to make stumble even those running at full stretch, unendurable ruin. (Aesch. *Eum.* 368–76)

These lines work as stage directions for the chorus's own dance by emphasizing violent jumping and stamping of their feet. The movement they describe and simultaneously enact is also reproduced through the paeonic rhythm of lines 372–76, so that, as Yopie Prins notes, "[the] emphasis on the last syllable both represents and *is* the foot coming down."[70] Henrichs observes that, by referring to their own dancing in this way, the Erinyes fulfill their own choral identity: their feet "epitomize their choral identity as performers of the dance; at the same time, their feet function as instruments of destruction that physically perform the incantation in an act of sympathetic magic. Ritual performance and choral self-referentiality thus go hand in hand, reinforcing each other."[71]

We can see this sort of overlap between choral character and self-reflexive emphasis on musical performance in some of the fragments of Aeschylus's plays as well. In a fragment of Aeschylus's *Nereids* the titular chorus sing of "crossing the expanse of the dolphin sea."[72] A series of vases from the second half of the fifth century B.C.E. shows Nereids riding on dolphins as they carry armor for Achilles, and we can assume that the chorus of Aeschylus's play are referring to this same

69. ἄγε δὴ καὶ χορὸν ἄψωμεν, Aesch. *Eum.* 307.
70. Prins 1991: 189 (emphasis original). Cf. Visvardi 2015: 103–5 on how the chorus here enact the derangement they describe.
71. Henrichs 1994–95: 64. Cf. Calame 2013 on the performative nature of the song. See also Prins 1991 on its self-fulfilling language, which effects the Erinyes' full visualization.
72. δελφινηρὸν πεδίον πόντου / διαμειψάμεναι, Aesch. fr. 150.

activity, which is a central part of their own character and dramatic role.⁷³ In *Bassarids*, the second play of the Lycurgan tetralogy, the chorus is made up of Thracian devotees of Dionysus, and cultic music-making for the god must have been an important part of their ritual identity; it would also represent the sort of worship that Orpheus, the central character, has shunned.⁷⁴ One of the few surviving fragments of this play consists of the chorus's describing in (appropriately) bacchiac meter how Dionysus will take revenge upon Orpheus by "leaping forth upon him."⁷⁵ As in the Binding Song of the *Eumenides*, we can imagine the choreuts themselves performing some energetic dance moves to represent the violence of the god's attack.

A more extended metamusical passage survives from the first play of the same tetralogy, *Edonians*, but here performed and described *mousikē* do not coincide. This fragment details the overwhelming sounds of cultic music being performed for Dionysus: the cry of the *aulos* that "brings on frenzy," the crash of castanets, the "terrifying" bull-roarers, and the drum (*tympanon*) that sounds like underground thunder.⁷⁶ But the anapaestic (recitative) rhythm of these lines indicates that those delivering them—probably the chorus of Thracians—are not yet fully singing and dancing as they do so. They seem to be referring not to their own activity (or not yet) but rather to that of Dionysus's followers, who have just arrived with the god in Thrace. They focus on their own terrified response to the noises they hear, but unlike the chorus of *Seven Against Thebes*, they do not simultaneously produce those noises through their own song and dance. The mismatch between their own, more restrained performance and the one they describe underscores the resistance to Dionysus's cult among the Edonians, for which their king, Lyrcurgus, is about to be severely punished. It also points forward to the performance of ecstatic song and dance later in the play and through the rest of the tetralogy.

*Mousikē*, then, clearly plays a central role in much of Aeschylus's work. In part this is because it is often related to the chorus's identity, but Aeschylus was also experimenting with how different types of musical performance and imagery could interact with the dramatic narrative. We should then question his reputation for being old-fashioned and conservative when compared with the musically innovative Euripides. This reputation results in part from the showdown staged between the two tragedians in Aristophanes' *Frogs*, in which Euripides characterizes Aeschylus's lyrics as monotonous, conforming to a single rhythmic pattern,

---

73. On these vases and their link to Aeschylus's tragedy, see Richter 1936: 175–76; S. G. Miller 1986, esp. 161–62; Matheson 1995: 252.
74. For a reconstruction of the play's plot, see esp. West 1990: 26–50. On the importance of *mousikē* in the tetralogy as a whole, see Watson 2015.
75. προπηδήσεται †νιντ†, Aesch. fr. 23a.
76. μανίας ἐπαγωγὸν, Aesch. fr. 57.5; φοβεροί, 9; ὥσθ' ὑπογαίου / βροντῆς, 10–11.

and full of bombastic language.[77] But it also results from modern scholarship on the New Music, which highlights the increase of language about *mousikē* in the later plays of Euripides and his use of motifs inherited from the dithyrambic genre but tends to be rather silent about Aeschylus (and Sophocles). Aristophanes' *Frogs* demonstrates that by the end of the fifth century Euripides was regarded as "the beacon of innovative styles and controversial themes."[78] But even this selective study of the older tragedian's extant plays indicates that he too experimented with many of the musical effects that we find in Euripides' tragedies, such as the use of performative language to heighten the intensity of *choreia* and mold the audience's response to it, and the interplay of language, music, and dance to bring onstage scenes that are otherwise unseen. We would do well to remember, then, not only that Aristophanes constructs such a sharp old/new opposition between the two tragedians for his own dramatic (and comedic) purposes but also that he and his audience may have had comparatively little experience of Aeschylean tragedy in performance—the full effect of Aeschylus's live *mousikē* would have been less clear to them than that of Euripides' more recent plays.[79] Given Aeschylus's reputation for many other technical advances—ancient commentators talk of his increasing the number of actors, using mechanical devices, and even being the first to devise his choruses' choreography himself—it is hard to believe that he was not a musical innovator as well.[80]

For all Aeschylus's musical experimentation, however, it is striking that few of the choral images that we saw at work in archaic lyric appear in his surviving plays. In this respect his tragedies differ markedly from Euripides' later work, in which choruses frequently refer to archetypal musical figures like horses, dolphins, birds, Nereids, and Muses, encouraging a crossover between their own performance and the images they describe. This difference may simply be an accident of survival: as we have seen, the tantalizing fragment of Aeschylus's *Nereids* clearly draws on the choral—especially dithyrambic—imaginary, and presumably would prompt the audience to visualize the dramatic chorus as the dolphin-riding Nereids whose journey they narrate. But whereas in Bacchylides 17 the chorus only momentarily assume the identity of Nereids, in Aeschylus's play they speak, sing, and dance as Nereids through the whole performance: this archetypal choral group does not just exist within a scene far removed in place and time from the dramatic action but constitutes the chorus's own character within the tragedy. In contrast, as we will see

---

77. Ar. *Ran.* 907–1364, esp. 1249–97.
78. Griffith 2013a: 119.
79. On the question of whether the audience of *Frogs* (and indeed any audience in the late fifth century) would have seen productions of Aeschylus's tragedies, see Griffith 2013a: 116; also Scodel 2007: 130–33.
80. On such innovations, see *Vit. Aesch.* 14–16; Arist. *Poet.* 1449a15–18; Ath. 1.21e.

in the rest of this book, Euripides frequently integrates such choral figures without making them a consistent part of a chorus's characterization and so effects a more complex and layered form of mimeticism. As in archaic lyric, his choruses can momentarily assume one identity and then another within the same song, even when the figures with which they merge seem far from their own choral character—though no farther than Nereid maidens may seem from an all-male dithyrambic chorus. Aeschylus does make use of the interplay between described and performed *mousikē* in order to evoke images that are otherwise absent onstage, but Euripides much more often takes us into worlds beyond the immediate dramatic action and performance space through his chorus's use of imaginative suggestion.

## Sophocles

Sophocles is often overlooked in discussions of tragic *mousikē*.[81] Such neglect partly results from there being fewer references to music and dance in surviving Sophoclean tragedy than in the work of both Aeschylus and Euripides, as well as from the lower number of sung lines in general. Yet even if he was not associated with musical novelty as much as Euripides, Sophocles nevertheless had a strong reputation as a musician, and several of his plays exhibit markedly performative language that suggests moments of intense musicality.[82]

Surviving fragments and titles of Sophocles' tragedies indicate that *mousikē* could play a very prominent role. Though the subject of *Tympanistae* ("The Drummers") is far from certain, the title indicates that the chorus consisted of players of *tympana*, instruments like tambourines, probably in honor of Dionysus or Cybele.[83] We may conjecture that they would have sung about the *mousikē* of their cultic celebrations while simultaneously performing it, presumably with an emphasis on percussion. Several fragments of other plays include vivid descriptions of instrumental music. One from *Mysians* mentions the Phrygian *trigōnos* (a type of lyre) and "the doubly twanged harmony of notes of the Lydian *pectis*."[84] In an unattributed fragment someone remarks "for he's no longer blowing on small *auliskoi* but with wild blasts without a cheek strap."[85] Timothy Power notes that Sophocles seems here to be imag-

---

81. Important exceptions are Pintacuda 1978: 127–55; Henrichs 1994–95: 65–85 (on choral self-reference and projection); Scott 1996a, 1996b (primarily focused on metrical patterns); Wilson 2009: 59–69 (on *Thamyras*); Power 2012.

82. Sophocles himself is said to have "taken up and played the kithara" in his *Thamyras* (κιθάραν ἀναλαβὼν ἐν μόνωι τῶι Θαμύριδί ποτε ἐκιθάρισεν, *Vit. Soph.* 5). Wilson 2009: 61 observes that this tradition suggests "a perceived analogue between the tragic poet and the mythic musician."

83. On the possibility that this play dealt with the story of the Thracian king Phineus, see Lloyd-Jones 1996: 308–9; Rizzo 2002.

84. ἀντίσπαστά τε / Λυδῆς ... πηκτίδος συγχορδία, Soph. fr. 412.

85. φυσᾶι γὰρ οὐ σμικροῖσιν αὐλίσκοις ἔτι, / ἀλλ' ἀγρίαις φύσαισι φορβειᾶς ἄτερ, Soph. fr. 768. A cheek strap (*phorbeia*) was used to hold the two *aulos* pipes in the mouth.

ining "a virtuoso showman of the New Music."[86] Such musical commentary would also help to shape the audience's auditory reception of the aulete in the theater and presumably link his instrumentation to an event or character in the play.

Music must also have been central to the tragedy *Thamyras,* in which the titular character was the Thracian kitharode who brought about his own demise by boasting that he could beat the Muses with his singing. It seems likely that the play had a chorus of Muses, in which case it may have staged a musical showdown between them and Thamyras.[87] Certainly the surviving fragments demonstrate a strongly musical focus: of the seven attributed to the play, five concern the lyre, or music making more generally, or both.[88] One choral fragment focuses in particular on the close association of music and dance, pointing to the power of one to incite the other: "These tunes in which we celebrate you get the feet forward, running, moving, with hands, with feet."[89] The chorus here draw attention to the trochaic rhythm of their song through the "running" (*trochima*) movement it inspires, with a mimetic effect similar to that of the Erinyes' emphasis on the strike of their feet in Aeschylus's *Eumenides;* they simultaneously encourage the audience's own kinetic response to such fast-paced tunes. With such performative language they also highlight their own musicality, as would befit a chorus of Muses.

*Thamyras* provides a particularly clear example of how *mousikē* could be closely bound up with the plot of a tragedy both as a theme or subject and through its live performance. The singer's downfall is an explicitly musical one, as becomes clear in another lyric fragment, which may come from his own lament: "breaking the horn bound with gold, breaking the harmony of the strung lyre."[90] Power has suggested that the play may have then staged the triumph of the *aulos* over the kithara;[91] at the very least the sound of the *aulos* following Thamyras's defeat would underscore the silence of his own instrument.

Several of Sophocles' surviving tragedies also indicate a close relationship between references to *mousikē* and the dramatic narrative. In *Ajax,* for example, the chorus sing a so-called joy-before-disaster ode—that is, they perform a particularly exuberant song shortly before the protagonist's downfall, at a moment of misguided optimism.[92] As Henrichs has emphasized, such songs tend to be remarkably performative, with descriptions of and directions for the chorus's own *mousikē* that suggest a strong ritual self-awareness: "It is here, at the climactic

---

86. Power 2012: 297.
87. On the Muse chorus, see Wilson 2009: 63–64. The Sophoclean title *Mousae* may refer to the same play: see ibid.; Lloyd-Jones 1996: 103.
88. Frr. 238, 240, 241, 244, 245.
89. πρόποδα μέλεα τάδε σε κλέομεν / τρόχιμα βάσιμα χέρεσι πόδεσι, Soph. fr. 240.
90. ῥηγνὺς χρυσόδετον κέρας, / ῥηγνὺς ἁρμονίαν χορδοτόνου λύρας, Soph. fr. 244.
91. Power 2012: 300.
92. Soph. *Aj.* 693–718.

turning point of the action, that these choruses comment self-referentially on their performance as dancers, and compare their own ecstatic dancing to the dancing associated with Dionysiac ritual."[93] Ian Rutherford has demonstrated that such songs can also have a paeanic coloring, as is again clear in the second stasimon of *Ajax*, when, in reaction to the hero's "deception speech," the chorus call on both Pan and Apollo to join them:[94]

> ἔφριξ' ἔρωτι, περιχαρὴς δ' ἀνεπτάμαν.
> ἰὼ ἰὼ Πὰν Πάν,
> ὦ Πὰν Πὰν ἁλίπλαγκτε, Κυλ- (695)
> λανίας χιονοκτύπου
> πετραίας ἀπὸ δειράδος φάνηθ', ὦ
> θεῶν χοροποι' ἄναξ, ὅπως μοι
> Μύσια Κνώσι' ὀρ-
> χήματ' αὐτοδαῆ ξυνὼν ἰάψῃς. (700)
> νῦν γὰρ ἐμοὶ μέλει χορεῦσαι.
> Ἰκαρίων δ' ὑπὲρ †πελαγέων†
> μολὼν ἄναξ Ἀπόλλων
> ὁ Δάλιος εὔγνωστος
> ἐμοὶ ξυνείη διὰ παντὸς εὔφρων. (705)

I've shuddered with desire and flown up in great delight. *Iō iō* Pan, Pan! O Pan, Pan, sea-wanderer, from the snow-beaten rocky ridge of Cyllene appear, O chorus leader of the gods, lord, so that you may be with me and send forth your Mysian, Cnosian self-taught dances. For now I am keen to dance! And, coming over the Icarian seas, lord Apollo, the Delian one, easy to recognize, may he be with me always in kindness. (Soph. *Aj.* 693–705)

Here the chorus describe the beginnings of their own dance as well as the mental state that provokes it, creating a clear correlation between their words and their musical performance. At the same time, they call upon Pan to appear as their chorus leader, followed by Apollo, whose imagined epiphany forms the strophe's climax. They thus generate a sense of the gods' presence through their own *choreia*, with Pan's (and Apollo's) dancing merging with their own, as if they really are performing to his lead. As we will see in chapter 4, *choreia* is often associated with epiphany through its ability to induce both performers and audience to imagine that a god is really present.[95] (And as we saw in the case of Aeschylus's *Persians*, it can

---

93. Henrichs 1994–95: 73. Cf. Rutherford 1994–95; Power 2012: 296.
94. Rutherford 1994–95, esp. 124–27. On the association of Pan as well as Apollo with the paean, see Rutherford 2001: 12 n. 8. Kowalzig 2007b: 235 emphasizes the merging of Pan, Apollo, and Dionysus in this song. See also Weiss forthcoming b on the ode's generic hybridity.
95. On this presencing effect of *choreia* in archaic poetry, see Mullen 1982: 70–89; Burnett 1985: 8–14; Kurke 2012, 2013.

bring a ghost physically into the theater.) In *Ajax* the effect of such a performance is to draw the audience into virtually experiencing the epiphany that the chorus describe, so that they too are encouraged to interpret Ajax's words optimistically, even though they know them to be otherwise.

In *Women of Trachis* the device of premature choral jubilation occurs sometime before the moment of tragic reversal and forms part of the drama's carefully constructed musical arc.[96] Following the news of Heracles' imminent arrival, the chorus burst into song, combining multiple choral genres (hymenaeal, parthenaic, paeanic, dithyrambic) in their enthusiasm to get everyone singing and dancing:[97]

| | |
|---|---|
| ἀνολολυξάτω δόμος | (205) |
| ἐφεστίοις ἀλαλαγαῖς | |
| ὁ μελλόνυμφος· ἐν δὲ κοινὸς ἀρσένων | |
| ἴτω κλαγγὰ τὸν εὐφαρέτραν | |
| Ἀπόλλω προστάταν, | |
| ὁμοῦ δὲ παιᾶνα παι- | (210) |
| ᾶν' ἀνάγετ', ὦ παρθένοι, | |
| βοᾶτε τὰν ὁμόσπορον | |
| Ἄρτεμιν Ὀρτυγίαν, ἐλαφαβόλον, ἀμφίπυρον, | |
| γείτονάς τε Νύμφας. | (215) |
| αἴρομαι οὐδ' ἀπώσομαι | |
| τὸν αὐλόν, ὦ τύραννε τᾶς ἐμᾶς φρενός. | |
| ἰδού μ' ἀναταράσσει, | |
| εὐοῖ, | |
| ὁ κισσὸς ἄρτι Βακχίαν | |
| ὑποστρέφων ἅμιλλαν. | (220) |
| ἰὼ ἰὼ Παιάν· | |
| ἴδε ἴδ', ὦ φίλα γύναι· | |
| τάδ' ἀντίπρωιρα δή σοι | |
| βλέπειν πάρεστ' ἐναργῆ. | |

Let the house raise a shout of *ololygē*, with shouts of *alalai* by the hearth, [the house] that is to be united in marriage. And let the collective cry of men go up to the one of the fair quiver, Apollo the protector, and you, O maidens, together raise up the paean, the paean, call upon his sister, Artemis the Ortygian, deer-shooter, bearer of the double torch, and the neighboring nymphs. I'm lifted up and will not reject the *aulos*, O tyrant of my mind. Look, the ivy shakes me up—*euoi!*—turning me round just now in the Bacchic contest. *Iō iō Paean!* Look, look, O dear lady: You can see these things clearly, right in front of you. (Soph. *Trach.* 205–24)

---

96. Henrichs 1994–95: 84.
97. On the mix of genres here, see Henrichs 1994–95: 80–84; Power 2012: 293–95; Weiss forthcoming b.

The chorus bring into their own *choreia* the divine participants whom they call upon to join them—Apollo, Artemis, the nymphs, even Dionysus, who becomes synonymous with the *aulos* as the "tyrant of my mind" (216). The epiphanic climax of their song comes when they direct Deianeira to see "these things" there before her—not, as it turns out, Heracles himself, but a procession of captives led by the herald Lichas. Later in the play, after Deianeira has instructed Lichas to give Heracles her magic robe, the chorus sing an ode again focused on Heracles' arrival. They envisage his return in musical terms, imagining a future celebration that is already present through their own *choreia*:

> ὁ καλλιβόας τάχ' ὑμῖν αὐλὸς οὐκ ἀναρσίαν (640)
> ἀχῶν καναχὰν ἐπάνεισιν, ἀλλὰ θείας
> ἀντίλυρον μούσας.

> Soon the beautiful shout of the *aulos* will rise up for you again, not sounding out an unharmonious clamor, but [the sound of] divine music, responding to the lyre. (Soph. *Trach.* 640–42).

The sound they describe here is the one already being heard in the theater—the tune of the *aulos*, to which they are singing and dancing. Like their earlier, astrophic outburst, the song thus heralds and also vividly enacts the appearance of Heracles, though perhaps, as Henrichs suggests, with a hint of premonition—the fear of "unharmonious clamor" rather than celebratory *mousikē*.[98]

When Heracles does finally come onstage, however, the chorus's *mousikē* is very different. In contrast with their earlier jubilant performance in anticipation of his arrival, now, as the dying hero is carried in, they sing a lament like that of the "shrill-voiced nightingale."[99] As we will see in chapter 4, this musical figure is often referred to in the context of tragic lament and can frame the audience's reception of the sounds they hear: indeed, the chorus in Aeschylus's *Suppliants* even describe how someone who hears their mourning song would think he is listening to that of the bird.[100] The chorus of *Women of Trachis* then break off their lament as they turn to see the long-awaited Heracles and focus on the silence of his entrance instead: the steps of those carrying him are "noiseless"; he himself is "speechless."[101] As William Scott observes, "the music that characterizes the first section of the play is purposefully silenced; both singer and song are replaced by the new music of Heracles."[102] The shift from *choreia* to the hero's own painful singing, and then to an intimate exchange between him and his son, stresses the poignant contrast

---

98. Henrichs 1994–95: 85.
99. ὀξύφωνος ὡς ἀηδών, Soph. *Trach.* 963.
100. Aesch. *Supp.* 58–71.
101. ἄψοφον, Soph. *Trach.* 967; ἀναύδατος, 968.
102. Scott 1996a: 15.

between the public celebration that the chorus previously envisaged (and prematurely enacted) and the reality of his fate.

As this selective survey of musical language and performance in Sophocles' tragedies makes clear, there is frequently a close correlation between the verbal and musical elements of *choreia*, whereby the chorus to a large degree enact the music and dance that they describe, often with a powerful dramatic effect. There are very few moments, however, when the chorus describe in any sustained way a scene of music making that is far from their own, without any self-referential markers that explicitly link it to the here and now of their own *mousikē*. Moreover, like Aeschylus, in his surviving work Sophocles seldom makes use of the network of choral associations that we saw in archaic lyric—associations that become so prominent in Euripides' later tragedies. A rare example of such choral imagery occurs in *Antigone*, in the closing antistrophe of the chorus's hymn to Dionysus:

ἰὼ πῦρ πνεόντων
χοράγ' ἄστρων, νυχίων
φθεγμάτων ἐπίσκοπε,
Ζηνὸς γένεθλον, προφάνηθ',
ὤναξ, σαῖς ἅμα περιπόλοις (1150)
Θυίασιν, αἵ σε μαινόμεναι πάννυχοι
χορεύουσι τὸν ταμίαν Ἴακχον.

*Iō* chorus leader of fire-breathing stars, overseer of voices of the night, offspring of Zeus, appear, lord, together with your attendant Thyiads, who in their frenzy dance in choruses all night long in honor of you, their master, Iacchus! (Soph. *Ant.* 1146–52)

Vividly metamusical language is again used to produce an epiphany, this time of the god Dionysus, to whose choruses of stars and Thyiads (maenads) the dramatic chorus's own performance is assimilated.[103] As we have seen, the image of a star chorus may already be suggested in Alcman's first *Partheneion*; it appears in many other fifth- and fourth-century texts and images, including several of Euripides' later tragedies.[104] The Thyiads here function rather like nymphs or Nereids, as a group of female dancers associated with Dionysus whose *choreia* crosses over with that of the dramatic chorus. As a human chorus, however, their identity merges rather more easily with the dramatic one of Theban Elders, who are themselves calling on the god with their song and dance. Moreover, as Athenian citizens the dramatic chorus are also performing for Dionysus in his theater, so their epiphanic

---

103. This hymn can be viewed as another so-called joy-before-disaster ode, since it is immediately followed by the entrance of the messenger, who announces the deaths of Electra and Haemon. There is no more *choreia* for the rest of the play: as in *Women of Trachis*, it is replaced by distraught monody—Creon's lament for his son and, following the news of Eurydice's suicide, his wife. On this musical structure, see Scott 1996a: 59–64.

104. On such celestial choruses, see Csapo 2008; Ferrari 2008.

invocation works extradramatically to bring the god of the City Dionysia onstage. Here, then, as in other examples of Sophoclean metamusicality, the process of imaginative suggestion requires little effort on the part of the audience to visualize the chorus in a particular way by linking the verbal and musical aspects of their performance.

While there is similarly little evidence of Aeschylean choruses evoking figures of the choral imaginary that are not immediately associated with their own dramatic identity, Sophocles' use of metamusical language nevertheless differs from that of his predecessor. Aeschylus's choruses often vividly describe their own ritual performance to great dramatic effect, but, as we saw in the case of both *Seven against Thebes* and *Agamemnon*, the tragedian also deploys the acoustic and visual effects of *choreia* to bring a past or otherwise offstage scene into the theater. When Sophocles' choruses use language that alludes to their own musicality, however, they tend to draw the audience's attention to the here and now of their performance, often at a moment of painfully premature jubilation. This is not to say that Sophocles does not experiment with musical effects—on the contrary, as far as we can tell from the fragments that survive of some of his lost plays, *mousikē* often played an important dramatic role, and not just in the obvious case of his *Thamyras*.[105] As we have seen, the surviving fragments of *Inachus* and *Ichneutae* suggest that he may have experimented even more freely with musical effects in his satyr plays. But the relationship between words, music, and dance in Sophoclean choral lyric tends to be more obviously mimetic than suggestive, keeping the audience focused on the present *choreia* rather than encouraging them to be simultaneously transported to a scene beyond the immediate action of play itself. Metamusical effects in this tragedian's work thus contribute to the thematic immediacy of his choral odes, which, unlike those of Euripides' late plays, tend not to stretch far from the immediate dramatic situation.[106] In this respect, then, just as Aristotle suggests in his *Poetics*, Sophocles' choral lyric does appear to be more immediately integrated within the action of a play.[107]

## Euripides

This book is focused on four plays that date from the last fifteen years of Euripides' life, a period from which his tragedies display an extraordinary abundance of references to *mousikē*. It is largely as a result of this emphasis on musical performance in the language of his later tragedies, in addition to some of the metrical character-

---

105. Cf. Goldhill 2012 (84–133) and 2013 on the integration of the chorus's lyric voice within the dramatic narrative of Sophoclean tragedy.

106. A rare exception is the so-called Cypris Ode in *Women of Trachis*, when the chorus recall the fight for Deianeira between Heracles and Achelous (498–530).

107. Arist. *Poet.* 1456a25–31.

istics of these plays' lyrics and Euripides' own reputation in antiquity, that they have been viewed as examples of the so-called New Music. Yet while the frequency with which Euripides' choruses from the late 420s onward make these musical allusions is certainly striking, such metamusicality in tragedy is not in itself new. As we have seen, both Aeschylus and Sophocles experiment with the interplay of the verbal and the musical in order to create certain dramatic effects, particularly in their choral odes. In doing so, they inherit the conceptualization of *choreia*, as well as *mousikē* more broadly, as a totality of words, music, and dance.

Such metamusical play is likewise not confined to the later plays of Euripides. Indeed, references to *mousikē* in his three earliest surviving works, *Medea, Children of Heracles*, and *Alcestis*, indicate that already in the 430s (if not earlier) he was beginning to experiment with the interaction between the verbal and musical elements of *choreia*, and with the different ways in which musicality could be integrated within a play as a whole. In *Medea*, produced in 431 B.C.E., the theme of musical revolution underscores the sense of a complete upheaval of norms and hierarchies, including those of gender. Early on in the play, before Medea's entrance, the nurse dismisses former musicians as unable "to stop Stygian pain with music and many-stringed songs," thereby implicitly calling for a new type of therapeutic song.[108] The chorus take up this call for musical change in the first stasimon, when they envision a new kind of song that no longer dwells on female infidelity (410–28). It is tempting to wonder if this focus on a revolution in *mousikē* may point to Euripides' own musical novelty on display in the performance of this tragedy, which could in turn stress the startling nature of Medea's crime.[109] At the very least, the discourse concerning musical change in the first half of *Medea* suggests that Euripides was already interested in the relationship of *mousikē* (both described and performed) to the plot. Such interest should come as no surprise, given how closely both Aeschylus and Sophocles, Euripides' older contemporary, worked *mousikē* into the dramatic narrative of their own tragedies. Indeed *Women of Trachis*, which,

---

108. στυγίους... λύπας / ... μούσηι καὶ πολυχόρδοις / ὠιδαῖς παύειν, Eur. *Med.* 195–97. Gurd 2016: 123–25 sees this in terms of Euripides' "pessimistic vision in which music had no positive effects and could even destroy" (124).

109. Drawing on D'Angour's suggestion (2006: 276–83; 2011: 203) that Euripides was the first to break free from the traditional matching of word pitch to musical pitch, Thomas forthcoming argues that the chorus of *Medea* enact musical novelty through employing melodic as well as metrical responsion. Beyond the language of musical change in the play itself, the only evidence for this having been the first tragedy to display such melodic responsion is a passage of Athenaeus concerning Callias's *Alphabetic Tragedy*: Larensius claims that the syllables of this comedy's choral odes "all have the same meter and tune in antistrophes, with the result that Euripides is not only suspected of having composed his *Medea* in its entirety from that source, but has clearly transferred the tune itself" (τό τε μέτρον καὶ τὸ μέλος ἐν ἀντιστρόφοις ἔχουσι πᾶσαι ταὐτόν, ὥστε τὸν Εὐριπίδην μὴ μόνον ὑπονοεῖσθαι τὴν Μήδειαν ἐντεῦθεν πεποιηκέναι πᾶσαν, ἀλλὰ καὶ τὸ μέλος αὐτὸ μετενηνοχότα φανερὸν εἶναι, 10.453d–e). This claim may derive from Callias's comedy itself: see Rosen 1999; Gagné 2013.

as we have seen, exhibits an especially effective musical narrative intertwined with its dramatic one, is generally considered one of Sophocles' earlier works, produced perhaps as much as two decades before Euripides' *Medea*.[110]

The third stasimon of *Children of Heracles* provides another early example of Euripides experimenting with the dramatic role of *mousikē*. In the second half of this ode, as they pray to Athena to keep her city safe, the chorus describe songs and dances performed for her there:

> ἐπεί σοι πολύθυτος ἀεὶ
> τιμὰ κραίνεται οὐδὲ λά-
> θει μηνῶν φθινὰς ἁμέρα
> νέων τ' ἀοιδαὶ χορῶν τε μολπαί.           (780)
> ἀνεμόεντι δ' ἐπ' ὄχθωι
> ὀλολύγματα παννυχίοις ὑπὸ παρ-
> θένων ἰαχεῖ ποδῶν κρότοισιν.

Since for you the honor of many sacrifices is always offered, and we don't forget the waning day of the month and the songs of youths and tunes of choruses. On the windy hillside loud shouts of joy resound all night long to the beats of maidens' feet. (Eur. *Heracl.* 777–83)

Here, as in the hymn to Dionysus in Sophocles' *Antigone*, the description of choral celebration is almost explicitly self-referential, since the dramatic chorus are themselves singing and dancing to the goddess. Through this performative crossover with the *choreia* of the Athenian youths and maidens, the chorus's prayer seems to become even more powerful as they join forces with their imagined counterparts. Unlike Sophocles' ode, this one, through such an emphasis on the performance of *choreia*, has an efficacious power, as it is immediately followed by the messenger's announcement that the Athenians have defeated the Argive army. This is an example of the generative power of *choreia*, which we saw at work in Aeschylus's *Libation Bearers*; as we will see in the following chapter, Euripides also exploits this for dramatic effect in *Electra*, produced roughly a decade later.[111] When the chorus of *Children of Heracles* next refer to *mousikē*, in the final stasimon of the play, they mark the success of their earlier prayer by emphasizing their enjoyment in their own celebratory *choreia*, singing, "To me choral dancing is sweet, if the shrill delight of the *lōtos* pipe †at a feast† ..."[112]

---

110. On the date of Sophocles' *Women of Trachis*, see esp. Easterling 1982: 19–23, with further bibliography. As she concludes, any date between 457 and 430 is possible.

111. The dates of both plays are uncertain. The metrical pattern of *Children of Heracles* suggests that Euripides wrote it within a few years of *Medea*, perhaps ca. 430: see Cropp and Fick 1985.

112. ἐμοὶ χορὸς μὲν ἡδύς, εἰ λίγεια λω- / τοῦ χάρις †ἐνὶ δαΐ†, Eur. *Heracl.* 892–93. Henrichs (1996: 51–54) sees these descriptions of *choreia* as part of a consecutive pattern of choral self-reference throughout the play, through which the chorus "can validate their own performance in the here and now of the City Dionysia" (53).

In *Alcestis*, which was produced in 438 B.C.E., seven years earlier than *Medea*, we find an extended description of music making foreshadowing the sort of metamusical play that appears so frequently in Euripides' later tragedies. Following the arrival of Heracles, the chorus begin the third stasimon by remembering Apollo's stay at Pherae, when he exchanged his kithara for the syrinx (panpipes):

> ὦ πολύξεινος καὶ ἐλευθέρου ἀνδρὸς ἀεί ποτ'
>   οἶκος,
> σέ τοι καὶ ὁ Πύθιος εὐλύρας Ἀπόλλων (570)
> ἠξίωσε ναίειν,
> ἔτλα δὲ σοῖσι μηλονόμας
> ἐν νομοῖς γενέσθαι,
> δοχμιᾶν διὰ κλειτύων (575)
> βοσκήμασι σοῖσι συρίζων
> ποιμνίτας ὑμεναίους.
>
> σὺν δ' ἐποιμαίνοντο χαρᾶι μελέων βαλιαί τε
>   λύγκες,
> ἔβα δὲ λιποῦσ' Ὄθρυος νάπαν λεόντων (580)
> ἁ δαφοινὸς ἴλα·
> χόρευσε δ' ἀμφὶ σὰν κιθάραν,
> Φοῖβε, ποικιλόθριξ
> νεβρὸς ὑψικόμων πέραν (585)
> βαίνουσ' ἐλατᾶν σφυρῶι κούφωι,
> χαίρουσ' εὔφρονι μολπᾶι.

O house of a hospitable and ever generous man, even Pythian Apollo of the lovely lyre deigned to dwell in you and submitted to become a shepherd in your pastures, playing on his syrinx wedding songs for your herds on the slanting hillsides.

And, in joy at his songs, both spotted lynxes began to be shepherded, and, leaving the vale of Othrys, a tawny troop of lions came, and the dappled fawn, stepping beyond the tall fir trees, danced to your kithara with its light foot, rejoicing in the joyful song. (Eur. *Alc.* 569–87)

The chorus bring this scene of Apollo's musical performance to life through their own singing and dancing in the theater. Though the character Apollo is no longer onstage, he nevertheless becomes present through the crossover of his piping as described by the chorus in the opening strophe and that of the aulete heard by the audience. In the antistrophe the god's characteristic instrument then reappears, as the chorus sing of him as an Orpheus figure, charming wild beasts with the music of his kithara, to which they dance in a chorus (*choreuse*, 583). The emphasis on dancing here continues the process of imaginative suggestion by encouraging the audience to associate the animals' *choreia* with that of the dramatic chorus. And though the syrinx has been replaced by the kithara, the *aulos*, to which the dramatic chorus are dancing, represents both instruments, producing the epiphanic effect of Apollo's presence in the theater.[113]

It may not be a coincidence that this highly metamusical passage appears in a play that contains many satyric traits, including its position as the fourth drama in Euripides' tetralogy, the scene of Heracles' drunkenness, and the pastoral character of the third stasimon.[114] Since a pronounced emphasis on musicality seems to have been a hallmark of satyr drama, this early experimentation with the merging of performed and imagined *mousikē* in a tragedy may also be a result of Euripides' mixing of the two genres.[115] Unfortunately, too few of Euripides' plays survive from the 430s for us to know the extent to which *Alcestis* was unusual in sharing these elements with satyr play. But its generic ambiguity reminds us that, like Sophocles with the musical discourse of *Ichneutae*, Euripides could well have been already developing various metamusical effects to dramaturgical ends in the third quarter of the fifth century, but perhaps limiting such experimentation to satyr play more than tragedy. It is only from around 420 onward that we find such sustained descriptions of music making in works that are more strictly defined as tragic.

Even if moments of explicit metamusicality are absent from Euripides' other tragedies from this earlier period, however, the process of imaginative suggestion through *choreia* can still be at work. Choral narratives of travel in particular encourage an associational relationship between the choreuts' words and bodily movements. In *Hippolytus*, for example, when the chorus begin the second stasimon with a wish to fly over the sea (732–51), we can imagine that their own bodily movement may suggest the enactment of this impossible desire, particularly given the choral associations of birds evident in archaic lyric and art. Alternatively, the chorus's choreography could be more static, thus highlighting the impossibility of their travel or transformation. In *Helen*, produced sixteen years later, in 412 B.C.E., the correlation between the chorus's wish to fly and their own song and dance is more explicitly indicated through their metamusical description of cranes following their syrinx-playing leader, to whom the aulete in the theater is assimilated.[116] In the second strophe of the *Hippolytus* ode the chorus shift from imagining their own journey through the air to dwelling on Phaedra's sea voyage from Crete to

---

113. On the crossover of *aulos* and syrinx here, see Weiss forthcoming a.

114. On *Alcestis* as satyric or prosatyric, see esp. Marshall 2000; Slater 2005; Shaw 2014: 94–105. On pastoral elements as typical of satyr drama, see esp. Griffith 2015: 146–69. For a more skeptical approach to this sort of generic classification, see Mastronarde 2010: 56–57.

115. This sort of cross-fertilization between satyr drama and tragedy may have partly resulted from their generic boundaries' being more fluid than we tend to assume: as Mastronarde notes, such elements would not necessarily have been recognized as "inherently satyric and non-tragic" by fifth-century audiences (2010: 56).

116. *Hel.* 1478–94. See Padel 1974 for a detailed analysis of the similarities between these two odes.

Athens (752–63).[117] Here again the emphasis on movement encourages a degree of correspondence with the chorus's choreography—an effect that, occurring as it does at the moment of Phaedra's suicide offstage, makes the scene they describe of her arrival in Greece as a "most unhappily married boon" jarringly vivid.[118] Yet however natural it may be for an audience of *Hippolytus* to see these voyages represented in the chorus's own movements, the surviving text lacks any clearly musical markers or choral imagery, leaving us able only to conjecture about such a correlation taking place in the tragedy's performance.

In comparison with his later tragedies, then, Euripides' earlier work contains fewer and less extended references to *mousikē*, and so tends to draw less attention to the associational process whereby the chorus physically interact with the scenes they simultaneously describe. And yet, as this brief survey demonstrates, we should not split his career in two by positing a sudden jump from his earlier plays to the marked, sustained emphasis on *mousikē* that is evident from *Electra* onward. We see in *Alcestis* early signs of Euripides beginning to play with the effects of combining imagined *mousikē* with the performance of the chorus in the *orchēstra*, thereby bringing to life through *choreia* a scene otherwise far from the scope of the drama and, in doing so, transforming the performance space. And the integration of references to *mousikē* within the narrative arc of both *Medea* and *Children of Heracles* suggests that Euripides was already experimenting with the dramatic role of *mousikē* in the late 430s B.C.E.

It is likewise important to note a continuity in tragic *mousikē* from the second quarter of the fifth century onward rather than see Euripides' later plays as representing an unprecedented musical departure. The tragedies of both Aeschylus and Sophocles include highly metamusical passages that, for their full dramatic effect, rely on the interplay of described and performed *mousikē*. Aeschylus seems to be more inclined than Sophocles to use the combination of metamusical language and live performance to encourage the audience to experience through the chorus's song and dance scenes and events that are offstage, or outside the time frame of the dramatic narrative, or both. But for both tragedians, *mousikē* could clearly play an important and dramatically integrated role. In Aeschylus's work, it is often essential to a particular choral character, but it can also contribute to an overarching theme, such as the *nomos anomos* of *Agamemnon*. In Sophocles' tragedies, *mousikē* is frequently used to manipulate audience expectations and create a sense of painful irony as choruses burst prematurely into intensely musical and metamusical celebration shortly before a protagonist's downfall. The remaining

---

117. A similarly associational relationship between a narrative of sea travel and the chorus's own choreography may also be at work in the first stasimon of *Hecuba* (444–83), when the chorus of Trojan women imagine where in Greece they will be taken as captives.

118. κακονυμφοτάταν ὄνασιν, Eur. *Hipp.* 756.

fragments of *Thamyras* also suggest that music could play a crucial role within a tragedy by being closely associated with a protagonist's identity. Finally, the fragments of *Ichneutae* indicate that Sophocles' greatest musical experimentation may have occurred in satyr play, the dramatic genre perhaps most prone to metamusical displays.

Yet however much Euripides shares these uses of *mousikē* with and develops them from the older tragedians, the musical language of his later plays is also markedly different. As the following four case studies will demonstrate, much of Euripides' novelty lies in his particular recuperation and adaptation of traditional, nondramatic *choreia* for the tragic stage. Unlike Aeschylus and Sophocles, he increasingly evokes the choral imaginary's repertoire of traditional musical figures that are frequently at work in archaic lyric, such as dolphins, birds, horses, Nereids, and Sirens. In this respect Euripides' "new music" is a form of archaizing, a reinvention of those familiar motifs for tragic theater. Such evocations of the choral imaginary often occur within songs that, unlike Sophoclean lyric, seem to stretch far from the immediate dramatic action, and for this reason it has been tempting for older scholars to deem them irrelevant, emblematic of the *embolima* that Aristotle criticizes for being disconnected from the tragedy's *mythos*. This book aims to demonstrate that such songs are skillfully integrated within the dramatic narrative of a play, even as they create a wider imaginative space for the play and its audience to inhabit.

2

# Chorus, Character, and Plot in *Electra*

*Electra* is the earliest tragedy of Euripides in which music and dance play a central role. As we saw in the previous chapter, already in the 430s Euripides was beginning to experiment with the dramatic functions of *mousikē* and the effects of markedly metamusical language. But *Electra*, which was probably produced in the late 420s or early 410s, marks a turning point, at least among the plays that have survived. Its songs (choral and solo) repeatedly refer to dance and music making, both explicitly and through musical tropes that are typical of the choral imaginary, such as dolphins and Nereids. This sustained, self-conscious engagement with *mousikē* in many ways shapes and directs the dramatic narrative in which it is firmly embedded. It also contributes to the protagonist's characterization by vividly demonstrating Electra's construction of her own social position, and in doing so plays on the sort of enactment of choral relations that we saw at work in Alcman's first *Partheneion*.

*Electra* has long been regarded as an example of Euripides' involvement with the so-called New Music of the late fifth century B.C.E., ever since Walter Kranz in 1933 labeled the first and second stasima as dithyrambic and therefore typical of "das neue Lied."[1] More recently, Eric Csapo has explored in some detail the New Musical character of these songs, particularly the first stasimon.[2] Based on a possible reference in the play to the relief expedition that sailed from Athens to Sicily in 413, scholars used to place it later in Euripides' career, and this dating supported Kranz's view that he only started to be musically innovative in 415, with the

1. Kranz 1933: 238, 241–42, 254. Cf. Panagl 1971: 79–118.
2. Csapo 2003 (71–73), 2008 (277–80), 2009.

production of *Trojan Women*, in which the chorus declare they will sing "new songs."[3] But a study of the play's metrical patterns—the rate of resolutions in the play's iambic trimeters and its lack of trochaic tetrameters—has suggested instead that *Electra* was first performed some years earlier, perhaps in 420/19.[4] At least within Euripides' surviving corpus, then, it is this play that seems to mark a new musical direction, though its earlier dating should also prompt us to view it within a more extended period of experimentation with *mousikē*.

But the scholarly preoccupation with the musical innovation showcased in these songs, which have often been deemed too remote from the play's action to have any dramatic relevance at all, can lead us to neglect how they work within the tragedy itself. This is an innovative play, and not only in musical terms: many have discussed its extraordinary antiheroic realism, with the appearance of Electra in rags, as a peasant's wife living in a hut outside Argos, and her logical dismissal of the various tokens of recognition by means of which she and her brother are successfully reunited in Aeschylus's *Libation Bearers*.[5] And yet, like Euripides' transformation of the setting and characters, the unprecedented focus on musical performance is closely bound up with the dramatic fabric of the tragedy as a whole.

The chorus's musicality also extends beyond the vivid allusions to *mousikē* in the first two stasima to encompass and define their character and role in the play as women on their way to join the choral celebrations at the Argive festival of Hera. In doing so, it demarcates Electra's own character through the sharp and repeated contrast between the chorus's enthusiastic performance and her refusal to join their song and dance. I explore this link between *choreia* and characterization in the first part of this chapter, demonstrating how the chorus's references to their own musical performance highlight the social isolation of Electra even as they become increasingly invested in the outcome of her and Orestes' plot. Their musical relationship also underscores the ambiguity of Electra's status as a married virgin who is neither a *parthenos* (maiden) nor a *gynē* (woman). *Choreia* here functions as a mechanism for social demarcation and thus contrasts with the strong sense of communality expressed through the shared performances of the female protagonists and sympathetic female choruses in other Euripidean tragedies as well as in parthenaic lyric more generally.

The second half of the chapter moves from character to plot, as I examine the role of all three choral stasima in both anticipating and enacting pivotal moments in the dramatic structure of *Electra*. The importance of imaginative suggestion in

---

3. Kranz 1933: 228 on *Tro.* 512. On the later dating of *Electra*, see Denniston 1939: xxxiii-iv.
4. On the earlier dating of *Electra*, see Cropp and Fick 1985: 23, 60–61; Cropp 1988: l-li.
5. On Euripides' innovations in his staging of the Electra story, see esp. Arnott 1973; Michelini 1987: 181–206; Cropp 1988: xlvii-iii; Papadimitropoulos 2008.

terms of the dramatic effect of *mousikē* is especially clear in the first stasimon, in which a series of images interact with the choreographic movement of the chorus in the *orchēstra*. Such a convergence of described and performed *mousikē* contributes, I suggest, to the song's increasingly disturbing connection to the action of the play. The following two odes are also carefully integrated within the tragedy's dramatic fabric, and the references to music and dance in the second stasimon in particular lead the audience not only to the tyrannicide that Orestes has just gone to commit but to the death of Clytemnestra. This second murder—the matricide—becomes the focus of all three stasima, and indeed of the play as a whole.

## ELECTRA AND THE CHORUS

Even before the chorus enter the *orchēstra*, Electra marks herself apart from their *choreia* in her opening monody, establishing a disconnect between her performance and theirs. Euripides had already experimented with an actor singing in advance of the parodos in both *Andromache* and *Hecuba*. As we shall see in the next two chapters, variations of this pattern occur in several later plays too, particularly those with female leads who, like Electra, begin by singing a lament. In *Trojan Women*, Hecuba mourns her troubles by singing increasingly lyrical anapaests before being joined by the chorus, who then sing antiphonally with her. In *Helen*, the title character unusually begins the parodos herself with a song she characterizes as a *goos*, a solo cry of lament; the chorus then respond in the antistrophe. *Andromeda* unusually opens with the heroine's mournful monody followed by a lyric dialogue with the chorus.[6] In Sophocles' *Electra*, perhaps influenced by Euripides' version (or vice versa), the princess enters singing astrophically one of her "songs of lament";[7] the chorus soon come into the *orchēstra* and start singing too, sharing each strophe and antistrophe with her (86–250).[8] Euripides' version is unusual, however, in having an actor perform an extended strophic song that is

---

6. *Andr.* 103–16; *Hec.* 59–89; *Andromeda* frr. 114–22. See chapter 3, pp. 107–13, on *Tro.* 98–234; chapter 4, pp. 145–56, on *Hel.* 167–251. Cf. also *Med.* 96–167, where Medea delivers short, exclamatory anapaests from behind the *skēnē* in a lyric dialogue first with the nurse, who is onstage, then with the chorus as they begin their parodos. In *Hypsipyle* the chorus enter as Hypsipyle is singing to the baby Opheltes and then perform responsively with her (frr. 752f, 752h). Occasionally a male protagonist begins singing before the chorus in Euripidean tragedy, as in *Ion* 82–183; Amphion may enter singing before the parodos in the fragmentary *Antiope* (fr. 182a; see Collard and Cropp 2008a: 172). Prometheus sings an astrophic monody just before the chorus's entrance in [Aesch.] *PV* 88–127.

7. θρήνων ᾠδάς, Soph. *El.* 88.

8. The similarities between Euripides' *Electra* and Sophocles' version strongly suggest that one is responding to the other, but it is impossible to determine with any certainty which was produced first. On the various arguments about priority, see Denniston 1939: xxxiv–ix; Michelini 1987: 199–206; Cropp 1988: xlviii–lx.

longer than the shared parodos that follows. The only other character in Euripides' surviving work who performs such a long initial monody with at least a partially strophic structure is Ion, singing as he tends Apollo's temple before the entrance of the chorus.[9] It is possible that Andromeda's opening song was also strophic and of similar length, but certainly Electra's is likely to have been the earliest—or one of the earliest—instances of this particular dramatic structure. It would therefore be particularly arresting for the audience, who would be expecting such a song from the chorus, not from an actor. Electra's initial takeover of their opening performance establishes her as musically self-sufficient, a soloist who can sing without the presence of a chorus.

Electra's solo lament in Euripides' play is also distinctive for its extraordinarily self-referential focus on her *mousikē*, and in this respect too it seems to replace the expected lyrics of the entering chorus and present its singer as one who does not need a chorus to perform with her. She begins the first strophe and antistrophe by directing her own choreography: "Hasten on (it is time) the spring of the foot: O, step on, step on, weeping aloud."[10] In the mesode between these two stanzas, she bids herself to "raise the same lament [*goos*], raise up the pleasure full of tears";[11] the second mesode starts with the order "tear the face!"[12]

Though hers is a solo song of mourning—which she marks as such with the word *goos*—these repeated directions also resemble those that the leader of a communal lament may give to the accompanying mourners. In the closing scene of antiphonal lamentation in Aeschylus's *Persians,* for example, Xerxes leads the chorus by giving them a series of orders regarding their performance:

| | | |
|---|---|---|
| {Ξε.} ἔρεσσ' ἔρεσσε καὶ στέναζ' ἐμὰν χάριν. | | [6th Antistrophe] |
| {Χο.} διαίνομαι γοεδνὸς ὤν. | | |
| {Ξε.} βόα νυν ἀντίδουπά μοι. | | |
| {Χο.} μέλειν πάρεστι, δέσποτα. | | |
| {Ξε.} ἐπορθίαζέ νυν γόοις. | | (1050) |
| {Χο.} ὀτοτοτοτοῖ· | | |
| μέλαινα δ' αὖ μεμείξεται | | |
| οἲ στονόεσσα πλαγά. | | |
| {Ξε.} καὶ στέρν' ἄρασσε κἀπιβόα τὸ Μύσιον. | | [7th Strophe] |
| {Χο.} ἀνία ἀνία. | | (1055) |
| {Ξε.} καί μοι γενείου πέρθε λευκήρη τρίχα. | | |
| {Χο.} ἄπριγδ' ἄπριγδα μάλα γοεδνά. | | |
| {Ξε.} αὔτει δ' ὀξύ. {Χο.} καὶ τάδ' ἔρξω. | | |

---

9. Eur. *Ion* 82–183.
10. σύντειν' [ὥρα] ποδὸς ὁρμάν· ὤ, / ἔμβα ἔμβα κατακλαίουσα, Eur. *El.* 112–13 = 127–28.
11. ἴθι τὸν αὐτὸν ἔγειρε γόον, / ἄναγε πολύδακρυν ἀδονάν, 125–26.
12. δρύπτε κάρα, 150.

*Xerxes:* Ply, ply [your strokes] and groan for my sake!
*Chorus:* I weep, being full of mourning.
*Xerxes:* Cry out now, sounding in response to me!
*Chorus:* It is my concern, my lord.
*Xerxes:* Lift up [your voice] now in lamentation!
*Chorus: Otototototoi!* And mixed in again—*oi!*—will be black, groaning beating.
*Xerxes:* And strike your breast and cry out the Mysian shout.
*Chorus:* Painful, painful!
*Xerxes:* And tear the white hair from your beard!
*Chorus:* With [hands] clenched tight, clenched tight, very mournfully!
*Xerxes:* And call out shrilly! Chorus: This too I will do. (Aesch. *Pers.* 1046–58)

The Persian king not only specifies the particular gestures of mourning here (the striking of the head, the tearing of hair) but explicitly bids the chorus to sing in alternation with himself ("Cry out now, sounding in response to me!"), thereby drawing attention to the shared, antiphonal nature of their performance. Hecuba and the chorus of Trojan women perform similarly directed antiphonal laments in *Trojan Women*, particularly in the final scene of extended mourning with which the play ends.[13] As Xerxes' reference to *gooi* (1050) suggests, the distinction in terminology between the individual performances of the dead man's female relatives and the professionally performed group lament (*thrēnos*) tends to be blurred by the fifth century B.C.E.—so much so that Helen in her eponymous tragedy asks if she should perform her *goos* along with *thrēnoi* before embarking on the parodos.[14] In the last book of the *Iliad* the description of Andromache, Hecuba, and Helen "leading" ([*ex*]*archein*) the *goos* indicates that even in the archaic period this sort of performance was not a solo, but instead involved the participation of a wider group.[15] But Electra's *goos* is exclusively her own: she herself responds to her directions for the gestures and sounds of ritual mourning, acting as her own *exarchos* rather than assuming this role with the chorus.[16]

Electra's *mousikē* thus constitutes an important part of her self-presentation, demonstrating her exaggerated preoccupation with solitary mourning. Her emphatic declamation of her name and lineage in the opening strophe of her lament makes the link between her mourning and dramatic identity especially clear:

---

13. See chapter 3, pp. 134–37, on *Tro.* 1226–37, 1287–1332.
14. On the blurred boundary between *thrēnos* and *goos*, perhaps even in the archaic period, see Swift 2010: 301–3. See chapter 4, pp. 146–47, on *Hel.* 164–66.
15. Hom. *Il.* 24.723, 747, 761: see Swift 2010: 301–3.
16. Cf. Cropp 1988: 107 ("[Electra] is alone but acts like an *exarchos*, dictating movement, song and gesture to herself").

ἐγενόμαν Ἀγαμέμνονος (115)
καί μ' ἔτικτε Κλυταιμήστρα
στυγνὰ Τυνδάρεω κόρα,
κικλήσκουσι δέ μ' ἀθλίαν
Ἠλέκτραν πολιῆται.

I am Agamemnon's [child], and Clytemnestra, the hated daughter of Tyndareus, bore me, and the citizens call me wretched Electra. (115–19)

Lament, at least at this point in the play, therefore seems to be Electra's main and defining activity, just as it is in Sophocles' tragedy, in which the princess explicitly presents herself as a perpetual mourner and repeatedly rejects the pleas of the chorus and her sister Chrysothemis that she cease lamenting.[17] In Euripides' version too Electra's mourning is presented as a repetitive activity, as she directs herself to sing "the same lament."[18] The metrical monotony of her song heightens this impression, as does the repetition of language between the first strophe and antistrophe.[19]

Electra makes her self-presentation as a perpetual mourner particularly vivid in the second mesode by comparing her crying song to that of a swan calling out to its captured father:

οἷα δέ τις κύκνος ἀχέτας
ποταμίοις παρὰ χεύμασιν
πατέρα φίλτατον καλεῖ,
ὀλόμενον δολίοις βρόχων
ἕρκεσιν, ὣς σὲ τὸν ἄθλιον, (155)
πάτερ, ἐγὼ κατακλαίομαι

Just as a shrill swan by the river streams calls out to her dearest father, as he dies in the treacherous snares of nets, so I lament you, my wretched father. (151–56)

Although the swan elsewhere appears in connection with death and mourning, it usually laments its own impending death, not another's.[20] The distortion of this musical model here, whereby the swan mourns the loss of its father instead, reflects Electra's own obsession with the murder of Agamemnon. Along with the echo of *m' athlian* (118) in *se ton athlion* (155), this swan simile also suggests that she equates her father's death with her own demise, thus augmenting the self-preoccupied nature of her song.

---

17. E.g., Soph. *El.* 103–4, ἀλλ' οὐ μὲν δὴ / λήξω θρήνων στυγερῶν τε γόων.
18. τὸν αὐτὸν ... γόον, 125. Cf. Raeburn 2000.
19. On the song's metrical uniformity, see Dale 1969: 3; Cropp 1988: 108.
20. Cf. *Ag.* 1444–46, Pl. *Phd.* 84e3–85b4, Arist. *Hist. an.* 615b2–5. The swan's association with mourning adds a note of unease to the chorus's celebratory mix of paeanic and epinician song at the arrival of Heracles in Eur. *HF* 692–94. On the bird's link with self-lament see Cropp 1988: 109–10; Arnott 2007: 123.

The parodos, which immediately follows Electra's monody, heightens our impression of her isolation in mourning. Instead of sharing her lament, the Argive women enter singing excitedly of a different event altogether:

Ἀγαμέμνονος ὦ κόρα, ἤλυθον, Ἠλέκτρα,
ποτὶ σὰν ἀγρότειραν αὐλάν.
ἔμολέ τις ἔμολεν γαλακτοπότας ἀνὴρ
Μυκηναῖος οὐριβάτας· (170)
ἀγγέλλει δ' ὅτι νῦν τριταί-
αν καρύσσουσιν θυσίαν
Ἀργεῖοι, πᾶσαι δὲ παρ' Ἥ-
ραν μέλλουσιν παρθενικαὶ στείχειν.

O daughter of Agamemnon, I have arrived, Electra, at your rather rustic courtyard. A milk-drinking man has come, come, a Mycenaean mountain walker. He reports that the Argives are now proclaiming a sacrifice in two days, and all the maidens [*parthenikai*] are about to process to Hera's temple. (167–73)

This chorus is far from that of Aeschylus's *Libation Bearers,* whose primary role is to perform lament, and who display their solidarity with both Electra and Orestes by singing the long *kommos* with them.[21] In both Sophocles' and Euripides' versions, Electra takes on the Aeschylean chorus's role, while the Argive women refrain from mourning with her, thus highlighting her stubbornly solitary preoccupation. Whereas in Sophocles' play the chorus nevertheless respond to her lament by advising her against it, Euripides' chorus do not even acknowledge her mourning in their opening lyrics, instead describing the celebrations at the *Heraia* festival that is about to be held in Argos, so that their performance seems completely disconnected from hers. Kim Chong-Gossard calls the *amoibaion* that follows an "antidialogue," similar to the longer version that occurs in the parodos of Sophocles' play: instead of having the chorus sing the strophe and Electra the antistrophe (or vice versa), both Euripides and Sophocles divide each stanza between them, so that they musically respond only to themselves in their singing, not to each other.[22] The resulting disconnect between the lyrics of Electra and those of the chorus presents a striking contrast with the kind of close musical relationship displayed by the chorus and female protagonist in the parodos of *Helen* and *Iphigenia in Tauris*;[23] the surviving fragments of lyric

---

21. Aesch. *Cho.* 306–478.
22. Chong-Gossard 2003: 217. Cf. Carson 2001: 48 on the parodos of Sophocles' *Electra:* "They are each talking to themselves. Musically, it is an anti-dialogue."
23. See chapter 4, pp. 145–56. on how the responsive singing of lament by Helen and the chorus in *Hel.* 167–251 underscores their intimacy at this initial point of the tragedy, presenting Helen as the women's *chorēgos.* In the parodos of *Iphigenia in Tauris* (126–235) the chorus highlight their responsive antiphony with Iphigenia by describing their mournful songs as "twanging in response" to hers (ἀντιψάλμους, 179).

dialogue between the chorus and Andromeda in her eponymous play indicate a similar intimacy through their shared mourning.[24] Though the chorus in *Electra* can be seen as another example of the trend in Euripides' work (and perhaps in tragedy in general in the late 400s B.C.E.) toward matching a sympathetic female chorus to a female protagonist, their lack of *mousikē* shared with Electra creates a divide between them that is unparalleled in Euripidean tragedy.[25]

Not only do the chorus refuse to engage in Electra's song of lament, but she rejects their invitation to the festival, refusing in particular to join the sort of parthenaic *choreia* that they propose. In doing so, she marks her "isolation from the civic life of the *polis*";[26] in refusing to dance both at the festival and within the play itself, she simultaneously enacts such isolation, making it visually clear to the audience. Though they focus on the participation of maidens (*parthenoi*) at the festival, the chorus do not specifically mention *choreia* in their invitation. Electra, however, sees choral participation as the primary activity that would be required of her there, and in response makes it clear that she is to perform continuous lament rather than dance in a chorus:

οὐκ ἐπ' ἀγλαΐαις, φίλαι, (175)
θυμὸν οὐδ' ἐπὶ χρυσέοις
  ὅρμοις ἐκπεπόταμαι
τάλαιν', οὐδ' ἱστᾶσα χοροὺς
Ἀργείαις ἅμα νύμφαις
εἱλικτὸν κρούσω πόδ' ἐμόν. (180)
δάκρυσι νυχεύω, δακρύων δέ μοι μέλει
δειλαίαι τὸ κατ' ἦμαρ.
σκέψαι μου πιναρὰν κόμαν
καὶ τρύχη τάδ' ἐμῶν πέπλων, (185)
εἰ πρέποντ' Ἀγαμέμνονος
κούραι τᾶι βασιλείαι
τᾶι Τροίαι θ', ἃ 'μοῦ πατέρος
μέμναταί ποθ' ἁλοῦσα.

Not at [the prospect of] festive splendor, friends, nor at golden chains have I, wretched me, flown forth in my heart, nor, setting up choruses alongside the Argive brides, will I beat my whirling foot. In tears I spend the night, and tears preoccupy me, unhappy me, throughout the day. Look at my dirty hair and these rags of my robes, [see] if they are seemly for Agamemnon's royal daughter and for Troy, which, taken once, remembers my father. (175–89)

---

24. Andromeda repeatedly refers to the chorus as sympathetic friends who share her lament (*Andromeda* frr. 117–20, 122).

25. On the sympathetic female chorus, especially in Euripidean tragedy, see Castellani 1989; Hose 1991: 17–20; Mastronarde 1999: 94–95 and 2010: 104; Foley 2003: 19–20.

26. Zeitlin 1970: 648.

Electra's focus on aspects of *choreia* here suggests that this is not just a general refusal to attend the *Heraia*, but a specific rejection of any choral participation—and indeed of the need for a chorus at all.[27] As we saw in the previous chapter, metallic radiance is a common motif within the Greek choral imaginary and is especially prominent in Alcman's first *Partheneion*, in which the chorus stress the brightness of their chorus leaders, likening Agido to the shining sun and Hagesichora's hair to pure gold; they also point to their own fine attire when singing of their purple clothes, golden jewelry, and Lydian headbands.[28] Prototypical divine choruses of *parthenoi* like the Nereids and Muses are also frequently described as golden, both in archaic lyric and in Euripidean tragedy: in Bacchylides 17 Theseus admires the Nereids' gleaming limbs and golden ribbons; in the parodos of *Iphigenia in Aulis*, the chorus describe the sight of the golden Nereids on the sterns of the Myrmidons' ships, thereby merging the maidens' traditional association with gold with the statues' actual material.[29] We also saw that flying and avian imagery are common features of the choral imaginary, and these seem to have become especially pronounced in contemporary fifth-century dithyramb, at least according to Aristophanes' parodies: in his *Birds*, for example, the dithyrambist Cinesias repeatedly sings of flying up into the air and claims that the best parts of dithyrambs are airy and flapping with wings.[30] Even before Electra states explicitly that she will not dance, then, her claim not to be interested in the "splendor" of the festival or "golden chains," nor to have "flown forth," can be understood as a rejection of the imagery typically associated with *choreia*.[31] The chorus of Alcman's *Partheneion*, through a process of imaginative suggestion, use such images to identify and draw attention to their leaders, as well as their own relationship to them. Electra, however, mentions these choral motifs to deny any possibility of her acting as a *chorēgos*, as well as to accentuate the disconnect between their traditional context and her own situation.

---

27. We could see Electra's rejection of *choreia*, a core component of the tragic genre, as part of her realist perspective on tragedy itself, as demonstrated most clearly in the recognition scene, with her rejection of the Aeschylean tokens that indicate Orestes' presence. On the tension between tragedy and "reality" in the play, see esp. Goldhill 1986: 245–58; Wohl 2015: 63–88.

28. Alcm. fr. 1 *PMGF*, 40–43, 51–54, 64–69. Alcman's chorus also mention a golden necklace: ποικίλος δράκων / παγχρύσιος, 66–67; cf. Alcm. fr. 91 *PMGF*, χρύσιον ὅρμον ἔχων ῥαδινᾶν πετάλοισι καλχᾶν.

29. See chapter 1, pp. 31–32, on Bacchyl. 17.101–8; chapter 5, pp. 198–201, on *IA* 239–41; cf. p. 213 on the "golden-sandaled" Muses at the wedding of Peleus and Thetis (*IA* 1042).

30. τῶν διθυράμβων γὰρ τὰ λαμπρὰ γίγνεται / ἀέρια καὶ σκότι' ἄττα καὶ κυαναυγέα / καὶ πτεροδόνητα, Ar. *Av.* 1388–90.

31. Cf. Ar. *Nub.* 333, *Pax* 830–31; also Eur. *Hipp.* 732–51, *IT* 1138, *Hel.* 1478–94; Soph. *Trach.* 953–59, *OC* 1081–83. On flight imagery in archaic lyric, see chapter 1, pp. 29–30; also chapter 4, pp. 185–87, on Eur. *Hel.* 1478–94.

It is also possible that "golden chains [*hormoi*]" could refer to a particular type of dance. Lucian, writing in the second century C.E., describes the *hormos* as "a dance shared by ephebes and *parthenoi*, dancing side by side and thus truly resembling a chain," and then interprets the dance's name metaphorically, as a reflection of the mix of male courage and female self-restraint that the young men and maidens display through their movements.[32] Drawing on Iris's promise to Eileithyia of a dedication at Delos of "a great *hormos*, strung with golden threads, seven cubits long" in the *Homeric Hymn to Apollo*,[33] Lillian Lawler suggested that the *hormos* may have a more literal origin, originally denoting "a cult dance in which a large garland, *hormos*, was carried in solemn procession by youths and maidens, alternating in a line."[34] There is no evidence in the Delian inventories that garlands called *hormoi* were in fact dedicated to Eileithyia; Nicholas Richardson suggests instead that the nine-cubit *hormos* "is mentioned as an *aition* for an actual necklace dedicated to Eileithyia in her sanctuary before the hymn was composed."[35] Whether it originally referred to the offering of a garland or to a necklace, the *hormos* described by Lucian could nonetheless derive from the sort of processional dance that Lawler envisages. Electra's mention of golden chains in Euripides' play therefore not only suggests a typical element of the Greek choral imaginary but could signify a particular form of *choreia*, as well as actual adornments and even offerings to Hera, all of which she rejects.

Electra goes on to refuse specifically to dance as a *chorēgos*, making it clear that she will not take on in this play the role that other Euripidean female protagonists (Helen above all) assume in theirs. In doing so, she underscores the extraordinary disconnect between her singing and that of the chorus in the play so far, as well as her unwillingness to join them in the near future. Her claim in line 178 that she will not "set up" choruses refers to the role of choral leader that she would typically undertake as a young female member of the royal house.[36] By then using the verb *helissō* in her refusal to "beat my whirling foot" (180), she appropriates language typical of choral choreography within her own uncompromising rejection of any movement associated with *choreia*. Despite such performative language, then, we can probably assume that the actor would remain motionless during this song. The resulting dissonance between choreographic referentiality and Electra's lack of movement onstage would visually emphasize her stubborn refusal to dance, par-

32. ὁ δὲ ὅρμος ὄρχησίς ἐστιν κοινὴ ἐφήβων τε καὶ παρθένων, παρ' ἕνα χορευόντων καὶ ὡς ἀληθῶς ὅρμωι ἐοικότων, Luc. *De Salt*. 12.
33. μέγαν ὅρμον / χρυσείοισι λίνοισιν ἐερμένον ἐννεάπηχυν, *Hymn. Hom. Ap*. 103–4.
34. Lawler 1948a: 4. Cf. Hedreen 2011: 500.
35. Richardson 2010: 97.
36. On the verb ἵστημι referring to the assembling of a chorus by its leader, see Calame 1997: 45–46; cf. Cropp 1988: 113. On the link between choral leadership and royalty, see Nagy 1990: 345–49 on Hagesichora and Agido in Alcm. fr. 1 *PMGF*. Cf. Halporn 1983: 110.

ticularly in contrast with the chorus, who, as they come onstage singing the opening of the parodos, would at the very least be performing some sort of processional dance. By drawing attention to her filthy hair and rags, Electra further undermines any possibility of assuming the role of the *chorēgos*, who is traditionally distinguished from the rest of a chorus by means of her beauty, as Nausicaa is in the *Odyssey* and Helen at the end of Aristophanes' *Lysistrata*.[37] Of course the irony here lies in the fact that she is nevertheless singing with the chorus, splitting a strophe of their parodos with them, yet her repeated claims not to join them in their dancing simultaneously prevent any sense of her participation in their *choreia*.

The chorus interpret Electra's refusal to accompany them to the festival in terms of her stubborn insistence on mourning and therefore advise her to honor the gods with prayers rather than continue with groans of lamentation.[38] Her response to their invitation also, however, highlights the ambiguity not only of her royalty—can this woman in rags fulfill the role of *chorēgos*, to which, as Agamemnon's daughter, she should be entitled?—but also of her virginal status.[39] In his opening prologue her husband tells the audience that she is still a *parthenos* (43–44); Orestes then says he has heard she "lives yoked in marriage and no longer remains a virgin."[40] Both the chorus and Electra underscore this ambiguity in their lyric dialogue, they by inviting her to a festival where "all the maidens are about to process to Hera's temple" (173–74); she by describing such choral dancers as *nymphai* (179)—young (or at least prospective) brides, who would naturally dance at the festival of a goddess associated with marriage and family.[41] So while the chorus see her as a potential member of a maiden chorus, Electra through her refusal to join the dancing excludes herself from either category, and simultaneously underscores her lack of choral participation within the drama itself.[42]

She reiterates her unclear position toward the end of the tragedy too, when she wonders into what chorus or marriage she may enter:

ἰὼ ἰώ μοι. ποῖ δ' ἐγώ, τίν' ἐς χορόν,
τίνα γάμον εἶμι; τίς πόσις με δέξεται
νυμφικὰς ἐς εὐνάς;                                             (1200)

---

37. Hom. *Od.* 6.99–109; Ar. *Lys.* 1315. See Calame 1997: 42–43.
38. οὔτοι στοναχαῖς / ἀλλ' εὐχαῖσι θεοὺς σεβί- / ζουσ' ἕξεις εὐαμερίαν, 195–96.
39. On Electra's reasons for avoiding such a festival, see esp. Michelini 1987: 192.
40. ἐν γάμοις / ζευχθεῖσαν οἰκεῖν οὐδὲ παρθένον μένειν, 98–99.
41. On the ritual celebrations at the *Heraia*, see Zeitlin 1970; Calame 1997: 114–20. On the meaning of *nymphē* as either a betrothed *parthenos* or a married woman before her first childbirth, see Calame 1997: 26; Larson 2001: 3.
42. Cf. Zeitlin 1970: 650: by creating a married Electra who is still a virgin, Euripides makes her an even greater "social misfit."

*Iō iō!* Where shall I go, into what chorus, into what marriage? What husband will receive me into his marriage bed? (1198–1200)

These questions demonstrate Electra's particular view of *choreia* as a parthenaic celebration linked to the preparation of young women for marriage. Such an association between *partheneia* and readiness for marriage is clear in the case of Nausicaa, who sees a potential bridegroom in Odysseus; it is also present in the surviving fragments of Alcman.[43] Indeed, depictions of female choruses frequently suggest the separation of one member of the group as she heads toward marriage.[44] In *Helen*, as we shall see in chapter 4, Euripides draws on these parthenaic associations of female *choreia* by presenting Helen as the choral leader par excellence. Electra, whose virginal status is no more ambiguous than Helen's, rejects this choral role for herself, even though the play actually ends with a resolution to her transitional state between *parthenos* and *gynē*, as Castor proclaims her betrothal to Pylades (1249).

The chorus never actually leave for the festivities of the *Heraia* that they so excitedly announce in the parodos, at least not during the dramatic action of the play itself. Instead they become enmeshed in Electra's crisis, looking in their next two odes both back toward Agamemnon's murder and forward to his children's revenge (432–86, 699–746). They also perform a short, astrophic victory song in celebration of Orestes' arrival (585–95) and, later, a burst of exuberant *choreia* in response to the news of Aegisthus's death (860–65, 874–78). Ironically, however, despite their increased involvement in the dramatic plot revolving around Electra, her refusal to join their *choreia* perpetuates the sense of a distance between them. Even after her reunion with her brother, her isolation is made visually and musically manifest through the contrast between her performance and that of the chorus.

Paradoxically, Electra's distance from the chorus is most evident at the moment of their mutual celebration following Orestes' murder of Aegisthus, when the chorus perform a brief, strophic victory song. As in the parodos, here Electra responds to their opening verses, but this time she does so with iambic trimeters rather than song (866–72). This is the only instance of such an interruption of choral strophic song by an actor in surviving Greek tragedy, and the stark contrast between the chorus's lyrics and Electra's speech emphasizes her continued refusal to participate in their *choreia*. Even as their mutually elated reaction to the messenger's speech suggests a closer relationship than that displayed in the parodos, Electra remains steadfastly separate from the chorus, displaying her isolation even at this moment of shared joy through her different style of performance. This contrast is all the

---

43. See Peponi 2007 on the enactment of such sexual maturation in Alcm. fr. 3 *PMGF*, with Astymeloisa's movement from female chorus to the broader community of the *asty*.

44. On this theme see Murnaghan 2013.

more striking as a result of the chorus's emphatic directions to Electra to join their *choreia*:

θὲς ἐς χορόν, ὦ φίλα, ἴχνος, ὡς νεβρὸς οὐράνιον
πήδημα κουφίζουσα σὺν ἀγλαΐαι. (861)
νικᾶι στεφαναφόρα κρείσσω τῶν παρ' Ἀλφειοῦ
ῥεέθροις τελέσας
κασίγνητος σέθεν· ἀλλ' ὑπάειδε
καλλίνικον ὠιδὰν ἐμῶι χορῶι. (865)

Set your foot to the choral dance, dear friend, like a fawn lightly leaping up to heaven with festive splendor. Your brother has completed and won a crown contest, greater than those by the streams of Alpheus. But sing the *kallinikos* song in accompaniment to my choral dance! (860–65)

This song is essentially an epinician, since the chorus sing in dactylo-epitrite meter and present Aegisthus's murder as a victory in a "crown contest" superior even to the games at Olympia; their direction to Electra to leap like a fawn (860–61) may also be epinician in tone, as we find a similar simile in one of Bacchylides' odes (13.84–90).[45] This framing of the murder contributes to what Geoffrey Arnott has termed the play's double vision, whereby Electra's view is consistently at odds with that of other characters: whereas in the messenger's account Orestes' attack on Aegisthus seems to be a cowardly and brutal stab in the back that mars the cult sacrifice being performed to the Nymphs, Electra presents it as an Olympic victory by repeatedly depicting Orestes as a heroic athlete.[46]

On the one hand, then, the fact that the chorus view the murder as Electra does marks the closeness of their relationship. Their shared focus here comes in marked contrast to their different preoccupations in the parodos: now the chorus's reference to "festive splendor" (*aglaïa*, 861, cf. 175, 192) refers to choral celebration for Orestes' victory as an athlete rather than that at the *Heraia*, in which Electra previously refused to participate. She responds to their epinician song with equal enthusiasm, announcing that she will crown her brother's head:

ὦ φέγγος, ὦ τέθριππον ἡλίου σέλας,
ὦ γαῖα καὶ νὺξ ἣν ἐδερκόμην πάρος,
νῦν ὄμμα τοὐμὸν ἀμπτυχαί τ' ἐλεύθεροι,
ἐπεὶ πατρὸς πέπτωκεν Αἴγισθος φονεύς.

---

45. On the song's epinician character see Zeitlin 1970: 656; Swift 2010: 159–60. Cf. Arnott 1981: 188; Cropp 1988: 158; Henrichs 1994–95: 87. The fawn imagery may also be Dionysiac: Henrichs 1994–95: 88.
46. Arnott 1981: 181–83, 186–89. References to Orestes as an athlete: 528, 781–82, 880–90, 953–56; the messenger contributes to this image by comparing Orestes' speed in stripping the bull's hide to a runner's in a race (824–25) and by describing how Aegisthus's servants garlanded Orestes' head after the murder (854–55). Epinician imagery is developed in nearly all the plays that deal with the Orestes myth, particularly in Aeschylus's *Oresteia* trilogy and Euripides' *Electra*: see Swift 2010: 156–70.

φέρ', οἷα δὴ 'χω καὶ δόμοι κεύθουσί μου (870)
κόμης ἀγάλματ' ἐξενέγκωμεν, φίλαι,
στέψω τ' ἀδελφοῦ κρᾶτα τοῦ νικηφόρου.

O light, O chariot-mounted blaze of the sun, O Earth and Night, whom I previously looked upon, now I am free to open my eyes, since Aegisthus, my father's murderer, has fallen! Come, friends, let us bring out such adornments for hair as I possess and are lying hidden away in my home, and I will crown the head of my victory-bearing brother! (866–72)

On the other hand, however, Electra marks the disconnect between herself and the chorus through her lack of response to their vivid directions that she dance and leap in the choral dance and perform a *kallinikos* song—a *kōmos* associated with Heracles that was sung for Olympic victors—to the accompaniment of their *choreia*.[47] Instead of sharing their strophe as she does in the parodos, she replies with speech, producing a kind of spoken version of a *kallinikos* song instead. She continues this after their antistrophe by addressing Orestes as *ō kallinike* in line 880, performing in iambics part of the refrain typically addressed to the victor within such a song.[48] Even though their address to her as "dear friend" makes it clear that their directions are for her, the chorus sing and dance instead, presumably making energetic movements similar to those they describe in lines 860–61 and thus creating a clear visual contrast with Electra's obstinately stationary pose.

The chorus explicitly comment on their different types of performance in their following antistrophe:

σὺ μὲν νυν ἀγάλματ' ἄειρε κρατί· τὸ δ' ἀμέτερον
χωρήσεται Μούσαισι χόρευμα φίλον. (875)
νῦν οἱ πάρος ἀμετέρας γαίας τυραννεύσουσι φίλοι βασιλῆς
δικαίως, τοὺς ἀδίκους καθελόντες.
ἀλλ' ἴτω ξύναυλος βοὰ χαρᾶι.

You then raise adornments upon his head; but our dancing, dear to the Muses, will go on. Now those dear ones who were previously kings of our land will rule it justly, having destroyed the unjust. But let the shout along with the *aulos* go out with joy! (874–78)

The *men . . . de* construction in line 874 makes clear for the first time the splitting of their role from Electra's: she can crown Orestes, but their job is to dance. These

---

47. Pindar makes the performance context of the *kallinikos* clear in the opening of his ninth Olympian ode: τὸ μὲν Ἀρχιλόχου μέλος / φωνᾶεν Ὀλυμπίαι, / καλλίνικος ὁ τριπλόος κεχλαδώς (*Ol.* 9.1–4); cf. Arch. fr. 324 W. The *kallinikos* is frequently evoked in Euripides' *Heracles* in reference to the hero's defeat of Lycus; in the second stasimon the chorus insist they will perform this song, old as they are (673–86; cf. 180, 570, 582, 785–89, 961, 1046): see Swift 2010: 145–47. On the nature of the *kallinikos* song, see Lawler 1948b; Swift 2010: 132–33.

48. Cf. Pind. *Ol.* 9.3; Arch. fr. 324.1–2 W, τήνελλα καλλίνικε / χαῖρε ἄναξ Ἡράκλεις.

lines are especially striking because the chorus so emphatically characterize themselves *as a chorus,* drawing further attention to their choral dancing as their sole preoccupation through the alliterative wordplay of *chōrēsetai* and *choreuma* in line 875.[49] Such explicit choral self-characterization is surprisingly rare in the extant tragedies of Euripides—more often they refer indirectly to their own singing and dancing through describing other scenes of music making, as they do in the first and second stasima of this play.[50] As we saw in the previous chapter, however, Aeschylean choruses, such as the Erinyes in *Eumenides,* more frequently refer to their own choral character, particularly when this is to a large degree defined by their musical and ritual performance. Here in *Electra* the chorus draw attention to their own choral activity, as well as to the *aulos* as their accompaniment, in order to accentuate the distance between themselves and the protagonist.

Electra and the chorus do come together in performance, however, near the end of the tragedy, when they lament along with Orestes following the murder of Clytemnestra (1177–1237). Yet they still do not show quite the sort of togetherness in mourning that we see in, for example, *Trojan Women,* in which, despite Hecuba's claim to have abandoned her role as *chorēgos* (*Tro.* 146–52), she and the chorus display an increasingly close relationship through their shared performances of lament. We shall see in the next chapter how, as these turn into full antiphonal mourning, the women's bond in suffering is presented even more strongly, with the result that Hecuba's separation from them as she departs for Odysseus's ship brings about a particularly painful end to the play, symbolizing once again the breakdown of any form of social cohesion in the aftermath of Troy's destruction.

In *Electra,* in contrast with their disregard for the princess's groans in the parodos, the chorus finally share in her and Orestes' song of mourning. Yet this is no longer a lament over the dead Agamemnon, like the lengthy *kommos* in Aeschylus's *Libation Bearers,* but instead an outburst of despair for the siblings' fate and a reliving of Clytemnestra's murder.[51] The chorus join their lyric iambics, but still seem rather detached from Electra's suffering, as they express critical judgment on the deed more than full sympathy for their plight: they accuse Electra of making her brother commit a terrible crime, even though he did not want to.[52] Admittedly, she ends up seeming to share their condemnation of her action when she admits "I

---

49. Cf. Henrichs 1994–95: 87, 89: he links the "performative future" χωρήσεται here with the chorus's reassertion of their choral identity.

50. See below on *El.* 431–86 and 699–746. In Euripides' *Phoenician Women* the Phoenician women's wish to become a whirling chorus (εἰ- / λίσσων ... χορὸς, 234–36) for Apollo is as much an enactment of their actual chorus-character as it is an instance of choral escapism, since they are in fact going to Delphi to serve Apollo there as (choral) offerings, ἀκροθίνια Λοξίαι, 203.

51. Aesch. *Cho.* 306–478.

52. δεινὰ δ' εἰργάσω, / φίλα, κασίγνητον οὐ θέλοντα, 1204–5. On this reversal of the chorus's perspective on the punishment inflicted on Clytemnestra, see Mastronarde 1999: 97, 2010: 121.

have committed the most terrible of sufferings," yet the oxymoron here of enacting sufferings implies that she is referring to her role in her and Orestes' own misfortunes rather than to the crime itself.[53] As in the parodos, the lack of strophic responsion between the chorus, Electra, and Orestes during this performance (they each metrically reply only to their own lyrics) may also heighten the isolation of each character, even at this moment of shared lament. Certainly it comes in marked contrast to the elaborate strophic structure of the *kommos* in *Libation Bearers*, which intensifies the sense of their collectivity and shared purpose.

We can see, then, that the degree of a protagonist's choral participation can be an important form of characterization in tragedy, and Euripides especially makes use of it as such in *Electra*. A comparison with Hecuba in *Trojan Women* can help us to understand how Electra is presented through her interactions with the chorus. As will become clear in chapter 3, Hecuba, like Electra, not only denies her role as chorus leader but similarly appropriates aspects of choral lyric within her monodic performance at the start of the play. Hecuba's rejection of her choral role, however, comes as a result of the lack of *choreia* altogether after the devastation of Troy: even though the Trojan women do sing and dance onstage, they simultaneously emphasize the absence of choral performance now that their city has been destroyed. At the same time Hecuba and the chorus display an increasing degree of solidarity through their performances of antiphonal lament, especially toward the end of the tragedy. The apparent absence of *choreia* in *Trojan Women* is very different from the chorus's repeated emphasis in *Electra* on its presence, which underscores the ambiguous nature of Electra's position. Her lack of choral participation, as well as the continued sense of distance between her and the chorus even in the final lament of the play, signifies both her actual social isolation and the sense of exclusion that she constructs for herself—a combination that has led to lengthy scholarly discussions of how far we should accept Electra's self-presentation in the drama and sympathize with her as a character.[54] Euripides' play with myth and innovation, heroism and realism, deliberately prevents a straightforwardly positive or negative response to Electra or Orestes in this tragedy; to adopt either as a critic is to underappreciate the complexity of Euripides' character portrayals.

---

53. δεινότατον παθέων ἔρεξα, 1226. MS L attributes line 1226, with the second person, ἔρεξας ("you committed"), to the chorus rather than to Electra, in which case they would also need to sing line 1232. It is more likely that both strophe and antistrophe would be evenly split between Orestes and Electra, with her singing the last three lines just as the chorus do in the previous strophic pair: see Cropp 1988: 178, following Diggle 1981. The first person, ἔρεξα, is an emendation by Seidler, but it is possible to retain the second person, in which case Electra would be addressing Orestes here: "now she laments the horror of the deed which *her* urging ... forced *him* to enact" (Cropp 1988: 181, emphasis original). This would continue the disconnect between her words and those of the chorus: whereas they tell her that she did "terrible things" (δεινά, 1204), she transfers primary responsibility onto her brother.

54. See, e.g., Arnott 1981; Lloyd 1986; Raeburn 2000; Papadimitropoulos 2008.

At the end of the tragedy, Electra detaches herself from the chorus entirely as she makes the transition away from Argos toward her new life with Pylades. Unlike Hecuba, whose extended antiphonal lament with the chorus brings *Trojan Women* to a close, Electra hardly interacts with the chorus at all in the final scene of her tragedy. After the chorus signal a new dimension of action with the coming of the gods through the sky (1233–37) and Castor delivers a long *rhēsis*, Orestes and Electra join together in dialogue with him (1292–1356). As she assumes her new social role as Pylades' bride, no longer in Argos and apart from her brother, Electra's previous refusal to participate in celebratory *choreia* or to think of herself as a marriageable *parthenos* is superseded. Now, responding to Orestes' request that she utter a *thrēnos* for him ("as if I were dead, at my tomb"), she utters quasi-funerary laments for the loss of her brother and city, as if resuming her mourning at the start of the play.[55] Her dialogue with Orestes and Castor, performed in recitative anapaests, is neither fully sung nor spoken, and does not involve the chorus at all (except for their final few lines of farewell with which the play ends). Instead, it seems to be directed upward and outward, to the gods in the *mēchanē* and the world beyond Argos. In this final closing scene, then, the question of Electra's choral role (or lack thereof) no longer seems significant, as she becomes completely disconnected from her social and communal ties at Argos and heads toward her new life as Pylades' wife in Phocis.[56] Like Helen, who abandons her chorus in Egypt as she is reunited with Menelaus and departs with him to Sparta, Electra leaves the chorus of Argive women behind, but without ever having assumed the role of their leader in the first place.

## PERFORMED ECPHRASIS

The chorus in this play perform three odes separately from Electra, each one at a pivotal point in the action of the play: the first stasimon, just before Electra recognizes Orestes with the help of the Old Man (432–86); the second and third as the murders of Aegisthus and then Clytemnestra take place offstage (699–746, 1147–64). Despite occurring at such critical moments, however, the first two stasima begin by dwelling on scenes that are apparently far from the immediate situation in Argos, transporting the audience initially to the ships carrying Achilles to Troy, and then in the second stasimon to the celebrations in Argos at the discovery of

---

55. θανόντος δ' / ὡς ἐπὶ τύμβωι καταθρήνησον, 1325–26.

56. Griffith 2011 (esp. 199–200) argues that this marriage arrangement (like those of many Greek tragedies) provides an uncomfortably undemocratic but predictable resolution whereby superelite families regroup after a series of catastrophes and begin to rebuild (often with Olympian support). So Electra, though she ends up being completely disconnected from her previous local support systems and community obligations (the city of Argos, her Mycenaean husband, the chorus of Argive women), is able to start up again in another location as the high-status wife of her prosperous cousin, Pylades.

the Golden Fleece. Both songs thus heighten the dramatic tension by seeming to delay the action to which each third of the play is leading—the reunion of Electra and Orestes, and the murder of Aegisthus.

For much of the twentieth century, scholars tended to view the first and second stasima as escapist fantasies that contrast with the realism with which Electra has thus far been depicted. Because they seem to be self-contained narratives at a remove from the dramatic action, they have typically been categorized as dithyrambic.[57] As we shall see, they also display the sort of self-referential musicality that has often been associated with the New Music and dithyramb. The first stasimon in particular has struck many as bizarrely detached from the surrounding drama—"the classic case of pictorial irrelevance."[58] George Gellie presents an extreme version of this view:[59]

> It is not connection that the ode seeks; it is disconnection. We are being reminded, for the sake of argument, of a special world, a wide-screen technicolor world that is crowded, fast and brilliant. It is the world the play rejects. There are no ideas or feelings in the ode, just images and tableaux.

According to this interpretation, then, the point of such songs lies in their disconnection, so that they seem paradigmatic examples of the *embolima* that Aristotle bemoans in *Poetics*.

Given the chorus's otherwise increasing concern for the dramatic action through the course of the play, complete choral detachment in these two stasima would be rather surprising. As we noted, their victory songs celebrating first Orestes' return (585–95) and then his murder of Aegisthus (699–746) demonstrate quite how embedded they are within the dramatic narrative surrounding Electra, even if a sense of distance remains between them and her. And in fact, as several scholars have pointed out, there is an ominous change of tone in both odes, which, far from contributing to a sense of detached escapism, involves a shift in focus from an idealized world in the opening stanza toward the realities of the events in Argos by the end.[60] In the second half of the first stasimon the chorus turn away from "a delightful dream of heroic mythology" toward the unsettling emblems

---

57. Kranz 1933: 238, 241–42, 254; Kubo 1967: 15; Cropp 1988: 128, 149. Cf. Csapo 2003: 71–73, 2009.
58. Barlow 1971: 20.
59. Gellie 1981: 7. Cf. esp. Kitto 1939: 360, 363; Barlow 1971: 20–21. Rode 1971: 111 notes the link to the surrounding drama through the address to Clytemnestra at the end of the ode but states that otherwise the mythological content "mit dem Thema des Dramas nur in sehr lockerem Zusammenhang steht und dadurch dem Lied einen gewissen Eigenwert gibt." In contrast, Walsh 1977 explores the apparent contradiction of "thematic relevance to the dramatic situation, and contrast with it," stating "it is the combination of the two that determines the ode's dramatic function" (278).
60. See esp. O'Brien 1964; Morwood 1981; Cropp 1988: 128–29, 149; Csapo 2009. Cf. Mastronarde 2010: 139–40.

displayed on Achilles' armor, and finally in the epode move from his sword to Clytemnestra's murder of Agamemnon and her impending punishment (476–86).[61] Csapo suggests that this turning point begins with the mention of the sons of Atreus in the closing line of the first strophic pair, creating an emphatic end to the preceding enjambment.[62] Likewise in the second stasimon images of pastoral celebration at the start turn into a description of Thyestes' treachery and its cosmic repercussions; the chorus eventually turn to Clytemnestra with a direct address, just as they do in the first stasimon (745–46).

The odes' *mousikē*, both in language and in performance, contributes significantly to this pattern, tying them to the surrounding drama in addition to augmenting their initial removal from it. The marked musicality displayed in the two songs has received little attention in Euripidean scholarship, except insofar as it can be used to demonstrate their dithyrambic character.[63] Yet the first stasimon in particular is full of allusions to choral dance, and these help both to transport the audience chronologically and geographically away from the present dramatic action and then to bring them back to disturbing events at Argos. Whether they deem it dramatically relevant or not, scholars have been struck by the "pictorial" quality of this ode—its series of "images and tableaux"—from the Nereids dancing around the Greek ships to the Gorgon, sphinxes, and Chimaera depicted on Achilles' armor.[64] These ecphrastic scenes do not, however, merely form a static verbal frieze, since their choreographic focus indicates that they would also be enacted through the chorus's own performance. That is, the chorus would not only describe such scenes in the words of their song but would simultaneously suggest them through their choreographed movements onstage.[65]

The first strophic pair of this song takes us away from Argos to Agamemnon's ships en route to Troy, then to the Nereids bringing Achilles' armor from Euboia to Cheiron's cave on Mount Pelion. The abundance of musical images in the initial strophe enhance this spatial and temporal movement away from the present action in Argos and back to a time before the bloodshed of and following the Trojan War.

κλειναὶ νᾶες, αἵ ποτ' ἔβατε Τροίαν [1st strophe]
τοῖς ἀμετρήτοις ἐρετμοῖς
πέμπουσαι χορεύματα Νηρῄδων,
ἵν' ὁ φίλαυλος ἔπαλλε δελ- (435)

---

61. Morwood 1981: 363.
62. Csapo 2009: 97.
63. As in Csapo 2003: 71–73. Csapo 2009 links the ode's paratactic sequence of images to the New Music but not to its actual performance. Csapo 2008 only indirectly connects references to star choruses in the first two stasima to circular dancing in the *orchēstra* (277–80).
64. Barlow 1971: 20; Gellie 1981: 7.
65. Cf. Walsh 1977: 280: "All of this may be vividly evoked by the dancing of the dramatic chorus itself."

φὶς πρώιραις κυανεμβόλοι-
σιν εἱλισσόμενος,
πορεύων τὸν τᾶς Θέτιδος
κοῦφον ἅλμα ποδῶν Ἀχιλῆ
σὺν Ἀγαμέμνονι Τρωίας						(440)
ἐπὶ Σιμουντίδας ἀκτάς.

Νηρῇδες δ' Εὐβοΐδας ἄκρας λιποῦσαι			[1st antistrophe]
μόχθους ἀσπιστὰς ἀκμόνων
Ἡφαίστου χρυσέων ἔφερον τευχέων,
ἀνά τε Πήλιον ἀνά τ' ἐρυ-						(445)
  μνὰς Ὄσσας ἱερὰς νάπας
  Νυμφαίας σκοπιὰς
†κόρας μάτευσ'† ἔνθα πατὴρ
ἱππότας τρέφεν Ἑλλάδι φῶς
Θέτιδος εἰναλίας γόνον						(450)
ταχύπορον πόδ' Ἀτρείδαις.

> Glorious ships, which once went to Troy with countless oars, escorting the choral dances of the Nereids, where the *aulos*-loving dolphin would leap, whirling by the dark-blue prows, carrying Thetis's son, Achilles, swift in the leap of his feet, with Agamemnon to the banks of the Simois, Troy's river.
> The Nereids, leaving Euboea's headlands, were carrying the shield-labors of Hephaestus's anvils, golden armor, up to Pelion and the holy dells of steep Ossa, the Nymphs' watch-tower, †seeking maidens† where his father, the horseman, was bringing up as a light for Greece the son of sea-dwelling Thetis, fast-moving on his feet for the sons of Atreus. (432–51)

The opening address to the "glorious ships" is left without any predicate, thereby becoming the sort of hanging apostrophe that seems to have been a typical feature of new Euripidean choral lyric and perhaps New Music in general—at least, this is what Aristophanes would have us believe in *Frogs*, when Aeschylus, parodying Euripidean verse, invokes halycons and spiders before submerging them with a series of relative clauses.[66]

The spotlighting of the ships through the address here sets the focus on maritime travel, which continues through the rest of the strophe. This is closely connected with choral dance, creating an interplay between words, music, and movement that brings the scene to life onstage. As we saw in the previous chapter, other Euripidean choral lyric also suggests the choreographic associations of seafaring: the first and second stasima of *Iphigenia in Tauris*, for example, combine descriptions of travel by sea (and horses) with imagery of choral dancing; the chorus in the third stasimon of *Helen* initially focus on the Phoenician ship carrying Helen to Sparta, picturing it as

---

66. See Dover 1993: 352 and Csapo 2003: 72 on this feature in Eur. *El*. 434–41 and Ar. *Ran*. 1309–19.

the *chorēgos* of dancing dolphins.⁶⁷ The link between seafaring and *choreia* may result in particular from the association of the dithyramb and Dionysus more generally with maritime travel. We see this association in Herodotus's story of Arion, the founder of the dithyramb, and also in the *Homeric Hymn to Dionysus*, in which pirate traders are transformed into a sort of dolphin chorus.⁶⁸ Depictions of dolphin choruses also appear on the series of archaic and early classical vases that I discussed briefly in chapter 1. These further indicate a nexus of associations between seafaring, dolphins, *choreia*, and Dionysiac cult, one that seems to be an essential part of the dithyrambic imaginary.⁶⁹

In the first stasimon of *Electra* the musical connotations of the opening theme become clear as the chorus sing of how the ships escorted the "choral dances of the Nereids," with the "*aulos*-loving dolphin" whirling and leaping alongside (434–37).⁷⁰ As we saw in the case of Bacchylides 17, Nereids almost always appear in connection with dancing in Greek literature; their number (usually fifty) can in particular link them to the chorus of the dithyramb. This is the first time that they are mentioned in Euripides' extant work, but from this point onward they appear quite frequently, suggesting his increasing experimentation with metamusical language and imagery.⁷¹ Their appearance here may be a sign of Euripides' own musical innovation in employing choral imagery associated with Dionysus, but we should not necessarily then see references to Nereids in tragedy as a mark of the New Music more generally. Indeed, as we saw in the previous chapter, Nereids actually appeared on the tragic stage at least fifty years before Euripides produced *Electra*: in Aeschylus's *Nereids*, a chorus of them enter in the parodos carrying Achilles' arms and singing of how they have crossed "the expanse of the dolphin

---

67. Eur. *IT* 393–466, 1089–1152; *Hel.* 1454–55.

68. Hdt. 1.23–24; *Hymn. Hom. Bacch.* 48–53. See also *Hymn. Hom. Ap.* 399–439, when Apollo in dolphin form steers the Cretan ship toward Crisa, and the pseudo-Arion hymn (probably a dithyramb), quoted in Ael. *NA* 12.45. Cf. Kowalzig 2013: 31–34.

69. On these vases see Csapo 2003. Kowalzig 2013 argues that the link between the dithyramb and maritime travel reflects and even enacts increased economic connectivity across the Greek Mediterranean in the archaic period.

70. Rather than follow Diggle's emendation, Willink 2009: 206–7 (cf. 1999) proposes that we retain the MS L reading πέμπουσαι χοροὺς μετὰ Νηρῄδων in line 434, arguing that this phrase has the meaning of "processing in association with." The more standard meaning of πέμπειν does not, however, seem particularly jarring here, since the idea instead seems to be that the Nereids and dolphin are dancing around the ships (and so being carried along with them), while the image of the ships carrying the maiden choruses contributes to the simultaneous merging of the dramatic chorus with the soldiers, Nereids, and dolphin that I discuss below.

71. Cf. Eur. *Ion* 1081–86; *IT* 263–64, 427–29; *IA* 239–40, 1055–57, 1078–79. References to the Nereids' choral dancing outside of choral lyric: *Andr.* 1267, *Tro.* 2. On Nereids' association with dancing, the dithyramb, and the New Music, see Csapo 1999–2000: 422 and 2003, esp. 73–78.

sea."[72] The description of the Nereids' choral dances and the dancing dolphin in the *Electra* ode, which goes on to recount how the maidens brought Achilles his armor, must refer back to Aeschylus's older tragedy as much as it also points to a new departure in Euripides' own use of *mousikē*.[73]

Unlike Aeschylus's chorus, however, this one is not actually made up of Nereids. Instead, by referring to these archetypal performers of *choreia*, the choreuts appear to merge with them—this is the doubling effect of imaginative suggestion, whereby the dramatic chorus can temporarily appear to embody the one they describe. Such an effect would have been particularly strong for those members of the Athenian audience who knew Aeschylus's play and its chorus of Nereids, but the crossover between the dramatic chorus and the Nereids depicted in the words of their song would also be a natural one given the frequency with which the dithyrambic chorus is imagined in this way.[74] By assuming the identity of the Nereids, then, the chorus do not simply describe the ships' voyage but also to a large degree enact it through their own choral performance. For the audience this scene thus becomes live, as the chorus, through the combination of words, music, and dance, draw them away from the Argos of the dramatic present back toward Troy of the heroic past.

With the "*aulos*-loving dolphin" the chorus's performance onstage similarly merges with the one they describe in their song. The unusual adjective *philaulos* (435) immediately establishes a link between the sea creature and the chorus, who are likewise dancing to the accompaniment of the *aulos*. It also alludes to the playing of the *aulos* on the Greek ships to provide a rhythm for the men rowing with "countless oars" (433) and so heightens the impression that the chorus are performing the sea journey they describe. We have already seen that dolphins are frequently associated with choral dance (especially the dithyramb) in archaic and classical Greek literature and art. Depictions of dolphin choruses on vases often follow the shape of the vessels, thus suggesting a circular dance formation. Euripidean choral lyric frequently depicts Nereids in this way too—in the third stasimon of *Iphigenia in Aulis*, for example, the Nereids are imagined as "whirling in circles" in their dance.[75] The combination of the "whirling" (*heilissomenos*) dolphin in the *Electra* ode and the dancing Nereids also suggests circular movement, in terms of the choral formation as a whole and perhaps also of the individual turns of the choreuts, so that the chorus again seem to be enacting in their dance what they describe in their

---

72. δελφινηρὸν πεδίον πόντου, Aesch. fr. 150. On the Aeschylean chorus, see S. G. Miller 1986: 162; Michelakis 2002: 53–54; Csapo 2003: 73. On the dating of the *Achilleis* trilogy to the second decade of the fifth century, see Snell 1971: 3 n. 5; Taplin 1977: 62 n. 4 and 456 n. 2.

73. On Euripides' allusion to Aeschylus's *Nereids* here, see Kenner 1941: 17; S. G. Miller 1986: 162–63; Csapo 2003: 73.

74. On the question of to what extent the Athenian audiences of the late fifth century could be expected to appreciate the interconnectivity of different plays, see Revermann 2006b, esp. 115–20.

75. εἱλισσόμεναι κύκλια, Eur. *IA* 1055.

song. Aristophanes' parody of this passage (combined with parts of *Hypsipyle* and *Meleager*) in *Frogs* highlights this particular aspect of the performance:

αἵ θ' ὑπωρόφιοι κατὰ γωνίας
εἱειειειειειλίσσετε δακτύλοις φάλαγγες
ἱστότονα πηνίσματα, (1315)
κερκίδος ἀοιδοῦ μελέτας,
ἵν' ὁ φίλαυλος ἔπαλλε δελ-
φὶς πρώιραις κυανεμβόλοις
μαντεῖα καὶ σταδίους.

And you spiders who beneath the roof, in the crannies, whi-i-i-i-irl [*heieieieieilissete*] with your fingers the loom-stretched threads, the works of the singing shuttle, where the *aulos*-loving dolphin would leap by the dark-blue prows for oracles and race tracks. (Ar. *Ran.* 1313–19)

The deliberate showcasing of melisma here, when Aeschylus's character stretches the initial syllable of the second person plural indicative form out over several notes (*heieieieieieilissete*), indicates that both the vocabulary of whirling and its enactment were especially striking aspects of the performance of Euripidean choral lyric, and of the *Electra* ode in particular. Euripides may have highlighted the verb's meaning similarly, perhaps matching the mimetic acoustic effect of melisma with the simultaneous twirling of each choreut. The chorus also imagine the dolphin as leaping, using another verb (*epalle*, 435) that is choreographically resonant and could therefore apply to their own movements in the *orchēstra*. In this invitation to the audience to visualize the choreuts as dolphins as well as Nereids, we see the flexibility of imaginative suggestion, whereby a chorus can adopt multiple overlapping identities in quick succession, asking the audience to hold all these images in mind at the same time.

Archaic and early classical vases show not just dolphin choruses but dolphin-human hybrids, which suggest that Greek audiences were accustomed to conflate choral (especially dithyrambic) performers with these dancing creatures.[76] An unattributed Attic black-figure krater of ca. 550 B.C.E. (fig. 1), which shows a chorus of men on the outside and dolphins on the inside of the rim, suggests a similar aesthetic crossover through *choreia*: as Barbara Kowalzig points out, "when looked at from the most usual angle, that is to say, slightly from above, the two lines of choral dancers blur into one and the same, the 'real' and the 'imagined' choros become almost indistinguishable."[77] This is a visual representation of the process of imaginative suggestion in the performance of a dithyramb: when a chorus sing of

---

76. On vase depictions of dancing dolphin-men see Csapo 2003: 79–86. He rightly stresses that such images should not be read merely as illustrations of the pirates who metamorphose into dolphins in the *Homeric Hymn to Dionysus*.

77. Kowalzig 2013: 35.

FIGURE 1. Attic black-figure cup-krater, ca. 550 B.C.E., with dolphins depicted along the inside rim. On the outside is a processional dance of men; below this is a frieze of horse riders. Musée du Louvre, Paris, CA 2988. (Photo: courtesy of RMN–Grand Palais / Art Resource, NY.)

dolphins, as Euripides' one does in *Electra,* they prompt the audience to visualize them as these archetypal dancers.

By assimilating themselves to the dancing dolphin as well as to the Nereids, the chorus could also represent through their performance the Greek soldiers on their way to Troy. While some dolphin vases have Nereids as riders, others show armed men on these animals, following the circular shape of the vessel, often with an *aulos*-player standing between them.[78] An especially clear example is the Oltos Psykter (fig. 2), which I mentioned in chapter 1: on this vase we see riders in full hoplite armor; each one appears to be singing, with the words *epi delphinos* ("upon a dolphin") coming out of his mouth, perhaps suggesting the opening words of a choral song.[79] Kowalzig argues that such riders represent a hoplite phalanx, which,

---

78. On vases showing Nereid riders, see Barringer 1995: 30–39. There is no need to claim, as she does, that this motif was a direct result of Aeschylus's *Nereids* (see also Matheson 1995: 252): these vases, the depictions of dolphins, and Aeschylus's play all draw on and reflect a shared cultural imaginary linked to the dithyramb.

79. Sifakis 1967 suggests that this is an image of a comic chorus and that the inscription ἐπὶ δελφῖνος could come from a song in which they describe themselves. Cf. Green 1994: 32–33, who further

FIGURE 2. Attic red-figure psykter attributed to Oltos, ca. 520–510 B.C.E., showing six hoplites riding on dolphins. Metropolitan Museum of Art, New York, Gift of Norbert Schimmel Trust, 1989, inv. 1989.281.69.

by winding around the walls of the vase like a chorus, seems to enclose its contents rather as it would in battle. She suggests that the association of the dithyrambic choral imaginary with that of the hoplite phalanx lies in their shared significance as images of civic solidarity and community integration.[80] At the same time, the fact that these men are also riders suggests "the contemporary military change

---

conjectures that these words are from a chorus's anapaestic parodos. The idea that the vase refers to a particular comedy is based on the assumption that it shows a chorus actually coming onstage as dolphin riders, but it could instead reflect a more widespread choral imaginary within which choruses were associated with dolphins. On the Oltos Psykter and related images, see also Vidali 1997: 60–64.

80. Kowalzig 2013: 37–47.

from knight to hoplite and the integration of exchange by sea and traditional modes of elite display in a new visual reference system."[81] By the time of Euripides' *Electra*, the specific identification of choral dolphin riders as knights-turned-hoplites may have been less resonant, but the first stasimon suggests that the more general association between dolphins and traveling soldiers remained within the choral imaginary. Moreover, the dolphin in this ode is not merely accompanying the Greek army on their way to Troy, but *carrying* Achilles (*poreuōn*, 438), just as the creatures on the vases are shown carrying soldiers.[82] If this image evoked for the late fifth-century Athenian audience a sense of community cohesion similar to what Kowalzig sees in the dolphin rider vases of a century earlier, the effect of escapism in the ode's initial strophe would be particularly pronounced, coming in sharp contrast with the past and impending civic turmoil at Argos.

For an audience familiar with the cultural nexus of (dithyrambic) chorus, dolphins, maritime travel, and hoplite soldiers, the chorus of *Electra* would therefore appear to merge through their *choreia* not only with the Nereids and the dancing dolphin, but also with Achilles himself, as he rides on its back to Troy. The focus in the subsequent lines on Achilles' own famously swift movement, with the description of him as "swift in the leap of his foot" (439) adds to this impression: by describing the actual movement of the leaping feet, the elaboration of the standard Homeric epithet "swift-footed" draws attention to the chorus's own energetic movement, not just Achilles' "youthfulness, athletic physique and readiness for action."[83] A similar effect results from the pleonasm of "fast-moving on his feet" at 451, which achieves particular emphasis through its position at the very end of the antistrophe.

Other than this reference to Achilles' speed, however, the antistrophe contains markedly less choreographic language and fewer verbs of movement than the preceding strophe. The dramatic chorus may fuse again with the stanza's main subject, as now the focus shifts further back in time to the Nereids bringing arms fashioned by Hephaestus from Euboia to Achilles on Pelion. Just like the strophe, the first six lines of the antistrophe are concerned not only with the Nereids but also with travel, so that any repeated dance movements in the chorus's performance of this verse could similarly match the content of their song.[84] The chorus can thus con-

---

81. Kowalzig 2013: 46.
82. I therefore see no reason to follow Willink's proposed emendation πορεύοντας τὸν Θέτιδος in line 438 (2009: 207). Since Achilles is clearly the direct object of πορεύων in line 439, these lines do not seem to depict the Nereids as dolphin-riders instead, as S. G. Miller 1986: 162 suggests the strophe and antistrophe do.
83. Cropp 1988: 130. Csapo 2003: 73 suggests the choreuts may themselves leap at this point.
84. Wiles 1997: 96–103 argues for strict choreographic symmetry between strophe and antistrophe in tragic choral odes by schematically examining the same examples that Dale 1968: 212–14 used to claim otherwise (*Bacch.* 977–1017, *Hec.* 923–42, *Ion* 205–37). But just as lines of the same metrical form

tinue to enact the scene that they describe, even without the sorts of verbal allusions to performance that we find in the strophe. Their performance visually and acoustically situates the audience in a scene that seems far removed from the immediate action of the play.

In the second strophic pair the chorus sing of Achilles' armor and in doing so begin an ominous shift in the ode back toward the bloodiness at Argos. In contrast to the strong sense of movement and travel in the first strophe and antistrophe, now the song's focus seems more static and pictorial. Yet the chorus once again enact what they describe through their own song and dance, thereby vivifying the armor in a kind of performed ecphrasis. By embodying through their choreographed performance the images that they describe in words, the chorus redirect the audience toward the dramatic present, to which the epode finally turns.

| | |
|---|---|
| Ἰλιόθεν δ' ἔκλυόν τινος ἐν λιμέσιν | [2nd strophe] |
| Ναυπλίοις βεβῶτος | |
| τᾶς σᾶς, ὦ Θέτιδος παῖ, | |
| κλεινᾶς ἀσπίδος ἐν κύκλωι | (455) |
| τοιάδε σήματα †δείματα | |
| Φρύγια† τετύχθαι· | |
| περιδρόμωι μὲν ἴτυος ἕδραι | |
| Περσέα λαιμοτόμαν ὑπὲρ ἁλὸς | |
| ποτανοῖσι πεδίλοις κορυφὰν Γοργόνος ἴσχειν, | (460) |
|    Διὸς ἀγγέλωι σὺν Ἑρμᾶι, | |
| τῶι Μαίας ἀγροτῆρι κούρωι. | |
| ἐν δὲ μέσωι κατέλαμπε σάκει φαέθων | [2nd antistrophe] |
| κύκλος ἀλίοιο | (465) |
| ἵπποις ἄμ πτεροέσσαις | |
| ἄστρων τ' αἰθέριοι χοροί, | |
| Πλειάδες Ὑάδες, †Ἕκτορος | |
| ὄμμασι† τροπαῖοι· | |
| ἐπὶ δὲ χρυσοτύπωι κράνει | (470) |
| Σφίγγες ὄνυξιν ἀοίδιμον ἄγραν | |
| φέρουσαι· περιπλεύρωι δὲ κύτει πύρπνοος ἔσπευ- | |
| δε δρόμωι λέαινα χαλαῖς | |
| Πειρηναῖον ὁρῶσα πῶλον. | (475) |
| ἄορι δ' ἐν φονίωι τετραβάμονες ἵπποι ἔπαλλον, | [epode] |
| κελαινὰ δ' ἀμφὶ νῶθ' ἵετο κόνις. | |
| τοιῶνδ' ἄνακτα δοριπόνων | |
| ἔκανεν ἀνδρῶν, Τυνδαρί, | (480) |

---

did not need to be melodically identical (D'Angour 2006 and 2011: 203), so the repetition of the strophe's choreography in the antistrophe, while certainly possible in the cases Wiles analyzes, need not have been an absolute rule.

σὰ λέχεα, κακόφρον κόρα.
τοιγάρ σοί ποτ' οὐρανίδαι
πέμψουσιν θανάτου δίκαν.
ἔτ' ἔτι φόνιον ὑπὸ δέραν (485)
ὄψομαι αἷμα χυθὲν σιδάρωι.

> I used to hear, from someone who came from Ilium to the harbor of Nauplia, that on the circle of your famous shield, O son of Thetis, were wrought these emblems, †terrors for the Phrygians†: on the surrounding base of the shield's rim, Perseus the throat cutter, over the sea with winged sandals, was holding the Gorgon's head, with Hermes, Zeus's messenger, the rustic son of Maia.
>
> In the center of the shield the gleaming circle of the sun was shining on winged horses, and the heavenly choruses of stars, Pleiades, Hyades, turning back †the eyes of Hector†; and upon his gold-beaten helmet were Sphinxes, carrying in their talons song-caught prey. On the rib-encircling hollow a fire-breathing lioness sped at a run with her claws, seeing Peirene's colt.
>
> On the bloody sword four-footed horses were leaping, and about their backs black dust was thrown up. The lord of such spear-toiling men your [adulterous] bed killed, evil-minded daughter of Tyndareus! For this the heavenly gods will one day [soon] send to you the punishment of death. Still, still beneath your bloody throat I shall see blood pouring forth at the sword. (452–86)

After the escapism of the initial strophic pair, now the chorus describe a series of increasingly ominous "emblems" (*sēmata*, 456) depicted on Achilles' shield, dominated by threatening, man-killing female monsters (the Gorgon, Sphinxes, Chimaera), which help to bring us back in the epode to Clytemnestra, who elsewhere in the play is likened to the Gorgon and lioness.[85] By pointing toward Clytemnestra's act of murder as well as her own death, these symbols contribute to a conflation of Troy and Argos, then and now, thereby moving us back toward the dramatic present.

The chorus's choreography would play an important role in pushing the audience into the present by making otherwise static images come to life onstage. The emphasis on circularity in the second strophe and antistrophe suggests that the shield could be visualized through the chorus's own circular performance—a for-

---

85. Eur. *El.* 1221–23, 1163 (cf. Aesch. *Ag.* 716–36, 1258–59): see O'Brien 1964; Cropp 1988: 129; Csapo 2009: 100. The Chimaera is typically represented as a fire-breathing lioness in classical art, with a goat growing from its back and a snake's head on its tail. All three female monsters could appear as apotropaic symbols on real weaponry: see Csapo 2009: 99–100. It is possible, as Csapo suggests (101–2), that the images of the dolphin and Nereids in the opening strophe could already hint at a more ominous theme, since both had apotropaic and funerary associations, appearing frequently on weaponry and in funereal art. When these creatures appear in dithyrambic and tragic choral lyric, however, such associations generally seem to be absent, and here they could become resonant only in retrospect, as the ode explicitly turns to more disturbing subjects.

mation in which they likely would already be moving, given the dithyrambic character of the ode's opening and the description of the whirling dolphin in the initial strophe.[86] The emphatically placed expression "in a circle" (*en kyklōi*) at the end of line 455 could reflect their choreography as well as the shape of the shield itself. This correspondence between the sung description and dance formation would be particularly clear to those spectators higher up in the *theatron*, looking down upon the chorus's circle.[87] Such interplay would continue when the chorus sing of the face of the shield's rim, describing it as *peridromōi* in line 458. Although this adjective tends to be translated as "surrounding" or "encircling," its literal meaning is "running around," which is reflected by the line's highly resolved glyconic meter, with the resolution of the first two syllables of *peridromōi* followed by the short anceps coming at the very start ($\smile\smile\smile-\smile\smile\smile\smile\smile-$). We can imagine some sort of quickened dance movement to match the meter (perhaps a turning around on the spot), but the interaction between what the chorus describe in their song and what they perform onstage need not be strictly mimetic. Instead the correspondence between description and performance works through imaginative suggestion, whereby the existing and even conventional choreography involving circular movements can suggest and be visualized as the images pictured in the chorus's lyrics.

The correspondence between ecphrastic description and choral choreography is more explicit in the antistrophe, with the initial image of the circle (*kuklos*) of the sun shining in the middle of the shield, along with its "winged horses" and the "heavenly choruses of stars" (465–67). The combination of the adjective *phaethōn* ("gleaming") and the reference to horses could allude to the myth of Phaethon, who was destroyed after losing control of the sun's chariot.[88] If so, as Csapo demonstrates, a third star chorus, the Heliades, may be suggested here, in addition to the Pleiades and Hyades; all three result from maidens being catasterized while mourning dead male relatives.[89] (The Heliades were Phaethon's sisters.) These lines can also, however, help to merge the scene depicted on the shield with the chorus dancing in the theater. As we saw in chapter 1, references to both horses and flying often appear in passages of highly self-referential choral lyric: in Alcman's first *Partheneion*, for example, Agido and Hagesichora are likened to different breeds of horses in their dancing and beauty; in Euripides' *Helen* the chorus sing of their wish to fly as birds through the air from Egypt to Sparta, following their syrinx-

---

86. On the circular formation of the dithyrambic chorus, see esp. D'Angour 1997.

87. Cf. Marshall 2014: 135 on choral dance formations more generally: "a spectator with an elevated view from the seating area is more likely to appreciate the movement and dance of the chorus than is the one seated near the level of the performance area."

88. As suggested by Denniston 1939: 107; Mulryne 1977: 42; Csapo 2008: 278 and 2009: 101.

89. Csapo 2009: 100–101.

playing chorus leader; in *Iphigenia in Tauris* equine and flying imagery are combined in the chorus's frequent singing of travel across the sea, which they imagine with vividly choreographic and musical language.[90] The choral associations of such imagery would therefore encourage the audience to see the chorus as the heavenly bodies they describe. The "gleaming" circle of the sun could also direct attention to the inner of two concentric circles of choreuts, with the outer one representing the choruses of stars, though it bears repeating that imaginative suggestion through *choreia* can work without a precisely mimetic correspondence between the described and performed images. Brightness is often associated with *choreia*, especially *partheneia*, as we saw in Electra's rejection of such choral imagery in the parodos. Here it could also allude to aspects of the chorus's actual costume, or the astral images on the shield could be evoked through the presence of the aulete playing in the center (*en de mesōi*, 464) of the circular chorus, shining like the sun in his elaborate robes.[91]

The sun and stars on Achilles' shield also evoke Dionysiac imagery, further prompting a correlation between the verbal and choreographic elements of the song. The depiction of these celestial bodies (particularly the Pleiades and Hyades) goes back to the ecphrasis in the *Iliad* (which may in turn derive from an early Greek tradition of star shields),[92] but the idea of their choral formation may derive both from Dionysiac cult and from the sort of Pythagorean eschatology that Plato draws on in the visions of cosmic *choreia* and harmony in the *Timaeus* and *Republic*.[93] In surviving fifth-century tragedy star choruses twice appear in connection with Dionysian cult and the Eleusinian Mysteries: in Sophocles' *Antigone* the god is addressed as "chorus leader of stars breathing fire and overseer of nighttime utterances"; in Euripides' *Ion* the chorus imagine Ion as an uninitiated foreigner witnessing "Zeus's starry-faced aether" starting up the choral dance, as well as the dancing of the moon and Nereids for Demeter and Kore.[94] The image of the sun and star choruses on Achilles' shield therefore picks up on the Dionysian/

90. Alcm. fr.1 *PMGF*, 58–59; Eur. *Hel.* 1478–94; Eur. *IT* 1138–52 (cf. 192, 408–38).

91. On the aulete's conspicuous attire, see Wilson 2002: 51.

92. Hom. *Il.* 18.483–89. On the link between the Iliadic ecphrasis and early Greek star shields, see Hardie 1985: 12–13.

93. Nikolaidou-Arabatzi 2015: 33–34 suggests that Euripides was the first to invent the idea of the Pleiades as a star chorus. But even if Alcman's first *Partheneion* does not refer to the Pleiades, their appearance in *Electra*, one of the few surviving tragedies, is not sufficient evidence for such an innovation on Euripides' part. Nikolaidou-Arabatzi also disregards the broader significance of star choruses in Dionysiac cult and Pythagorean eschatology.

94. ἰὼ πῦρ πνεόντων / χοράγ' ἄστρων, νυχίων / φθεγμάτων ἐπίσκοπε, Soph. *Ant.* 1146–48; Διὸς ἀστερωπὸς / ἀνεχόρευσεν αἰθήρ, Eur. *Ion* 1078–79. Cf. Zarifi 2007: 227–28; Csapo 2008: 267–72. The Pleiades may also appear as a chorus in Alcm. fr. 1 *PMGF*, 60–63: see chapter 1, p. 28. Also cf. Eur. *Phaethon* fr. 773.19–21.

dithyrambic imagery of the opening strophe, creating a natural movement from choruses of Nereids to those of stars. At the same time it suggests the sort of cosmic harmony that the revolving circles of heavenly bodies in Plato's dialogues represent: in *Timaeus* the Demiurge is said to have created two concentric circles of stars and planets, which perform *choreia* around the Earth; in Book Ten of the *Republic* Socrates describes eight concentric whorls revolving around the spindle of Necessity, like the stars and planets around the Earth, with a Siren on each one, together producing a single *harmonia*.[95] The description of Hephaestus fashioning the heavens on the Iliadic shield gives a similar impression by resembling a cosmogony, while the following depictions of the two cities (one at peace and one at war), agricultural fertility, and *choreia* suggest a link between cosmic and social order among men.[96] Within the context of *Electra*, however, such an image of cosmic regularity, simultaneously enacted onstage by means of the chorus's own dancing, is an ironic one, undermined by the description of the star choruses as *tropaioi* in line 469, causing the rout of Hector, and then by the images of the Sphinxes carved on Achilles' helmet and the Chimaera on his breastplate—creatures who lead us back to the murder at Argos.

Such irony is particularly pronounced as the chorus shift to these more ominous images not only in the words of their song but in their *mousikē* too, as they describe them with language that again allusively suggests their own performance. The Sphinxes' "song-caught prey" (471) positions the singing choreuts as these monsters who catch men through their song, while the depiction of the Chimaera that "sped at a run [*dromōi*]" along Achilles' corselet, the "rib-encircling [*peripleurōi*] hollow" (472–74), continues the emphasis on movement and circularity (especially the adjective *peridromos*) from the rest of the strophic pair. This effect of interaction between the images described and the chorus's own performance extends into the opening image of the epode—the horses galloping along Achilles' bloody sword. The reference to horses, following that in the preceding antistrophe, prompts us to link them to the dancing choreuts, yet these beasts are now far more terrifying than the flying ones on the shield. Similarly, the verb *pallō* ("leap") reminds us of the movement of the dancing dolphin at the start of the ode (*epalle*, 435), but now any mimetic movement in terms of the chorus's leaping suggests a much more disturbing image than the *aulos*-loving dolphin.[97] By then describing the dust, dark with blood, kicked up around the horses (477), they make us recall Hector's body being dragged around

---

95. Pl. *Tim.* 40b4–d1, *Rep.* 616c4–617d1. On the choral associations of the latter passage, see Peponi 2013b: 18–20.

96. Hom. *Il.* 18.490–606.

97. Cf. Csapo 2009: 103 ("The symmetry . . . creates a strong opposition between the joyful dance of innocent dolphins and the charge of warhorses"); also King 1980: 207–8.

Troy,[98] and this association then leads into Clytemnestra's murder of Agamemnon, another hero of the war, and the chorus's wish for her own bloody death.

With their address to Clytemnestra in lines 480–81,[99] the chorus move directly to the present situation. All self-reflexive allusions to their own choreography cease now that the chorus are no longer bringing to life scenes and images of the world beyond the play itself—a shift that they could physically enact by being stationary for the final lines of the ode.[100] These lines pull the whole ode into the immediate dramatic present, replacing the image of the Gorgon and her severed throat with that of Clytemnestra's own "bloody neck," and the blood on Achilles' sword with that on the iron used to kill her (485–86). By vividly taking us away from the present in the initial strophic pair and then leading us back to it through their own *choreia*, until they finally address Clytemnestra herself and look forward to her death, the chorus generate a sense of dark foreboding that was previously absent from the play, while also adding to its suspense, as we too become increasingly expectant of the siblings' revenge.

This ode does not therefore remain at a remove from the surrounding drama, as a series of pictorial images situated in a heroic-mythical world far from that of the play itself. The escapist opening of the song enables the return to the dramatic present to be particularly forceful, and indeed the change of tone away from the dithyrambic opening achieves a kind of chilling potency, as it leads us to Clytemnestra's bloody murder.[101] The chorus's own transformation through their *choreia* reflects and vivifies this change of tone, as they shift from appearing as the unthreatening Nereids and dolphin in their dance to visualizing the "terrors" (456) on Achilles' shield; like the choruses of stars, they themselves seem to become *tropaioi* (469), things that turn Hector around and cause his defeat. As a result, they increasingly appear as part of a killing machine, so that when they finally turn their full focus to the queen's imminent death, they seem already to be effecting it.[102] With the entry of the Old Man immediately after the epode, it really does

---

98. Cf. Csapo 2009: 103–4.

99. Some scholars have argued that the vocative Τυνδαρί (480) refers to Helen instead, though most now agree on Clytemnestra as the addressee: see the discussion by O'Brien 1964: 16–17 n. 7; also Cropp 1988: 133; Csapo 2009: 104–5; Gagné and Hopman 2013b: 12. There may, as Csapo argues, be some deliberate ambiguity here, but the following wish for revenge and vision of murder (483–86) clearly refer to Clytemnestra, and these lines are thus mirrored by the second-person address to the queen at the end of the second stasimon (745–46).

100. On the stationary performance of a choral epode, cf. Mullen 1982: 90–142 on Pindar's epinician odes. On the shift through the ode from the remote to the immediate, cf. Eisner 1979: 164; King 1980: 198.

101. Cf. King 1980 on the turn toward violence in the ode's final stanzas.

102. Such a transformation is not too far from that of Electra herself, who first appears as a completely defenseless outcast, only to become the joint murderer of her mother, grasping the sword alongside Orestes (1224–25).

seem as if the chorus's song has played a part in pushing the plot along toward Clytemnestra's death, since he becomes the crucial agent for facilitating the recognition of Orestes by Electra and so also their joint revenge.[103] Following the chorus's claim that "the heavenly gods will one day [soon] send to you the punishment of death," his arrival confirms the efficacy of their song.[104]

## CHORAL ANTICIPATION AND ENACTMENT

The dramatically generative effect of *choreia* that we see in the first stasimon becomes even more potent in the following two choral odes, which are performed at the same time as Aegisthus and then Clytemnestra are killed offstage. The second stasimon in particular anticipates and virtually enacts the murders of both Aegisthus and Clytemnestra, leading the audience to these bloody events rather in the same way as the first stasimon encouraged us to anticipate Clytemnestra's death through a shift from an escapist beginning to much more ominous images and predictions in the second half of the ode. Unlike the previous stasimon, however, the shift in this later song is also an integral element of the chorus's narrative about the Golden Fleece and Thyestes' extreme reversal of fortune, which they make especially vivid through their own *mousikē*. Their performance of this reversal not only parallels what they envisage for Aegisthus and in particular Clytemnestra but marks a pivotal moment in the play as Electra and Orestes begin to carry out their long-anticipated revenge on Thyestes' son and the queen.

Like the first stasimon, the second begins with a past scene of seemingly carefree *mousikē* that is brought to life through the chorus's own singing and dancing:[105]

| | |
|---|---|
| ἀταλᾶς ὑπὸ †ματέρος Ἀργείων† | [1st strophe] |
| ὀρέων ποτὲ κληδὼν | (700) |
| ἐν πολιαῖσι μένει φήμαις | |
| εὐαρμόστοις ἐν καλάμοις | |
| Πᾶνα μοῦσαν ἡδύθροον | |
| πνέοντ', ἀγρῶν ταμίαν, | |
| χρυσέαν ἄρνα καλλίπλοκον | (705) |
| πορεῦσαι. πετρίνοις δ' ἐπι- | |
| στὰς κᾶρυξ ἰαχεῖ βάθροις· | |
| Ἀγορὰν ἀγοράν, Μυκη- | |

---

103. Walsh 1977: 283–88 argues that the ode's evocation of heroic times also looks forward to the recognition scene and following events of the play, since the images of monster-killing represent the sort of morally unambiguous heroism that Electra hopes she and Orestes will achieve through the murders of Clytemnestra and Aegisthus.

104. ποτ' οὐρανίδαι / πέμψουσιν θανάτου δίκαν, 483–84.

105. In rendering line 719, "†in praise†" is a translation of Wecklein's emendation of εὐλογίαι for the meaningless ἐπίλογοι: see Cropp 1988: 150.

ναῖοι, στείχετε μακαρίων
ὀψόμενοι τυράννων (710)
φάσματα †δείματα.
χοροὶ δ᾽† Ἀτρειδᾶν ἐγέραιρον οἴκους.

θυμέλαι δ᾽ ἐπίτναντο χρυσήλατοι, [1st antistrophe]
σελαγεῖτο δ᾽ ἀν᾽ ἄστυ
πῦρ ἐπιβώμιον Ἀργείων· (715)
λωτὸς δὲ φθόγγον κελάδει
κάλλιστον, Μουσᾶν θεράπων,
μολπαὶ δ᾽ ηὔξοντ᾽ ἐραταὶ
χρυσέας ἀρνὸς †ἐπίλογοι†
Θυέστου· κρυφίαις γὰρ εὐ- (720)
ναῖς πείσας ἄλοχον φίλαν
Ἀτρέως, τέρας ἐκκομί-
ζει πρὸς δώματα· νεόμενος δ᾽
εἰς ἀγόρους αὐτεῖ
τὰν κερόεσσαν ἔχειν (725)
χρυσεόμαλλον κατὰ δῶμα ποίμναν.

From beneath its tender †mother in the Argive† mountains, as the rumor remains among gray-haired tales, Pan, guardian of fields, blowing on well-fitted reeds sweet-strained music, once brought forth the golden fine-fleeced lamb. And standing on a stone platform, the herald cries out: "Make your way to the agora, to the agora, Mycenaeans, to see the blessed royals' prodigies, †terrors." And choruses† began to honor the house of the Atreidae.

Altars of beaten gold were spread, and through the Argives' city the fire on the altar was gleaming. And the sound of the *lōtos* pipe was resounding, most beautiful, the Muses' servant, and lovely songs were swelling forth, †in praise† of the Golden Fleece of Thyestes: for having persuaded the dear wife of Atreus in secret union, he carries the portent out to his house. And coming into the agora he shouts that he has the horned, golden-woolled sheep at his home. (699–726)

The combination of the description of the god's *mousikē* and its simultaneous enactment in the theater brings to life the initial scene of pastoral simplicity, as Pan carries the Golden Fleece to Argos from the mountains. As they sing of him playing his syrinx (panpipes), the characteristic instrument of herdsmen, the audience would hear the tune of the *aulos*. As we shall see in chapters 4 and 5, Euripides elsewhere suggests a mimetic merging of the *aulos* in the theater with the syrinx described in choral lyric: such an acoustic crossover is especially clear in the first stasimon of *Iphigenia in Aulis*, when the chorus picture Paris "piping foreign tunes on the syrinx, blowing on the reeds imitations of the Phrygian *auloi* of Olympus."[106]

---

106. βάρβαρα συρίζων, Φρυγίων / αὐλῶν Οὐλύμπου καλάμοις / μιμήματα †πνέων†, Eur. *IA* 576–78. On the relationship between the syrinx and *aulos* in Euripidean theater, see Weiss forthcoming a.

Timothy Power suggests that Sophocles too may have exploited the "mimetic intimacy" of the two instruments in his *Inachus*, in which the actor impersonating Hermes could mime playing the syrinx while the aulete would supply its sound.[107] A similar merging of *aulos* and syrinx is also suggested in *Prometheus Bound*, when Io in her monody sings of Hermes' pipe playing: "And the clear-sounding, wax-molded reed booms forth a tune that brings sleep."[108] In *Electra* the chorus's description of the syrinx with its "sweet-strained music" (703) similarly shapes the audience's reception of the sound of the *aulos*, so that it can momentarily represent for them Pan's piping. The metonym of "well-fitted reeds" (702) aids the merging of described and performed *mousikē*, since reeds were associated with the *aulos* as well as with the syrinx.[109] This mimetic effect helps to transport the audience to a peaceful, bucolic scene, far from the imminent bloodshed of the dramatic present.

The ode continues to focus on this past scene of seemingly untroubled celebration but moves away from the pastoral simplicity with which it began and into the city of Argos. Just as the aulete imitates Pan playing his syrinx, so the chorus impersonate the herald, reperforming in direct speech his summoning of the Argives to the agora. With the mention of the *choroi* honoring the Atreidae (712), the dramatic chorus through their own singing and dancing then represent the *choreia* they describe, performing themselves a song in celebration of the Golden Fleece. This crossover between described and performed *mousikē* continues into the antistrophe, with its vivid synaesthetic focus both on the brightness of gold and fire and on the sound of the *aulos* and singing. As in the preceding strophe, the chorus place particular emphasis on instrumental noise—now that of the *lōtos* pipe, a name often given to the *aulos* in Euripidean tragedy:[110] "the sound of the *lōtos* pipe was resounding, most beautiful, the Muses' servant" (716–17). This description of the *aulos* comes in exact responsion with the lines in the strophe describing the syrinx, further encouraging a sense of merging between the two instruments. We can assume that the tune of the auletic accompaniment would be similar (or even identical) for both the strophe and antistrophe, yet its sound is imagined as two different but closely related instruments within the same song.[111]

---

107. Power 2012: 297.

108. ὑπὸ δὲ κηρόπλαστος ὀτοβεῖ δόναξ / ἀχέτας ὑπνοδόταν νόμον, [Aesch.] *PV* 574–75.

109. Syrinx associated with *kalamoi*: Eur. *IA* 577, 1038; *El.* 702; *IT* 1125–27; Ar. fr. 719 KA, καλαμίνην σύριγγα. The syrinx was also linked with *donakes*: Eur. *Or.* 146; [Longinus], *Subl.* 2.34.2–3; Nonnus, *Dion.* 11.105–6, 19.294. *Aulos* and *kalamoi*: Theophr. *Hist. pl.* 4.6; Ar. fr. 144 KA; Theoc. *Id.* 5.6–7; Ath. 4.176c, 4.182c.

110. Cf. Eur. *Heracl.* 892, *Tro.* 544, *Hel.* 170–71, *Phoen.* 787, *Bacch.* 160, *IA* 438, 1036; *Erechtheus* fr. 370.8; cf. [Aesch.] *PV* 574–75.

111. Cf. Gagné and Hopman 2013b: 8: "As the scene changes from the wild mountains of Pan to the public space of the city, the wind instrument continues to be heard, and both reeds of song are embodied by the *aulos* of performance."

With the *aulos* are "lovely songs" (718) about the Golden Fleece—songs that coincide with the song of the dramatic chorus, so that they again seem to be reperforming the celebrations that they so vividly describe.[112]

The transition from there to here, country to city, mountains to Argos, is thus enacted musically through the transition from the rustic syrinx to the urban *aulos* and the *choreia* it accompanies. It also brings us from then to now, from the carefree pastoral past to the more disturbing dramatic present. This shift may have a particularly powerful effect now that the described sound matches the *aulos* playing in the here and now of the performance, since the audience do not need to work hard to hear one as the other. The movement back toward the adultery and murder in Argos becomes clear through the language of the song as well, as Csapo has shown: the reality of the dramatic situation first intrudes through the prominently positioned *Thyestou* in line 720 (Thyestes has the fleece, not Atreus); the chorus then explain how Thyestes stole the fleece after luring Atreus's wife to bed.[113] Not only do the last few lines of the antistrophe thus shift from celebration to conflict; they prompt us to remember Atreus's gruesome revenge on his brother, even though this is not explicitly mentioned here.[114] The focus on Thyestes' affair with Aerope also encourages us to see this older crime as a mirror for Clytemnestra's infidelity with Thyestes' son, Aegisthus, who stole the throne from Agamemnon, Atreus's son, just as his father had taken the Golden Fleece.[115] And as Thyestes suffered a terrible punishment for his crime, so Aegisthus at this very moment in the play is being punished for his.

With this disturbing shift in tone, the chorus's self-reflexive references to celebratory *mousikē* cease, and, in contrast with the first strophic pair, they make no clear allusions to their own singing and dancing in the following strophe. Now they describe not Atreus's revenge but that of Zeus, who is said to have reversed the movement of the sun and stars, thus also changing the climates so that the north became wet and the south dry:[116]

| | |
|---|---:|
| τότε δὴ τότε ⟨δὴ⟩ φαεν- | [2nd strophe] |
|   νὰς ἄστρων μετέβασ' ὁδοὺς | |
| Ζεὺς καὶ φέγγος ἀελίου | |
| λευκόν τε πρόσωπον ἀοῦς, | (730) |
|   τὰ δ' ἕσπερα νῶτ' ἐλαύνει | |
| θερμᾶι φλογὶ θεοπύρωι, | |
| νεφέλαι δ' ἔνυδροι πρὸς ἄρκτον, | |

---

112. Cf. Gagné and Hopman 2013b: 9.
113. Csapo 2009: 98.
114. Cropp 1988: 149 suggests that the suppression of the story's horrific culmination "[matches] the suppression of thought about the horror of matricide within the play."
115. On this parallel see Cropp ibid.; Gagné and Hopman 2013b: 14.
116. Cf. Eur. *Or.* 1001–6.

ξηραί τ' Ἀμμωνίδες ἕδραι
φθίνουσ' ἀπειρόδροσοι, (735)
καλλίστων ὄμβρων Διόθεν στερεῖσαι.

Then indeed, then did Zeus turn around the gleaming courses of the stars and the light of the sun and the white face of dawn, and he drives the western skies with warm, divinely kindled flame, and the clouds [become] heavy with rain toward the north, and the dry seats of Ammon wither, not tasting the dew, deprived of the most beautiful rains from Zeus. (727–36)

This movement away from the carefree *mousikē* of the past, which was so vividly reenacted in the chorus's own performance onstage, highlights the terrible consequences of Thyestes' theft and a more general sense of the complete reversal of fortune. Moreover, the chorus's description of Zeus's punishment continues the parallel set up in the previous stanza between the two generations, suggesting that Orestes' retribution on Aegisthus is also a form of cosmic justice.[117]

The chorus's choreography could, however, still emphasize the reversal they describe, even though there are no more explicit references to *mousikē*. As a result of the cosmic dance in the first stasimon (464–68), the audience are already primed to see in the *choreia* onstage a representation of a star chorus, and indeed of the circle of the sun itself. When the chorus sing here of how Zeus turned around the courses of the stars, sun, and dawn (727–29), they may likewise reverse the direction of their circular dance, thereby enacting the astral change as if they themselves are a chorus of stars again.[118] We can only speculate regarding such choreographic directions, but certainly this seems a natural one given the language of change and reversal here. This opening image of cosmic reversal recurs in the following antistrophe, even as the chorus claim not to have much trust in such tales:

λέγεται ⟨τάδε⟩, τὰν δὲ πί-                      [2nd antistrophe]
   στιν σμικρὰν παρ' ἔμοιγ' ἔχει,
στρέψαι θερμὰν ἀέλιον
χρυσωπὸν ἕδραν ἀλλάξαν- (740)
   τα δυστυχίαι βροτείωι
θνατᾶς ἕνεκεν δίκας.
φοβεροὶ δὲ βροτοῖσι μῦθοι
κέρδος πρὸς θεῶν θεραπείαν.
ὧν οὐ μνασθεῖσα πόσιν (745)
κτείνεις, κλεινῶν συγγενέτειρ' ἀδελφῶν.

---

117. As Wohl 2015: 77–79 emphasizes, this myth of cosmic restitution also unsettlingly contrasts with the actual nature of Aegisthus's murder, which is portrayed as a perverted sacrifice.
118. Gagné and Hopman 2013b: 9–10 also suggest that the chorus's circular dance would reverse direction as they sing of stars' new "roads" (728).

> These things are said, but they hold little trustworthiness for me, that the golden-faced sun changed its warm seat for human misfortune, for the sake of mortal punishment. Fearful tales benefit men in encouraging worship of the gods. Unmindful of them you kill your husband, sister of glorious brothers. (737–46)

The verbs of turning and changing in lines 740–41 (the emphatically placed infinitive *strepsai* and the participle *allaxanta*) could again draw attention to and be reflected by the chorus's own choreography, particularly if their movements here were to correspond with those in the preceding strophe.

It is possible that this image of change and reversal could be represented not only choreographically but also acoustically, through melodic modulation. Vocabulary of turning and twisting, especially with the roots *streph-* (which we find here) and *kamp-*, often seems to refer to modulation in fifth-century critiques and commentaries on New Musical practice: in the famous fragment from Pherecrates' *Chiron*, for example, Music complains how Phrynis, a kitharode from Mytilene who was active in Athens in the mid-400s, "ruined me completely through his bending [*kamptōn*] and twisting [*strephōn*], having twelve tunings on his five strings."[119] We can only speculate about the *melos* of *Electra*'s second stasimon, but certainly any such modulation here would, along with the choreography, give further vivid force to the image of cosmic reversal that the chorus describe in their song. Not only the verbal account, then, but also the enactment of this cosmic shift in response to Thyestes' crime mirror the simultaneous killing of Aegisthus offstage, as Orestes punishes him for Agamemnon's murder.

The chorus end this stasimon, like the previous one, with a direct address to Clytemnestra (745–46), thus explicitly linking her imminent death, not just that of Aegisthus, with the celestial reversal that they have just described. The apostrophe in the final two lines mirrors the one at the end of the first stasimon, adding to the similarities between the two odes' structures: in both, a mythic narrative initially draws us into a more carefree scene, but then the chorus bring us back with increasingly ominous images toward the dramatic present, finally making an explicit connection with the events of the play through an invocation of Clytemnestra.[120] As a result of this final focus on the queen, the second stasimon looks forward to her punishment even as it mirrors and symbolically enacts that of Aegisthus. As in the first stasimon, then, *choreia* here seems both anticipatory and dramatically genera-

---

119. κάμπτων με καὶ στρέφων ὅλην διέφθορεν, / ἐν πέντε χορδαῖς δώδεχ' ἁρμονίας ἔχων, Pherecrates fr. 155.15–16 KA, quoted in ps.-Plut. 1141d–42a; cf. esp. Ar. *Nub.* 333, 969–70, *Thesm.* 100. On the complaint against modulation in the Pherecrates fragment, see Barker 1984: 94, 237 nn. 200, 201; Power 2010: 507; Franklin 2013: 229–30. On *kampai* as practiced by the New Musicians, see Franklin 2013: 229–31.

120. On this structure, see Kranz 1933: 197–98; Csapo 2009: 98; Mastronarde 2010: 139–41. On the similarity between the mention of Clytemnestra in the second stasimon and the chorus's address to her at the end of the first, see Gagné and Hopman 2013b: 11–12.

tive. Indeed it appears even more efficacious than it was in the previous ode, since this one is immediately followed by the sounds of Aegisthus's murder: the chorus cease their singing with a cry of *ea ea* and shift into iambic trimeters in reaction to the shouts that they can hear offstage (747–50); there follows an urgent exchange with Electra concerning the nature and source of the sounds that they are hearing (751–60). Even while it both represents and leads up to the death of Aegisthus, however, the ode keeps us focused on the imminent murder of Clytemnestra, pushing the plot forward to that climactic event of the play.

The third stasimon (1147–64) is also performed at a crucial moment in the plot, just as Orestes and Electra have entered the hut to kill Clytemnestra. In this brief song, which consists of just one strophic pair, the chorus apply the imagery of change and reversal from the previous stasimon to the immediate situation: they begin by singing "Repayments for evils [are being made]: turning about, the winds of the house blow"; they draw on such imagery at the start of the antistrophe too, singing of how justice is "flowing back."[121] Though this ode lacks the richly musical images of the previous two, some correspondence between the metaphors of reversal at the start of each stanza and the chorus's own dancing would powerfully reinforce the impression of a turning point in the plot. As they sing of winds switching direction and streams of justice reversing their course, the chorus's movements, in addition to their words, could link such change to the parallel moment they enacted in the previous stasimon.

Partly in virtue of its placement at the moment of Clytemnestra's death, this final choral ode also shares with the first and second stasima a sense of dramatic efficacy. Following the images of reversal at the start of each stanza, the chorus focus on the queen's murder of Agamemnon, which mirrors and coincides with that of Clytemnestra at the hands of Electra and Orestes, Agamemnon's avengers. Like the second stasimon, this song is immediately followed by the sounds of the very event that the chorus have envisaged through their images of reversal: their singing is interrupted by Clytemnestra's offstage cries, which parallel those of Agamemnon, which the chorus have just reenacted (1165–67; cf. 1151–54).[122]

It also soon becomes clear that the theme of reversal in this ode not only anticipates Clytemnestra's death but points to a change in the mood of the play as a whole. Upon hearing her cries, the chorus express pity for the first time, lamenting the form of her punishment, even if it is just (1168–70). Then, as Orestes and Electra enter, they begin their *amoibaion* of lament over the matricide, which contrasts markedly with the chorus's exuberant song of victory following the death of

---

121. ἀμοιβαὶ κακῶν· μετάτροποι πνέου- / σιν αὖραι δόμων, 1147–48; παλίρρους . . . δίκα, 1155.

122. Cf. Michelini 1987: 223. The meter can also have such a generative effect: as Finglass 2007: 502 points out, excited dochmiacs often precede an offstage killing in tragedy (cf. Soph. *El.* 1384–97; Eur. *HF* 735–46).

Aegisthus earlier in the play. The imagery in the third stasimon of winds and water changing direction as retribution is carried out therefore seems to mark a point of transition in the drama from celebration to lament and regret—a shift that also becomes clear through its *mousikē*.

All three stasima, then, each of them occurring just prior to the culmination of one of the play's three movements—the recognition scene between Electra and Orestes, the killing of Aegisthus, and, finally, the matricide—are closely integrated within the dramatic structure of *Electra*, working to push the *mythos* forward by anticipating and even enacting these pivotal events.[123] The odes work together to achieve this effect. The shape of the first and second stasima, whereby the audience are led away from the immediate dramatic context so as to be brought back with a hard-hitting jolt, increases their anticipation and foreboding of the murders about to be committed. In the second and third stasima the imagery of reversal, which the chorus's singing and dancing bring to life, similarly both generates suspense for and reflects these key moments in the *mythos*. And in all three songs the chorus make vivid through their own performance images and scenes that both remind us of the death of Agamemnon and at the same time look toward the revenge taken by his children. The escapist character of the first and second stasima, which some critics have seen as part of these odes' disconnection from the surrounding *mythos*, is what makes their ultimate relevance so powerful and dramatically effective.

In addition to generating the action of the play, the chorus's musical performances also help to define the character of its protagonist. As we have seen, the lack of any singing or dancing on Electra's part following her exchange with the chorus in the parodos, when she rejects their invitation to participate in *choreia* at the *Heraia*, underscores her exclusion from the communal rites of the *polis*—a form of social exclusion that she in part constructs for herself. The musically self-referential character of the first and second stasima, both of them replete with images that correspond with the chorus's performance in the theater, also contributes to the picture of Electra's isolation, since the chorus draw repeated attention to their own song and dance, which she refuses to perform. The first stasimon may in particular draw out this contrast between the chorus's engagement with communal ritual and Electra's lack of social integration, since the description of Achilles' armor could recall the shield contest (*agōn chalkeios*) that was apparently a significant element of the *Heraia* festival.[124] The celebrations at Argos that the chorus describe and reperform in the second stasimon, as they remember the festivities surrounding the introduction of the Golden Fleece into the city, could also parallel the *Heraia* in the dramatic present.[125] In both odes, then, the chorus would

---

123. On the division of the play into these three movements, see Cropp 1988: xxxviii.
124. Zeitlin 1970: 659–60.
125. Cf. Zeitlin 1970: 653.

appear to be enacting the very form of ritual celebration that Electra has refused to attend. In doing so, they set up a division between them that is unparalleled in other surviving tragedies with a female protagonist and female chorus.

*Choreia* can therefore frame the audience's understanding of a central character, and it especially seems to work in this way in plays with this combination of female protagonist and chorus—we shall see in the following chapters how it shapes our reception of Hecuba in *Trojan Women*, of Iphigenia in *Iphigenia in Aulis* and, in particular, of Helen in *Helen*. In *Electra* Euripides deploys the traditional dynamics and images of female chorality in order to define Electra against a larger social group. Drawing on parthenaic motifs in particular, he underscores the contradictory nature of a female protagonist who tries to reject her chorus.

*Choreia* in *Electra* has a presencing effect too, since the enactment of the deaths of Aegisthus and Clytemnestra in the three stasima (especially the last two) brings offstage action into the theater for the audience to experience more powerfully, even while the scenes depicted simultaneously appear at a remove from the immediate *mythos*. In chapter 1 we saw how Aeschylus makes vivid use of the presencing power of *choreia*, bringing onstage through the chorus's song and dance a crucial event or scene that is otherwise unseen, like the army approaching in *Seven against Thebes*. Euripides continues to exploit this effect, as will become clear in my discussion, in the next chapter, of the closing scene of *Trojan Women*. In chapter 4 I explore how *choreia* can also have an epiphanic force, which can be likened to the sort of anticipatory potency it displays in *Electra*. Its dramatic power demonstrates the close relationship between *choreia* and *mythos* in this play and suggests that, in contrast to the traditional view that actors' song becomes dominant in his later tragedies at the expense of *choreia*, Euripides continues to emphasize the role of the chorus—even in a play in which an actor not only sings prior to the chorus's entrance but shares their parodos with them.

3

# Musical Absence in *Trojan Women*

*These two ideas—dance and 9/11—don't necessarily go together. I was living in Little Italy during 9/11, about 20 blocks from the World Trade Center, so I saw the whole thing. . . . I thought: After something like this, dance—which to me is something joyous, ecstatic, athletic—what can dance do after this disastrous time?*

*It's precisely that question—it seems like that Adorno line: "To write poetry after Auschwitz is barbaric." The Titanic is drowning; are we still playing our violins here? What is an artist's response to this?*

What dance, what music can we perform in the wake of utter destruction and loss?[1] In an interview on the ten-year anniversary of 9/11, the dancer and choreographer Sarah Skaggs explained how this question lay behind her installation piece *9/11 Dance—A Roving Memorial*. In seven different locations across New York, Washington, and Shanksville, fifteen dancers slowly and seemingly spontaneously gathered like a flash mob, demonstrating "the power of bodies coming together in public spaces."[2] In doing so, they produced a "reflective, beautiful thing" out of and in response to disaster.[3]

Euripides addresses this same question in *Trojan Women*, produced in 415 B.C.E. The play is set in the immediate aftermath of the Trojan War, as the captive women wait to be divided up among the Greeks, with the smoldering ruins of Troy behind them. Structured around the interactions of Hecuba with the Greek herald, Talthybius, and with a series of three women of Troy, Cassandra, Andromache, and Helen, the tragedy is remarkable for its lack of action, offering instead a relentlessly immobile picture of the captive women's misery.[4] In this bleak postwar environment, the women repeatedly question the possibility of any musical performance beyond lament. Above all, they highlight the absence of *choreia*, which

---

1. The epigraph to this chapter: Sarah Skaggs as quoted in *The Washington Post*, August 26, 2011.
2. As quoted in *nj.com*, September 4, 2011.
3. As quoted in *The Washington Post*, August 26, 2011.
4. Cf. Mastronarde 2010: 78–79.

functions as a symbol for the civic strength and stability that has now been destroyed. Indeed, not only is there hardly any action or movement in this extraordinary play, but the audience is even led to wonder if it will feature any choral song and dance at all. Yet even while they emphasize the lack of such *mousikē*, the chorus simultaneously sing and dance, and so effect a dissonance between the verbal content and live performance of their *choreia*. At the same time they produce a musical performance that can induce pleasure in the audience, even if such a response is impossible for the characters themselves.[5]

*Trojan Women* is also deeply unsettling for any audience—and perhaps especially for its original Athenian one. It has often been understood as a pointed criticism of Athenian actions just a few months before in Melos, where they slaughtered all the adult men and enslaved the women and children.[6] Some of those who carried out these atrocities must have been in the audience of the play's first production, and the tragedy may have prompted them to reflect on their actions, whether or not Euripides meant it as a direct response to this particular event. We may also interpret it as a warning to Athens on the eve of the massive—and disastrous—Sicilian Expedition, with the annihilation of nearby Plataea twelve years earlier still serving as a powerful reminder of what defeat by the Peloponnesians could entail.[7] The Athenian audience could therefore respond to the play as potential victims as well as perpetrators of the sort of civic destruction it depicts so vividly, even if the focus on a non-Greek city's fall still keeps such destruction at a tolerable distance.[8]

Lament, which so dominates this play, heightens the uncomfortable stagnancy of its dramatic action. Although lament is often performed in tragedy, it is not usually sustained throughout a drama: in *Helen*, for example, mourning dominates the songs of the chorus and female protagonist for the first part of the play, but other types of *mousikē* take over as the possibility of escape becomes more real; a similar musical structure is evident in *Iphigenia in Tauris*. In the case of *Trojan Women*, however, the antiphonal lament of Hecuba and the chorus opens and closes the tragedy, and sung lament repeatedly interrupts spoken dialogue throughout. When the chorus are not performing formal mourning, their songs still contain elements of lament:

---

5. On the paradoxical nature of such tragic pleasure, see Segal 1993: 13–36, esp. 20–22.
6. As recounted in Thuc. 5.84, 114–16. On *Trojan Women* as a response to Athenian actions at Melos, see, e.g., Conacher 1967: 136; Lee 1976: ix–x; Barlow 1986: 26–27; Croally 1994: 232–34; Easterling 1997: 173; Dué 2006: 148; Goff 2009: 27–34. This interpretation is complicated by the fact that Euripides must have conceived of this play before the slaughter of the Melians in the winter of 416/15: see Kip 1987; Kovacs 1997: 162–66; Mastronarde 2010: 77 n. 27. Wohl 2015: 42–49 emphasizes the more general analogy between imperial Athens and the conquering Greeks in the play, which makes the audience responsible for the suffering it has watched and enjoyed.
7. For this interpretation of the play, see esp. Easterling 1997: 173; Dué 2006: 148–50; Torrance 2013: 234–37.
8. Cf. Easterling 1997: 173.

their first stasimon, for example, is framed as a "funereal song";[9] in the third they reproduce the mourning cries of the Trojan children at the gates (1089–92). Even in their closing lines the chorus continue to sing a lament for the city without reverting to a recitative meter as they usually do at the end of Euripidean plays.[10] By continuing in lyric iambics, they finish the play without ever seeming to cease their mourning song. In this respect Euripides' play resembles Aeschylus's *Persians*, which closes with an extended antiphonal performance of non-Greek lament sung by Xerxes and the chorus and includes briefer songs of mourning throughout.

Mourning song thus becomes the defining activity of the play, and of Hecuba, the chorus, and Andromache.[11] The dominance of this song type is linked to the dominance of female Phrygian characters in the tragedy. In fifth-century Athenian culture lament was conceptualized as an especially female type of performance, associated with displays of extreme emotion by women as well as by foreigners;[12] in Euripidean and Aeschylean tragedy Greek male (nonchoral) characters seldom lament or even sing at all.[13] As a result of Solon's restrictions on large-scale public displays of mourning within Attica, such a performance in the theater would be a marker of otherness—as it is both in Aeschylus's *Persians* and in *Trojan Women*—even while it could powerfully move its Athenian audience.[14] Lament in this play thus corresponds with the protagonists' gender and foreignness, but at the same time the women's songs evoke prior forms of women's music making within Troy, offering us glimpses of a functioning civic life that contrasts sharply with the desolation of the present. Lament appears to be the only song left for a city that has lost all its men.

Their style of song therefore sharply distinguishes the Trojan women from Talthybius and Menelaus, the two male characters in the play. Both men speak almost

---

9. ὠιδὰν ἐπικήδειον, 514.
10. See Dunn 1996: 101–14 on the play's lack of generic markers of closure.
11. On lament as the primary mode of expression in *Trojan Women*, see Suter 2003, Dué 2006.
12. Hall 1989; Loraux 1986, 1998; Holst-Warhaft 1992: 98–126.
13. On lament as a female activity in tragedy, see esp. McClure 1999: 40–47; Foley 2001: 19–56; Loraux 2002; Weiss 2017. When men do sing (and lament) in the tragedies of Aeschylus and Euripides, either they tend to be non-Greek (like Xerxes in Aeschylus's *Persians*, the Phrygian slave in Euripides' *Orestes*, or Polymestor in *Hecuba*) and portrayed effeminately or their speech devolves into song at a moment of extreme emotion (as when Orestes joins in the *kommos* with Electra and the chorus in Aeschylus's *Libation Bearers* and Amphitryon sings antiphonally with the chorus in Euripides' *Heracles*): see Hall 1999: 112–18. On the other hand, Sophoclean heroic protagonists, like Ajax and Heracles, often sing lyrics when in physical or emotional pain: ibid. 112; Suter 2008. On the lyricism (more broadly defined) of such Sophoclean characters, see also Nooter 2012.
14. On the regulations on mourning instituted by Solon, see Plut. *Sol.* 21.4–5; M. Dillon 2002: 271–72. See also Thucydides' account of public burial rites in Athens (Thuc. 2.34), through which the Greek city takes over the act of mourning from the women of the deceased's family. Loraux 1986 (esp. 44–46) and 1998 sees Solon's legislation against mourning practices as an attempt to control the dangers with which feminine excess was imagined to threaten the city.

exclusively in iambic trimeter, marking through their lack of song not just their gender and Greekness but their status as victors rather than mourning captives.[15] When Talthybius addresses Astyanax, Hecuba's grandson, in anapaests (782–89), this single slippage by a male character out of iambic trimeter emphasizes the emotional intensity of the moment, as the messenger bids the child to go to the battlements, from which he will be thrown down to his death. The contrast between the song of Trojan women and the speech of Greek men is particularly marked by the entrance of Menelaus immediately following the second stasimon: from this point until his exit two hundred lines later, all characters (including the women) speak in iambic trimeter. This interlude from lament and song is dominated by the *agōn* of Helen and Hecuba, who, with their opposing speeches concerning culpability for the war, engage in a particularly male form of oratory (though the debate also comes as the culmination of previous speeches by female characters, including Cassandra and Andromache).[16]

Despite the dominance of lament in *Trojan Women*, scholarship concerning the play's *mousikē* has concentrated instead on the possibility that it showcases Euripides' musical innovation. This idea stems from Walter Kranz's interpretation of the "new songs" announced by the chorus at the start of the first stasimon (512) as programmatic for Euripides' New Musical experimentation in the latter half of his career.[17] Yet we fully appreciate the implications of the chorus's claim as well as the dramatic impact of their song only if we take into account the *mousikē* of the play as a whole and situate this remarkable ode within the context of the lament that governs the rest of the drama. As we shall see, their proclamation of "new songs" is as much a response to the question of what music can be performed following Troy's destruction as it is an indication of Euripides' own innovation. To demonstrate how pervasive that question is, I begin this chapter by exploring the motif of absent *choreia*, especially in Hecuba's opening monody, the parodos, and Cassandra's solo performance of her *hymenaios*. I then turn to the first stasimon and discuss both the chorus's representation of their past *choreia* and the various implications of their very self-consciously performative claim, not only in terms of Euripides' musical style at this point in his career but also within the drama itself. In the final section I shift from absence to presence as I examine how the chorus and Hecuba reproduce scenes of Troy's destruction through their own singing and dancing, bringing onstage these otherwise inaccessible sights and sounds for the

---

15. Cf. Suter 2003: 11.
16. On the formal elements of this *agōn*, see esp. Lloyd 1992: 99–112. Following her frenzied singing, Cassandra delivers her *rhēsis* at *Tro.* 353–443; Andromache speaks about her relationship with Hector at 634–83 and then bids farewell to her son, Astyanax, with another speech at 740–79.
17. Kranz 1933: 228. For discussions of Kranz's claim and the meaning of "new songs" in the first stasimon, see Neitzel 1967: 42–50; Biehl 1989: 223–24; Hose 1991: 303–4; Quijada 2006; Sansone 2009. Battezzato 2005b offers a more holistic interpretation of the play's *mousikē*.

audience to experience in the theater. Yet even this moment of presencing underscores the lack of *choreia*, suggesting that the only *mousikē* that can still be performed is the enactment of the destruction itself.

## THE PARADOX OF ABSENT *CHOREIA*

*Trojan Women* is a play of loss, negation, and absence. The repetition throughout the tragedy of the words *phroudos* ("gone, vanished") and *erēmos* ("desolate, void"), as well as other expressions of privation, such as *apolis* ("cityless") and *aphilos* ("friendless"), underscores the sense of total loss experienced by the Trojan women—loss of their husbands, children, homes, city, freedom; even loss of their traditional worship of the gods.[18] Their loss is also articulated through the motif of absent *choreia*—a motif that often seems paradoxical, since the chorus do in fact sing and dance onstage. When they begin the third stasimon by telling Zeus "Gone [*phroudai*] are your sacrifices and the cheerful cries of choruses," they seem to point explicitly to this disconnect between their actual performance and their declaration of its absence.[19] But as we shall see, the trope of absent or lost *choreia* is most powerful in the first stasimon, when the chorus remember their past performances at Troy, emphasizing the absence of such *mousikē* while also reviving it through their own song and dance.

This focus on the lack of *choreia* may form a thematic link with the sense of lost *mousikē* that Euripides seems to have emphasized in *Palamedes*, the second tragedy of the trilogy. In the first tragedy, *Alexander*, Paris, who was abandoned as a baby because it was portended that he would bring destruction on Troy, returns to the city to participate in games and is finally recognized as the son of Hecuba and Priam and received in the royal palace.[20] *Palamedes* then dramatized the death of the famous Greek inventor as a result of Odysseus's false accusation of treason.[21] One of the few surviving fragments, in which the chorus (or possibly Oeax) represent Palamedes' death as that of the Muses' songbird, indicates that musical performance may have been a powerful theme of the play:[22]

---

18. Poole 1976.
19. φροῦδαί σοι θυσίαι χορῶν τ' / εὔφημοι κέλαδοι, 1071–72. Torrance 2013: 228 also notes the irony here.
20. Frr. 41a–62i.
21. Frr. 578–89.
22. Cf. fr. 580, in which "friends of *mousikē*" (οἵ τε μουσικῆς φίλοι) seems to be a reference to Palamedes: Scodel 1980: 51. On the possibility that fr. 580 is from Oeax's song rather than the chorus's, see ibid. 59. Scholars usually assume that the play had a chorus of Greek soldiers, but they may instead have been Trojan women, for whom a lament like this one would be more suitable: Kannicht 2004: 597–98.

On the translation of ἀηδών (*Pal.* fr. 588.3) as "songbird" rather than "nightingale," see chapter 4, p. 158. This is the only extant reference to Palamedes' Muse-derived skills as a singer: he is more usually associated with writing, counting, currency, and board games.

> ... ἐκάνετ' ἐκάνετε τὰν
> πάνσοφον, ὦ Δαναοί,
> τὰν οὐδέν' ἀλγύνουσαν ἀηδόνα Μουσᾶν.

You killed, you killed, O Greeks, the Muses' all-wise songbird, who harmed no one. (Eur. *Pal.* fr. 588)

Unlike the loss of one man's music in *Palamedes*, however, the devastation depicted in *Trojan Women* is much more far-reaching. In this play the collective *mousikē* of the whole city is destroyed.[23]

### Loss of City, Loss of Choreia

The emphasis on the absence of *choreia* in the play is in part explained by the departure of the gods in the prologue. Poseidon declares that he is leaving the city and his altars there, since such desolation causes divine worship to cease:

> λείπω τὸ κλεινὸν Ἴλιον βωμούς τ' ἐμούς· (25)
> ἐρημία γὰρ πόλιν ὅταν λάβηι κακή,
> νοσεῖ τὰ τῶν θεῶν οὐδὲ τιμᾶσθαι θέλει.

I am leaving the famous Ilium and my altars: for whenever evil desolation takes hold of a city, the rites of the gods grow ill and do not tend to be honored. (25–27)

The lack of any divine presence in the rest of the play reinforces this statement of the collapse of cult worship—a collapse entailing the abandonment of *choreia* too, since sacrifices and choruses together constitute an essential unit in divine worship.[24] It is in this godless environment, devoid of traditional divine worship, that Hecuba must utter her famous "new" prayers to Zeus, addressing him as "either necessity of nature or mind of mortals."[25]

In addition to symbolizing divine absence both at Troy and in the play itself, the lack of *choreia* suggests the complete breakdown not only of culture and religion but of social cohesion. The idea that choral performances (such as dithyrambs) are crucial for reflecting and maintaining a well-ordered community was prevalent throughout ancient Greece—its most obvious manifestation is in the long discussion of *choreia* in Plato's *Laws*, demonstrating the essential role of choral culture in the creation and running of the city.[26] *Trojan Women* illustrates by the contrary

---

23. The killing of Palamedes also seems bound up with the theme of murder of the innocent that runs throughout the trilogy (in the attempt to kill Paris in *Alexander* and the slaying of Astyanax in *Trojan Women*): see Scodel 1980: 73–76.

24. Kowalzig 2004: 49–55; 2007b: 70–72. See also Kurke 2012: 221–22. Sacrifices and *choreia* form a minimal pair in *Tro.* 1071–72.

25. εἴτ' ἀνάγκη φύσεος εἴτε νοῦς βροτῶν, 886.

26. On *choreia* as a medium of social cohesion in archaic and classical Greece, see esp. Bacon 1994; Wilson 2003. On *choreia* in Plato's *Laws*, see esp. Peponi 2013a, 2013b: 21–23; Prauscello 2014; Folch 2015.

this same idea: the loss of *choreia* comes hand in hand with *erēmia* (26), the complete loss of the Trojan community.[27] Since choral performances—paeans above all—were closely tied to the construction of a city's built environment (especially its temples), the apparent absence of *choreia* in the play also highlights the physical destruction of Troy.[28] Far from representing the sorts of performances associated with the founding and ordering of civic structures, *Trojan Women* is instead an extended lament for the whole city.[29]

### Hecuba's Chorusless Woes

The motif of lost *choreia* produces a paradox of performed absence, whereby the chorus's performance in the theater enacts the lack of that performance for the characters in the play. This paradox resembles the trope of negated or unmusical song, which is often used to characterize lament in tragedy. Depictions of lament tend to emphasize the lack of *mousikē*, and singers of lament frequently describe their song with privative adjectives like "lyreless" or "chorusless," even while they are performing impressive lyrical showpieces; a fragment of Euripides' *Ino* even contains the noun "unmusic" (*amousia*).[30] Euripides is particularly fond of this motif in his later work and likes to point to the paradox of the supposedly unmusical song being performed on the stage. As we shall see in the next chapter, this contradiction is especially pronounced in *Helen*, when the chorus represent Helen's opening song as "a pitiful noise, a lyreless song" even as the audience have a contrary aesthetic experience.[31]

In *Trojan Women*, however, Euripides develops the motif not of negated song per se but of negated or absent *choreia*. The emphasis on the lack of *choreia* is used not

---

27. Cf. Henrichs 1994–95: 65–73 on the sense of ritual crisis expressed at Soph. *OT* 896, when the chorus asks "Why should I dance?" (τί δεῖ με χορεύειν;).

28. Pindar's *Paean* 8, for example, was probably commissioned to celebrate the new Alcmaeonid temple at Delphi in the early fifth century. On its relationship to the physical environment of its performance, see Rutherford 2001: 214–31 (esp. 230–31); Power 2011; Weiss 2016. The fourth-century paean of Philodamus of Scarpheia included an announcement that construction of the sixth Delphic temple was to be resumed, suggesting that it was composed for the temple's inauguration: Rutherford 2001: 131–32, 230. On the physical embeddedness of this song within Delphi, see LeVen 2014: 304–17. *Mousikē* in general could play a role in the founding of cities: the mythic construction of Thebes was said to occur through Amphion's lyre playing, as Hermes predicts at the end of Euripides' *Antiope* (fr. 223.90–95).

29. On laments for cities in the Greek tradition, see Alexiou 1974: 83–101.

30. ἄλυρος in contexts of lament: Soph. *OC* 1222; Eur. *Phoen.* 1028, *IT* 146, *Hel.* 185. ἄχορος, ἀχόρευτος: Aesch. *Supp.* 681; Soph. *OC* 1222; *Tro.* 122. ἀμουσία: Eur. *Ino* fr. 407 (cf. *Her.* 676). Cf. παράμουσος, Aesch. *Cho.* 468; νόμος ἄνομος, Aesch. *Ag.* 1142 (on this as a theme in the *Oresteia*, see Fleming 1977: 230). On negated song in tragedy, see Segal 1993: 16–20; Weiss 2017; also Wilson 1999–2000: 433, who suggests that the description of song as lyreless both stresses the absence of the lyre and hints at the presence of the *aulos* instead. See too Barker 1984: 69–71 on sorrow as the negation of music.

31. οἰκτρὸν ὅμαδον . . . ἄλυρον ἔλεγον, Eur. *Hel.* 184–85.

merely to denote lament but to produce the paradoxical impression of its absence even while the chorus sing and dance in the theater.[32] Such performed absence has the dramatic function of emphasizing how much the women have lost now that Troy has been destroyed. It also, as we shall see, is closely tied to their memory of their previous lives and plays an important part in their recollections of different moments in Troy's history. Even when the chorus repeat through their singing and dancing in the first stasimon the celebratory *choreia* that they have now left behind, there remains a disturbing disconnect between their past and present performances.

The motif of the absence of *choreia* is emphasized at the very beginning of the tragedy, in the opening lines of the prologue. As soon as he comes onstage, Poseidon declares that he has come to Troy from where "choruses of Nereids whirl about the most beautiful trace of the foot."[33] This description of the Nereid choruses dancing at his home in the Aegean Sea sets up a contrast between such celebratory *mousikē* and the reality of the dramatic present—a contrast that is in play throughout the drama. Now he is amid the ruins of Troy, where instead of singing the only sounds are the cries of the captive women, echoed by the river Scamander: "Scamander cries out with the many wailings of the captive women as they are assigned by lot to their masters."[34]

But it is Hecuba who explicitly emphasizes the lack of choral performance in these desolate surroundings. She enters immediately following the divine prologue, mourning her troubles and expressing the wish to perform a lament:

οἴμοι κεφαλῆς, οἴμοι κροτάφων (115)
πλευρῶν θ᾽, ὥς μοι πόθος εἰλίξαι
καὶ διαδοῦναι νῶτον ἄκανθάν τ᾽
εἰς ἀμφοτέρους τοίχους μελέων,
ἐπιοῦσ᾽ αἰεὶ δακρύων ἐλέγους.
μοῦσα δὲ χαὔτη τοῖς δυστήνοις (120)
ἄτας κελαδεῖν ἀχορεύτους.

O my head, O my temples, my side! How I long to whirl about and to turn my back and spine now to this, now to that side of my limbs, always to the accompaniment of my tears' dirges. Even this is music [*mousa*] to the wretched, to cry out chorusless [*achoreutous*] woes. (115–21)

The adjective *achoreutos* (literally "without *choreia*") seems programmatic, suggesting that the *mousa* (music, Muse) of this play lacks choral song and dance. The

---

32. Cf. Segal 1993: 29–32 on "the paradox of embodied absence," a concept taken from Cole 1985: 9. Murnaghan 2011 observes that many tragedies begin with a situation where choral activity seems impossible and shows how the return to circumstances favorable to choral performance can mirror the resolution of conflict in a plot as a whole.
33. Νηρῄδων χοροὶ / κάλλιστον ἴχνος ἐξελίσσουσιν ποδός, 2–3.
34. πολλοῖς δὲ κωκυτοῖσιν αἰχμαλωτίδων / βοᾶι Σκάμανδρος δεσπότας κληρουμένων, 28–29.

prospect of Hecuba's own distorted dance movements intensifies the absence of the chorus, particularly since, as we have repeatedly seen, depictions of choral choreography in Euripides' later work often include "whirling" movement; the verb here (*hēlissō*) has already appeared in Poseidon's description of the Nereid choruses in the opening lines of the play.

Hecuba's lament for the weakness of her body, which prevents her from whirling around, is reminiscent of Sappho's description of how her advanced age prevents her from dancing as a *chorēgos*:[35]

νῦν δὴ μ' ἔτι Μοίσαν ἰ]οκ[ό]λπων κάλα δῶρα, παῖδες,
φίλημμι δὲ φωνὰ]γ φιλάοιδον λιγύραν χελύνναν·

νῦν γὰρ μ' ἄπαλον πρὶν] ποτ' [ἔ]οντα χρόα γῆρας ἤδη
κατέσκεθε, λεῦκαι δ' ἐγ]ένοντο τρίχες ἐκ μελαίναν·

βάρυς δέ μ' ὀ [θ]ῦμος πεπόηται, γόνα δ' [ο]ὐ φέροισι, (5)
τὰ δή ποτα λαίψηρ' ἔον ὄρχησθ' ἴσα νεβρίοισι.

τὰ ⟨μὲν⟩ στεναχίσδω θαμέως· ἀλλὰ τί κεν ποείην;
ἀγήραον ἄνθρωπον ἔοντ' οὐ δύνατον γένεσθαι.

[Now there are still for me] the beautiful gifts of the violet-bosomed [Muses], girls, and [I love] the song-loving [voice] of the melodious lyres.

[For now] old age [has taken hold of my once tender] flesh, and my hair has turned [white] from dark.

And my heart's become heavy, and my knees don't support me, which once were swift at dancing, just like fawns.

These things I often bewail. But what should I do? To be an ageless human isn't possible. (Sappho fr. 58.1–8)

But whereas Sappho can still play the lyre and, as she states at the end of this song, can still enjoy the "brightness and beauty of the sun,"[36] Hecuba has no such musical or aesthetic consolation, since all that remains for her is to "cry out chorusless woes." Moreover, she even rejects any element of chorality for the choreographic movement she wishes to perform: it is to be accompanied by her "tears' dirges" (120) rather than any form of choral song or instrumental accompaniment. The characterization of her song as chorusless therefore not only suggests a contrast

---

35. Sappho fr. 58 = P.Köln inv. 21351.9–20 + 21376; POxy. 1787. I have printed here the restoration suggested by Lidov 2009, which is similar to that of Gronewald and Daniel 2004. It seems very likely that Sappho is referring to her own lyre playing in the opening lines: see Lidov 2009; Lardinois 2009 (contra West 2005). For an alternative reading, see Di Benedetto 2004.

36. τοῦτο καί μοι / τὸ λά[μπρον ἔρως ἀελίω καὶ τὸ κά]λον λέ[λ]ογχε, fr. 58 Voigt 25–26. On the question of whether the poem ended with these lines, which are included on the Oxyrhynchus papyrus, see esp. Boedeker 2009; Lardinois 2009. ἀελίω in the last line could be constructed with ἔρως instead (i.e., "love of the sun provides me with brightness and beauty").

between her past role as a chorus leader and her current isolated lament but seems to rule out any possibility of choral performance at all. The audience is left wondering whether this singing actor really has replaced the tragic chorus.[37]

As her anapaests then become less regular and more lyrical, Hecuba fulfills the characterization of her *mousikē* as *achoreutos* by performing a monody before the entrance of the chorus.[38] Her astrophic song also emphasizes their absence by drawing on typically choral motifs within this monodic performance, beginning with an address to the "prows of ships" that went to Troy:

πρῷραι ναῶν, ὠκείαις
Ἴλιον ἱερὰν αἳ κώπαις
δι᾽ ἅλα πορφυροειδῆ καὶ
λιμένας Ἑλλάδος εὐόρμους          (125)
αὐλῶν παιᾶνι στυγνῶι
συρίγγων τ᾽ εὐφθόγγων φωνᾶι
βαίνουσαι †πλεκτὰν Αἰγύπτου
παιδείαν ἐξηρτήσασθ᾽†,
αἰαῖ, Τροίας ἐν κόλποις          (130)
τὰν Μενελάου μετανισόμεναι
στυγνὰν ἄλοχον, Κάστορι λώβαν
τῶι τ᾽ Εὐρώται δύσκλειαν,
ἃ σφάζει μὲν
τὸν πεντήκοντ᾽ ἀροτῆρα τέκνων          (135)
†Πρίαμον, ἐμέ τε μελέαν Ἑκάβαν†
ἐς τάνδ᾽ ἐξώκειλ᾽ ἄταν.

Prows of ships, which with swift oars to holy Ilium over the dark purple sea and the fair harbors of Hellas, to the hateful paean of *auloi* and the voice of fine-sounding syrinxes, traveling, †you hung the twisted handiwork of Egypt†—*aiai*—in the bays of Troy, pursuing the hateful wife of Menelaus, disgrace to Castor and ill repute for Eurotas, who is the murderer of †Priam,† the father of fifty children, and brought †me, wretched Hecuba,† to this shore of misery. (122–37)

References to ships and sailing pervade the whole play, as Hecuba and the chorus frequently mention the Greek vessels that are about to take them away. The invocation of the ships' prows here, however, does not have a merely thematic significance. As we saw in the case of the first stasimon of *Electra*, descriptions of

---

37. Battezzato 2005b: 81 emphasizes how the phrase "chorusless woes" points to the change from Hecuba's past *mousikē* to "the monotonous music of sorrow." Torrance 2013: 241 observes that this sentiment "announces metatheatrically Hecuba's shift into song while she is still unattended by the chorus."

38. On the metrical changes here, see Dale 1968: 57–59; Lee 1976: 80; Hose 1991: 287. On the (sometimes blurry) distinctions between recitative anapaests and lyric or melic anapaests, see Dale 1968: 47–54; Hall 1999: 106–7.

maritime travel in choral lyric often reflexively refer to the chorus's own *mousikē*, especially their dancing and the music of the *aulos*.³⁹ Hecuba's opening address is in fact very like that of the *Electra* ode, which also begins with a hanging apostrophe to the ships traveling to Troy; a similar invocation, this time to the Phoenician ship carrying Helen back to Sparta, opens the third stasimon of *Helen*, which is likewise full of choral imagery.⁴⁰ Hecuba's monody thus appropriates the performative language and imagery that usually appears in choral odes instead. And like the chorus of *Electra*, Hecuba describes how the ships made their way to an instrumental accompaniment—"to the hateful paean of *auloi* and the voice of fine-sounding syrinxes" (126–27).

Hecuba's description of the Greek ships traveling to Troy with musical accompaniment is the first of several references to past scenes of *mousikē* that contrast with the present one of lament and recall different stages of the Trojan War. As we shall see, this contrast between past and present *mousikē* is particularly pronounced in the first stasimon, when the chorus describe the Trojans' celebrations around the Greek horse on the night of Troy's fall. This later depiction is of the women's Trojan *mousikē*, emphatically characterized as such by the Libyan *lōtos* pipe and "Phrygian songs." Here, however, Hecuba describes the battle paean, the song of Greek men, and in doing so marks the moment of the Greeks' invasion in terms of their ominous music. The aulete, even if not yet present onstage, could at this point be already playing in accompaniment to Hecuba's anapaests.⁴¹ If so, the sound picture of the Greeks' arrival in Troy would be especially vivid, with "the hateful paean of *auloi*" merging with the actual tune of the *aulos* in performance.⁴²

The scene of an invading Greek army in Phrygia performing a paean is inherited from Aeschylus's *Persians*. In that play, the messenger's description of this type of song as he recounts the king's defeat at Salamis also emphasizes the ethnic distinction between the Greeks and the Persians:⁴³

πρῶτον μὲν ἠχῆι κέλαδος Ἑλλήνων πάρα
μολπηδὸν εὐφήμησεν, ὄρθιον δ' ἅμα
ἀντηλάλαξε νησιώτιδος πέτρας (390)
ἠχώ, φόβος δὲ πᾶσι βαρβάροις παρῆν
γνώμης ἀποσφαλεῖσιν· οὐ γὰρ ὡς φυγῆι
παιᾶν' ἐφύμνουν σεμνὸν Ἕλληνες τότε,
ἀλλ' ἐς μάχην ὁρμῶντες εὐψύχωι θράσει.

39. See chapter 2, pp. 77–84, on *El.* 432–41.
40. See chapter 4, pp. 180–82, on *Hel.* 1451–64.
41. On the *aulos* accompanying actors' anapaests in tragedy, see Hall 1999: 106–7.
42. Battezzato 2005b: 81–82 argues that the Greek *auloi* invade by disrupting the old songs of Troy. But since no previous *mousikē* has yet been mentioned, such a musical displacement is not clear at this point in the play.
43. On the acoustic contrast here, see Scott 1984: 154–55; Gurd 2016: 65–66.

> First a sound from the Greeks rang resonantly in triumph, in full song, and at the same time echo shouted clearly in response from the island rock. But there was fear among all the barbarians, balked of their purpose: for not as if in flight were the Greeks singing the solemn paean at that time, but hastening into battle with goodhearted courage. (Aesch. *Pers.* 388–94)

Like the Phrygian queen in *Trojan Women*, a Persian describes the paean as a distinctively Greek song, though his depiction is far more positive than the "hateful paean" that Hecuba remembers.

In his version of the battle at Salamis, Timotheus, possibly writing within only a few years of the production of *Trojan Women*, similarly stresses the contrast between the Greeks and the Persians through the performance of a paean:[44]

> οἱ δὲ τροπαῖα στησάμενοι Διὸς
> ἁγνότατον τέμενος, Παιᾶν᾽
> ἐκελάδησαν ἰήιον
> ἄνακτα, σύμμετροι δ᾽ ἐπε-
> κτύπεον ποδῶν                                                                (200)
> ὑψικρότοις χορείαις.
>
> But they, after setting up trophies to establish a most holy sanctuary for Zeus, celebrated loudly Paean, the healer lord, and in simultaneous measure they stamped in high-beating choral dances of feet. (Tim. fr. 791 *PMG*, 196–201)

But whereas Timotheus's nome then itself transitions into a quasi-paeanic song, as he calls on "healer Paean" to aid him in his singing,[45] Hecuba's description of the Greeks' paean accentuates the disconnect between the *mousikē* she describes and her own performance—a disconnect that in turn underscores her own position as a defenseless female foreigner.

Despite her initial emphasis on the lack of a chorus, Hecuba finally calls on the chorus of Trojan women to lament with her:[46]

> ἀλλ᾽ ὦ τῶν χαλκεγχέων Τρώων
> ἄλοχοι μέλεαι
> †καὶ κόραι δύσνυμφαι†,
> τύφεται Ἴλιον, αἰάζωμεν.                                                (145)
> μάτηρ δ᾽ ὡσεὶ πτανοῖς κλαγγὰν
> †ὄρνισιν ὅπως ἐξάρξω ᾽γώ

---

44. On the date of Timotheus's *Persians*, see Hordern 2002: 15–17.
45. ἰήιε Παιάν, Tim. fr. 791 *PMG*, 205.
46. I see no reason to replace the manuscripts' διερειδομένα (150) with Herwerden's emendation of the genitive διερειδομένου. In line 151 I agree with Lee 1976: 90 in keeping Φρυγίαις, rather than following Wilamowitz's emendation of Φρυγίους (which would then agree with the gods, not the beats). The characterization of aspects of the Trojan queen's *mousikē* as Phrygian is not surprising: cf. Φρύγια . . . μέλεα in line 545.

μολπὰν οὐ τὰν αὐτὰν†
οἵαν ποτὲ δὴ
σκήπτρωι Πριάμου διερειδομένα (150)
ποδὸς ἀρχεχόρου πλαγαῖς Φρυγίαις
εὐκόμποις ἐξῆρχον θεούς.

But, O wretched wives of bronze-speared Trojans, †and ill-betrothed maidens†, Ilium is smoldering; let us wail *aiai*! And I, just as a mother ⟨raises⟩ her cry for her winged †birds, so I will start up the song, not the same† as the one that I once started up for the gods, leaning on Priam's scepter, with the fine-sounding Phrygian beats of my chorus-leading foot. (143–52)

Even as the chorus enter, Hecuba stresses the absence of *choreia* through this negative contrast with past music making. The vivid description of her role as *chorēgos* in Troy, setting the rhythm with the beat of her feet and asserting her royal authority through Priam's scepter, works in sharp juxtaposition with her current performance, as she summons the chorus to join her not in celebratory *choreia* for the gods but in an antiphonal lament in a land the gods have now abandoned. The repetition of the verb *exarchō* ("start up, lead") emphasizes that she is still a musical leader, though now it refers not to a choral performance but to mourning, just as it does at the end of the *Iliad*, when she, Andromache, and Helen each take up the lament by Hector's body.[47]

The image of the mourning mother bird is typically used in tragedy to intensify the musicality of a sung lament, like in the address to the "most songful bird, melodious songbird full of tears" in the first stasimon of Euripides' *Helen*.[48] Here, however, Hecuba employs the image so as to undermine any such euphony by comparing her song to the screeching sound of the bird's cry (146), thereby accentuating a feeling of dissonance—a disjunction between her portrayal of past *mousikē* and her present performance. Through this simile Hecuba also links the loss of her role as chorus leader to her inability to produce a melodious voice, thereby adding vocal weakness to her earlier image of bodily frailty. The result is an inverse of the chorus's self-description in Alcman's first *Partheneion*, when they present themselves as an owl powerlessly screeching from the rafters now that they have lost

---

47. Hom. *Il*. 24.747. On the use of *exarchō* in lament, see Alexiou 1974: 131–32. This verb frequently refers to the leading of choral song and dance: see, e.g., *Hymn. Hom.* 27.18; Archil. frr. 120, 121 W; Arist. *Poet*. 1449a10. Gregory 1991: 162 suggests that by leading the lament here, Hecuba is able to "sustain social bonds and uphold her former authority." Her role as leader in lament certainly reflects her (former) status as queen, but it also constitutes a deliberate contrast with her earlier role as leader of *choreia*, and the social ties and positions once held by the Trojans seem to have little significance now that they are captives.

48. τὰν ἀοιδοτάταν / ὄρνιθα μελωιδὸν / ἀηδόνα δακρυόεσσαν, Eur. *Hel*. 1109a–10. On the association of nightingales with lament, see Weiss 2017.

their leader, Hagesichora.[49] Hecuba, the former chorus leader, simultaneously assumes the persona of the abandoned chorus. She thus undermines the presence of the actual chorus at the same time as she calls upon them to join her lament.[50]

By the time the chorus finally do start singing, then, their song has been paradoxically framed as a nonchoral performance. The impression of the absence of *choreia* is furthered both by the continuation of regular anapaests rather than a fully lyric meter and by the splitting of the first strophic pair between the two semichoruses that emerge separately from the *skēnē*, each singing their own antiphonal lament with Hecuba.[51] It is also possible that the chorus and Hecuba would not in fact dance at all in this whole ode, singing (or wailing) the anapaests and producing a performance that is indeed *achoreutos* (that is, without choral dance). Moreover, their song, even as it picks up the motif of sea travel begun by Hecuba in her monody, includes no self-reflexive choral imagery like the descriptions of naval voyages do in *Electra, Helen,* and *Iphigenia in Tauris*. Instead the women express their anxious uncertainty about their own impending sea journey and the different parts of Greece to which they may come as slaves (176–234), and they give no hint of such travel including any possible choral scenarios. The lack of any musical self-reference in this parodos intensifies the sense that full *choreia* has not yet been performed and that the *mousikē* of this play is *achoreutos* even when the chorus are in fact present.[52]

### Cassandra's Chorusless Hymenaios

Following the parodos and a brief exchange between Hecuba and Talthybius, who tells her she will be Odysseus's slave, the motif of absent *choreia* continues through another monody, this time performed by Cassandra. The musical stagnancy of lament is suddenly broken as she rushes onstage, singing her own *hymenaios*—a much more energetic and lyrical song with a highly resolved dochmiac-iambic meter. The fact that she sings this without the chorus is particularly striking given that *hymenaioi* tended to be choral performances.[53] Indeed, the typically choral refrain of *Ō Hymenaie (anax)*, similar to the repeated cry of *hymēnaon* that we find

---

49. [ἐ]γὼν μὲν αὐτὰ / παρσένος μάταν ἀπὸ θράνω λέλακα / γραύξ, Alcm. fr. 1 *PMGF* 85–87.

50. On the owl image in Alcm. fr. 1 *PMGF*, see esp. Stehle 1997: 76–77.

51. Though not indicated in the manuscripts, the division of the chorus here seems likely based on the content of lines 166 and 176: Lee 1976: 90–91; Hose 1991: 288.

52. Croally 1994: 244 notes that Hecuba's statement that Troy's troubles are undanceable is "both self-referential and inappropriate in a medium which was dominated formally by the presence and songs of the chorus ... it declares its self-consciousness by questioning its ability to represent what it is in fact representing."

53. On *hymenaioi* as typically choral songs, see Lardinois 1996: 151 n. 4; Swift 2010: 241–49. On Cassandra's solo performance of her *hymenaios*, see Rehm 1994: 129–30: she utters the *makarismos* herself (313–13) and carries her own bridal torches (320–21).

in one of Sappho's wedding songs, explicitly highlights the bizarreness of Cassandra, as the supposed bride, singing this *hymenaios* herself.[54] Of course the silence of the chorus here not only underscores the apparent lack of *choreia* so far in the play, but also poignantly undermines Cassandra's crazed performance, reminding us quite how far such a marriage celebration is from the reality of her fate.[55] In tragedy the subversion of wedding ritual and corresponding destruction of the household is often expressed in terms of maenadism.[56] The characterization of Cassandra immediately before and after her song as a raving maenad (307, 342; also 169–73), in addition to her own Dionysiac cultic cry *euan euoi* (326), therefore further undermines her self-presentation as a bride.

The idea that the distortion or absence of a proper *hymenaios* signals both the hopelessness of the union and the bride's own destruction may have been a common one in archaic and classical Greek thought. As we shall see in chapter 5, the performance of a marriage song in the third stasimon of Euripides' *Iphigenia in Aulis* ironically highlights the lack of any such celebratory *choreia* for Iphigenia, who is to be led to her sacrifice rather than her wedding. Pindar also evokes this idea in *Pythian* 3, in which the account of Coronis's adultery against Apollo and consequent death begins with the observation that she waited neither for the marriage feast nor for the *hymenaioi*:

οὐκ ἔμειν' ἐλθεῖν τράπεζαν νυμφίαν,
οὐδὲ παμφώνων ἰαχὰν ὑμεναίων, ἅλικες
οἷα παρθένοι φιλέοισιν ἑταῖραι
ἑσπερίαις ὑποκουρίζεσθ' ἀοιδαῖς·

She waited neither for the marriage feast to come, nor for the cry of full-voiced *hymenaioi*, the sorts of things with which maiden companions of the same age love to murmur in evening songs. (Pind. *Pyth*. 3.16–19)

As David Young has pointed out, Pindar places a particular emphasis on the importance of *hymenaioi* in this marriage, and so "establishes the absence of song

---

54. Sappho fr. 111 Voigt.
55. On the ominously ironic nature of Cassandra's song, see esp. Barlow 1986: 173–74; Rehm 1994: 129–30. Dué 2006: 144 interprets the song as "a horrible conflation of a wedding hymn and a funeral dirge," but this scene's painful irony results from the contrast between her performance and the lament that so dominates the rest of the play.
56. Seaford 1994: 330–62, esp. 356. See also Foley 2001: 43 on the links between lament and Dionysiac performance. Papadopoulou 2000: 515–21 notes that the hymenaeal nature of Cassandra's song is also undermined by her addresses to Hecate (323) and Apollo (329). Andromache is described as a maenad in the *Iliad* at the moment when, upon seeing her husband's dead body, she flings from her head the *krēdemnon* that Aphrodite gave to her on her wedding day (22.468–72). In doing so, she not only symbolically reverses that marriage ritual but also represents her own rape in the future, since the loss of this veil often acts as an analogy for the loss of chastity: Nagler 1974: 44–58; Seaford 1994: 333–34.

as the primary motif in the disastrous nature of Coronis's new union."⁵⁷ In *Trojan Women* the lack of *hymenaioi* sung by a chorus of *parthenoi* (rather than by the bride herself) similarly heralds Cassandra's doom.

The unsettling disjunction between the intended performance context for this song and the actual one onstage becomes especially powerful in the antistrophe, when Cassandra calls on the chorus and her mother as their leader to dance:⁵⁸

> πάλλε πόδ' αἰθέριον, ⟨ἄναγ'⟩ ἄναγε χορόν— (325)
> εὐὰν εὐοῖ—
> ὡς ἐπὶ πατρὸς ἐμοῦ μακαριωτάταις
> τύχαις. ὁ χορὸς ὅσιος.
> ἄγε σύ, Φοῖβε, νῦν· κατὰ σὸν ἐν δάφναις
> ἀνάκτορον θυηπολῶ. (330)
> Ὑμὴν ὦ Ὑμέναι' Ὑμήν.
> χόρευε, μᾶτερ, χόρευμ' ἄναγε, πόδα σὸν
> ἕλισσε τᾶιδ' ἐκεῖσε μετ' ἐμέθεν ποδῶν
> φέρουσα φιλτάταν βάσιν.
> βόασον ὑμέναιον ὦ (335)
> μακαρίαις ἀοιδαῖς
> ἰαχαῖς τε νύμφαν.
> ἴτ', ὦ καλλίπεπλοι Φρυγῶν
> κόραι, μέλπετ' ἐμῶν γάμων
> τὸν πεπρωμένον εὐνᾶι (340)
> πόσιν ἐμέθεν.

Shake the foot high in the air, ⟨lead⟩, lead the dance—*euan euoi!*—as if for my father's most blessed fortunes. The dance is holy. Come now, Phoebus: it is in your temple, [crowned] in laurels, that I make a sacrifice. *Hymēn Ō Hymenaios Hymēn!* Dance, mother, lead the choral dancing, whirl [*helisse*] your foot this way and that together with mine, moving the lovely step of feet. Shout out the *hymenaios*, O, with blessed songs and cries, for the bride. Come, O Phrygian maidens in your beautiful robes, sing of my husband, the one who is destined to share my marriage bed. (325–41)

These vivid choreographic directions, instructing the chorus to leap in the air and Hecuba to whirl her feet, use vocabulary that, as we have seen, tends to correspond with the actual dancing of the chorus in Euripides' later tragedies.⁵⁹ Here, however, they go unanswered. Cassandra's song comes to an end with a "mundane and

---

57. Young 1968: 35.
58. I follow Lee 1976 here in keeping the manuscripts' νῦν in line 329 rather than Musgrave's emendation of νιν.
59. On the choreographic import of the verb *pallein* (325), see esp. chapter 5, p. 198, n. 25. On *helissein* (333), see the introduction, p. 9, and chapter 2, pp. 80–81.

almost banal" couplet from the chorus leader, encouraging Hecuba to stop her daughter's frantic dancing:[60]

βασίλεια, βακχεύουσαν οὐ λήψηι κόρην,
μὴ κοῦφον ἄρηι βῆμ' ἐς Ἀργείων στρατόν;

Queen, won't you check the maiden who is frenzied as a Bacchant, lest she take her light step to the Argives' army? (341–42)

Hecuba then tells the chorus to remove Cassandra's torches and replace her wedding songs with tears, and so the *mousikē* of the play must revert to the lamentation with which it began.[61] Yet the immediate effect of these orders seems to be an absence of song altogether, since, in great contrast with Cassandra's highly lyrical performance, all characters speak predominately in iambic trimeters for the next 170 lines: Cassandra talks of Trojan and Greek sufferings (353–443), and then her iambic trimeters turn briefly into more agitated trochaic tetrameters just before she leaves to join Agamemnon (444–61); Hecuba then speaks about the loss of her children (466–510). The sudden contrast of wild song and coherent speech is presumably modeled on Cassandra's similar transition in Aeschylus's *Agamemnon*, when she abandons her riddling, prophetic singing and speaks clearly with the chorus (1178–1330). In the context of *Trojan Women*, however, this speech is all the more striking given the predominance of song in the play as a whole. Moreover, whereas in *Agamemnon* the chorus end up sharing Cassandra's lyric performance, shifting from iambic trimeter to singing in responsion with her (1130–77),[62] in *Trojan Women* the silencing of her song stresses the failure of her attempt to make the chorus and Hecuba sing and dance with her. Even with the chorus present in the *orchēstra*, then, it is unclear whether this tragedy will contain any *choreia* at all.

## NEW SONGS AND PAST PERFORMANCES

Finally, however, the chorus do sing and dance. They break the extended section of speech after Cassandra's departure by performing their first "proper" choral ode, shifting from their earlier anapaests to a more lyrical mix of dactylo-epitrite and iambic rhythms. Most discussions of this first stasimon stem from Kranz's argument that it heralds the beginning of Euripides' dithyrambic style and engagement with the New Music, though few now accept that the reference to "new songs" in

---

60. Lee 1976: 132.
61. δάκρυά τ' ἀνταλλάσσετε / τοῖς τῆσδε μέλεσι ... γαμηλίοις, 351–52. Cf. Papadopoulou 2000: 518.
62. On this transition from speech to song in *Agamemnon*, see Scott 1984: 7–8.

line 512 has the sort of programmatic force that he saw in it,[63] and the likely dating of *Electra* (as well as *Heracles*) demonstrates that Euripides was displaying an increasingly self-conscious musical style before the production of *Trojan Women* in 415 B.C.E.[64] As we shall see, the integration of this song within the musical fabric of the play as a whole further complicates its categorization as a typical example of the supposedly freestanding narrative-style odes found in the later work of Euripides.[65]

Like many of the other songs that Kranz saw as dithyrambic and that Csapo has deemed representative of the New Music, this ode has an intensely musical focus, since in the antistrophe and epode the chorus describe their singing and dancing on the night when the Greeks' horse was brought into Troy. But its metamusicality is of a different character than that of the many odes in Euripides' plays that feature particular images and tropes typical of the Greek choral imaginary, such as dancing dolphins, Nereids, or Muses. In contrast with those songs, the musical scene described here is very close in time and place to the dramatic chorus's own current situation and moreover is one in which they themselves are the principal performers. The ode's novelty therefore partly lies in Euripides' use of the first-person perspective in this musical description.[66] By singing of their own *choreia* in the recent past, which they performed within the city that is now the backdrop to their song, the Trojan women bring to life a moment of their personal history. This focus on the *mousikē* of their own devastating past and near-present, which continues throughout the play, does not allow for any form of choral escapism, leaving no moment of respite for the audience nor any prospect of a choral future for the women themselves.[67] To apply the term "choral projection" to their choral memory here would be misleading, since it suggests a less immediate overlap between described and performed *mousikē*. But the process of imaginative suggestion is still at work, even though the shift from vision to visualization required of the audience—from seeing the chorus as they are now to picturing them as they were then—seems more straightforward. At the same time, the two performances, produced at moments of such extreme contrasting emotions, do not overlap

---

63. Kranz 1933: 228–29: "Das ist wie das Programm einer anderen Zeit, denn nicht nur von dem einen Stasimon gilt dieses Wort, sondern ein unerhörtes Aufblühen der chorischen Kunst zeigt das Chorlied des ganzen letzten euripideischen Jahrzehnts; es ist das Zeitalter des Alkibiades und des Agathon, das Zeitalter einer neuen Musik." Wilamowitz also remarked on the song's dithyrambic elements (Wilamowitz-Moellendorff 1921: 174). Against Kranz's interpretation, see esp. Neitzel 1967: 44–49; Csapo 1999–2000 (406–7) and 2009: 95–96; Battezzato 2005b: 89–90; Sansone 2009: 193–94.

64. On *mousikē* in *Heracles*, see Wilson 1999–2000.

65. Kranz 1933: 254 ("völlig absolut stehende balladeske Erzählung").

66. Cf. Hose 1991: 303–4 on the distance between the narrative perspective characteristic of epic and dithyramb, and the personal perspective of this stasimon; also Quijada 2006: 844–46.

67. Cf. Goff 2009: 46–47 on the play's lack of escape odes.

comfortably with each other, and the resulting disconnect between them adds to the overwhelming sense of the loss of *choreia*—and loss of city—in the dramatic present.

### Performing Trojan Choreia (and Its Loss)

The chorus begin the first stasimon with an address to the Muse, before going on to sing of the night of Troy's fall, when they brought the horse into the city:

| | |
|---|---|
| ἀμφί μοι Ἴλιον, ὦ | [strophe] |
| Μοῦσα, καινῶν ὕμνων | |
| ἄισον σὺν δακρύοις ὠιδὰν ἐπικήδειον· | |
| νῦν γὰρ μέλος ἐς Τροίαν ἰαχήσω, | (515) |
| τετραβάμονος ὡς ὑπ' ἀπήνας | |
| Ἀργείων ὀλόμαν τάλαινα δοριάλωτος, | |
| ὅτ' ἔλιπον ἵππον οὐράνια | |
| βρέμοντα χρυσεοφάλαρον ἔνο- | (520) |
| πλον ἐν πύλαις Ἀχαιοί· | |
| ἀνὰ δ' ἐβόασεν λεὼς | |
| Τρωϊάδος ἀπὸ πέτρας σταθείς· | |
| Ἴτ', ὦ πεπαυμένοι πόνων, | |
| τόδ' ἱερὸν ἀνάγετε ξόανον | (525) |
| Ἰλιάδι Διογενεῖ κόραι. | |
| τίς οὐκ ἔβα νεανίδων, | |
| τίς οὐ γεραιὸς ἐκ δόμων; | |
| κεχαρμένοι δ' ἀοιδαῖς | |
| δόλιον ἔσχον ἄταν. | (530) |
| πᾶσα δὲ γέννα Φρυγῶν | [antistrophe] |
| πρὸς πύλας ὡρμάθη, | |
| πεύκαν οὐρεῖαν, ξεστὸν λόχον Ἀργείων, | |
| καὶ Δαρδανίας ἄταν θεᾶι δώσων, | (535) |
| χάριν ἄζυγος ἀμβροτοπώλου· | |
| κλωστοῦ δ' ἀμφιβόλοις λίνοιο ναὸς ὡσεὶ | |
| σκάφος κελαινὸν εἰς ἕδρανα | |
| λάϊνα δάπεδά τε, φονέα πατρί- | (540) |
| δι, Παλλάδος θέσαν θεᾶς. | |
| ἐπὶ δὲ πόνωι καὶ χαρᾶι | |
| νύχιον ἐπεὶ κνέφας παρῆν, | |
| Λίβυς τε λωτὸς ἐκτύπει | |
| Φρύγιά τε μέλεα, παρθένοι δ' | (545) |
| ἄειρον ἅμα κρότον ποδῶν | |
| βοάν τ' ἔμελπον εὔφρον', ἐν | |
| δόμοις δὲ παμφαὲς σέλας | |
| πυρὸς μέλαιναν αἴγλαν | |
| †ἔδωκεν ὕπνωι†. | (550) |

ἐγὼ δὲ τὰν ὀρεστέραν　　　　　　　　　　　　　　　　　　[epode]
τότ' ἀμφὶ μέλαθρα παρθένον
Διὸς κόραν ἐμελπόμαν
χοροῖσι· φοινία δ' ἀνὰ　　　　　　　　　　　　　　　　　　(555)
πτόλιν βοὰ κατέσχε Περ-
　γάμων ἕδρας· βρέφη δὲ φίλι-
　α περὶ πέπλους ἔβαλλε μα-
　τρὶ χεῖρας ἐπτοημένας.
λόχου δ' ἐξέβαιν' Ἄρης,　　　　　　　　　　　　　　　　　(560)
κόρας ἔργα Παλλάδος.
σφαγαὶ δ' ἀμφιβώμιοι
Φρυγῶν ἔν τε δεμνίοις
καράτομος ἐρημία
νεανίδων στέφανον ἔφερεν　　　　　　　　　　　　　　　(565)
Ἑλλάδι κουροτρόφον,
Φρυγῶν δὲ πατρίδι πένθος.

About Troy, O Muse, sing for me a funeral ode of new songs, with tears: for now I will cry out a song to Troy, telling how I was ruined by a four-footed vehicle, [becoming] the Argives' wretched captive, when the Achaeans left at our gates the horse, making a rumbling noise up to the sky, with its trappings of gold and armed within; and the people shouted out from the Trojan rock, standing there, "Go, you who have ceased from toils, bring this holy image to [the shrine of] the Zeus-born maiden of Troy!" Who of the young women didn't come, what old man didn't [come] from his house? Rejoicing with songs they received treacherous ruin.

And the whole race of Phrygians hastened to the gates, to give to the goddess this pinewood from the mountain, this polished hiding-place of Argives, and Dardania's ruin, a gift for the unwedded [goddess] with her immortal steeds; and with encircling ropes of spun flax [they dragged it] like the dark hull of a ship to the stone temple of the goddess Pallas and set it on the floor, [to be the] murderer of their country. And when nighttime darkness came upon their toil and joy, the Libyan *lōtos* pipe was sounding as well as Phrygian songs, and maidens raised together the beat of their feet and sang and danced a cheerful cry, and in the halls an all-blazing gleam of fire †shed a dark glow on sleep.†

And I to the mountain maiden, the daughter of Zeus, around the halls I was singing and dancing then in choruses; but a bloody cry through the town took hold of the seat of Pergamon; and dear babies threw their frightened arms about their mothers' skirts. And out from his ambush place came Ares, the handiwork of maiden Pallas. And slaughters of Trojans around the altars and, in the beds, desolation resulting from beheadings brought a victory crown of young women, to bear sons for Greece, but [a source of] grief for the Phrygians' fatherland. (511–67)

The motif of the Trojans' celebratory song and dance in response to the horse is not in itself new. In Euripides' *Hecuba,* produced at least eight years earlier than *Trojan Women,* the chorus of captive women briefly mention the songs and "sacrifices that produce dancing" that the Trojans performed immediately prior to the Greeks' attack.[68] But in the later play Euripides develops this motif into a much more detailed picture of the Trojans' premature elation, thereby characterizing this crucial turning point of the war in musical terms.

As in Hecuba's monody, the *aulos* occupies a central place in this sound picture. But whereas it was previously a marker of the Greek paean, the description of the instrument as a "Libyan *lōtos* pipe" (544) draws on its non-Greek associations instead, just as it does in the parodos of *Bacchae*, when the chorus stress the Phrygian location of Dionysus's music.[69] Like the "Phrygian beats" of Hecuba's own dancing feet (151–52), as well as the "Phrygian shouts and cries" that join the *lōtos* pipe in *Bacchae*,[70] the "Phrygian songs" (545) in this ode further stress the foreignness of such *mousikē*. Since Phrygian music tended to be especially associated with Dionysiac revelry, the focus on the ethnicity of the *mousikē* here may support Kranz's classification of the ode as dithyrambic. However, unlike the explicitly Dionysiac context of the Phrygian performances described (and enacted) in *Bacchae*, this musical characterization in *Trojan Women* reflects the actual identity of the Trojan (Phrygian) performers and so the reality of the dramatic situation.[71]

It is possible that the aulete in the theater would at this point have exchanged his previous instrument for a Phrygian *aulos*, which not only seems to have had a deeper pitch than the Greek one but would have been visually distinct, since one of its two pipes apparently ended in a bell made of horn.[72] It is just as likely, however, that the same *aulos* would be used throughout the play but that through its characterization in the singing of Hecuba and the chorus it could assume different ethnic characteristics—it was, after all, considered to be the most mimetic of all instruments.[73] In either case, the chorus's depiction of the *mousikē* performed after the horse was brought into Troy becomes particularly vivid through the crossover of the sound of the *aulos* and "Phrygian songs" that they describe with what the audience would actually be hearing in the theater—the *aulos* accompanying the singing of this Trojan chorus.

68. χοροποιὸν / θυσίαν, Eur. *Hec.* 916–17.

69. Eur. *Bacch.* 135–69. On the Libyan *lōtos*, see Barker 1984: 67 n. 34; 268 n. 38; Biehl 1989: 234–35; West 1992: 113 n. 145. Cf. Eur. *Hel.* 170–71, *IA* 1036. For *lōtos* as a designation for the *aulos*, cf. Eur. *Heracl.* 892, *El.* 716, *Phoen.* 787, *Bacch.* 160, *IA* 438, *Erechtheus* fr. 370.8; also Pind. fr. 94b.14. See also Theophr. *Hist. pl.* 4.3.3–4 on the Libyan *lōtos* as an apt material for *auloi*; Ath. 14.618c1–4 on why the *aulos* is called Libyan.

70. ἐν Φρυγίαισι βοαῖς ἐνοπαῖσί τε, Eur. *Bacch.* 159.

71. Cf. Barker 1984: 82 n. 132.

72. For ancient sources on the Phrygian *aulos*, see West 1992: 91–92. Battezzatto 2005b: 87–89 suggests that the Phrygian *harmonia* may have been used in the performance of the first stasimon. Since this *harmonia* was apparently used for most tragic music (Aristox. fr. 79 Wehrli; Psellus, *De Trag.* 5), its use here may not have been especially striking.

73. On the *aulos* and mimesis, see Weiss forthcoming a.

The chorus continue to merge *mousikē* of the (described) past and (performed) present by focusing on the *choreia* of *parthenoi*, who "raised together the beat of their feet and sang and danced a cheerful cry" (546–47). The resolved rhythm of these lines could encourage a correspondence between words and movement, with the chorus energetically beating the floor of the *orchēstra* with their feet, thus physically evoking their past performance. The resulting association of the Trojan women of the chorus with *partheneia* continues into the epode, when the chorus shift from the third to the first person (*egō*, 551), strengthening the merging of described and performed *choreia* by explicitly referring to their own choral singing and dancing in honor of the *parthenos* Artemis (551–55). The repetition of the verb *emelpoman* here (cf. *emelpon*, 547) reinforces the inclusion of the chorus's own performance in this scene of choral celebration. As Laura Swift has shown, the self-characterization of these women as *parthenoi*—women whom Hecuba previously addressed as the "wretched wives of bronze-speared Trojans" (143)—frames their enslavement by the Greeks in terms of ritual transition: "these women when raped and abducted are envisaged as though they were *parthenoi* once more, and are described in imagistic terms as girls whose transition to maturity becomes perverted into violence rather than legitimate marriage."[74] Andromache later similarly pictures herself now as a *parthenos* entering marriage, saying with bitter irony, "I am going to a fine wedding, having lost my own child."[75] Now that they are the Greeks' childbearing trophies (565–66), the women retrospectively seem to lose their former status as Trojan wives.[76]

We can therefore understand the women's parthenaic image of themselves as another marker of absence and loss. Within Performance Studies performance is often understood as a reenactment of absence, particularly when it presents acts of the past: because of the distorting effects of memory, these can never be exactly reproduced.[77] As Charles Batson writes of theatrical performance (with particular reference to a 1924 production by Ballet Suédois entitled *Relâche*), "the thing that was once present has become absent to be re-rendered present in its remembrance." Since such remembrance is inevitably faulty, "it is therefore the absence

---

74. Swift 2010: 192. Cf. Eur. *Hec.* 462–69, 923–25, 933–35.

75. ἐπὶ καλὸν γὰρ ἔρχομαι / ὑμέναιον, ἀπολέσασα τοὐμαυτῆς τέκνον, 778–79. Cf. 569–94; Eur. *Andr.* 100–110. On the representation of Andromache's abduction from Troy as a perverted marriage ritual, see Seaford 1987: 129–30; 1994: 335.

76. This loss of former status may explain the metrically problematic †καὶ κόραι δύσνυμφαι† in Hecuba's address (144): as soon-to-be concubines to their Greek captors, the Trojan wives are also "ill-betrothed maidens."

77. On performance as disappearance, embodied absence, substitution, or both, see esp. Phelan 1993: 146–66; Gilpin 1996; Diamond 1996: 1–2; Roach 1996 (esp. 2–3); Franko and Richards 2000; Lepecki 2004: 4–6; Batson 2005: 221–48.

that is again pointed to, that is re-presented, in the repeated misrememberings."[78] In *Trojan Women* both the chorus's description of their past *choreia* and their actual performance onstage re-present such absence. The disconnect between the Trojan women's current identity and the depiction of their former selves as *parthenoi*, as they reperform through their present song and dance the *choreia* that they, as mature women, would most likely not have performed in Troy, intensifies the overwhelming sense of loss, as their act of remembering in this song fails to reproduce their original performance.

The reperformance of these musical celebrations through the chorus's own song and dance repeats not only the end of Troy but the end of Trojan *choreia*, providing an aetiology for the apparent absence of choral song and dance in the dramatic present. The "bloody cry" (555–56) that interrupts the women's choral song and dance, replacing their "cheerful cry" (547) with a much more sinister sound, marks the beginning of the Greeks' attack on the city, after which there is no further reference to *choreia* either in the song or in the play as a whole—except for the chorus's lament that it has vanished (*phroudos*) at the start of the third stasimon. Luigi Battezzato sees the first stasimon as "the first occasion the women have for *singing* after the interruption during the fall of Troy" and argues that they now resume their previous song with a distinctively Greek tone that replaces their earlier Phrygian music.[79] The merging of that past *mousikē* with the present performance, however, causes this "new" song still to seem foreign, with the *aulos* in the theater representing the "Libyan *lōtos*" and the chorus's singing and dancing reproducing the "Phrygian songs." No *mousikē* other than lament has replaced this Phrygian *choreia*, which has been destroyed along with the city itself. Paradoxically, however, the audience can more powerfully feel the absence of *choreia* through its presence in the performance onstage, as the chorus reenact the *mousikē* of the past amid the desolation of the present.

The disappearance of Troy's past musical performances would have been especially powerful for the Athenian audience if the first stasimon continued the topos of Trojan *mousikē* from *Palamedes*, the tragedy that preceded *Trojan Women*, and perhaps also from *Alexander*, the trilogy's opening play.[80] One of the surviving fragments of *Palamedes* suggests that the Greek chorus of this drama evoked Dionysiac music that was strongly linked to the Trojan setting:[81]

---

78. Batson 2005: 241. *Relâche* was a Dadaist production that explicitly played with the idea of performance as absence (the title itself means "show canceled"). Batson's discussion is influenced by Derrida's (1976: 154) concept of the trace as an "absent presence."

79. Battezzatto 2005b: 88 (emphasis original).

80. On thematic correspondences between the three tragedies, see Scodel 1980, esp. 64–121.

81. The chorus of *Palamedes* may even have been Trojan maenads rather than Greek soldiers: Kannicht 2004: 597–98, and above, p. 104 n. 22.

In fr. 586.2 I follow the emendation of Collard and Cropp 2008b.

†οὐ σὰν† Διονύσου
†κομᾶν† ὅς ἄν' Ἴδαν
τέρπεται σὺν ματρὶ φίλαι
τυμπάνων ἰάκχοις.

†. . . (hair?)† of Dionysus, who over Mount Ida delights with the dear mother in the Iacchus songs of the drums. (Eur. *Pal*. fr. 586)

While allusions to the cultic *mousikē* performed for Dionysus and the Great Mother (here the "dear mother") occur in plays set in Greek cities too (and, in the case of *Helen*, in Egypt), its Phrygian associations are nevertheless especially topical in a tragedy set just outside Troy. The reference to Ida, the mountain above Troy, further strengthens the relevance of this musical depiction to the Trojan environment. None of the surviving fragments of *Alexander* alludes to *mousikē* of any sort, but given the many representations of Paris playing the chelys lyre on archaic and classical vases, as well as the mention of his kithara in the *Iliad* (3.54), it would not be surprising if the chorus of this play referred to his music making too.[82] If *Palamedes* and *Alexander* did already develop a picture of Trojan *mousikē* for the audience, the cessation of such music making as (re)enacted in *Trojan Women* would also represent a cessation of performances that the audience themselves would have witnessed earlier in the trilogy. By thus sharing the chorus's memory of such *mousikē*, the audience would experience its loss all the more powerfully.

### What's New?

Given that the first stasimon describes and accounts for musical absence and loss, what, then, are we to make of its simultaneous emphasis on musical novelty? In the opening lines the chorus bid the Muse to sing "a funeral ode of new songs, with tears" (512–14), thereby characterizing their own *mousikē*—and framing the audience's response to it—in a strikingly self-referential way. Their stress on the newness of their songs seems as pointed as Timotheus's boast, "I do not sing the old songs, for my new ones are better."[83] In the voice of a tragic character, however, the chorus's characterization of their song as new (*kainos*) is at one remove from the kitharode's first-person statement as both composer and singer, and can refer both extradramatically to the novelty of Euripides' *mousikē* and intradramatically to that of the chorus's performance at this point in the play. Although the first stasimon is not necessarily dithyrambic in style, the chorus's request to the Muse to provide "new songs" may still suggest musical novelty within both the ode and the

---

82. On depictions of Paris as a musician, see esp. Bundrick 2005: 65–66; cf. Eur. *IA* 573–78.

83. οὐκ ἀείδω τὰ παλαιά / καινὰ γὰρ ἁμὰ κρείσσω, Tim. fr. 796 *PMG*. On the possible allusion to Timotheus's *sphragis* here, see Power 2010: 272–73. The emphasis on the novelty of Euripides' song is further pronounced if we follow the punctuation of Biehl's 1970 Teubner edition and understand this as an address to the Muse of new songs (Μοῦσα καινῶν ὕμνων).

play as a whole, thus integrating this performance within the larger musical narrative while also pointing beyond it.

As many have noted, some of the song's novelty lies in its conflation of an epic subject and a tragic setting, above all in the opening address to the Muse ("About Troy, O Muse, sing," 512–14).[84] This sort of invocation—typical of epic and the Homeric hymns, but unique in extant tragedy—transposes the Muse of hexameter poetry into tragic lyric. The inclusion of some dactylic rhythms in these first three lines creates a sense of the tragic appropriation and transformation of epic and hymnic style as well as content. Moreover, although the *Iliad* ends with the mourning of Hecuba, Andromache, and Helen, the poetry itself is never framed as a lament, and neither is the Muse ever called upon to inspire such a song as she is here.[85] As David Sansone has noted, Kranz did not comment on the fact that the chorus ask the Muse for "new songs" that belong to a funeral ode accompanied by tears (513–14), a type of performance that is as far from the dithyramb as the association of the Muse with lament is from epic.[86] The first-person female perspective that becomes explicit in the epode further distorts traditional epic treatments of Troy's fall, as well as distinguishing this ode from narrative kitharodic or dithyrambic songs.[87] Wilamowitz suggests that the opening phrase of the ode (*amphi moi*) evokes a kitharodic song type, in which case the ode becomes a new mix of not just epic but also kitharodic song, all performed to the accompaniment of the *aulos,* the instrument of the theater (tragedy, comedy, satyr play, and dithyramb).[88] The rare compound adjectives and riddling phrases that follow may have a dithyrambic flavor.[89] We can even detect a trace of epinician in the final lines of the ode, when, in a horrible distortion of a victory song, the women claim that the bloodshed at Troy produced a childbearing crown (*stephanos*) for Greece (565–66).

---

84. Cf. esp. *Hymn. Hom.* 19.1, 20.1, 33.1; this use of ἀμφί with the accusative of a song's subject also occurs at *Hymn. Hom.* 7.1, 22.1. On the novelty of this epic address within tragic lyric, see Neitzel 1967: 44; Lee 1976: 164; Hose 1991: 303; Quijada 2006: 844; D'Angour 2011: 194. On further parallels between the *Trojan Women*'s first stasimon and the *Iliad,* see Sansone 2009. Torrance 2013: 219–28 argues that the "new songs" denote a new version of Demodocus's song about the wooden horse and destruction of Troy (Hom. *Od.* 8.426–534).

85. Cf. Neitzel 1967: 44–47; Biehl 1989: 226.

86. Sansone 2009: 194.

87. Cf. Barlow 1986: 184; Hose 1991: 303; Croally 1994: 245; Quijada 2006: 844–47.

88. Wilamowitz-Moellendorff 1921: 173; cf. Neitzel 1967: 44; Power 2010: 272. According to schol. Ar. *Nub.* 595, Aristophanes' use of ἀμφί μοι αὖτε at the start of the chorus's antistrophe in the parabasis of *Clouds* imitates the prooimia of both kitharodists and dithyrambists (μιμεῖται τῶν διθυραμβοποιῶν καὶ κιθαρῳδῶν τὰ προοίμια).

89. On the ode's dithyrambic language (e.g., the compound adjective χρυσεοφάλαρον at 520; the phrase τετραβάμονος ... ὑπ' ἀπήνας at 516), see Wilamowitz-Moellendorff 1921: 174; Neitzel 1967: 45; Battezzato 2005b: 89; cf. Kranz 1933: 243.

Although the first stasimon does not itself enact the sort of Greek takeover of Trojan *mousikē* that Battezzato suggests, the allusions to epic, hymnic, kitharodic, dithyrambic, and epinician styles of performance do point to the beginnings of these song types in the wake of Troy's destruction. Hecuba later makes this idea more explicit when she remarks on how the women's sufferings will provide material for future song:[90]

> εἰ δὲ μὴ θεὸς
> ἔστρεψε τἄνω περιβαλὼν κάτω χθονός,
> ἀφανεῖς ἂν ὄντες οὐκ ἂν ὑμνηθεῖμεν ἂν
> μούσαις ἀοιδὰς δόντες ὑστέρων βροτῶν.

> But if god had not wheeled us around, casting what was above the earth beneath it, we, being invisible, would not be celebrated in song, providing songs for the music of men to come. (1242–45)

The conflation of different types of song within the choral ode therefore suggests a departure from *all* previous *mousikē* with this performance, and in this respect the chorus seem to sing "new songs."[91]

The sort of mixing of genres on display here was apparently a feature of the New Music, at least according to the complaints of the Athenian stranger in Plato's *Laws*:

> προϊόντος τοῦ χρόνου, ἄρχοντες μὲν τῆς ἀμούσου παρανομίας ποιηταὶ ἐγίγνοντο φύσει μὲν ποιητικοί, ἀγνώμονες δὲ περὶ τὸ δίκαιον τῆς Μούσης καὶ τὸ νόμιμον, βακχεύοντες καὶ μᾶλλον τοῦ δέοντος κατεχόμενοι ὑφ' ἡδονῆς, κεραννύντες δὲ θρήνους τε ὕμνοις καὶ παίωνας διθυράμβοις, καὶ αὐλῳδίας δὴ ταῖς κιθαρῳδίαις μιμούμενοι, καὶ πάντα εἰς πάντα συνάγοντες.

> But as time went on there arose leaders of unmusical unlawfulness, poets who, though by nature poetical, were ignorant about what is just and lawful in music, being full of Bacchic frenzy and possessed by pleasure more than is fitting, and they mixed both dirges with hymns and paeans with dithyrambs, and represented *aulos* songs with kithara songs, and brought together everything with everything. (Pl. *Leg.* 700d3–9)

It is therefore not so much Euripides' new *dithyrambic* style that the song heralds as it is his experimentation with the mixing of various musical genres, including the dithyramb. This is neither the first instance of this sort of generic conflation nor the most explicit. In the second stasimon of *Heracles*, for example, which was

---

90. This idea recalls Helen's statement in the *Iliad* that Zeus has inflicted sufferings on her and Paris so that they may become future subjects of song (ὡς καὶ ὀπίσσω / ἀνθρώποισι πελώμεθ' ἀοίδιμοι ἐσσομένοισι, 6.357–58): see Kovacs 1997: 175–76; Segal 1993: 31–32.

91. Though Sansone 2009: 194 argues that the ode asserts the role of tragedy as successor to epic poetry, the novelty it advertises is not clearly that of an entire genre: the combination of so many musical styles may be more representative of Euripides' *mousikē* than it is of tragedy as a whole.

probably produced a year or two before *Trojan Women,* the chorus sing of how they are combining the kithara and *aulos,* epinician, paean, lament, and Dionysiac *mousikē* in their celebration of Heracles' achievements.[92] Nevertheless, *Trojan Women* is one of the earlier plays to exhibit such a marked mixing of song types, and the chorus's announcement of "new songs" in the first stasimon can in this respect be understood as an advertisement for Euripides' musical innovation, even if it does not begin with this particular ode.

The similarities between this stasimon and Agathon's song in Aristophanes' *Women at the Thesmophoria,* which was probably produced in 411 B.C.E., four years later than *Trojan Women,* suggest that there may have been a new trend in late fifth-century Athens for representing performances of female *choreia* at Troy.[93] Agathon, Euripides' young contemporary, known as much for his effeminacy as for the novelty of his tragic compositions, sings this choral ode himself, taking on the roles of both chorus leader and chorus:[94]

> ἱερὰν χθονίαιν
> δεξάμεναι λαμπάδα, κοῦραι, ξὺν ἐλευθέραι
> πραπίδι χορεύσασθε βοάν.
> —τίνι δαιμόνων ὁ κῶμος;
> λέγε νιν. εὐπείστως δὲ τοὐμὸν (105)
> δαίμονας ἔχει σεβίσαι.
> —ἄγε νῦν ὄλβιζε μοῦσαι
> χρυσέων ῥύτορα τόξων
> Φοῖβον, ὃς ἱδρύσατο χώρας
> γύαλα Σιμουντίδι γᾶι. (110)
> —χαῖρε καλλίσταις ἀοιδαῖς,
> Φοῖβ', ἐν εὐμούσοισι τιμαῖς
> γέρας ἱερὸν προφέρων.
> —τάν τ' ἐν ὄρεσι δρυογόνοισιν
> κόραν ἀείσατ' Ἄρτεμιν ἀγροτέραν. (115)
> —ἕπομαι κλήιζουσα σεμνὰν
> γόνον ὀλβίζουσα Λατοῦς,
> Ἄρτεμιν ἀπειρολεχῆ.
> —Λατώ τε κρούματά τ' Ἀσιάδος (120)
> ποδὶ παράρυθμ' εὔρυθμα Φρυγίων

---

92. Eur. *HF* 680–94. On the mixing of genres here, see Wilson 1999–2000: 435; Weiss forthcoming b. Other critics have tended to focus almost exclusively on the ode's epinician character: Parry 1965; Rehm 1996: 53; Swift 2010: 129–31.

93. On the comedy's date, see Henderson 2000: 444. On kitharodic accounts of the sack of Troy, see Power 2010: 267–73.

94. I follow Henderson 2000 and Austin and Olson 2004 both in retaining ὀλβίζουσα (ms R) in line 117 and in the division of speakers (all played by Agathon himself) at 126–29. On the reading [kithara] (κιθάριος) in line 120, see Austin and Olson 2004: 94.

διὰ νεύματα Χαρίτων.
—σέβομαι Λατώ τ' ἄνασσαν
κίθαρίν τε ματέρ' ὕμνων
ἄρσενι βοᾶι δόκιμον, (125)
—τᾶι φάος ἔσσυτο δαιμονίοις
ὄμμασιν, ἁμετέρας τε δι' αἰφνιδίου ὀπός. ὧν χάριν
ἄνακτ' ἀγάλλετε Φοῖβον.
—χαῖρ', ὄλβιε παῖ Λατοῦς.

[As chorus leader] Receive the holy torch of the underworld pair, maidens, with free heart dance a cry!
[As chorus] For which of the gods is our revel? Name him/her. I'm in a state that's easily persuaded to worship gods.
[As chorus leader] Come now, with song bless the drawer of golden arrows, Phoebus, who founded our country's vales in the land of the river Simois.
[As chorus] Rejoice in our most beautiful songs, Phoebus, bringing forth your holy gift amid musical honors.
[As chorus leader] And sing of the maiden in the oak-bearing mountains, wild Artemis.
[As chorus] I follow, glorifying, blessing the revered child of Leto, Artemis, inexperienced in sex.
[As chorus leader] Both Leto and the strummings of the Asian [kithara], keeping time with the foot against the rhythm thanks to the Phrygian Graces' nodding heads.
[As chorus] I revere both Queen Leto and the kithara, mother of songs that are renowned for their male cry.
[As chorus leader] At which a light darted from divine eyes, and through our quick voice. For the sake of these things glorify lord Phoebus!
[As chorus] Hail, blessed son of Leto! (Ar. *Thesm.* 101–29)

The identification of the singers impersonated by Agathon as Trojan (109–10) and the probable allusion to Troy's liberation ("with free heart," 102–3) suggest that this song celebrating Apollo, Artemis, and Leto is also meant to be set on the night of the city's fall, when the Trojans believe the Greeks have departed and bring the horse within their walls.[95] Agathon's own performance of this choral celebration further resembles the one described by the chorus in *Trojan Women* in its emphasis on *partheneia*: Agathon as chorus leader calls on his fellow "maidens" (102) and invokes the maiden Artemis (115), stressing her virginity—and thus also that of the chorus he imitates—by describing her as "inexperienced in sex" (119). As in

---

95. Bothe 1845: 111 suggested that this song parodies a choral passage from a play (otherwise unattested) by Agathon on the fall of Troy. Cf. Muecke 1982: 46. The command to dance "with free heart" (Ar. *Thesm.* 102–3) resembles the call to beat the ground "with free foot" in the opening lines of Horace's famous ode celebrating the fall of Cleopatra ("nunc pede libero / pulsanda tellus," *Carm.* 37.1–2), though of course in Agathon's song it is highly ironic, since the city is about to be destroyed.

Euripides' ode, in which the chorus remember how they raised their feet and beat the ground together as they danced, Agathon's song includes an intensely rhythmical focus on choreography (120–22) when in the role of the chorus he describes how the kithara's strumming (*kroumata*, a word that also evokes the beating of feet) keeps time with the dance, aided by the Graces nodding their heads. The fact that Aristophanes has Agathon perform his version of this choral celebration in the presence of Euripides himself, the very man who had depicted a similar scene on the same stage just a few years earlier, strengthens the connection between the two men, as Agathon replaces those "new songs" with his own.

As I have already indicated, however, the newness of the chorus's song in *Trojan Women* does not lie just in its extradramatic implications: in addition to pointing toward *mousikē* that is new regardless of its context, the appeal for "a funeral ode of new songs" highlights musical change within the drama itself. This first proper choral ode brings new music to the play in its combination of hymnic, epic, kitharodic, and dithyrambic elements within a narrative-style song and so provides a contrast to and brief respite from the chorus's previous performance of lament. This ode's interruption within the lament of the tragedy as a whole is an inverse of what is described in the song itself, but the juxtaposition of the two types of performance still underscores the poignant contrast between the Trojans' own celebratory *mousikē* before Troy's fall and the mourning that follows. The fact that the ode provides an explanation for the lack of *choreia* in the present dramatic situation, however, ironizes this impression of a new musical departure, creating a disconnect between the chorus's own singing and dancing and the *mousikē* that they describe even as the two performances seem to merge with each other onstage. Although for the audience this is the first full *choreia* of the play, the ode stresses the disappearance of such *choreia* at Troy.

The type of performance that would seem new to these Trojan women, now that they have abandoned their *choreia,* is lament. In this respect the call for "a funeral ode of new songs" does not so much apply to the ode itself, which does not feature any traditional markers of lament, but to the dominant song type of the surrounding drama.[96] The ode thus describes and simultaneously enacts through the chorus's own performance the transition from the celebratory *choreia* of the past to the mourning of the present; this mourning is immediately renewed in the following scene, when Andromache and Hecuba sing an antiphonal lament together (577–606). We can therefore view the invocation of the Muse as an appeal for musical inspiration for the play as a whole—a play that is unusual in the surviving tragic corpus for being so full of lament from start to finish. In this respect the

---

96. *Contra* Neitzel 1967: 47 ("besteht die Neuartigkeit des Liedes eben darin, daß es ein 'Totenlied' ist"). Suter 2003: 5, 14, sees the first stasimon as a "reduced lament" for Troy based on its subject matter. See also n. 103 below.

call for "new songs" is laden with irony, since it heralds not a new departure but a reversion to lament, the originary song type from which all other *mousikē* is typically thought to derive.⁹⁷ When the chorus then say "for now I will cry out a song to Troy" (515), they signal a different type of song from the one that they request from the Muse. As the conjunction *gar* ("for") signals, this song will explain why lament is now the only type of *mousikē* that can be performed, since *choreia* has been abandoned amid the ruin of their city.

The first stasimon also brings the *mousikē* of the play back to lament after Cassandra's frenzied *hymenaios,* with her distorted solo performance of *choreia*. So the call for new music refers not only to the change from the *mousikē* performed in the past to that of the dramatic present but also to a change within the play itself, as mourning takes over from her failed attempt to perform a wedding song with the chorus. Such a transition from a *hymenaios* to lament is reminiscent of a similar shift described in the second stasimon of Aeschylus's *Agamemnon:*⁹⁸

Ἰλίωι δὲ κῆδος ὀρ-
θώνυμον τελεσσίφρων (700)
Μῆνις ἤλασεν, τραπέζας ἀτί-
μωσιν ὑστέρωι χρόνωι
καὶ ξυνεστίου Διὸς
πρασσομένα τὸ νυμφότι- (705)
μον μέλος ἐκφάτως τίοντας,
ὑμέναιον ὅς τότ' ἐπέρ-
ρεπε γαμβροῖσιν ἀείδειν.
μεταμανθάνουσα δ' ὕμνον
Πριάμου πόλις γεραιὰ (710)
πολύθρηνον μέγα που στένει, κικλήσκου-
σα Πάριν τὸν αἰνόλεκτρον
†παμπρόσθη πολύθρηνον
αἰῶν' ἀμφὶ πολιτᾶν† (715)
μέλεον αἷμ' ἀνατλᾶσα.

To Ilium, fulfilling its will, wrath drove a rightly named *kēdos* [sorrow/marriage alliance], exacting at a later time payment for the dishonor done to the table of hospitality and to Zeus of the hearth from those who celebrate loudly the bridal song, the *hymenaios,* which at that time fell to the bridegroom's kin to sing. But, starting to learn a different song, one full of lamentation, Priam's old city wails it loudly, calling Paris the "terribly wed," having endured †a life entirely destroyed, full of lamentation because of† the wretched blood †of her citizens†. (Aesch. *Ag.* 699–716)

---

97. On lament as a prototypical form of song, see Feld 1990; Ford 2010; Steiner 2013; Weiss 2017.
98. Line 716 could instead be translated "having endured wretched bloodshed."

The change in Troy's *mousikē* that the Argive chorus in *Agamemnon* describe, from the wedding celebrations for Paris and Helen to the songs "full of lamentation" (714) for the slain, is reperformed in *Trojan Women* through the musical transition from Cassandra's *hymenaios* to the mourning of the chorus, Hecuba, and Andromache.[99] The first stasimon, though not itself a lament, accounts for this transition, thereby also providing an aetiology for the dominant *mousikē* of the play as a whole. Unlike Aeschylus's ode, it also looks outward, to the different types of music that can be performed and combined in the theater, yet such pointers to Euripides' own musical innovation become part of the song's programmatic force within the play itself.

### PERFORMING THE FALL OF TROY

As we have seen, Hecuba's opening monody and the chorus's first stasimon together describe and reperform the beginning and the end of the Trojan War: the Greeks' voyage to Troy accompanied by the *aulos* and syrinx; the moment of Troy's fall, when the "bloody cry" interrupts the Trojans' choral celebrations as the Greeks come out from the horse. In the second stasimon, which the chorus perform after Astyanax is taken away to his death and his mother to the ships, the chorus initially rehearse another moment of Troy's past, this time looking further back to its sack by Telamon. They begin the ode from a strongly Greek perspective, addressing the hero with epinician language and celebrating his connection with Athens:

μελισσοτρόφου Σαλαμῖνος ὦ βασιλεῦ Τελαμών,
νάσου περικύμονος οἰκήσας ἕδραν                                                  (800)
τᾶς ἐπικεκλιμένας ὄχθοις ἱεροῖς, ἵν' ἐλαίας
πρῶτον ἔδειξε κλάδον γλαυκᾶς Ἀθάνα,
οὐράνιον στέφανον λιπαραῖσί ⟨τε⟩ κόσμον Ἀθάναις,
ἔβας ἔβας τῶι τοξοφόρωι συναρι-
στεύων ἅμ' Ἀλκμήνας γόνωι                                                        (805)
Ἴλιον Ἴλιον ἐκπέρσων πόλιν
ἁμετέραν τὸ πάροιθεν ⟨ . . . ⟩
[ὅτ' ἔβας ἀφ' Ἑλλάδος]·

O king of bee-nourishing Salamis, Telamon, you who made your home in a sea-girt island lying near the holy hills, where Athena first revealed the shoot of grey olive, a heavenly crown and glory for gleaming Athens, you came, you came, doing great exploits together with the arrow-bearing son of Alcmene, to sack Ilium, Ilium, our city, in days gone by ⟨ . . . ⟩ [when you came from Hellas]. (799–808)

---

99. Cf. Battezzato 2005b: 84–85. He likens the description of the Trojans' abandonment of Helen's *hymenaios* in Aeschylus's play to the way Hecuba and the chorus in *Trojan Women* must unlearn their former songs and take up a new tradition of Greek *mousikē* instead.

But after reasserting their own Phrygian perspective with the emphatically placed "our city" (806–7), the chorus vividly describe in the first antistrophe the violent destruction wrought by Telamon at Troy, and in doing so they bring their focus forward in time by merging the two scenes of destruction, past and present:[100]

κανόνων δὲ τυκίσματα Φοίβου
πυρὸς ⟨πυρὸς⟩ φοίνικι πνοᾶι καθελὼν                                                (815)
  Τροίας ἐπόρθησε χθόνα.
δὶς δὲ δυοῖν πιτύλοιν τείχη πέρι
Δαρδανίδας φονία κατέλυσεν αἰχμά.

And having brought down with the crimson breath of fire, ⟨fire,⟩ Phoebus's stonework produced by the rule, he laid waste to the land of Troy. And twice in two attacks the murderous spear has killed Dardanians around their walls. (814–19)

The rest of the ode continues to combine allusions to the past (Ganymede and Zeus in the second strophe, Eos and Tithonus in the final antistrophe) with vivid scenes of the dramatic present, marking a transition in the tragedy's song as a whole: from this moment on the chorus and Hecuba shift away from *re*performing Troy's past toward performing in real time its present. Their song and dance increasingly reflect, intensify, and make present onstage the final destruction of the city burning behind them, thus producing a sort of auditory and choreographed *skēnographia* for the audience of a scene that would not otherwise be physically represented in the theater.[101]

The chorus's performance of Troy's fall is also a lament for the city. As the chorus begin to reflect directly on the present again, so their style of song shifts back to that of lament, away from the narrative and generic mixing of the first stasimon. Though it begins with epinician language and motifs, the second stasimon becomes what Ann Suter calls a "reduced lament," containing some stylistic elements of lament without developing into a full mourning song.[102] The song's status as a partial or reduced lament becomes particularly clear through its repetitive language, like the doubling of words at the start of a line (*ebas ebas*, 805; *Ilion Ilion*, 806; *pyros* ⟨*pyros*⟩, 815; *Erōs Erōs*, 841) and the alliterative polyptoton of *dis de duoin* ("twice in

---

100. On the double fall of Troy here, see Torrance 2013: 232–33. The alliterative tautology at the start of line 817 (δὶς δὲ δυοῖν πιτύλοιν; cf. Pind. *Nem.* 8.48) further encourages a sense of doubling. Pind. *Ol.* 8.30–46 similarly merges these two sacks of Troy.

101. Cf. Bassi 2005: 259 on visual perception in tragedy, drawing from Bühler's (1934) concept of *Deixis am Phantasma*: "the dramatic script inscribes two (or more) levels of visual absence: the play in performance as available to the bodily eye of a putative spectator, and verbal references to what is *not* seen." Cf. chapter 5, pp. 193–203, on the parodos of *IA*. On the representation of the fall of Troy in *Trojan Women*, see Hose 1991: 325–29.

102. Suter 2003: 3–4 (drawing on the unpublished work of Elinor Wright); *contra* Biehl 1989: 303–4, who sees the content of the ode's first half as typical of an epinician.

two," 816).¹⁰³ The language of loss, destruction, and absence that pervades the ode further enhances the impression of a lament.¹⁰⁴

As the chorus focus on the present scene of destruction in the second strophe, however, their mourning becomes much more striking, since they perform not only their own lament but that of the place itself, thus merging their own voices with those of the Trojan landscape:

ἠϊόνες δ' ἅλιαι
ἴακχον οἰωνὸς οἷ-
ον τέκνων ὕπερ βοῶσ', (830)
ἄι μὲν εὐνάς, ἄι δὲ παῖδας,
ἄι δὲ ματέρας γεραιάς.

The salty shores shout out a cry, just as a bird [cries] for her children, here for marriage beds, here for sons, here for old mothers. (826-32)

Parts of the physical environment are often said to echo or resound in Greek poetry: in the context of battle, as when the waters and banks of the river Xanthos ring amid the confusion of drowning Trojans in the *Iliad*; or in response to a character's pain, such as when the rocky cave cries out in response to the groans of the blinded Polyphemus in the *Odyssey*.¹⁰⁵ In the musical context of Hesiod's description of the Muses' singing in the *Theogony*, the sounds produced by the landscape suggest its participation in the performance of *choreia*: Zeus's halls laugh with joy at the goddesses' voices, while the peak of Olympus resounds; as they make their way toward Olympus, "around them the black earth cried out as they sang."¹⁰⁶ That this sort of pathetic fallacy extends to the participation of the physical environment in a lament is not surprising given the intensity of emotion experienced and displayed through such a performance and the fact that the lament is for a whole city rather than an individual. These lines of *Trojan Women* are striking, however, for the comparison that the chorus make between the sound produced by the shores of Troy and the cry of a mother bird for her children. As we have seen, the analogy of the songbird singing for the loss of her children appears earlier in the play too, in the monody of Hecuba (146–48). Here in the second stasimon, a simile that more naturally applies to the chorus's own singing, comparing their lament to that of the bird, is attached instead to the Trojan landscape. The effect of this crossed identification is a merging

---

103. On repetitive language as a feature of lament, see Alexiou 1974: 97, 151; also Suter 2003: 3; Weiss 2017. The extended laments in Aeschylus's *Persians* are full of such repetition: see esp. lines 918–1076.

104. E.g., καθελών (815), ἐπόρθησε (815), κατέλυσεν (820), δαίεται (825), βεβᾶσι (835), ὤλεσ' (840), ὄλεθρον (851), φροῦδα (859).

105. Hom. *Il*. 21.9-10; *Od*. 9.395.

106. ἠχεῖ δὲ κάρη νιφόεντος Ὀλύμπου, Hes. *Theog*. 42; περὶ δ' ἴαχε γαῖα μέλαινα / ὑμνεύσαις, 69–70. Sarah Olsen pointed out to me the similarity between these instances of the physical world responding to *choreia* and Orpheus's ability to charm trees, rocks, and animals with his song: see esp. Simonides fr. 62 *PMG*; Eur. *Bacch*. 561–64, *IA* 1211–12.

of the women and their land, an assimilation of their voices.[107] The following cries of lament intensify the fusing of chorus and landscape, since they themselves perform the shores' cries (831–32). Their lament *for* Troy becomes the lament *of* Troy itself.

We should note here the use of the word *iakchon* (829) to mean the cry produced by Troy's shores. Although commentators on *Trojan Women* usually gloss it as a general shout of distress, elsewhere it tends to refer specifically to the *Iacchus* song for Dionysus or to the god himself.[108] There is no reason to deny the Dionysiac character of this particular sound-word, particularly as it intensifies the polyphonic effect, with the shores emitting a cry that is usually performed by a chorus. As when the chorus later describe Hecuba's mourning as a *Iacchus* cry of the dead (1230), the reference to this type of song occurs not in the context of a civic cult but instead within a lament for the city. Though Dionysiac imagery is more usually associated with the destruction of the household in tragedy (as it is, for example, in *Heracles*) rather than with that of the whole city, in *Trojan Women* it is used to emphasize the total annihilation of both.[109]

The motif of enclosed lament, whereby the chorus perform the lament of others within their own song of mourning, recurs in the third stasimon, which they sing after Menelaus has left with Helen. Like the first stasimon, this ode initially evokes the history of Trojan worship and performance, from the incense burning on Zeus's altar to the sacrifices and choruses performed in his honor (1060–80). Like the second stasimon, however, it includes repetitions typical of lament (*Idaia t' Idaia*, 1066; *melei melei*, 1077; *boai boai*, 1090) and increasingly focuses on the present destruction of Troy, though the women also look to their uncertain future and in the second antistrophe wish for Menelaus to be shipwrecked on his way home (1100–1117). In the second strophe they picture their children at the city gates, crying out their own lament to their mothers:

τέκνων δὲ πλῆθος ἐν πύλαις
δάκρυσι †κατάορα στένει† βοᾶι βοᾶι (1090)
Μᾶτερ, ὤμοι, μόναν δή μ' Ἀχαιοὶ κομί-
ζουσι σέθεν ἀπ' ὀμμάτων.

But a crowd of children at the gates with tears †hanging down wails†, cries, cries, "Mother, alas! the Achaeans are taking me, alone indeed, away from your sight." (1089–92)

---

107. Barlow 1986: 32 notes how closely the women identify themselves with Troy itself, frequently addressing the city as if it were one of them (e.g., 173, 780, 1278, 1324).

108. Ἴακχον is an emendation by Hartung; ms V prints ἴαχον (the third person plural imperfect form of ἰάχω), but the tense seems odd in this otherwise present context. For ἴακχος as a reference to the *Iacchus* song for Dionysus, see, e.g., Eur. *Cycl.* 69, *Bacch.* 725; cf. Hdt. 8.65.9.

109. On Dionysiac music in Euripides' *Heracles*, see Wilson 1999–2000: 433–39. On the use of Dionysiac imagery in tragic portrayals of the destruction of the family, see Seaford 1994: 328–62. Loraux 2002: 73 notes that ἰακχέω and related words are often associated with the cry of lament.

The women thus perform the cries of the children as well as their own, and by vivifying this imagined scene through such polyphony they extend the audience's view of Trojan suffering to include those who are not physically present onstage.[110]

This reduced lament soon turns into full antiphonal mourning, which reaches its culmination as Hecuba and the chorus hear the crashes of Troy falling in the closing lines of the play. After Talthybius brings Hecuba the corpse of Astyanax and she addresses it in grief (1123–1215), the chorus repeatedly interrupt her iambic trimeters with cries (*e e, aiai aiai, oimoi, iō moi moi*) and emotional dochmiacs (1215–38), drawing her into their lament for Astyanax by directing her to perform the ritual sounds and gestures of mourning:[111]

{Χο.} αἰαῖ αἰαῖ·
πικρὸν ὄδυρμα γαῖά σ', ὦ
τέκνον, δέξεται.
στέναζε, μᾶτερ {Εκ.} αἰαῖ.
{Χο.} νεκρῶν ἴακχον. {Εκ.} οἴμοι. (1230)
{Χο.} οἴμοι δῆτα σῶν ἀλάστων κακῶν.
{Εκ.} τελαμῶσιν ἕλκη τὰ μὲν ἐγώ σ' ἰάσομαι,
τλήμων ἰατρός, ὄνομ' ἔχουσα, τἄργα δ' οὔ·
τὰ δ' ἐν νεκροῖσι φροντιεῖ πατὴρ σέθεν.
{Χο.} ἄρασσ' ἄρασσε κρᾶτα (1235)
πιτύλους διδοῦσα χειρός.
ἰώ μοί μοι.

*Chorus:* *Aiai aiai!* You, a cause for bitter mourning, O child, the earth will receive. Wail, mother...

*Hecuba:* *Aiai!*

*Chorus:* ... the cry of the dead!

*Hecuba:* *Oimoi!*

*Chorus:* *Oimoi* indeed for your unforgettable sorrows!

*Hecuba:* Your wounds I shall heal with bandages, a wretched healer, having only the name and not the deeds. But your father will care for things among the dead.

*Chorus:* Beat, beat the head, applying your hand's strikes. *Iō moi moi!* (1226–37)

Whereas previously Hecuba led their mourning, now the chorus direct this performance with their orders to "wail ... the cry of the dead" (1230) and "beat the head" (1235). As a result, they seem to urge both Hecuba and the drama itself to abandon speech altogether and devolve into lament alone—as the Trojan women

---

110. Biehl 1989: 389 sees these lines as an example of "Phantasia-Darstellung," in which the mothers recall the moment when they last saw their children. The chorus's depiction of the lamenting children seems to combine this memory with their vision of what is happening in the present, when the children, like their mothers, are being taken as slaves to different Greek ships (1094–99).

111. On the contrast of iambics and dochmiacs here, see Barlow 1986: 224.

themselves do for the last 120 lines of the play.[112] Battezzato sees the chorus's words at 1226–37 as a distortion of the traditional form of ritual mourning whereby they would follow the orders of a leader.[113] We can see from the extended lament in Aeschylus's *Persians* (935–1076) that the actor as leader tends to give directions for mourning to the chorus, who respond by confirming that they are indeed performing these sounds and gestures: when Xerxes bids them, "cry out now, sounding in response to me," they respond by singing, "this is my care, my lord."[114] Battezzato argues that the chorus's takeover of the role of leader in lament here in *Trojan Women* emphasizes "the breakdown of family and society, a breakdown that affects even the rituals used by society to deal with mourning."[115] If the traditional structure of ritual lament does seem to break down here, the effect is temporary, since Hecuba leads the mourning again in the final, extended scene of antiphonal lamentation with which the play ends. But the chorus's active role in encouraging lamentation is striking for how it pushes this type of *mousikē* into the play, interrupting the rhythms of speech with these lyrical outbursts of grief. As in the *kommos* scene of Aeschylus's *Libation Bearers*, when the chorus's vivid description of their wailing and beating (423–28) helps to escalate the feelings of sorrow and anger expressed by Orestes and Electra, in *Trojan Women* the chorus's self-referential focus on the sounds and ritual gestures of mourning further heightens the emotional intensity of their lament.

In the closing scene of the play the characters do finally abandon speech altogether and break down into a full antiphonal lament that accompanies, reflects, and magnifies the complete destruction of Troy. The chorus interrupt Hecuba's iambic trimeters again at 1251–59 with a short lament in lyric anapaests, punctuated by the cries of *iō iō* and *ea ea*.[116] There follows the last scene of spoken dialogue in the play, when Talthybius tells the Greek captains to burn Troy to the ground and bids Odysseus's servants to take Hecuba away (1260–86). Then, beginning with Hecuba's anguished cry of extreme grief (*otototototoi*, 1287), she and the chorus sing a long antiphonal lyric iambic lament for Troy, beginning with a depiction of the fire devouring the city (1287–1301). In the second strophe they concentrate on their own gestures of lament, before bewailing Hecuba's fate:

{Εκ.} ἰὼ γᾶ τρόφιμε τῶν ἐμῶν τέκνων.
{Χο.} ἒ ἔ.
{Εκ.} ὦ τέκνα, κλύετε, μάθετε ματρὸς αὐδάν.

---

112. The directions for the gestures of lament here recall those of Hecuba in response to the news that she will be Odysseus's slave (ἄρασσε κρᾶτα κούριμον / ἕλκ' ὀνύχεσσι δίπτυχον παρειάν, 279–80).
113. Battezzato 2005b: 79–80.
114. {Ξε.} βόα νυν ἀντίδουπά μοι. / {Χο.} μέλειν πάρεστι, δέσποτα, Aesch. *Pers.* 1048–49.
115. Battezzato 2005b: 77.
116. See Lee 1976: 273 on the probability that these lines are meant to be sung, despite some non-lyric features.

{Χο.} ἰαλέμωι τοὺς θανόντας ἀπύεις.
{Εκ.} γεραιά γ' ἐς πέδον τιθεῖσα μέλε' ⟨ἐμὰ⟩ (1305)
καὶ χερσὶ γαῖαν κτυποῦσα δισσαῖς.
{Χο.} διάδοχά σοι γόνυ τίθημι γαίαι
τοὺς ἐμοὺς καλοῦσα νέρθεν
ἀθλίους ἀκοίτας.
{Εκ.} ἀγόμεθα φερόμεθ' {Χο.} ἄλγος ἄλγος βοαῖς. (1310)

Hecuba: Iō! Land, nourisher of my children!
Chorus: E e!
Hecuba: O children, listen, note your mother's voice!
Chorus: In your lament you call on the dead.
Hecuba: Placing ⟨my⟩ old limbs on the ground and beating the earth with my two hands.
Chorus: Following you, I place my knee on the ground, summoning my wretched husband from below.
Hecuba: I am being led away, carried away!
Chorus: Pain, pain you cry! (1301–10)

Following the vivid description in the previous antistrophe of Troy falling to the ground, engulfed by flames (1298–99), the cries, kneeling, and beating of the ground described and (we assume) simultaneously performed by Hecuba and the chorus in this strophe seem to (re)produce sonically and visually the scene of Troy's sinking to ruin.

The second antistrophe strengthens this mimetic effect of the women's performance, whereby the sounds and gestures of their lament not only express their own suffering but also enact the demolition they so vividly describe. Now, instead of calling on her children to hear her cries (1303), Hecuba uses the same language (*emathet'*, *ekluete*, 1325) to refer to the sound of the citadel falling down in the final words of the play:

{Εκ.} ἐμάθετ', ἐκλύετε; {Χο.} περγάμων ⟨γε⟩ κτύπον. (1325)
{Εκ.} ἔνοσις ἅπασαν ἔνοσις {Χο.} ἐπικλύζει πόλιν.
{Εκ.} ἰὼ ⟨ἰώ⟩, τρομερὰ τρομερὰ
μέλεα, φέρετ' ἐμὸν ἴχνος· ἴτ' ἐπὶ
δούλειον ἁμέραν βίου. (1330)
{Χο.} ἰὼ τάλαινα πόλις. ὅμως
δὲ πρόφερε πόδα σὸν ἐπὶ πλάτας Ἀχαιῶν.

Hecuba: Do you note, do you hear? Chorus: The crash of Troy's citadel.
Hecuba: Shaking, shaking . . . Chorus: . . . overwhelms the whole city.
Hecuba: Iō ⟨iō⟩! Trembling, trembling limbs, carry my step: go to your life's day of slavery.
Chorus: Iō wretched city! Nevertheless carry your foot forward to the ships of the Achaeans. (1325–32)

The noun *ktypos* ("crash, din, noise," 1325) recalls Hecuba's use of the related verb *ktypeō* in the previous stanza to refer to the sound of her beating the ground with her hands (1306), and often appears in Euripidean tragedy to express the percussive element of lament.[117] As we found in chapter 1, a similar synaesthetic application of *ktypos* occurs in Aeschylus's *Seven against Thebes*, in which it refers to the sound of the approaching Argive army and the chorus's own physical movement. Here in *Trojan Women* the sound produced by Hecuba and the chorus in their mourning is transformed into that of the city crashing to the ground. By following her reference to the shaking (*enosis . . . enosis*, 1326) that overwhelms the city with a similarly repetitive description of her own quivering limbs (*tromera tromera / melea*, 1328–29), Hecuba correlates her own and the chorus's movements with those of Troy itself; the highly resolved meter of lines 1326–29 intensifies this effect by rhythmically imitating such trembling. Hecuba's instructions to her limbs to "carry my step" (1329), which the chorus then take up in their closing line ("carry your foot," 1332), also, however, mark the end of their lament by replacing their directions for the gestures of mourning from the previous strophe. The choreography of lament turns into the movements of Hecuba as she makes her way toward the Greek ships.

At the beginning of this chapter I noted how the continuance of Hecuba's and the chorus's singing right up until the end of the play gives the impression that the mourning that has dominated the whole drama, especially its closing scene, will never cease. At the same time, the departure of Hecuba, the chorus's leader, who has been onstage for almost the entire drama, also signals the end of their lament together, as well as the end of the tragedy itself. Up until this point the performance of and allusions to lament have intensified the stagnancy of the women's position: they have remained in the one place on the shore outside Troy, waiting to be assigned as slaves to their new Greek masters. Now that Hecuba is finally moving from this stationary position toward the ships, leaving her chorus behind, their lament cannot continue. Since their songs of and about mourning have defined the whole tragedy, this too must now come to a close.

A running theme of this chapter has been that *Trojan Women* is about absence, and that such absence becomes clear through the performance of *mousikē*. Lament so dominates the play that Hecuba's claim that her music is *achoreutos* appears to hold true; even after the chorus enter, their focus on mourning seems to deny the audience the enjoyment of full *choreia* being performed onstage. Yet they *do* sing and dance, and do so not just in performances of lament but in three choral stasima, the first of which, as we have seen, is a complex mix of different musical genres (dithyrambic, epic, hymnic, kitharodic). The chorus's *mousikē* thus produces the paradoxical effect of performed or present absence as they emphasize through their own *choreia* the loss of these sorts of choral performances in the

---

117. Cf. Eur. *Alc.* 87; *Andr.* 1211; *Supp.* 87, 605; *Phoen.* 1351; *Or.* 963, 1467; also Aesch. *Cho.* 427.

dramatic present. This performance of the abandonment of *choreia* emphasizes—even enacts—the obliteration of Troy, demonstrating quite how essential *choreia* is to the cultural, social, religious, and physical structure of the city.

But even while the *mousikē* of the play underscores a sense of absence, it also has a presencing effect, as the chorus and Hecuba make what is *not* onstage come to life. The merging of the ritual gestures and sounds of lament with the vivid depiction of Troy's fall in the final, antiphonal lament of Hecuba and the chorus brings this scene into the theater for the audience to experience visually and sonically. We saw in the previous chapter examples of scenes that are not physically present but become as if so through the chorus's own singing and dancing: the Nereids leaping to the tune of the *aulos*-playing dolphin around the Greek ships as they made their way to Troy, and the music making in Argos upon Thyestes' appropriation of the Golden Fleece. In the first stasimon of *Trojan Women* the chorus produce a similar effect when they describe their own former *mousikē*, which they reenact in their present performance. Such presencing is part of the imaginative suggestion achieved by and through *choreia*, whereby the singing and dancing of a chorus encourage the audience to assimilate what they see and hear onstage to what is described in song—though in *Trojan Women* this process is seldom comfortable or straightforward. The representation of some of the visual and sonic effects of Troy falling to the ground in the final scene of lament, as well as the chorus's enactment of the cries of the city's shores and children in the second and third stasima, is also a form of presencing through *choreia*, demonstrating that this phenomenon need not solely concern the suggestion of *mousikē* performed outside the temporal and geographical scope of the play itself. Choral performance can thus function like a messenger's speech or herald's report, providing an alternative mode of vividly presenting offstage scenes and events to the audience—we will see it working in this way in *Iphigenia in Aulis* too. In *Trojan Women* the musical representation of scenes happening concurrently with the events onstage or, like the night the horse was brought into the city, in the very recent past, underlines the inability of both Hecuba and the chorus to escape from the devastation of the present.

Sarah Skaggs, the choreographer with whom I began this chapter, responded to the question "What can dance do after this disastrous time?" by creating a piece that represented the reformation of community in the wake of 9/11. Fifteen dancers came together to form a chorus of sorts, and in their slow, contemplative movements, they invited the audience to reflect and heal. By performing in thriving public spaces, they also reaffirmed the strength and vibrancy of the civic community. In his postwar vision, in which neither the city survives nor the women's status within it, Euripides allows for no such healing or cohesion. His play is a chilling reminder of the destruction of war, for both its perpetrators and its potential victims, and we can reasonably assume that it made its original Athenian audience wonder about the fate of their own city as well as reflect on their recent actions at

Melos. Euripides' fifteen choreuts sing and dance, yet while seeming not to do so at all; they perform *choreia* while denying its very possibility in the wake of their city's destruction. And the departure of Hecuba, their leader, at the end of the drama heralds the dispersion of them all—the final fracturing of the Trojan community. The play (and perhaps even the trilogy as a whole) has enacted the end of *choreia* and so too the end of the city. Even lament is at the final moment abandoned as the women depart, so that the play ends on a bizarre and devastatingly bleak note of silence. Can any form of *mousikē* now be performed? All that can follow is something completely different altogether—the singing and dancing of the satyr chorus in *Sisyphus,* the final drama of the tetralogy.

# 4

## Protean Singers and the Shaping of Narrative in *Helen*

τρὶς δὲ περίστειξας κοῖλον λόχον ἀμφαφόωσα,
ἐκ δ' ὀνομακλήδην Δαναῶν ὀνόμαζες ἀρίστους,
πάντων Ἀργείων φωνὴν ἴσκουσ' ἀλόχοισιν.

*Three times you went around the hollow ambush, feeling it all around,
and you called aloud the names of the Danaans' chieftains,
making your voice like that of all the Argives' wives.*

—ODYSSEY 4.277–79

We may know Helen of Troy for her beauty, but in the Greek tradition her voice was just as powerful. In the *Iliad* she is an "expert lamenter," the last of the three women to lead a mourning song over Hector's corpse in the closing scene of the poem.[1] In the *Odyssey*, in the passage quoted above, we hear of her uncanny ability to imitate the voices of the Greeks' wives as she circles the Trojan horse and tries to lure the men out. This extraordinary vocal performance resembles that of the Deliades, the archetypal chorus, in the *Homeric Hymn to Apollo*—maidens who "know how to represent the voices and rhythmic motions of all men."[2] Helen switches from one voice to another, representing them all at once in a strangely singular and protean choral performance to which the Greek men yearn to offer an antiphonal response.[3]

The choral character of her vocal dexterity in this *Odyssey* scene points to Helen's close association with chorality, which is evident in later Greek literature as well as in myth and cult more broadly.[4] As this chapter will make clear, *choreia*

---

1. Hom. *Il.* 24.761–76. On Helen as an expert lamenter, see Martin 2008.
2. πάντων δ' ἀνθρώπων φωνὰς καὶ κρεμβαλιαστὺν / μιμεῖσθ' ἴσασιν, *Hymn. Hom. Ap.* 161–62; Martin 2008: 119–20.
3. Hom. *Od.* 4.280–89.
4. On Helen as a chorus leader, see esp. Calame 1997: 191–202; Martin 2008: 119–26; Murnaghan 2013. I discuss her identification as a *chorēgos*, particularly in Spartan cult, further below.

plays a prominent role in Euripides' *Helen*, of 412 B.C.E., centering on Helen's position as the chorus leader par excellence. Aristophanes' *Lysistrata*, produced just one year later, in addition to parodying Euripides' play, reveals Helen's central role within the Athenian conceptualization of Spartan *choreia* as it ends with the Spartan delegate singing of girls dancing by the river Eurotas with Helen, their "pure and lovely chorus leader."[5] In Theocritus's epithalamium for her, she appears as a supremely musical figure more generally: "No one knows how to strum the lyre and sing to Artemis and broad-chested Athena like Helen does."[6]

In Euripides' play, the *choreia* that surrounds Helen in her role as a *chorēgos* generates a musical narrative closely intertwined with the dramatic one. In the previous two chapters we have seen Euripides experimenting in different ways with the relationship between music and plot: in *Electra*, choral song and dance anticipate and generate the dramatic action while also characterizing the protagonist; in *Trojan Women* they intensify the lack of action or movement through the entire drama. Despite *choreia*'s central role in the dramatic narrative, however, the protagonists of both those plays have an uneasy relationship with it: Electra continuously rejects the role of chorus leader and refuses to participate in the chorus's musical performances; Hecuba, the former chorus leader, can sing only "chorusless woes" against the backdrop of her destroyed city.[7] In *Helen*, produced a few years after *Trojan Women*, Euripides weaves a remarkably tight choral narrative around Helen's state and physical location at each point of the drama and beyond, from being a leader of lament in the parodos to becoming a leader of *choreia* back in Sparta following her escape there with Menelaus. The powerful presence of *choreia* in this play therefore complements Helen's position as the consummate *chorēgos* in the Greek imagination—a position that she continues to occupy even when she has left her chorus behind in Egypt.

The musical narrative of *Helen* is partly created through a transition from one type of performance to another: as we shall see, responsive lament transitions into more celebratory *mousikē* with a strongly Dionysian flavor, mirroring the plot's movement toward a happy resolution. In this respect it is similar to the musical patterning of *Iphigenia in Tauris*, which also has a plot structure very close to that of *Helen*: both plays focus on the plight of the central heroine in a barbarian land (Egypt/Tauris), then begin to look toward a more positive outcome once she is reunited with a newly arrived Greek hero (Menelaus/Orestes) with whom she

---

5. ἀγνὰ χοραγὸς εὐπρεπής, Ar. *Lys*. 1315.
6. οὐ μὰν οὐδὲ λύραν τις ἐπίσταται ὧδε κροτῆσαι / Ἄρτεμιν ἀείδοισα καὶ εὐρύστερνον Ἀθάναν, / ὡς Ἑλένα, Theoc. *Id*. 18.35–37.
7. *Tro*. 121.

finally escapes back to Greece.⁸ And in both the heroine is a prominent singer for the first half of the drama, but, after forming an escape plan, she then leaves the chorus to sing without her. *Andromeda*, which was performed within the same tetralogy as *Helen*, had a similar plot structure, with Perseus's rescue of the Greek heroine from Ethiopia.⁹ It may have had a similar musical narrative as well: it too begins with a lament and shares some musical imagery with *Helen*, though too little of the play survives to conjecture any further as to its *mousikē*.

The musical narrative of *Helen* is also generated by means of a series of images that tie the choral songs together through their association with Helen and her *mousikē*. These images—from the Sirens to the mourning nightingale, the Great Mother, and the syrinx-playing crane—all ultimately refer to Helen herself, who thus becomes a multiform figure, appearing in different musical guises at different stages of the narrative. Musical metamorphosis therefore contributes to the theme of doubling that, as has often been observed, pervades the whole play, based as it is on the premise of two Helens: here we have a Helen who never went to Troy but was instead whisked away by Hermes to Egypt while her phantom (*eidōlon*) went off with Paris.¹⁰ The play's protean nature is even made physically manifest through its setting by Proteus's tomb: as C. W. Marshall observes, "Euripides literally buries Proteus, the embodiment of shape-shifting and the blurring of limits, into his stage."¹¹ Helen herself not only is and has a double; in Euripides' version of her origin story she is even born from a moment of metamorphosis: as she tells us in the prologue, Zeus flew after her mother, "assuming the shape of a swan, fleeing the chase of an eagle";¹² later she wonders about the story that Leda gave birth to an egg

---

8. On the structural similarities between *Helen* and *IT*, see esp. Platnauer 1938: xv-xvi; Matthiessen 1964; Mastronarde 2010: 73-74; Marshall 2014: 45-49. On the relationship between *Helen* and *Andromeda*, see Marshall 2014: 140-87. The dating of *Helen* and *Andromeda* to the City Dionysia of 412 is based on scholia on Aristophanes (test. iia-c). Cropp and Fick dated *IT* on metrical grounds to 417-12 (1985: 23); Cropp later narrowed this window down to 414-12 (2000: 60). Based on the thematic and structural similarities between the three plays, Wright (2005: 43-55) has argued that they were all performed together in 412 as an "escape trilogy." Others have on the same basis claimed that *IT* was not produced in the same year as *Helen*, and in general Wright's argument has met with skepticism: see Hose 1995: 14-17, 190-92; Foley 2006; Gregory 2006; Kyriakou 2006; Marshall 2009 and 2014: 12.

9. The similarities between *Helen* and both *Andromeda* (performed within the same tetralogy) and *IT* suggest that in the late 410s Euripides was experimenting with exotic settings and a new type of plot structure, which may previously have been more common in satyr drama than in tragedy. On the links between *Helen* and satyr play, especially Aeschylus's *Proteus*, see Marshall 1995 and 2014: 55-95.

10. On doubling and the play between illusion and reality in *Helen*, see esp. Solmsen 1934; Burnett 1960; Zuntz 1960; Segal 1971; Downing 1990; Pucci 1997; Wright 2005: 278-337; Zeitlin 2010. Not only does Helen herself become a copy (μίμημα, 74) of the *eidōlon*, but the nature of the *eidōlon* itself is multiplied: it is a cloud (νεφέλη, 705, 1219), an apparition (δόκησις, 36, 119), a substitute (διάλλαγμα, 586), a statue image (ἄγαλμα, 705, 1219), and a copy (μίμημα, 875).

11. Marshall 2014: 88.

12. Λήδαν κύκνου μορφώματ' ὄρνιθος λαβών, / . . . ὑπ' αἰετοῦ / δίωγμα φεύγων, Eur. *Hel.* 19-21.

(258).[13] As we shall see, this avian heritage becomes a musical motif in the play as Helen and her chorus merge with a succession of singing and dancing birds.

Helen's multiform nature makes her the ideal character for Euripides' play with the merging of imagined and performed *mousikē* that lies at the heart of the Greek choral imaginary, within which choruses (and chorus leaders) are frequently assimilated to particular animals, objects, and archetypal musical performers through their own live *choreia*. In Helen's case the shift from vision to visualization, from seeing her as one thing to imagining her as another, is a natural one, since both in myth and especially within this tragedy she is the ultimate shape-shifter as well as the ultimate *chorēgos*. The protean ability we saw in the *Odyssey*, whereby she assumes different vocal forms around the Trojan horse, is central to the interplay between her and the chorus, who continue to conjure her presence through various musical figures even when she has left them behind.

Such metamusical play around the figure of Helen is in one sense highly innovative, showcasing Euripides' bold experimentation with the different ways in which such musical imagery and performance may be integrated within a dramatic narrative. The play was famous for its novelty: just a year later, the character of Euripides' kinsman in Aristophanes' *Women at the Thesmophoria* calls the tragedy (or its protagonist) "that new Helen."[14] We may understand this reputation to derive as much from its *mousikē* as from Euripides' particular version of the myth, combined with the exotic setting in Egypt.[15] But the play's *mousikē* is also grounded in tradition. As we saw in chapter 1, both Aeschylus and Sophocles experimented with transitions from one type of choral performance to another in order to heighten a tragedy's dramatic impact. And as Sheila Murnaghan has demonstrated, the dynamics of *choreia* in

---

13. Cf. *Hel.* 215–16. The story of Helen's birth from an egg laid by Leda herself is first attested here: see Allan 2008: 148, 179–80. On Helen as a protean figure, see Zeitlin 2010, esp. 268: "As the undisputed emblem of beauty incarnate and sexual allure, she has by now become a figurative sign, even close to an abstraction, always available as a site of projection of fantasies, a receptor of the overflow of reality."

14. τὴν καινὴν Ἑλένην, Ar. *Thesm.* 850. On this statement, see esp. Arnott 1990; Allan 2008: 67. Given Helen's mimetic nature, it is perhaps not a coincidence that the kinsman claims he will imitate (μιμήσομαι, 850) Helen/*Helen*.

15. Neither the Egyptian setting nor Helen's phantom double may have been a complete innovation, but her situation as the play opens must still have seemed extraordinary to Euripides' Athenian audience. There is no iconographic evidence for a tradition of an Egyptian Helen, but in several literary sources Helen stays in Egypt, either with Menelaus (Hom. *Od.* 4; Hec. *FGrH* 4 F 153) or on the way to Troy with Paris (Hdt. 2.112–20; cf. Hom. *Il.* 6.289–92). Stesichorus's so-called *Palinode* apparently defended Helen, arguing that she did not go to Troy and perhaps proposing that her double did instead (Pl. *Phaedr.* 243a–b = fr. 192 *PMGF*; cf. Apollod. *Epit.* 3.1–5). Aeschylus's *Proteus* (the satyr play that followed the *Oresteia*) was also set in Egypt, but we know little else about this lost drama: on this play (including its possible relationship to *Helen*), see esp. Cunningham 1994; Marshall 1995 and 2014: 79–95; Sommerstein 2008: 219–22; Griffith 2015: 57–70. On how far Euripides' version of the Helen myth was new, see Wright 2005: 67, 80–113; Allan 2008: 18–22.

this play draw strongly from the parthenaic genre, with Helen cast as a displaced chorus leader caught between maidenhood and marriage.[16] Moreover, the tragedy's musical doubling draws at least in part from a traditional set of musical associations that we also see at work in archaic lyric, as well as from the tradition of Helen herself as a highly protean choral performer.

## BIRDSONG AND LAMENT

The parodos and first stasimon of *Helen* both begin with remarkable addresses to avian musical figures. As the chorus come onstage, Helen starts their responsive song by summoning them as Sirens (167–78); when the chorus next sing a strophic ode, almost a thousand lines later (1107–64), they call upon the nightingale to join their lament. Although both the Sirens and the nightingale often appear as models or comparisons for *mousikē* in archaic and classical Greek lyric, neither tends to be addressed directly: the main other example of this sort of invocation is that of the nightingale in Aristophanes' *Birds*—from which, as we shall see, Euripides probably derived the address in the first stasimon of *Helen*.[17] These addresses can be viewed as examples of the remote choral apostrophes that are particularly common in Euripides, like the address to Helen's ship in the third stasimon.[18] Here, however, I will explore how we can also understand them as invocations to characters within the play: the chorus as the Sirens; Helen as the nightingale.

The occurrence of two such unusual apostrophes to multivalent avian figures within songs of lament encourages us to view them not only in relation to each other but also within the broader pattern of bird imagery throughout the play. As we have seen, both the references to Zeus's rape of Leda in the form of a swan and the story of Helen's birth from an egg point to her protean nature as a figure who can assume different forms. References to flying and wings also suggest her own avian metamorphosis: she herself uses the metaphor of flying to indicate her delight at being reunited with Menelaus; the messenger describes her form as winged; and later Theoclymenus asks whether she escaped on wings or feet.[19] Though she never actually turns into a bird in the action of the play, she frequently seems on the verge of such a metamorphosis. Indeed, when she expresses envy of Callisto and the daughter of Merops, maidens who were turned into animals, and wishes her own beauty could have been similarly effaced (375–85), we begin to imagine her similarly transformed. But it is in the choral odes, through a succes-

---

16. Murnaghan 2013.

17. Ar. *Av.* 209–23, 676–85. Euripides' *Cresphontes* also seems to contain a second-person address to a nightingale (fr. 448a.82–86).

18. *Hel.* 1451–64. On remote choral apostrophes in Euripides, see Mastronarde 2010: 149–50.

19. ἀνεπτέρωσα, 633; ὑπόπτερον, 618; πτεροῖσιν ἀρθεῖσ' ἢ πεδοστιβεῖ ποδί; 1516. Podlecki 1970: 408 n. 23 also notes this motif.

sion of musical metamorphoses, that not only Helen but her chorus, through performing (or wishing to perform) with her, appear as birds: as Sirens, a nightingale, and finally, in the third stasimon, flying (dancing) cranes.

Such metamorphosis, combined with particular styles of musical performance, articulates Helen's position at each stage of the drama. Both the parodos and first stasimon are primarily forms of lament, which is the dominant song type in the first two-thirds of the play, mirroring Helen's plight in Egypt. The invocations to the Sirens and nightingale underscore this song type, though, as we shall see, the former also introduce a parthenaic coloring, creating a sense of musical hybridity to match Helen's own multiform nature. But these two musical figures also indicate the difference between these two points in the tragedy in terms of Helen's own position and her relationship to the chorus. The ability of the chorus to become like Sirens through joining Helen, their avian leader, in song and dance suggests their closeness to her, which also becomes clear through the responsive form of their opening lament. By the time the chorus sing the first stasimon, however, Helen has embarked upon her escape plan and no longer has need for lament. The chorus therefore sing without her, still marking their close relationship by enacting the mourning she is falsely performing offstage but also wistfully calling her back as a nightingale to lead them. As we shall see in the final part of the chapter, in the third stasimon the chorus mark the distance between themselves and their former *chorēgos* by enacting her journey back to Greece, which they can only wish in vain to join as birds to her syrinx accompaniment. But they also demonstrate a continued affinity to her by evoking through their own *choreia* the cultic dances that she will perform back in Sparta.

### The Siren Chorus

By the time the chorus enter the *orchēstra* to sing the parodos, it is clear that by far the most prominent voice of the drama, at least in its initial stages, is that of Helen herself. She delivers the opening monologue herself; in the stichomythic dialogue with Teucer that follows, she learns of Menelaus's supposed death and of the terrible reputation she holds as a result of her double, the *eidōlon* that went to Troy (68–163). Helen's vocal dominance continues into the parodos, an *amoibaion* of lament that, unusually, she begins. As we have seen, it is not uncommon for a female protagonist to perform a monody before the chorus enter with their strophic opening song: both Electra and Hecuba sing before being joined by the chorus; *Andromeda*, performed alongside *Helen*, even opens with the protagonist's song of lament. But nowhere else in surviving tragedy does an actor sing the first strophe of the parodos itself, answered by the chorus's antistrophe. Here they repeat this strophic exchange; then Helen concludes the song with the epode.[20]

---

20. On the unusual nature of this responsive parodos, see Kannicht 1969: 59; Willink 1990: 77; Burian 2007: 200; Allan 2008: 165–66; Ford 2010: 284.

With this anomalous parodos, Euripides highlights the novelty of his work, as he revolutionizes the standard structure of Athenian drama by having an actor begin the opening choral song.[21] At the same time, he grounds such novelty within the traditional imaginary of *choreia* through the character of Helen, a long-established singer and choral leader in archaic and classical Greek myth and ritual. Helen's performance of the opening and closing stanzas also stresses her close identification with the chorus, blurring the line between her roles as actor and as *chorēgos*. The metrical symmetry of this lyric exchange complements the high degree of repetitive language between the strophe and antistrophe, creating an impression of antiphonal and responsive lament shared between Helen and her chorus.[22]

But what type of lament is it? In the dactylic proode, Helen wonders about the precise nature of her song:

ὦ μεγάλων ἀχέων καταβαλλομένα μέγαν οἶκτον
ποῖον ἁμιλλαθῶ γόον ἢ τίνα μοῦσαν ἐπέλθω    (165)
δάκρυσιν ἢ θρήνοις ἢ πένθεσιν; αἰαῖ.

Oh as I begin a great lamentation for my great pains, what sort of lament should I strive for or what music [*mousa*] should I follow, with tears, or dirges, or mourning? *Aiai!* (164–66)

This sort of initial deliberation seems to have been common in formal threnody, but it may serve a further, metatheatrical purpose here, reflecting the audience's own uncertainty about the tragedy itself.[23] In this "new *Helen*," with its exotic Egyptian setting and a Helen who never went to Troy, composed by a tragedian who was increasingly experimenting with the role and form of *mousikē* in his plays, what indeed will the *mousa* (music/Muse) be?[24] As in the opening scenes of *Trojan Women*, in which the audience is left wondering whether the play's *mousa* will be choral at all, Euripides is playing here with the audience's expectations of the genre,

---

21. Cf. Marshall 2014: 27 on the parodos's untraditional elements. Euripides may be similarly experimenting with tragedy's lyric structure in *IT*, in which Iphigenia's initial three lines of song precede the parodos (if, *pace* Cropp 2000, we accept Diggle's assignment of lines 123–25 to her rather than to the chorus).

22. On the antiphonal structure of lament in the Greek tradition, see Alexiou 1974: 132–51, 158–60; Seremetakis 1990; Holst-Warhaft 1992: 45–53.

23. On this sort of threnodic opening, see Alexiou 1974: 161–65; Willink 1990: 78. On the ways the drama's structure plays with the audience's expectations of the tragic genre, see Marshall 2014: 24–45.

24. On the meaning of *mousa* here, see Dale 1967: 76; Kannicht 1969: 66; Willink 1990: 79; Allan 2008: 171; Ford 2010: 288 n. 17. Its primary meaning must be what kind of song she should adopt, but this does not exclude the secondary sense, "Muse," especially since Helen then calls upon Sirens, the Muses' chthonic counterparts, to aid her.

explicitly leaving the nature of the tragedy's music open to question until the moment it is actually performed.[25]

Still alone onstage, Helen then begins the first strophe of the parodos with an invocation to the Sirens to join her lament, bringing with them reciprocal song and musical accompaniment from Persephone in Hades:[26]

πτεροφόροι νεάνιδες,
παρθένοι Χθονὸς κόραι,
Σειρῆνες, εἴθ' ἐμοῖς
μόλοιτ' ἔχουσαι (170)
Λίβυν λωτὸν ἢ σύ- (171a)
ριγγας [ἢ φόρμιγγας] αἰλίνοις κακοῖς· (171b)
τοῖς ⟨δ'⟩ ἐμοῖσι σύνοχα δάκρυα,
πάθεσι πάθεα, μέλεσι μέλεα,
μουσεῖα θρηνήμα- (174a)
σι ξυνωιδὰ πέμψειε (174b)
Φερσέφασσα φόνια, χάριτας (175)
ἵν' ἐπὶ δάκρυσι παρ' ἐμέθεν ὑπὸ
μέλαθρα νύχια παιᾶνα
νέκυσιν ὀλομένοις λάβηι.

Winged maidens, virgin daughters of Earth, Sirens, may you come bringing the Libyan *lōtos* pipe or syrinxes [or phorminxes] to my woeful wails, and tears joined together with my tears, sufferings with sufferings, songs with songs, may Persephone send deadly concert halls singing in harmony with dirges, so that as a thanks offering she may receive from me in tears within the halls of night a paean for the perished dead. (167–78)

The chorus, who must enter while Helen is singing or just after, are imagined as Sirens, coming from Hades to provide dirges to complement and assist Helen's individual song of mourning (*goos*).[27] Helen's song in response to theirs thus becomes what Persephone will receive in turn as an offering of thanks—an offering that will be not a lament but a paean for the dead (174b–78). The appearance of

---

25. Kannicht 1969: 60 and Ford 2010: 286 both observe that Helen's question here, with its dactylic meter and metaphor of *kataballesthai* (literally, "lay down as a foundation"), resembles the proem of a kitharode, helping to focus the audience's attention on the song that follows.

26. This text follows that provided by Ford 2010: 287, which is largely based on Allan 2008, but I retain the metrically problematic [ἢ φόρμιγγας] in 171b. I follow Ford's reading in keeping πέμψειε in line 174b rather than the common emendation πέμψαιτε. (See esp. Willink 1990: 89.)

27. Barker 2007: 12–14 argues that the *thrēnēmata* of the Sirens comprise professional lamentation offered by them as expert musicians, as opposed to the individual *goos* of Helen as a family member. (Cf. Alexiou 1974: 10–14.) Such traditional practice may be hinted at here, but Helen's own mix of terminology in her proode precludes such a precise distinction. Moreover, as Swift 2010: 302–4 observes, *thrēnos* and *goos* are often used interchangeably in fifth-century tragedy (e.g., Eur. *Andr.* 92).

a paean in such a chthonic context is not unusual in tragedy;[28] it is also typical of Euripides' particular predilection for generic mixing, which we saw on display in the first stasimon of *Trojan Women*. But its effect here is to prevent any clear categorization of the nature of this musical performance and to leave the audience again wondering what sort of song will follow. And as we shall see, the parthenaic character of the chorus's antistrophe broadens the generic scope of the performance even further. In this way the play's doubleness also extends to its *mousikē*, which is multiform, just like Helen herself.

We are left in no doubt, however, of the song's antiphonal character, which is suggested even before the chorus begin their antistrophe. Helen's own repetitive, doubling language, especially in line 173 (*pathesi pathea, melesi melea*) gives the impression of some sort of musical reciprocity, as does her description of the music provided by the Siren chorus as *synocha* ("joined together with") and *xynōida* ("singing together with").[29] Such doubling, which is continued in the second strophic pair (191–228), not only draws our attention to the antiphony of this lament but also establishes a close relationship between Helen and the Sirens, performing responsively together as chorus leader and chorus.[30]

As Helen begins by framing the nature of the Sirens' song,[31] so the chorus, responding to her call, enter singing of the lament they have just heard come from Helen herself:[32]

κυανοειδὲς ἀμφ' ὕδωρ
ἔτυχον ἕλικά τ' ἀνὰ χλόαν                                                                (180)
φοίνικας ἁλίωι
πέπλους χρυσέαισιν
⟨τ' ἐν⟩ αὐγαῖσι θάλπουσ'

---

28. On tragic paeans sung to the dead (esp. Aesch. *Cho.* 149–51; Eur. *Alc.* 422–24), see Rutherford 1994–95: 119–24 and 2001: 118–20; also Swift 2010: 71–72. Rutherford stresses, *contra* Kannicht 1969: 70, that the chthonic παιᾶνα in *Hel.* 177 is not simply an oxymoron but that the song itself is a generic hybrid (1994–95: 124). Ford 2010: 290–94 suggests that, like the description of the nightingale's song in Ar. *Av.* 209–22, the transformation of Helen's song from a solo cry into a choral paean to the dead shows "a solitary outpouring of sorrow being sublimated into a fundamentally different kind of song" (293), marking Helen's own transformation from individual mourner into chorus leader. See also Murnaghan 2013: 174–75.

29. Cf. Ford 2010: 288.

30. On the song's call-and-response effect, see Marshall 2014: 102–3. Murnaghan 2013: 174 argues that the ode anticipates "Helen's restitution to her proper role as chorus leader."

31. Cf. Kannicht 1969: 67: "die Strophe ihrem Wesen nach selbst Mimesis der Sirenenklage ist."

32. This text follows Allan 2008. Ford 2010: 295 suggests an alternative translation of lines 188–89, reading a change of subject there and taking ὑπό in tmesis with ἀναβοαῖ: "and in accompaniment to the screams the rocky recesses shout aloud the marriage of Pan." This is tempting, as it suggests another level of antiphonal response, with the stony hollows also echoing the cries of the nymph/Helen. But the change of subject is awkward, and tmesis with a doubly compounded verb seems unlikely.

ἀμφὶ δόνακος ἔρνεσιν·
ἔνθεν οἰκτρὸν ὅμαδον ἔκλυον,
ἄλυρον ἔλεγον, ὅτι ποτ' ἔλακεν (185)
⟨- - ⌣⟩ αἰάγμα-
σι στένουσα νύμφα τις
οἷα Ναῒς ὄρεσι φύγδα
νόμον ἱεῖσα γοερόν, ὑπὸ δὲ
πέτρινα γύαλα κλαγγαῖσι
Πανὸς ἀναβοᾶι γάμους. (190)

Beside the dark-blue water and along the twisted grass I happened to be drying purple robes in the golden rays of the sun, by the young reed shoots; there I heard a piteous noise, a lyreless song, which she once shrieked with an *aiai* shout, a nymph groaning, just as a Naiad as she flees in the mountains sends forth a mournful strain, and within the stony hollows she cries out with screams [about] her rape by Pan. (179–90)

Such mutual framing of their lyrical performances highlights lament as the initial song type of the play and sets up its *mousikē* as reflective of the position of Helen and the chorus at each point of the dramatic plot. Helen's song is now reframed as the sort of shriek a Naiad nymph may make when chased, captured, and raped by Pan: an indistinguishable noise, not yet a song but a wail of *aiai*, which the chorus themselves shout out in the second antistrophe (211). This description comes in sharp juxtaposition with Helen's characterization of the chorus's *mousikē* as the "concert halls"[33] of Sirens accompanied by the *aulos* or syrinxes,[34] particularly given the explicit lack of any such instrumentation for her own singing as heard by the chorus. Their description of her song as "lyreless" (185) is a traditional way to denote lament,[35] but here it forms a striking contrast with the choice of instruments that could accompany their Siren song.

By the time Helen and the chorus embark upon the second strophic pair, then, they have each characterized the singing of the other in a particular way: the chorus are invited to perform as Sirens; Helen is heard as a Naiad nymph crying out at her rape. With these roles established, they progress into a full lament for Helen's sufferings, marked by the variation of twofold cries (*iō iō, aiai aiai, pheu pheu*) and by more repetitive doubling language that mirrors the metrical response, such

---

33. Not "singers" (Allan 2008: 172) nor simply "musical things" (Barker 2007: 11–12), since *mouseia*, as Dale (1967: 78) observes, is always local (as it is at *Hel.* 1108): cf. Eur. *Alcmene* fr. 88; Ar. *Ran.* 93. See also Ford 2010: 288–89.

34. Perhaps also phorminxes, if we accept the metrically superfluous ἢ φόρμιγγας in 171b. Dale (1967: 78) follows Hartung in omitting κακοῖς in 171b instead to keep the response with line 183. Cf. Kannicht 1969: 67–69.

35. Cf. *IT* 144–46. On this phrase see Kannicht 1969: 73; Allan 2008: 173.

as Helen's line "[a sailor] has come, has come [*emolen emole*], bringing tears upon tears [*dakrya dakrysi*] for me."[36]

These characterizations of musical performance in the first half of the parodos therefore draw our attention to the nature of Helen's and the chorus's song at this point in the play and also shape how we receive it. The dominant song type is lament, matching Helen's plight within the dramatic narrative, but the figures mentioned here allude to parthenaic performance too and in doing so establish Helen as a (musically) hybrid figure. By describing her like a Naiad the chorus reconfigure Helen as a *parthenos* or a new bride (*nymphē*), perhaps hinting at a link between the unwanted sexual advances of Theoclymenus and the divine abduction of a maiden. The theme of rape is then continued in the epode of the parodos, in which Helen sings of her abduction by Hermes from Sparta (245–49).[37] This parthenaic framing is further enhanced by the frequently noted parallel between the chorus's description of what they were doing when they heard the nymphlike cry (179–83) and Homer's account of the companions of Nausicaa, a maiden on the point of marriage, in the *Odyssey*.[38] The Homeric description of the girls washing the royal robes in the river before playing around the singing princess evokes a choral scenario, with Nausicaa as their *chorēgos*, distinguished among them as Artemis is among nymphs, leading their song and dance. The parallel between the two choruses suggests an identification between Nausicaa and Helen too, thereby configuring her as the chorus leader in a parthenaic performance, despite the context of lament. This musical framing both evokes the threat of Theoclymenus and prepares us for Helen's reunion with Menelaus, who will soon appear like the shipwrecked Odysseus, so unrecognizable that she will view him as a sexual predator (541–52).

The invocation to the Sirens can also be understood as a parthenaic framing of the song, the chorus, and Helen herself. The identity of these birdlike females as *parthenoi* is stressed through the tautology of Helen's opening address, when she calls them *neanides, parthenoi,* and *korai* (167–68). Sirens were traditionally associated with *partheneia*: as we saw in chapter 1, in Alcman's fragment 1 they are introduced as rival singers, but they are also a musical identity that the choreuts themselves seem to assume. They are potentially dangerous models for parthenaic performance, as Pindar's second *Partheneion* suggests: their "loud vaunt" (*kompos*) recalls the threatening knowledge and seductive power of the Odyssean Sirens, who destroy sailors through singing of "all that happens on the much-

---

36. ἔμολεν ἔμολεν δάκρυα δάκρυσί μοι φέρων, 195. See Ford 2010: 297–98 on paregmenon and anadiplosis as typical markers of lament here; also Kannicht 1969: 75.

37. Allan 2008: 173–74; Swift 2010: 225–26.

38. Hom. *Od.* 6.85–109. See Foley 2001: 306 n. 10; Burian 2007: 10–11; Ford 2010: 294; Murnaghan 2013: 174.

nourishing earth."[39] Both their destructive power of seduction and their ability to raise and silence winds (mentioned here and in the Hesiodic *Catalogue of Women*) go far beyond the parthenaic chorus's own ambit, which, they say, is "to think maiden thoughts and say them with my tongue."[40] So Sirens, though traditional models for *partheneia*, are also problematic ones, and Pindar's chorus here invoke them to demonstrate difference as well as similarity, neutralizing their threat by containing it within a proper parthenaic performance.[41]

Though the address to these creatures in Euripides' play does not reveal any explicit concern regarding their destructive aspect, it is nevertheless unsettling, since Helen does not attempt to draw any contrast between herself and them: instead she focuses on their commonality by stressing the shared nature of their *mousikē*. What does their association suggest about Helen as a character? We may see it as a subtle reminder of her own infamous—and equally destructive—powers of seduction, as well as the vocal mastery she is said to have displayed at Troy, in the *Odyssey* passage with which this chapter began. It may also point to her dangerous potential within the drama itself. Though apparently helpless here, she becomes an increasingly powerful figure through the course of the play: she later instigates the whole escape plan, tricking Theoclymenus into believing he will finally be able to marry her (1231–35) and encouraging Menelaus in the bloody slaughter of the Egyptian sailors on their ship (1589–1610).[42]

Helen's call to Persephone to send the Sirens, as if from one choral leader to another, also highlights both these singers' parthenaic identity and her own. Apollonius Rhodius records the tradition that the Sirens were the maiden Persephone/Kore's choral companions prior to her abduction by Hades, after which they apparently assumed birdlike forms;[43] their connection is confirmed by images of Sirens depicted with pomegranates found in southern Italy and mainland Greece.[44] The

---

39. ὅσσα γένηται ἐπὶ χθονὶ πουλυβοτείρηι, Hom. *Od.* 12.191. Cf. chapter 1, p. 33, on Pind. fr. 94b SM.

40. παρθενήια ... φρονεῖν / γλῶσσαί τε λέγεσθαι, Pind. fr. 94b SM, 34–35. We know of the reference to the Sirens in the *Catalogue of Women* from schol. *Od.* 12.168. On the mix of Odyssean and Hesiodic ideas here, see Stehle 1997: 96–97.

41. Referring to the mention of Sirens in Alcm. fr. 1 *PMGF*, 96–99, Bowie 2011: 51–56 suggests a threatening model of Sirens in *partheneia* due to a (hypothesized) myth complex in which they, like the Harpies, were associated with the abduction of girls ready for marriage. But although Sirens do appear as companions of Persephone at the moment of her abduction, there is no evidence that they were ever conceived of as abductors themselves.

42. Swift 2010: 224–25 sees the Sirens here as dangerous parthenaic models in terms of their perpetual maidenhood: like the Sirens, Helen has become a perennial *parthenos*, delaying her transition to sexual maturity.

43. Ap. Rhod. *Argon.* 4.898. Cf. Ovid, *Met.* 5.552; Claudian, *De Rapt. Pros.* 190. On this tradition, see Tsiafakis 2001: 19; Barker 2007: 10; Swift 2010: 225; Bowie 2011: 51.

44. On these vase depictions of Sirens with pomegranates (early sixth to mid-fifth century B.C.E.), see Tsiafakis 2001.

call to Persephone in the parodos therefore establishes a link between her and Helen as two parthenaic chorus leaders, each abducted by a god, the one to Hades and the other to Egypt. This twofold identification of the chorus and Helen with Persephone recurs in the second stasimon, when the chorus enact the parthenaic dances from which Hades snatched Kore (1312–14).[45] But in both songs the reference to Persephone/Kore points to Helen's hybrid character as both maiden and matron: Persephone as she is invoked in the parodos, as Hades' queen, is a *gynē* as well as a *parthenos*; in the second stasimon Helen is identified with both Kore and the Great Mother. The suggestion of this hybridity in the opening song points to her metamorphosis from the one to the other following the arrival of her husband, Menelaus—a metamorphosis that will set in motion the entire escape plan.[46]

As Persephone's attendants in Hades, the maiden Sirens are also chthonic, and this trait is emphasized in Helen's address to them as "virgin daughters of Earth" (168), encapsulating their joint association with maidenhood and death. Their chthonic aspect is particularly evident from how frequently they appear on gravestones from the late fifth century onward.[47] Given Helen's position by the tomb of Proteus, her call to the Sirens is therefore rather fitting, though it need not be prompted by their actual representation on the tomb, as some have suggested.[48] They are thus apt figures for lament as well as *partheneia*, seen as both sympathetic mourners and models for parthenaic song.[49] The invocation to them here captures the similarly hybrid nature of the song itself.

In a strikingly parallel context in the play performed alongside *Helen*, Andromeda also refers to the Sirens in their role as divine mourners. In a tantalizingly short fragment from her extraordinary monodic mournful prologue, which Andromeda performs just before the entrance of the chorus, she asks, "What teardrops, what Siren . . . ?"[50] In fragment 117, presumably from the same song, she then addresses the chorus as *parthenoi*. Depending on how soon they would then enter, it is possible that her reference to Sirens could indicate the chorus rather as Helen's address

---

45. On the link between Helen and Persephone in the play, see Robinson 1979: 165; Downing 1990: 2, 6; Foley 2001: 304–27; Barker 2007: 11–12; Swift 2009a and 2010: 218–38; Murnaghan 2013: 164–65. There also survives a tradition resembling the abduction of Persephone/Kore by Hades in which Helen is said to have been snatched by Theseus while dancing in a chorus (Plut. *Thes.* 31; Hellanicus *FGrH* 4 F 168a; Alcm. fr. 21 *PMGF*; see Calame 1997: 136; Bowie 2011: 46).

46. On Helen's dual status as both *parthenos* and *gynē*, and how the drama is structured around her transition from one to the other, see esp. Guépin 1968: 120–22; Foley 1992 and 2001: 325–27; Zweig 1999b: 227–30; Swift 2009a and 2010: 218–40; Murnaghan 2013.

47. See Weicker 1902: 171–72; *LIMC* s.v. "Seirenes" §4; Kannicht 1969: 67; Holford-Strevens 2006: 19; Barker 2007: 10.

48. Dale 1967: 78; Kannicht 1969: 67; also (more speculatively) Willink 1990: 78, 86.

49. Cf. Sophocles fr. 861, in which the Sirens' songs are described as "wailing the strains of Hades" (θροοῦντε τοὺς Ἅιδου νόμους). On Sirens as sympathetic female mourners, see Alexiou 1974: 102–3.

50. ποῖαι λιβάδες, ποία σειρήν, Eur. fr. 116.

does. Like the Siren chorus in *Helen*, the one in *Andromeda* enter both as *parthenoi* and as fellow mourners, whom Andromeda bids to grieve with her.[51]

Of course the mention of the Sirens in both *Andromeda* and *Helen* also helps to showcase the song that is actually being performed in the theater, since the Sirens, whatever song they sing, are renowned for their alluring, musical skill.[52] In the *Odyssey* they have the same attributes as the Muses, with their enticing song and prophetic ability;[53] later they were even said to be daughters of a Muse.[54] Their renowned musicality also led to their inclusion in the neo-Pythagorean theory of the harmony of the spheres. (Iamblichus calls the *tetraktys* "the harmony in which the Sirens reside.")[55] Plato had already adapted the Pythagorean theory in the cosmic system that Socrates describes at the end of the *Republic*, in which Sirens are positioned on the eight cosmic circles, together producing the octave scale:[56]

ἐπὶ δὲ τῶν κύκλων αὐτοῦ ἄνωθεν ἐφ' ἑκάστου βεβηκέναι Σειρῆνα συμπεριφερομένην, φωνὴν μίαν ἰεῖσαν, ἕνα τόνον· ἐκ πασῶν δὲ ὀκτὼ οὐσῶν μίαν ἁρμονίαν συμφωνεῖν.

And at the top of each of [the spindle's] circles stood a Siren, carried around together with it, emitting one voice, one pitch: and from all eight voices a single *harmonia* sounded in harmony. (Plato, *Republic* 617b4–7)

This passage also suggests a form of archetypal cosmic *choreia*, with the Sirens moving in circles, as if dancing, and together producing a single *harmonia*.[57]

When Helen addresses the dramatic chorus as Sirens, then, she frames how the audience should perceive not just the chorus's character and the generic associations of their song (as well as hers) but also the nature or quality of their *mousikē*, which is to appear as the captivating *euphonia* of the Sirens, the archetypal chorus.[58]

---

51. συνάλγησον, Eur. fr. 119.
52. On the bewitching charm (*thelxis*) of the Sirens' *mousikē*, see esp. Peponi 2012: 70–88.
53. Hom. *Od.* 12.39–54, 165–200. On the similarity between the Sirens and the Muses in the *Odyssey*, see Buschor 1944; Pucci 1979: 126–28 and 1987: 209–13; Ford 1992: 83–84; Dickson 1993: 26, 49; Doherty 1995b.
54. Their mother is Terpsichore in Ap. Rhod. *Argon.* 4.893; Melpomene in Apollod. *Bibl.* 1.3–4; Calliope in Servius *ad* Verg. *Aen.* 5.364. Muse and Siren are conflated in Alcm. fr. 30 *PMGF*.
55. Iambl. *VP* 82 (τετρακτύς· ὅπερ ἐστὶν ἡ ἁρμονία, ἐν ἧι αἱ Σειρῆνες).
56. West 1992: 224 even suggests that the eleven Sirens in Alcm. fr. 1 *PMGF* match the same number of "true and perfect notes," just as they represent the diatonic scale in Plato's *Republic*.
57. Of course if all eight notes of the scale sounded together the result would be cacophonous, but we need not then assume that "the Sirens are imagined as emitting the notes of a key or mode *in sequence*," rather than together at the same time (Halliwell 1988: 182). See Barker 1989: 58: "Though scalar *harmonia* is indeed sounded, it is not itself the celestial music, but constitutes the permanent framework... on which that music is based."
58. Steiner 2013: 177–78 argues that the Sirens' song is to be understood as a *thrēnos*, transforming Helen's *goos*, "the originary female cry of grief," into a more elaborate musical form, as Athena does with the Gorgons' cry in Pindar, *Pythian* 12. Cf. Ford 2010.

At the same time Euripides calls attention to his own music making and in doing so draws on a long tradition in Greek poetry of using the Sirens as self-reflexive musical models for both performance and composition.[59] They function in this way in both Alcman fragment 1 and Pindar fragment 94b, but above all in the *Odyssey*, in which they appear as figures whose knowledge and diction coincides with the content and style of the *Iliad* (and to a lesser extent that of the *Odyssey* itself), so that the description of their beguiling skill focuses the audience's attention on that of the epic poetry and frames their reception of the bardic performance.[60]

The invocation of the Sirens in the *Helen* parodos may also introduce a note of musical rivalry to the lyric exchange between Helen and the chorus. As we have seen, Alcman fragment 1 suggests that the Sirens are a competitive model for the performing parthenaic chorus; this aspect is recorded in myth too, in the story of a singing match between them and Muses.[61] It is tempting to see an allusion to this competitive element of the Sirens' song in the *agōn* metaphor in Helen's proode when she asks, "What sort of lament should I strive for [*hamillathō*]?" (165). This sort of imagery may be a traditional way to begin a lament or to describe the antiphonal exchange involved in such a song,[62] but by having Helen then call different singers onstage two lines later, Euripides also seems to engage with the tradition of the Sirens as musical rivals. As a result, he influences the audience's perception of Helen's musical ability as much as of the Sirens': her address to them implies that their *euphonia* is necessary for but also in competition with her own. This framing ensures not only that we see Helen as a supremely musical figure but that we view her in relation to the chorus, for the nature of this relationship evolves in tandem with her situation at each point in the drama.

The Sirens were not just models of supreme vocal skill: they were also associated with instrumental music, as Helen's request that they bring a "Libyan *lōtos* pipe or syrinxes" (171a–b) suggests. On archaic vases Sirens usually appear as more bird than human, singing and diving, but from the late sixth century they start to be represented more anthropomorphically: they have hands and often play instruments like the kithara or *aulos* in addition to (or instead of) singing.[63] They also

---

59. On the self-mirroring and metatheatrical reflection of the play's poetry, see Burnett 1971: 77–78; Downing 1990: 9; Pucci 1997: 70.

60. Cf. Pucci 1979 (= 1998: 1–10) and 1987: 209–13; Dickson 1993: 50; Doherty 1995a: 61–62 and 1995b. Helen in Hom. *Od.* 4 resembles the Sirens as a female narrator with a captivated audience, whose role merges with that of the poet himself: cf. Doherty 1995b: 86–87. Euripides develops Helen's story-making capability through her various references to the different *logoi* of her birth, and through the alternative *logos* that forms the premise of the entire play—that the "real" Helen never went to Troy.

61. As recorded in Paus. 9.34.2; Eust. *Il.* 1.135.

62. As in the parodos of Euripides' *Suppliants*: "Here comes another contest of laments answering laments" (ἀγὼν ὅδ' ἄλλος ἔρχεται γόων γόοις / διάδοχος, 71–72). Cf. Willink 1990: 79.

63. Holford-Strevens 2006: 18–19; Neils 1995: 180.

frequently appear as instrument-playing mourners on funerary monuments, indicating that by the late fifth and early fourth centuries their musical skill was associated with their chthonic presence.[64]

Helen's wish that the Sirens bring musical accompaniments with them, in addition to emphasizing their traditional musicality, may have a more specific dramatic reference too. The "Libyan *lōtos*" (171a) refers to the *aulos*, just as it does in the first stasimon of *Trojan Women*. It may then point as much to the *aulos* of the theater as it does to the common attribute of Sirens in Greek art, particularly since the aulete would probably be entering at this point with the chorus, striking up his tune as Helen begins the parodos. At the same time, the Libyan *lōtos* evokes not only the African setting but also the mythical lotus plant, which, like the Sirens, Odysseus must avoid in the *Odyssey*; in some accounts the Sirens are even conflated with the lotus, which they offer to unsuspecting men.[65] The implication here is that the music brought by the Sirens to Helen—and so also by the dramatic chorus and aulete to the audience—is meant to make its listener forgetful of cares, concentrating solely on the pleasure that it, like the lotus plant, brings. As a result, however, the allusion to the lotus suggests some danger too, perhaps implying that Helen, like those who eat this plant, may never leave this Egyptian land, performing in perpetuity a lament with her Siren chorus.

Helen's remarkable address to the Sirens therefore has several dramatic implications. On the one hand, the evocation of these supremely musical figures points to the musicality of the play itself, and to Euripides' own skill in combining different lyric genres in this self-consciously "new" tragedy. On the other hand, it heightens the musicality of both Helen and her chorus, thereby making clear the importance of her role as musical leader in the play and suggesting the possibility of her endlessly lamenting with them as a *parthenos* in Egypt—a scenario that only the arrival of Menelaus, her suitor-husband, can change. But the Sirens, whom Odysseus famously encounters on his journey back to Ithaca, are also strongly linked to the theme of *nostos* (homecoming), and in this respect they suggest the prospect of the women's return to Greece. Ironically, the Siren model fits Helen much better than the chorus, who remain stuck in Egypt: in the third stasimon, as

---

64. Neils 1995: 181. The inclusion of phorminxes in Helen's address, despite difficulties of responsion, therefore makes sense here and is not contradicted by the chorus's description of Helen's song as "lyreless" (ἄλυρος, 185: *contra* Willink 1990: 87–88; Allan 2008: 172). It is the Siren chorus, not Helen, who is to bring these lyres; more to the point, ἄλυρος is frequently used to describe lament without actually necessitating the lack of any such instrumentation. (Cf. Dale 1967: 79.) The mention of syrinxes may be more surprising here, since Sirens only rarely appear playing these in Greek art: for the few surviving examples from Etruria, southern Italy, and Cyprus, see Tsiafakis 2001: 19.

65. Lehnus 1984: 82 and Stehle 1997: 97 link the phrase αὐλίσκων ὑπὸ λωτίνων in Pind. fr. 94b SM, 14, to the mythical lotus plant. On the Egyptian origins of the lotus plant, see Hdt. 2.92.2–5, Diod. Sic. 1.34.6; on its location in the *Odyssey*, see Page 1973: 14.

we shall see, this Siren chorus can only fantasize about flying back to Greece with her. The link between the Sirens and Helen herself also prompts our expectation of her own dangerous potential, making us wonder how similar she may in fact be to the *eidōlon* that went to Troy in her place.

The invocation of the Sirens further contributes to the motif of mirror images in the play—the "protean, polytropic reality of doubling, changing and substituting shapes, fiction and appearance" that recurs throughout the tragedy and revolves around the duality of Helen and her *eidōlon*.[66] When she summons the Sirens in the parodos, Helen does not just link the chorus (and accompanying aulete) with these mythical birdlike singers: she encourages the audience to see and hear the entering chorus *as* Sirens, so that her address has a transformative, almost epiphanic effect. As Helen begins her lament by the tomb of Proteus, the archetypal figure of metamorphosis, the protean atmosphere of this Egyptian setting and of the play itself is materialized through the entrance of the chorus as both captive Greek women and Sirens. As we shall see, the chorus's own call to the nightingale at the start of the first stasimon has a similar effect, this time framing the audience's reception of Helen herself.

### The Deserted Chorus

Lament continues to be the primary song type in *Helen* for the first two-thirds of the play. Shortly after the parodos Helen further mourns both her own position (now that she believes Menelaus to be dead) and the destruction that her *eidōlon* has caused at Troy, in an astrophic lyric dialogue with the chorus that turns into a monody (330–85). The markers of lament that appeared in the parodos, like the repetitive language and exclamatory *iō*, recur in Helen's singing here, building up to her climactic image of all Greece performing a ritual lament:

> βοὰν βοὰν δ''Ελλὰς ⟨αἶ'⟩
> ἐκελάδησε ἀνοτότυξεν,
> ἐπὶ δὲ κρατὶ χέρας ἔθηκεν,
> ὄνυχι δ' ἀπαλόχροα γένυν
> ἔδευσεν φοινίαισι πλαγαῖς.

And the cry, cry the ⟨land⟩ of Greece shouted aloud [and] wailed, and put her hands on her head, and with her nails drenched her tender-skinned cheek with bloody strokes. (370–74)

Helen herself enacts this collective lament, using highly choreographic language to describe the typical gestures of mourning.[67] In doing so she becomes the personi-

---

66. Downing 1990: 5.
67. Typical, that is, in tragedy (cf., e.g., Aesch. *Cho.* 418–28; Eur. *Hec.* 652–56) and presumably in the performances of lament outlawed by Solon (Plut. *Sol.* 21).

fied Greece, able to transcend the distance between Egypt and her native land through this remarkable individual performance of *choreia*.

The close relationship between Helen and the chorus that has been established through the parodos and this lyric dialogue is further emphasized by the unusual exit of both Helen and the chorus, who leave the stage together to consult Theonoe, Theoclymenus's prophetic sister, for news of Menelaus.[68] This is the only example in surviving tragedy of a chorus's exit into the *skēnē* building, and one of only a few occasions when a chorus leave the stage in the middle of the action.[69] Their departure here allows Menelaus to enter a deserted stage, but it also underscores the extraordinarily close association between them and their *chorēgos*, Helen.

When the chorus return, they perform a brief, astrophic song (the epiparodos) reporting Theonoe's hopeful response (515–27). The spoken dialogue is again punctuated a hundred lines later by a lyric exchange, this time in the recognition *amoibaion* between Helen and Menelaus (625–97). Although this initially contains expressions of ecstatic joy upon their reunion, it also incorporates aspects of lament, particularly in the second half, when Helen responds lyrically to Menelaus's iambic trimeters. Within this performance, the frequently resolved dochmiac meter heightens the emotional intensity of her grief, as when she exclaims, "sufferings, sufferings over your house, Mother, alas!"[70] The fact that Helen now performs a lament before Menelaus, and separately from the chorus, marks the beginning of her departure from them as their leader now that she has been reunited with her husband. The context of her singing thus reflects the narrative arc of the tragedy.

This shift may partly explain the extraordinary silence of the chorus for six hundred lines and the delay of the first stasimon until the last third of the play, almost a thousand lines after the parodos.[71] As William Allan points out, the lack of *choreia* following the reunion of Menelaus and Helen allows the plot to move forward increasingly quickly and urgently as they form their escape plan, without any pause for choral reflection.[72] At the same time, since Helen and the chorus have previously been so closely united in their shared performance of lament, the absence of choral performance following Menelaus's arrival, as well as the moment of musical joy that she shares with him, reflects Helen's own movement away from

---

68. *Contra* Burian 2007: 212, who argues that the chorus leave the stage as Helen sings her monody, even though they have explicitly said that they will enter the house with her (327–28; cf. 330–34).

69. Cf. Aesch. *Eum.* 231–44; Soph. *Aj.* 814–66; Eur. *Alc.* 746–861, [*Rhes.*] 564–674. See Arnott 1973: 54; Allan 2008: 185. Marshall 2014: 29–31 suggests that Euripides uses this structural anomaly to create the effect of two plays here: following the chorus's departure, we have another prologue; their reentry then becomes another (albeit truncated) parodos.

70. τὰ δὲ ⟨σὰ⟩ κατὰ μέλαθρα πάθεα πάθεα, μᾶ- / τερ, οἴ 'γώ, 684–85.

71. Marshall 2014: 111 calculates that the chorus's silence for six hundred lines would constitute forty to sixty minutes of performance time.

72. Allan 2008: 265–66.

both the chorus and their song, anticipating her physical departure once her escape plan is put into action. When Helen next leaves the stage, she leaves the chorus to sing without her.

### Summoning the Nightingale

By the time the chorus do perform the long-delayed first stasimon (1107–64), then, the audience must be wondering what sort of song theirs will be: What will they sing after having been silent for so long? And what *mousikē* can they perform without Helen, their *chorēgos*? As it turns out, even in her absence they continue their earlier type of *choreia*, framing their song (at least initially) as a lament by calling on the "songbird full of tears" to aid their dirges (*thrēnoi*):[73]

> σὲ τὰν ἐναύλοις ὑπὸ δενδροκόμοις
> μουσεῖα καὶ θάκους ἐνί-
>   ζουσαν ἀναβοάσω,
> τὰν ἀοιδοτάταν
> ὄρνιθα μελῳδὸν
> ἀηδόνα δακρυόεσσαν, (1110)
> ἔλθ' ὦ διὰ ξουθᾶν γενύων ἐλελιζομένα
> θρήνων ἐμοὶ ξυνεργός,
> Ἑλένας μελέους πόνους
> τὸν Ἰλιάδων τ' ἀει-
>   δοῦσαι δακρυόεντα πότμον (1115)
> Ἀχαιῶν ὑπὸ λόγχαις,
> ὅτ' ἔδραμε ῥόθια πολιὰ βαρβάρωι πλάται
> ὃς ἔμολεν ἔμολε μέλεα Πριαμίδαις ἄγων
> Λακεδαίμονος ἄπο λέχεα
> σέθεν, ὦ Ἑλένα, Πάρις αἰνόγαμος (1120)
> πομπαῖσιν Ἀφροδίτας.

> You beneath your leafy-treed dens, sitting in your halls of music and on your throne, let me call upon you, the most songful bird, melodious songbird full of tears, O come trilling through your vibrant cheeks, a fellow worker of dirges with me, as I sing of the piteous travails of Helen and of the tearful fate of the Trojan women under the Achaeans' spears, when he sped over the gray sea breakers with his foreign oar, he who came, came bringing to Priam's sons his miserable bride from Lacedaemon, you, O Helen—the fatally wedded Paris, with the escort of Aphrodite. (1107–21)

The ode in part represents Helen's own offstage performance at this moment in the drama, as she pretends to mourn Menelaus's death so that Theoclymenus might let her perform the funeral rites at sea. Whereas every previous song has been domi-

---

73. I translate ἀηδών literally, "songbird," to reflect its etymological root (ἀείδειν, ἀοιδός). On the identification of ἀηδών with the nightingale, see Thompson 1936: 16–22; Arnott 2007: 1–2.

nated by her voice, here the substitution of the chorus for Helen underscores the absence of her own song onstage from this point onward in the play: the chorus now take over from her as the main singers of the tragedy, performing this lament without her as their leader and then singing two more odes in quick succession. The departure of Helen from song mirrors her impending departure from Egypt and so from the play itself, as she and Menelaus prepare to escape, leaving the chorus of captive Greek women behind to sing in her place. As the chorus envisage in the third stasimon, Helen will soon sing and dance elsewhere, in the choruses and revels (*kōmoi*) of the Leucippides and Hyacinthus in Sparta (1465–77).[74]

The remarkable similarities between this song and the chorus's earlier performance with Helen as their leader also suggest that they can in fact continue their song and dance without her physical presence among them. The address to the nightingale (the "songbird full of tears") in the first stasimon immediately establishes a reflexive correspondence between this song and the parodos: as Helen called on the Sirens to join her mourning, so the chorus call on the nightingale as their partner (*synergos*) in lament (1112). Similarities in language reinforce the sense of both continuation and mirroring between the two songs, especially between the two initial strophes, the one sung by the chorus, the other by Helen: *thrēnōn emoi xynergos* recalls Helen's description of the Sirens' tears as *tois ⟨d'⟩ emoisi synocha* (172–73) and their music as *thrēnēma- / si xynōida* (174a–b); as in the parodos, the opening strophe of the first stasimon contains polyptoton of words like *melea* (the adjective meaning "miserable" here rather than the noun "songs") and *emole* (1113, 1118). By mimicking Helen's own previous style and language of lament, the chorus seem both to replace her, acting out her false mourning while she is offstage, and to respond once again to her initial call to them in the parodos.

Andrew Barker suggests that, given the similarities between the opening lines of the parodos and first stasimon, the Sirens and nightingale are essentially copies of each other, providing another example of the theme of doubling in the play.[75] To a certain extent this is true, since both are used as paradigms of female *euphonia* in the context of lament, but the nightingale also has a separate set of musical associations that both overlap with and are independent of those of the Sirens. The complex nature of its song makes the nightingale a natural model for musical skill.[76] The length and repetitiveness of its singing may lie behind this bird's

---

74. Cf. Murnaghan 2013 on how the chorus articulate Helen's return to her role as *chorēgos* in Sparta.

75. Barker 2007: 14–15.

76. Already in the *Odyssey* we find an awareness of these different sorts of trilling sounds when Penelope describes how the nightingale "pours forth her many-toned voice, changing it frequently" (θαμὰ τρωπῶσα χέει πολυηχέα φωνήν, 19.521). This is also what Aristotle must mean by παντοδαπή and ταχεῖα when he describes the nightingale's song in the late spring (*Hist. an.* 632b24). Pliny gives the most expansive description of the bird's range of acoustic effects: its song can be "full, heavy, sharp, repeated, prolonged, ... quivering, high-pitched, medium, deep" (*plenus, gravis, acutus, creber,*

association with lament too, but it acquires this trait above all from the myth of Procne's transformation into a nightingale and her continuous mourning for her son, Itys, whose name she ceaselessly repeats.[77] Nightingales therefore frequently appear in Greek lyric to denote musicality (especially vocal skill), lament, or both:[78] so, for example, Sappho calls the bird "lovely-voiced";[79] Bacchylides refers to himself as the "honey-tongued Ceian songbird";[80] the chorus in Aeschylus's *Agamemnon* compare Cassandra's singing to the bird's endless cry of *Itys Itys*, and she responds with *iō iō*, a similar cry of lament, but rejects the comparison (1142–45);[81] in Sophocles' *Ajax* the chorus use the nightingale as a contrast, to emphasize how painfully *un*musical the sounds of mourning made by the hero's mother will be (622–34).[82]

As these examples show, the figure of the nightingale tends to frame the audience's perception of the song they are actually hearing, underlining the musicality of the poetry itself. Its use as a framing device is especially clear in the parodos of Aeschylus's *Suppliants*, when the chorus compare their own song to the nightingale's:[83]

εἰ δὲ κυρεῖ τις πέλας οἰωνοπόλων
ἔγγαιος οἶκτον ἀίων,
δοξάσει τιν' ἀκούειν ὄπα τᾶς Τηρεΐας (60)
†μήτιδος† οἰκτρᾶς ἀλόχου,
κιρκηλάτου γ' ἀηδόνος,

ἅ τ' ἀπὸ χώρων ποταμῶν τ' ἐργομένα
πενθεῖ μὲν οἶκτον ἠθέων,
ξυντίθησι δὲ παιδὸς μόρον, ὡς αὐτοφόνως (65)
ὤλετο πρὸς χειρὸς ἔθεν
δυσμάτορος κότου τυχών·

---

*extentus, ... vibrans, summus, medius, imus, HN* 10.81). On archaic and classical Greek perceptions of nightingales, see Nagy 1996: 7–38; Suksi 2001: 646–53; Barker 2004: 187–91; also Arnott 2007: 2; Weiss 2017.

77. Both Aristotle and Pliny emphasize the continuous nature of the bird's singing, claiming it sings nonstop for fifteen days and nights (Ar. *Hist. an.* 632b21; Plin. *HN* 10.81). The variant reading of πολυδευκέα at Hom. *Od.* 19.521 may also suggest the continuity of the bird's song (and that of the poet's own song making): Nagy 1996: 43–53.

78. Cf. Suksi 2001: 649–50.

79. ἰμερόφωνος, Sappho fr. 136 Voigt.

80. μελιγλώσσου ... / Κηΐας ἀηδόνος, Bacchyl. 3.98.

81. We find similar wordplay in Aristophanes' *Birds*, where the cries of ἰὼ ἰώ, ἴτω ἴτω, and ἰοὺ ἰού are used to mimic birdsong (*Av.* 228–29, 343, 820, 857, 1170). Cf. Rutherford 1995: 42–43.

82. Sophocles was the first to dramatize Procne's transformation into a nightingale in his *Tereus*: see Suksi 2001: 646–47. The nightingale also appears as a figure of musicality and lament at Soph. *El.* 107, 145–52; *OC* 18, 671–77; and *Trach.* 966: see Suksi 2001: 651–57.

83. I follow Sommerstein 2008a in reading νόμοισι ("tunes") rather than νομοῖσι "pastures") in line 69.

τὼς καὶ ἐγὼ φιλόδυρτος Ἰαονίοισι νόμοισι
δάπτω τὰν ἁπαλὰν Νειλοθερῆ παρειὰν (70)
ἀπειρόδακρύν τε καρδίαν.

But if there happens to be any bird-divining native nearby who hears our piteous cry, he'll think he's listening to the voice of †Metis†, Tereus's pitiful wife, the hawk-chased songbird, who, shut away from lands and rivers, laments piteously for her accustomed haunts, and composes the tale of her son's doom, how he died, killed by her own hand, encountering the rage of an unhappy mother. So I too, devoted to lamentation with Ionian tunes, tear my soft cheek, tanned by the Nile's sun, and my heart, inexperienced in tears. (58–71).

Here the chorus explicitly shape their audience's auditory reception of their performance, imagining that whoever is overhearing their song would think he is listening to that of the nightingale. As Gregory Nagy has shown, the use of the verb *xyntithēsi* ("composes") exemplifies how the nightingale also symbolizes the poet's act of composition, not just the performance.[84] By describing and reperforming the content of the bird's lament (63–67), the chorus then merge the two songs completely, so that the one virtually becomes the other, and as a result they create a heightened experience of their own euphonic lamentation. Avian imagery recurs elsewhere in the play too, in the chorus's later wishes to be able to fly away (392–95, 779–83, 792–99), just as in the third stasimon of *Helen* the chorus wish they could escape as cranes from Egypt to Greece (1478–94); but it is only with the extended comparison of the lamenting nightingale that the two identities, chorus and bird, can actually merge into one.[85]

Euripides makes use of the nightingale's association with skillful song and lament for similarly self-reflexive effects, as we can see in two of his fragmentary plays, *Cresphontes* and *Phaethon*.[86] The parodos of *Cresphontes* contains the only other example in extant tragedy of a direct address to a nightingale, as the chorus of old Messenians call on Procne as a comparison for their own plaintive song:[87]

φεῦ φεῦ· ὦ γῆρας· ὦ πα . δι . [
τάλα[ι]να [ . . . . . . ].ιμως πτερού[σ]σα
ἀείδο[υσ . . . .μέ]λη φιλοπροσωιδ[ί]αι

84. Nagy 1996: 15–16.
85. Cf. Rutherford 1995 on *POxy.* 2625 = *SLG* 460, where a reference to a nightingale is followed by the unusual choral refrain ἴτω ἴτω χορός. Reminiscent of Procne's repetitive lament of Ἴτυν Ἴτυν, this indicates a merging of birdsong and human song, even offering "an ornithological aetiology for processional song, and for song in general" (43).
86. See also Eur. *Hec.* 337–38, *Her.* 1021–22, *Tro.* 146–47, *Pho.* 1515–18, *Oed.* fr. 556, *Pal.* fr. 588; [*Rhes.*] 546–50.
87. The translation below is adapted from Collard and Cropp 2008a, following emendations by Haslam (ὦ Πανδίο[νος] τάλα[ι]να [παῖς, 82–83; [φωνᾶι τ' ἐπι]στρέφει, 85) and Bonnycastle-Koenen (ἀείδο[υσ' ὀξέα μέ]λη, 84).

ἀλεᾶι [ . . . . . . . . . ]στρεφει παρα[ ἀπο-  (85)
ζυγεῖ[σα .. παιδ]ὸς οὗ πόθωι στ[έ]νει(ς)·

*Pheu pheu*! O old age, O wretched [daughter of Pandion?] . . . feathered, sing[ing your shrill songs?] with futile fondness for modulation [and?] twisting [voice?] separated from your son, in longing for whom you groan. (fr. 448a.82–86)

The language used to describe the nightingale's song, with the remarkable hapax *philoprosōidiai* ("fondness for modulation")[88] and the adjective concerning twisting or turning (]*strephei*), stresses its complexity. It would thereby emphasize and augment the chorus's own performance (whether or not they likewise varied their pitch) and perhaps also their auletic accompaniment.[89]

The chorus of *Phaethon* also evoke the nightingale's song in the opening strophe of their parodos:[90]

ἤδη μὲν ἀρτιφανὴς
  Ἀὼς ἱ[ππεύει] κατὰ γᾶν,  (20)
ὑπὲρ δ᾽ ἐμᾶς κεφαλᾶς
Πλειά[δων πέφευγε χορός],
μέλπει δὲ δένδρεσι λεπ-
  τὰν ἀηδὼν ἁρμονίαν
ὀρθρευομένα γόοις  (25)
  Ἴτυν Ἴτυν πολύθρηνον.

Already Dawn, just appearing, [drives her chariot] over the earth, and above my head [the chorus of the] Pleiades [has fled], and the songbird sings in the trees her subtle mode, awake before dawn, much-wailing with her lament, "Itys, Itys." (fr. 773.19–26)

The appearance of the nightingale here demonstrates how the bird's association with lament can affect the audience's understanding of the surrounding narrative. On the one hand, it vividly establishes the temporal setting of the action, at dawn on the day of Phaethon's marriage, in part through the merging of the "subtle mode" of the nightingale's song with that of the chorus; a similar effect may arise from the reference to the Pleiades, a star chorus with whom the dramatic one can momentarily coincide. On the other hand, the description of the nightingale and her mournful cry for Itys, like that of the swan's song in the following antistrophe (32–33), also introduces an ominous strain of lament to a song that the chorus later

---

88. For the translation of *prosōidia* as "modulation" or "changing pitches," see *LSJ* s.v. 2.1; cf. Pl. *Rep.* 399a8.

89. Such a focus on modulatory style seems typical of the New Musicians (see esp. Franklin 2013: 229–31), but this is a relatively early example of highly metamusical language in Euripidean tragedy—at least if we accept Collard and Cropp's dating of *Cresphontes* to the mid-420s (2008a: 495).

90. In line 22 I give the supplement suggested by Diggle 1970.

claim to be a *hymenaios* (51-58)[91] and encourages identification between Procne and Phaethon's mother, Clymene, who will soon be mourning her son too.[92]

In *Helen* Euripides likewise draws on the nightingale's traditional association with extreme musicality and, as in *Phaethon,* uses her as a double for a character in the play—in this case Helen herself, the virtuoso musician who is now pretending to mourn for her husband. Like the Sirens, the nightingale both marks the generic type of the chorus's song (and Helen's offstage) and draws attention to the musicality of their performance. Although the chorus describe her as "tearful" and their "fellow worker in dirges" (1110, 1112), they above all emphasize the bird's musical skill.[93] Even the bird's home is pictured as full of music, as the chorus imagine her sitting in her "concert hall" (1108)—and in so doing they further link her with the Sirens by recalling Helen's use of the same word (*mouseia*) in the parodos (174a). They then address her not only as "melodious" (1109) but with the rare superlative "most songful" (*aoidotatan,* 1108);[94] they follow this description with the songbird herself (*aēdona*), thereby stressing the common root of the verb "to sing" (*aeidein*). In line 1111 they turn to her modulating style of singing with the phrase "trilling through your vibrant cheeks." The adjective *xouthos* ("vibrant"), which denotes not only color but also sound or rapid movement or both, suggests the acoustic as well as visual appearance of the bird, just as it does when the chorus in Aeschylus's *Agamemnon* compare Cassandra to "a vibrant songbird."[95] With the doubled *el-* sound, the onomatopoeic participle *elelizomena,* translated here as "trilling" but more literally denoting quivering like that of a lyre's strings, suggests both the bird's characteristic modulation and the repetitiveness of its song, and this moment of verbal mimicry links the chorus's own musical effects with those produced by the nightingale itself.[96]

Instead of proceeding to reproduce the content of the absent nightingale's song, however, the chorus call on her to join them as a partner (*xynergos*) in their own lament, to sing the same song together. Although, as we shall see, this motif is partly derived from Tereus's address to the nightingale as "my fellow singer" (*synnome moi*) in Aristophanes' *Birds*, such doubling of bird and dramatic singer,

---

91. See chapter 2, p. 64, on the association of swan song with lament.
92. Cf. Barlow 1971: 24 on the ode's ironic tone.
93. See Pucci 1997: 70-71 on the nightingale as a musical icon.
94. Cf. Theoc. *Id.* 12.6-7. On this superlative, see Allan 2008: 272.
95. τις ξουθά ... ἀηδών, Aesch. *Ag.* 1142-45. See Dunbar 1995: 206; Allan 2008: 272. ξουθός is used similarly in Aristophanes' *Birds* (214, 676).
96. Cf. Ar. *Av.* 213. (See below, pp. 165-66.) The same verb appears in an avian context in Euripides' *Phoenician Women* when Antigone asks whether any bird might mourn with her, ὡς ἐλελίζω (1514); but the primary meaning of the active form here may instead be "utter a shrill, mournful cry [ἐλελεῦ]": see Mastronarde 1994: 571-72. On the meaning of ἐλελιζομένη in Ar. *Av.* 213 and Eur. *Hel.* 1111, see Dunbar 1995: 204-5.

whereby the one is invoked to sing with the other the lament that then follows, is unparalleled.⁹⁷ The transference of singing (*aeidein*) from the "the most songful songbird" (*aoidotata aēdōn*) to the chorus (*aei- / dousai*, 1114–15) completes the union of nightingale and chorus in the lament over the sufferings of Helen and Trojan women.⁹⁸

Given the epiphanic nature of Helen's invocation to the Siren chorus in the parodos, we may expect the unusual apostrophe to the nightingale in the first stasimon also to result in this musical figure somehow becoming manifest onstage. Of course, as Pietro Pucci reminds us, the appeal here is metaphorical, but, just like the one to the Sirens, it could do more than function as "a mere verbal, musical icon" and instead pertain to a character within the play itself.⁹⁹ That character must be Helen, who until this point has been the chorus's leader and lamenter par excellence, and whose own *logos* of avian birth may encourage the audience more readily to identify her with the bird. The prominent use of the second-person pronoun *se* as the very first word of the ode strengthens this impression: as Helen has just exited after giving final instructions to Menelaus regarding their escape plan, this "you" seems to refer as much to her as to the imagined nightingale.¹⁰⁰ By the end of the first strophe the second-person apostrophe really is directed at Helen herself, and a similar address follows in the second strophe and antistrophe.¹⁰¹ The lamenting nightingale is thus embodied by and transformed into Helen, who, though she does not enter during the chorus's song, comes onstage again immediately afterward, this time with Theoclymenus and in mourning attire, physically transformed from when the audience saw her last. Just as the chorus momentarily became Sirens, so Helen merges with her own musical double, the nightingale and thus still seems to participate in the women's *choreia* even as she is separated from it. At the same time, the fact that she does *not* immediately appear underlines the disunion between Helen and the chorus now that her escape plan has been put into action. About to flee Egypt and leave her Greek chorus there behind, Helen

---

97. Ar. *Av.* 209. The apostrophe to the nightingale in *Helen* is not the first instance of an invocation to a nightingale to appear onstage, as Pucci 1997: 70–71 claims that it is: in Aristophanes' *Birds* Tereus tells the nightingale to come (ἄγε, 209), and she really does physically appear in response at 667; the sound of the *aulos* from the point when Tereus addresses her is probably also meant to represent her (Romer 1983; Barker 2004).

98. Ford 2010: 299 suggests that the metrical division of ἀει- / δοῦσαι across a line break indicates "the endlessness ["ever," *aei*] of her [the nightingale's] song." The participle actually applies to the chorus's song, but the sharing of musical traits between them and this avian model must be deliberate.

99. Pucci 1997: 71.

100. Cf. Marshall 2014: 112: "There is . . . a deliberate blurring of imagery, as Helen, the subject of the song, becomes its (absent) addressee." Ford 2010: 284 also notes that the chorus's invocation of the nightingale offers "a natural prototype for Helen as leader of a mourning chorus."

101. σέθεν, ὦ Ἑλένα (1120); σὺ Διὸς ἔφυς, ὦ Ἑλένα (1144); σὰν ἔριν, ὦ Ἑλένα (1160).

now has less cause to produce her own genuine lament, and so for the first time in the play the chorus must sing without her.

The identification between Helen and the nightingale also marks a transition in Helen's characterization between the parodos and first stasimon. The earlier framing of the chorus as Sirens denoted a parthenaic performance while they heard her cry out as a maiden Naiad nymph, but now the chorus imagine Helen as an archetypal *mater dolorosa*, emphasizing her matron role instead. This aspect of Helen is highlighted again in the second stasimon through the figure of the Great Mother, who, like the nightingale, laments for the loss of her child—though this identification is combined with a parthenaic one, through Helen's association with Persephone/Kore. In the third stasimon too her roles as parthenaic choral leader and mother are simultaneously emphasized as the chorus imagine her back in Sparta, dancing in honor of the Leucippides and Hyacinthus, and being reunited with her daughter, Hermione.

Those members of the Athenian audience who remembered the summoning of the nightingale in Aristophanes' *Birds* two years earlier would have been especially likely to link her with a soon-to-appear female character within the play itself.[102] It has often been noted that line 1111 of *Helen* ("trilling through your vibrant cheeks") recalls Tereus's invocation to the nightingale, in which he describes her production of song with very similar language (presumably echoing in turn Sophocles' *Tereus*, which was produced sometime before Aristophanes' play):[103]

> ἄγε σύννομέ μοι, παῦσαι μὲν ὕπνου,
> λῦσον δὲ νόμους ἱερῶν ὕμνων,                                    (210)
> οὓς διὰ θείου στόματος θρηνεῖς
> τὸν ἐμὸν καὶ σὸν πολύδακρυν Ἴτυν,
> ἐλελιζομένη διεροῖς μέλεσιν
> γένυος ξουθῆς.

> Come, my fellow singer, stop your sleep, and loosen the strains of your holy hymns, which through your divine mouth you give as a lament for my and your much-bewept Itys, trilling with liquid melodies from your vibrant cheeks. (Ar. *Av.* 209–14)

Two years later, Euripides uses the same onomatopoeic participle, *elelizomenē* ("trilling," *Hel.* 1111), to describe the nightingale and combines the expressions "through your divine mouth" (Ar. *Av.* 211) and "from your vibrant cheeks" (214) from Aristophanes' play in "through your vibrant cheeks" in *Helen*. As we have seen, the vocative *synnome* ("fellow singer," 209), used of Procne in *Birds*, also

---

102. On the question to what extent the Athenian audiences could be expected to appreciate the interconnectivity of different plays, see Revermann 2006b, esp. 115–20.

103. Fraenkel 1950: 175–77; Dover 1972: 148–49; Dunbar 1995: 205; Corbel-Morana 2004; Allan 2008: 272; Marshall 2014: 213. The date of Sophocles' *Tereus* is unknown, but we can assume it was produced before Aristophanes' *Birds* on the basis of Tereus's complaint in the latter about Sophocles' treatment of him (*Av.* 100–101).

resembles the epithet *xynergos* ("fellow worker," Eur. *Hel.* 1112) in the first stasimon of *Helen*, as well as the adjectives *synocha* ("joined together with," 172) and *xynōida* ("singing together with," 174b) used of the Sirens' music in the parodos.[104] It is possible that Euripides was also influenced by Sophocles' *Tereus*, of which only a handful of fragments survive. But the striking parallels between the first stasimon of *Helen* and Aristophanes' *Birds* indicate that the tragedian at least partly modeled the beginning of his first stasimon on Tereus's invocation in the comedy.

One more passage from *Birds* provides an intertext for the invocation of the nightingale in Euripides' play. Later in the comedy, once Procne is physically present onstage, she is addressed again, this time by the bird chorus:

ὦ φίλη, ὦ ξουθή, (676)
ὦ φίλτατον ὀρνέων,
πάντων ξύννομε τῶν ἐμῶν
ὕμνων, ξύντροφ' ἀηδοῖ,
ἦλθες, ἦλθες, ὤφθης, (680)
ἡδὺν φθόγγον ἐμοὶ φέρουσ'·
ἀλλ', ὦ καλλιβόαν κρέκουσ'
αὐλὸν φθέγμασιν ἠρινοῖς,
ἄρχου τῶν ἀναπαίστων.

O dear, O vibrant one, O dearest of all the birds, fellow singer of my songs, O my companion songbird, you've come, you've come, you're here to be seen, bringing sweet sound to me. But, O you who weave the fair-toned *aulos* with springtime voices, begin the anapaests! (676–84)

This song is notable for the way in which it emphasizes the nightingale's presence onstage, both with the repeated "with" (*syn-*) epithets denoting her companionship with them (as in *Helen*'s first stasimon) and with the repetition of "you've come" followed by the epiphanic "you're here to be seen" in line 680. In *Birds* the nightingale is therefore not merely called upon metaphorically or mentioned as an imagined figure offstage: rather, she is a character who enters just before this choral song and has most likely already been audibly present through the sound of the *aulos* from the moment when Tereus summons her.[105] So at least some of the audience of *Helen*, recalling the appearance of this avian *aulētris* in *Birds*, would be ready to understand the nightingale not only as a metaphor for song but also as a female character within the play who will (re)enter shortly afterward. It is unclear if Euripides could have intended or expected his audience to pick up on any further implications in the link between the famously attractive Helen and the prostitute *aulētris* of *Birds* here, but certainly the correspondence is amusing and

---

104. σύννομος at Ar. *Av.* 209 means both "marriage-partner" and "partner in melody" (Dunbar 1995: 203–4).

105. On the nightingale as aulete, see Romer 1983 (esp. 138); Barker 2004.

unflattering. At the same time, the association between the nightingale and the sound of the *aulos* in Aristophanes' play may encourage the audience of Euripides' *Helen* to imagine that they are already hearing the trilling bird in the auletic accompaniment to the chorus's song, even if she has not yet appeared onstage.[106]

The allusion to Aristophanes' *Birds* in *Helen*'s first stasimon is also significant for how it frames the chorus's relationship to Helen as their choral leader. In both addresses to the nightingale this bird is presented as an initiator of *choreia*: in his invocation to her, Tereus goes on to describe how in response to her song Apollo picks up his phorminx and starts leading choruses of the gods, who then start singing themselves (*Av.* 217–22); when the bird chorus later address her in person, they emphasize their own closeness to and reliance upon the nightingale, whom they ask to start up their anapaests (684). As we have seen, in Euripides' play Helen is similarly presented as chorus leader, especially in relation to the Siren chorus in the parodos. Through calling on the nightingale, the chorus call on her to lead their lament, just as she did in the parodos; they also simultaneously perform the nightingale's song themselves, enacting Helen's own false mourning offstage. But, though she does come back onstage after their song, Helen is no longer their *chorēgos* and will soon leave them to sing and dance in Sparta instead.

## NEW MUSIC

Following the first stasimon—and in contrast with their earlier silence—the chorus perform two more songs in quick succession, producing a flurry of *choreia* in the last third of the play. This extended burst of *choreia* both complements the suddenly fast-moving action as Helen and Menelaus engineer their escape plan and also indicates the chorus's increasing separation from it, as their leader arranges to leave without them. The second stasimon, the relevance of which within the surrounding drama has vexed so many scholars, encapsulates this combination of dramatic movement and choral distance.[107] Unlike their previous songs in the play,

---

106. The link between the nightingale and the *aulos* may have been traditional; it is also suggested in Eur. *Oed.* fr. 556, where the reeds of the river Melas in Boeotia are described as "the skillful nightingale of sweetly-blown *auloi*" (ἀηδόν' εὐπνόων αὐλῶν σοφήν). Pliny makes a similar connection, remarking that "in such a little throat are all the things which human skill has devised in the exquisite mechanisms of the pipes" ("omnia tam parvulis in faucibus, quae tot exquisitis tibiarum tormentis ars hominum excogitavit," *HN* 10.82).

107. E.g., Golann 1945; Burnett 1960: 155–56; Kannicht 1969: 327–59; Wolff 1973: 70–74; Rehm 1996: 57–58; Burian 2007: 270; Allan 2008: 292–95, 305–7, 309–10; Swift 2009a and 2010: 229–40. Many of these interpretations link the narration of the Great Mother's search for her daughter and eventual appeasement to the play's overarching *anodos* pattern and to Helen's own dual status within the drama and cult as both *parthenos* and *gynē*. Cf. Guépin 1968: 120–22 and Foley 1992 on *anodos* dramas; Zweig 1999b: 227–30 and Foley 2001: 325–27 on motifs of female rites of passage in the play.

which focus more directly on Helen's circumstances and are generically framed as laments, here the chorus sing a narrative ode recounting the search of the Great Mother (Cybele, who is syncretized with Demeter) for her daughter, Kore (Persephone).[108] As I will argue here, this change in *mousikē*, which continues into the third stasimon, heralds a corresponding shift toward the positive resolution of the dramatic plot.

On the one hand, the second stasimon has often been regarded as emblematic of Euripides' supposed *embolima* odes—a self-contained narrative lacking any integration within the dramatic narrative and a typical example of Kranz's dithyrambic choral stasima.[109] On the other hand, as we shall see, through this story of crisis and grief resulting in a happy resolution the ode enacts the positive shift in the surrounding *mythos*, in which Helen and a disguised Menelaus have just persuaded Theoclymenus to let them perform funeral rites at sea, thus contriving a way for them to escape from Egypt (1186–1300). Such correspondence between the narrative of the stasimon and the action of the play is highlighted through how the Great Mother, like the nightingale, resembles Helen as a *mater dolorosa*. The song also marks a corresponding change in the dominant *mousikē* of the play, which from this moment ceases to involve any markers of lament. The story of the calming of the Great Mother's frenzied grief enacts this change in the play overall as new, pleasing forms of music replace the discordant sounds described at the start of the ode. This song is therefore both intricately related to the surrounding drama and, like the chorus themselves at this point in the play, removed from it.

One of the most striking aspects of the second stasimon—and one of the reasons why it has seemed so dithyrambic—is the extraordinary abundance of musical images that it contains, from the roaring *krotala* (an instrument like slapsticks or castanets) during the Great Mother's search, the dancing and playing of the *tympana* (hand drums) and *aulos* that coincide with her appeasement, to the whirling *rhombos* spun in worship of the goddess and Dionysus.[110] Like the images of the Sirens and nightingale in the play's previous stasima, this focus on musical-

---

108. On the syncretism of the Great Mother and Demeter in fifth-century Athenian cult and beyond, see Parker 1996: 188–89 (esp. n. 134) and 2005: 344–45; Roller 1996: 312–13 and 1999: 174–76; Allan 2004: 143–46; Currie 2005: 394–96. Pucci 1997: 72 relates the syncretism of the two goddesses in *Helen*'s third stasimon to the theme of doubling in the play as a whole.

109. On the ode as an *embolimon*, see Decharme 1906: 314–15; Kranz 1933: 254; Golann 1945: 31–32; Dale 1967: xiii, 147; Kannicht 1969: 334–35; Whitman 1974: 64; Burian 2007: 270; Allan 2008: 40, 293–94; Mastronarde 2010: 141; Nikolaidou-Arabatzi 2015: 43–46. For an analysis of its dithyrambic character, see Battezzato 2013; cf. Panagl 1971: 140–64.

110. Panagl 1971: 140–64 also highlights the auditory richness of this ode; cf. Barker 2007: 15–20; Ford 2010: 300. On the syncretism of the Great Mother and Dionysus, for which the earliest surviving evidence is Pind. fr. 70b SM, 8–11, see Roller 1996: 313–16; Summers 1996: 351–53; Allan 2004: 131, 141–42.

ity reflects and intensifies both the chorus's own performance and the tragedian's skill, perhaps also drawing attention to Euripides' engagement with New Musical trends. The story of how music achieved the appeasement of the Great Mother therefore not only provides an aetiology for the inclusion of particular instruments within her cult (the *krotala, kymbala, tympanon,* and *aulos*), which is syncretized with the rites of both Demeter and Dionysus, but also functions as a sort of *aition* for the Dionysiac performance of the singing and dancing chorus of Athenian citizens in the *orchēstra*.[111] This is not to say, however, that the relevance of the ode therefore lies entirely beyond its immediate dramatic context: on the contrary, its musicality reflects and intensifies the positive shift away from lament as Helen and Menelaus start to engineer their escape.

The first strophe begins with an emphasis on swift and urgent movement, as the Great Mother frantically searches for her abducted daughter:[112]

ὀρεία ποτὲ δρομάδι κώ-
  λωι Μάτηρ ἐσύθη θεῶν
ἀν' ὑλᾶντα νάπη
ποτάμιόν τε χεῦμ' ὑδάτων
βαρύβρομόν τε κῦμ' ἅλιον                                      (1305)
πόθωι τᾶς ἀποιχομένας
ἀρρήτου κούρας.
κρόταλα δὲ βρόμια διαπρύσιον
ἱέντα κέλαδον ἀνεβόα,
θηρῶν ὅτε ζυγίους                                             (1310)
ζεύξασα θεὰ σατίνας
τὰν ἁρπασθεῖσαν κυκλίων
χορῶν ἔξω παρθενίων
κούραν ⟨- × - ⏑⏑ -⟩
μετὰ δ' ⟨ἤιξαν⟩ ἀελλόποδες,
ἃ μὲν τόξοις Ἄρτεμις, ἃ δ'                                    (1315)
ἔγχει Γοργῶπις πάνοπλος,
αὐγάζων ἐξ οὐρανίων
⟨Ζεὺς ὁ παντόπτας ἑδράνων⟩
ἄλλαν μοῖραν ἔκραινεν.

The mountain Mother of the Gods once with running foot rushed along the wooded glens and the river stream of waters and the deep-roaring breaker of the sea in longing for her absent daughter whose name is never spoken. And the roaring castanets [*krotala*], sending forth their piercing din, cried out, when she had yoked her chariot to a team of wild beasts and ⟨rushed off to save?⟩ her daughter, who'd been seized from the circling dances of maidens; after her ⟨darted⟩ storm-footed Artemis with

---

111. Cf. Downing 1990: 12: "the Mountain Mother ode yields an aetiology for choral celebration."
112. The text here follows Allan 2008.

her bows and the Grim-eyed One, fully armed with her spear. But seeing clearly from his heavenly ⟨seat, all-seeing Zeus⟩ brought about a different fate. (1301–18)

The opening image of the Great Mother rushing on running feet (1301–2) is enhanced by the resolution of the glyconic colon in the first line: the meaning of the adjective *dromadi* ("running") is matched by the speed at which the syllables must be sung; the word *kōlon*, here translated "foot," may be meant to point our attention toward this metrical effect. These initial two lines are self-referential too, pointing the audience's attention toward the fast-moving feet of the dancing chorus and assimilating the choral performance they are seeing in the *orchēstra* with the goddess's movement described in the song. When Artemis and Athena start to join the Great Mother in her quest, before they are even mentioned by name the speed of their feet is highlighted through the adjective "storm-footed" (1314), a high-lyric epithet that stresses the raw energy of this motion.[113] It may also deliberately suggest a confusion of environment and choreography, merging the storm implied by the gushing streams of water and the deep-roaring sea (1304–5) with the goddesses' movement through the air—and so also with the chorus's own dancing. The only vision we have of more orderly movement is the reference to the circular parthenaic dances from which Kore was snatched away, which again could correspond with the dramatic chorus's own choreographic formation; yet that dancing was in the past, at the moment when Kore was seized in the first place.[114]

This first strophe is also full of disturbing sound—an unsettling mix of vocal, instrumental, and environmental noises.[115] The "deep-roaring" (*barybromon*) breaker of the sea (1305) is followed by the roaring (*bromia*) *krotala* (1308), so that the two sounds—sea and percussion—blend together into a polyphonic confusion of acoustic images. Adjectives of the *brom-* root may seem more apt for the thundering of the sea, but the short, clattering sound produced by *krotala* (whether made of wood, bone, or bronze) could also resemble the clap of thunder;[116] the

---

113. Cf. *Hymn. Hom. Ven.* 217; Simon. fr. 10 *PMG*; Pind. *Pyth.* 4.18, *Nem.* 1.6, fr. 221 SM. The equine associations of this epithet, in addition to the metaphorical meaning of *aella* as "whirling," suggest that the maiden goddesses Artemis and Athena are even dancing: see chapter 1, pp. 29–30, on the association of horses with *choreia* (especially in *partheneia*).

114. The lightening of the rhythm through the choriamb in line 1312 after five long syllables, contrasting with the rushed movement elsewhere in the strophe, may also suggest the happier nature of the parthenaic dancing.

115. On sound as disturbance in Greek poetry, see Gurd 2016.

116. On the material from which *krotala* could be made and the type of noise they could produce, see Barker 1984: 76 n. 89; Mathiesen 1999: 163; Sadie 2001: 6.727; Allan 2008: 300. West 1992: 123, 125, distinguishes between *krotala* made of wood and those of bronze: the former were used in "popular, festive music-making . . . not in the theatre, in professional contests, or in cult" (123). But the description of the *krotala* in *Helen*'s second stasimon could encompass both the higher-pitched clashing of bronze "cymbal clappers" (125) and the clattering noise of wood or bone being knocked

description of them as *bromia* here suggests a merging of elemental and instrumental noise. The entirely resolved rhythm of line 1308 also conveys their clapping sound—a percussive effect that is sharply juxtaposed with the five long syllables in the previous line, and with the silent absence of the girl whose name cannot be spoken (1306–7).[117] The *krotala* and the *bromos* sound were also associated with the orgiastic rites of Cybele and with the frenzied celebration for both her and Dionysus,[118] whose title *Bromios* ("Roarer") appears in the final antistrophe (1365) and is also suggested by the repetition of *brom-* root words in the first strophe. As a result, the ode acts as an *aition* for the goddess's cultic *mousikē* from the start, not just in the description in the second strophe of her musical appeasement.

The sound picture of the *krotala* is also an uncomfortably mixed one of acoustic vocabulary piled up together. In addition to being described as "roaring," they are simultaneously producing a piercingly loud noise (1308–9). The adjective "piercing" (*diaprysion*) seems more appropriate for the effect of the *aulos*, the one instrument that (so far as we know) was actually played in accompaniment to the choral song. Imagined music (the *krotala*) can thus merge with and intensify what the audience would actually be hearing in the theater, despite the difference between the actual sounds of the two instruments.[119] The *krotala* are also shouting (1309), as if they themselves are crying for help, emitting a vocal, not just percussive, sound. Of course the clattering noise of the *krotala* is in part being produced by the rhythm of a purely human voice (as well as the chorus's hand clapping and foot stamping, presumably), so it is tempting to see here some self-referential commentary, as the chorus refer to their own ability to verbally conjure up instrumental sound. With such mingling of different pitches and timbres of sounds—elemental, instrumental, and vocal—Euripides displays his ability to use the human voice to

---

together. Rather than interpreting the reference to *krotala* in the *Helen* ode as a precise indication of a particular sort of instrument and the sound it produced, we should see it as an expression of a richly mixed sound experience.

117. Cf. Kannicht 1969: 337 on the series of short syllables in line 1308: "sind eine Periode und ersichtlich als metrische Darstellung des Geklappers der Korala zu fassen." Allan 2008: 300 also notes this "striking concatenation of sound words, with the fervent striking of the instruments expressed in the resolved iambic dimeters." This percussive sound effect may also draw attention to the chorus's dancing: according to Athenaeus (14.636c3–d3) *krotala*, like the closely related *krembala*, were used to produce rhythmical sound to accompany dancers; in vase painting they are also associated with dance movement. See Peponi 2009: 49–55.

118. Cf. *Hymn. Hom.* 14.3. On the playing of *krotala* for Dionysus as well as Cybele, see Pind. fr. 70b SM, 8–11, and Eur. *Cycl.* 205. See also Roller 1996: 308; Mathiesen 1999: 164–65; Sadie 2001: 6.727, 797.

119. There is no reason why the chorus may not at this point play *krotala* as they dance (or at least hold them as a visual prop), just as celebrants would in the rites of the Great Mother. If so, their description of the instrument would magnify the audience's reception of the sound actually being produced in the theater. But the dominant instrumental sound would still be that of the *aulos*.

represent a whole variety of noise, to represent even what seems to be unrepresentable.[120]

Such polyphonic confusion seems to have been a traditional element of the cult of the Great Mother. In the *Homeric Hymn to the Mother of the Gods* a multilayered sound picture is created through the description not only of instrumental noise (*krotala, tympana,* and *auloi*) but also of animal cries and the echoing landscape:[121]

> Μητέρα μοι πάντων τε θεῶν πάντων τ' ἀνθρώπων
> ὕμνει Μοῦσα λίγεια Διὸς θύγατερ μεγάλοιο,
> ἧι κροτάλων τυπάνων τ' ἰαχὴ σύν τε βρόμος αὐλῶν
> εὔαδεν, ἠδὲ λύκων κλαγγὴ χαροπῶν τε λεόντων,
> οὔρεά τ' ἠχήεντα καὶ ὑλήεντες ἔναυλοι. (5)

Celebrate, shrill Muse, the Mother of all gods and all men, daughter of great Zeus, whom the shriek of castanets [*krotala*] and hand drums [*tympana*] together with the roar of *auloi* pleases, and the howling of wolves and fierce lions, and the echoing mountains and wooded glens. (*Hymn. Hom.* 14.1–5)

Euripides' virtuosic display may also be a sign of his engagement with the so-called New Music—at least it is strikingly close to what Plato condemns in his *Laws* as apparently recent musical practice:

> ἔτι δὲ θηρίων φωνὰς καὶ ἀνθρώπων καὶ ὀργάνων καὶ πάντας ψόφους εἰς ταὐτὸν οὐκ ἄν ποτε συνθεῖεν, ὡς ἕν τι μιμούμενοι.

What's more, [the Muses] would never combine the cries of beasts and of humans and of instruments and all kinds of noises into the same piece, as a way to represent one thing. (Plato, *Laws* 669c8–d2)

This sort of exploitation of the mimetic ability of the voice also seems to lie at the heart of the criticism leveled by Socrates against the "baser" kind of imitation in speech in Book 3 of Plato's *Republic*:[122]

> πάντα ἐπιχειρήσει μιμεῖσθαι σπουδῆι τε καὶ ἐναντίον πολλῶν, καὶ ἃ νυνδὴ ἐλέγομεν, βροντάς τε καὶ ψόφους ἀνέμων τε καὶ χαλαζῶν καὶ ἀξόνων τε καὶ τροχιλιῶν, καὶ

---

120. Cf. E. Dillon 2006, who discusses obscene sound in Dante's *Inferno*: she observes that the sounds there, unlike those in *Purgatorio* and *Paradiso,* "shun any kind of fixed system of pitch and rhythm, and are unruly, unpredictable sounds, more heightened than speech, but not quite fully fledged into song" (70). In describing sounds that went beyond musical notation, Dante was "tackling the challenge of representing the unrepresentable" (59). Although the issue of what could and could not be notated is not pertinent to the *Helen* ode, a similar sort of challenge seems to lie behind Euripides' mimetic play with voice and music.

121. Cf. Pind. fr. 70b SM, 8–11.

122. Cf. Pl. *Rep.* 396b5–9, where the noise of rivers and roar of the sea are included among the sounds that the guardians should not imitate.

σαλπίγγων καὶ αὐλῶν καὶ συρίγγων καὶ πάντων ὀργάνων φωνάς, καὶ ἔτι κυνῶν καὶ προβάτων καὶ ὀρνέων φθόγγους.

[The speaker who uses much imitation] will attempt, seriously and in front of many, to imitate everything, both the things that we were just talking about, and claps of thunder and the noises of winds and hail and axles and pulleys, and the strains of trumpets and pipes and syrinxes and of all instruments, and besides the sounds of dogs and sheep and birds. (Plato, *Republic* 397a3–7)

Of course we cannot know whether the actual tune of the chorus's singing contained as much variation as the words did,[123] but we can hear in this opening strophe vocal imitation of a great range of sound sources that are deliberately confused with each other to convey the acoustic frenzy of the goddess's search for Kore. Such experimentation with imitative effects may be a display of musical novelty, but it is also rooted in the traditional representation of the Great Mother: Euripides characteristically blends old and new in this multilayered sound picture.

In the following antistrophe, after an initial reference to running feet (1319),[124] the narrative slows down as Cybele abandons her search and starts destroying mankind by making the earth infertile.[125] Turbulent *mousikē* is replaced by its absence. Instead of descriptions of sound and movement, the antistrophe is full of silent grief, negation, and verbs of stopping and dwindling.[126] The one violent movement on the part of the goddess is her headlong collapse in grief (1325). The infertility, sadness, and immobility of the aftermath of the goddess's fruitless search are thus reflected in the lack of references to *mousikē*, which is all the more pronounced after the noisiness of the initial strophe.

But with the new strophic pair new, more pleasing music begins, marking a shift in the larger musical and dramatic narrative of the play as a whole. The focus shifts from the barren world of mortals to the divine plane, as the gods use music to console the Great Mother: Zeus tells the Muses and Graces to sing and dance, and Aphrodite and the Great Mother herself join in the music making:[127]

ἐπεὶ δ' ἔπαυσ' εἰλαπίνας
θεοῖς βροτείωι τε γένει,
Ζεὺς μειλίσσων στυγίους
Ματρὸς ὀργὰς ἐνέπει·                                              (1340)

---

123. Cf. Pl. *Rep.* 397c.
124. The rhythm of δρομαῖον (‿ – –) itself seems to signify a slowing down of movement, in contrast to the three short syllables of δρομάδι in line 1301.
125. Cf. Allan 2008: 302.
126. ἔπαυσε (1320) in place of ἐσύθη in line 1302; φθείρει (1329); ἀπέλειπε βίος (1332); ἄφλεκτοι πελανοί (1334); ἀμπαύει (1335); πένθει ... ἀλάστωι (1337).
127. The text here follows Allan 2008.

Βᾶτε, σεμναὶ Χάριτες,
ἴτε, τὰν περὶ παρθένωι
Δηὼ θυμωσαμέναν
λυπᾶν ἐξελᾶτ' ἀλαλᾶι,
Μοῦσαί θ' ὕμνοισι χορῶν. (1345)
χαλκοῦ δ' αὐδὰν χθονίαν
τύπανά τ' ἔλαβε βυρσοτενῆ
καλλίστα τότε πρῶτα μακά-
  ρων Κύπρις· γέλασεν δὲ θεὰ
δέξατό τ' ἐς χέρας (1350)
βαρύβρομον αὐλὸν
τερφθεῖσ' ἀλαλαγμῶι.

But when she stopped feasts for gods and the mortal race, Zeus, trying to soothe the grim wrath of the Mother, said, "Step forth, holy Graces, go, and take Deo, who is angered for her daughter, away from her grief with the cry *alalai*, and you, Muses, with the songs of choruses." And the earthy voice of bronze and the drums [*ty[m]pana*] of stretched hide then for the first time Cypris, loveliest of the blessed ones, took up; and the goddess laughed and took into her hands the deep-roaring *aulos*, delighting in the *alalai* cry. (1338–52)

Zeus directs the Graces and Muses to perform *choreia*, with both the ritual cry *alalai* and "the songs of choruses."[128] His imperatives "step forth . . . go" (1340–41) seem to have a metachoreographic significance, addressed as much to the dancing dramatic chorus as to these divine maidens.[129] Following these directions, the introduction of instrumental sound makes it clear that the *mousikē* illustrated here is associated with delight and charm: Aphrodite, described as the most beautiful of the gods (1348–49), takes up the "earthy voice of bronze"—most likely *kymbala*, but perhaps bronze *krotala*—and the *tympana* of stretched hide (1346).[130] Again the resolved rhythm of line 1347, as well as the alliteration of the harsh *ch*- and *t*- consonants, produces a percussive effect, so that there is a brief mimetic interplay between the chorus's voice and the drumming music that they are describing. This performance then culminates in the laughter of the Great Mother and her delight in the sound of the *aulos* and the *alalai* cry, which, as Pucci has observed, replace Kore as the found object that enables reconciliation.[131]

---

128. As Kannicht 1969: 350 points out, the Graces' cry *alalai* is only nominally separated from the Muses' *hymnoi*. For the association of this cry with cultic celebration for Cybele and Dionysus, see also Pind. fr. 70b SM, 12.

129. On *bainō* as a verb used to describe dancing, see Naerebout 1997: 281.

130. See Burian 2007: 273 on the *kymbala*. Cf. Barker 1984: 76 n. 93. On the "earthy" (and chthonic) sound of bronze, see Kannicht 1969: 353–54.

131. Pucci 1997: 73–74. Such laughter as a sign of the goddess's abandonment of solitary grief also augments the syncretism between Cybele and Demeter, whose laughter at Iambe's jesting in the

This musical aetiology accounts for the inclusion of various instruments (including the *krotala* of the first strophe) within the orgiastic cults of the Great Mother as well as in those of Dionysus, on whom the final antistrophe focuses: Aphrodite plays the *kymbala* and *tympana* for the first time in order to appease the Great Mother, who herself takes up the *aulos* as if it is a new thing. At the same time, the shift from grief to delight, from disturbing noise to new, more pleasing *mousikē*, indicates a change for the music of the play too, as the chorus no longer perform lament and instead take up a new kind of song. The enactment of this different type of *mousikē* by the dramatic chorus at the same time as they describe it brings this transition into the present of the play, merging the aetiological myth with the surrounding drama.[132]

It is striking that in this account of the Great Mother's musical appeasement the *aulos* signifies the climax of the whole ode—the moment when the goddess finally shifts from grief to delight in its sound and is herself pictured as an aulete as she takes the instrument into her hands (1350–52). Recalling the similar-sounding "deep-roaring breaker of the sea" (*barybromon... kym' halion,* 1305) in the first strophe, the "deep-roaring *aulos*" (*barybromon aulon,* 1351) here stresses the contrast between the delightful sound of the *aulos* among the gods and the cacophony that previously accompanied the goddess's frenzied search. It may seem surprising for the *aulos* to be described as "deep-roaring," but this adjective could denote the Phrygian version of the instrument, which was said to have a deeper pitch than the Greek one and would suit the worship of the Great Mother, whose cult originated in Phrygia.[133] (The *bromos* of *auloi* in the *Homeric Hymn to the Mother of the Gods* may suggest the same instrument.) The Greek *aulos* being played in the theater could have had a similarly low pitch,[134] but even if it did not, it could be imagined to produce such a sound, for this instrument was conceptualized as being able to imitate anything, low or high.[135] Perhaps more significant than the acoustic sound

---

*Homeric Hymn to Demeter* marks a similar shift in the narrative (202–5). See Burian 2007: 274; Allan 2008: 305; Marshall 2014: 117.

132. On the reenactment of aetiological myth in choral performance, see Kowalzig 2007a and 2007b.

133. Kannicht 1969: 353; Barker 1984: 76 n. 95 (cf. 74 n. 79) and 2007: 19–20. For ancient sources on the Phrygian *aulos*, which seems usually to have been a pair of unequal pipes, one ending in a bell made of horn, see West 1992: 91.

134. Cf. Allan 2008: 213, who points to the description in Aristophanes' *Clouds* of the choral accompaniment at the City Dionysia as "the deep-roaring music of *auloi*" (μοῦσα βαρύβρομος αὐλῶν, 313). We cannot, however, use this passage as conclusive evidence for the use of lower-pitched *auloi* in the theater, since the use of *brom-* words also relates the instrument to Dionysus Bromios. The explicit reference to Phrygian *auloi* in Euripides' *Bacchae* complicates this issue still further, since there they are not described as deep-sounding at all: instead their "sweet-crying breath" is "high-stretched" (σύντονος, 126).

135. On the *aulos*'s reputation for mimetic versatility, see esp. Barker 1984: 51; Wilson 1999: 87–93; Weiss forthcoming a.

implied by the word *barybromos* is how it continues the wordplay of the first strophe, associating the *mousikē* described here with Dionysus's cultic title *Bromios*.[136] These alliterative effects have an epiphanic power as they lead to the actual appearance of Dionysus, addressed as *Bromios*, in the final antistrophe (1364–65). They also help to link the musical experience described in the myth with that of the audience, hearing the *aulos* in the Theater of Dionysus during the City Dionysia.

The description of the *aulos* here also suggests its surprisingly *vocal* sound, which again points to its imitative versatility. When the goddess is said to delight in the cultic cry *alalai*, it is unclear whether this is the sound of the Muses (as at 1344) or of the *aulos* itself; the chorus's own performance of this cry may represent both. Unlike the discordancy described in the first strophe, however, here the fusion of vocal and instrumental sound, chorus and *aulos*, causes delight, and the instrumental sound causing the most pleasure in the narrated myth is the very one being played in the dramatic performance. So the goddess is not the only one who delights in this sound: the audience may see a similar response in the physically present aulete, whose tune they themselves are encouraged to enjoy along with the chorus dancing to it.[137] As a result, the song creates an aetiology as much for the present performance in the theater as for the orgiastic *mousikē* of the Great Mother's rites.[138]

Musical revelry continues in the antistrophe, but it is now transferred to the mortal realm—and, it seems, to the drama itself—with a warning to Helen that the sacrifices of the Great Mother should be honored. The form in which she should be worshipped becomes clear through the following scene of ritual celebration, which describes the dancing and music making of mortals in honor of Dionysus and the Great Mother, whose cult is completely syncretized with Demeter's at Eleusis (and perhaps also at Sparta):[139]

†ὧν οὐ θέμις οὔθ' ὅσια
ἐπύρωσας ἐν θαλάμοις,†
μῆνιν δ' ἔχεις μεγάλας (1355)

---

136. We see similar wordplay in Aristophanes' *Clouds*: the βαρύβρομος music of the *auloi* is mentioned as part of the god's festivities, described as βρόμια χάρις ("the grace of Bromios," 311–13).

137. Marshall 2014: 118 also suggests that the Great Mother is to be associated with the aulete in the *orchēstra*.

138. Cf. Wilson and Taplin 1993 on *Oresteia*: they suggest its musical themes culminate in an aetiology for "the incorporation of tragedy itself within the city of Athens" (175).

139. On the second stasimon as evidence for the Eleusinian syncretism of the Great Mother and Demeter, see Allan 2004: 144–45 and 2008: 295. The rites of the Great Mother at Agrai in Attica were seen as a prelude to the Mysteries at Eleusis: see Parker 1996: 188; Allan 2004: 143. For evidence for the cult of Demeter, Dionysus, and the Great Mother at Sparta, see D'Alessio 2013: 130–31; Battezzato 2013: 106; Prauscello 2013: 78. Battezzato thinks that the ritual activity described in the second stasimon of *Helen* refers specifically to Spartan cult.

Ματρός, ὦ παῖ, θυσίας
οὐ σεβίζουσα θεᾶς.
μέγα τοι δύναται νεβρῶν
παμποίκιλοι στολίδες
κισσοῦ τε στεφθεῖσα χλόα                    (1360)
νάρθηκας εἰς ἱεροὺς
ῥόμβου θ' εἰλισσομένα
κύκλιος ἔνοσις αἰθερία
βακχεύουσά τ' ἔθειρα Βρομί-
  ωι καὶ παννυχίδες θεᾶς.                   (1365)
†εὖ δέ νιν ἅμασιν
ὑπέρβαλε σελάνα
μορφᾷ μόνον ηὔχεις.†

†Offerings neither right nor holy you burned in inner rooms,† and you have incurred the wrath of the Great Mother, my child, by not honoring the sacrifices of the goddess. Great is the power of the dappled fawn skin robes, and the shoot of ivy wound about the holy narthex wands, and the whirling, circular shaking of the *rhombos* high in the air, the hair streaming in Bacchic joy for Bromius, and the nightlong festivals of the goddess. †But when well by day the moon surpassed her, you gloried in your beauty alone.† (1353–68)

As we have seen, the previous strophe brought the divine music narrated in the myth closer to what the audience would be experiencing in the theater. Now, with this transference to the mortal celebration of Dionysus and the Great Mother (and Demeter), the *mousikē* described at the end of the stasimon merges with the Athenian audience's own ritual experience, as well as with the Dionysian musical imaginary.[140] The description of characteristically Dionysian festivity is highly visual, with references to the celebrants' long hair (1364) and their accoutrements of dappled deerskins and ivy wound around the *narthex* (1359–61). The synaesthetic experience of this cultic celebration is encapsulated by the *rhombos*, a spatulate blade (usually made of wood) that produced a sound by being whirled through the air on a string in a circular motion.[141] This instrument comes in responsion with the most music-focused part of the second strophe (1362–63 ≈ 1346–47), which describes the sounds of the *kymbala* and *tympana*, yet the *rhombos* is depicted in purely visual terms, conveying a vivid impression of its fast, circular movement through the air. The "whirling [*heilissomena*], circular shaking of the *rhombos*" may also draw the audience's attention to the circular dancing of the chorus in the *orchēstra*, particularly since, as we have repeatedly seen, words of the *heliss-* root often have a choreographic resonance in Euripides' later plays. The resolved

---

140. On the worship of the Great Mother, Demeter and Dionysus at the "lesser" and "greater" Mysteries, see Parker 2005: 344–45.

141. On the *rhombos* or bull roarer, see West 1992: 122; Sadie 2001: 4.598–99.

rhythm of line 1363 could simultaneously give the impression of fast movement (whether or not this would have been part of the performance). The chorus's song and dancing thus suggest a fusion of the aural and visual aspects of performance, evoking the synaesthetic experience of ecstatic cultic celebration. The suggestion of circular dancing, which as the typical formation of the dithyramb was linked to Dionysus, may further strengthen the syncretism of the god and the Great Mother.[142] With the inclusion of the *rhombos,* the chorus have now sung of all the instruments associated with the orgiastic rites of the two divinities—the *krotala, kymbala, tympana, aulos,* and *rhombos*—and, in doing so, they combine in their own live performance both divine and mortal archetypes of *choreia.*

But why should this description of cultic celebration be framed as a warning to Helen? The cause for this reprimand has been much debated, and textual problems in the opening and closing lines of the final antistrophe make its precise meaning impossible to grasp. Kannicht suggests that Helen is addressed here not just as a dramatic character but as a metaphor for improper human behavior regarding the Mysteries.[143] Others argue that the warning is much more integrated within the themes of the play as a whole: in particular, Allan and Swift both suggest that Helen is being rebuked for persisting in her figurative role as a *parthenos* and refusing to enter sexual maturity.[144] If Helen as "a figure of parthenaic allegory" does lie behind the anger of the Great Mother,[145] this reason can be only implicit at best, and the identification between Helen and the Great Mother, not just Kore, problematizes such an interpretation. Barker instead sees the warning to Helen in terms of the difference between the musical character of this ode and the parodos and first stasimon, suggesting that she is being rebuked for omitting ecstatic rites and for instead concentrating on lamentation.[146] Given the dominance of musical imagery in the second stasimon, this interpretation seems rather more plausible. The warning itself is another instance of doubling identity and misleading appearances, since it points to another Helen, one who glories in her beauty (1368), far from the charac-

---

142. On the circular formation of the dithyramb, see D'Angour 1997. On the Dionysiac connotations of vocabulary concerning circular movement in late Euripidean tragedy, see Csapo 1999–2000: 418–24 and 2003: 69–73.

143. Kannicht 1969: 334.

144. Allan 2008: 295, 306–7. Swift 2009a: 433–34 and 2010: 236–38. Robinson 1979: 70 interprets the second antistrophe as a threat that the Great Mother will detain Helen in Egypt because she never worshipped her in Sparta. Podlecki 1970: 412 finds verbal connections between this stanza and other passages in the play, concluding that these last lines are addressed to Persephone, not Helen, and concern her inability to leave Hades after tasting the pomegranate. (Cf. Pearson 1903: 170.)

145. Swift 2010: 237.

146. Barker 2007: 21. Cf. Pucci 1997: 73–74, who emphasizes the "relieving power" of such orgiastic music. Barker's suggestion that the previous song type is rejected because "le lamentazioni di tipo tradizionale esprimono un atteggiamento incauto nei confronti della morte" is less convincing, especially since Helen's attitude toward death is not a major theme in the play.

ter presented onstage, who earlier wished for her beauty to be effaced (262–63), and who has just appeared with a shorn head and dressed in mourning clothes.[147]

The reprimand also, however, concludes the musical change described and performed through the ode, thus redirecting the *mousikē* of the play as a whole. The chorus's description of Dionysian celebration draws attention to the difference between the sort of musical performance now being enacted and the lament revolving around the figure of Helen that dominated the parodos and first stasimon, as well as Helen's shorter lyric exchanges with the chorus and Menelaus. Like the Great Mother, who abandoned her grief, rejoicing in the ecstatic *mousikē* of her rites, Helen no longer has need for lamentation, and will soon sing and dance in cultic celebrations back in Sparta, just as the chorus depict her doing in the next and final song of the play (which the second stasimon therefore anticipates).[148] The ode as a whole, then, reflects a crucial transition in the plot of the tragedy, marking a shift from lament to more celebratory *mousikē*, just as Helen and Menelaus are finally able to escape from Egypt.

The ritual *choreia* that the chorus describe at the end of the second stasimon will also be performed for Helen herself. In the closing scene of the play the Dioskouroi announce that she will receive offerings as a goddess (1666–69), and her cult at Sparta was famous enough for Aristophanes to describe her choral dances there in *Lysistrata* (though this play, performed just one year after Euripides' *Helen*, draws from and parodies the tragedy); she was worshipped in some parts of Attica too.[149] The parallel between the goddess and Helen is also evident in their geographical movement toward Greece. Although the Great Mother's cult was well established in Greece by the late fifth century, she was still seen as an exotic import from Phrygia.[150] Helen will arrive in Greece from the equally exotic land of Egypt, bringing her *mousikē* with her.[151]

## TRAVEL AND EPIPHANY

The chorus perform the third stasimon within just a hundred lines of the second, as Menelaus and Helen depart on the ship that Theoclymenus has unwittingly

---

147. Cf. Zweig 1999a: 170. She sees in the warning a tension between the Helen of myth and the Helen of Spartan ritual worship.

148. Cf. Battezzato 2013: "The stasimon is . . . an invitation to Helen to perform a religious rite, once she returns to her homeland (106)." He understands the rebuke in terms of Helen's absence from Sparta: she is to resume the rituals in honor of the goddess there upon her return.

149. Ar. *Lys.* 1296–1321. On Helen's role in Greek (esp. Spartan) cult, see Farnell 1921: 323–25; Larson 1995: 69–70, 80–81; Calame 1997: 191–202; Zweig 1999a: 162–63; Allan 2008: 14–15.

150. On this paradox, see Allan 2004: 120–21, 140–46.

151. Cf. Murnaghan 2013: 169–71. She sees Helen's return to Sparta as "also a musical return, to one of tragedy's points of origin, in the non-dramatic choral lyric genres of the Peloponnesus" (169).

provided. In this final burst of song and dance, they imagine the return of Helen to Sparta, wishing that they could travel there themselves, rather as the chorus of *Iphigenia in Tauris* sing of the escape of Iphigenia, Orestes, and Pylades to Athens.[152] This focus on the immediate present and future of the play makes the ode seem a far cry from the lament that dominated the parodos and first stasimon and from the narrative aetiology of the song that they have just sung. At the same time, however, there is a sense of continuity between the third stasimon and the chorus's previous songs. Not only is the aeolo-choriambic meter of this ode similar to that of the previous one, but as we shall see, it develops some of the imagery of Dionysiac cultic celebration that appeared in the second stasimon, displaying the different kind of *mousikē* to which that song propelled us. Moreover, like the previous stasima, this one is dominated by images of *choreia*, which continue to articulate the relationship between Helen and the chorus, and so also Helen's position at this point in the dramatic narrative. As in the first stasimon, in which the chorus represented the mourning being performed by Helen offstage, here, through their highly choreographic description of Helen's travel, they enact the journey being made beyond the space of the dramatic action.[153] They then look beyond the play's temporal scope, imagining and simultaneously representing through their own performance Helen's participation in *choreia* back in Sparta. In doing so, the chorus seem to bring her back into the play, transcending the distance between Egypt and Greece by conjuring up her presence amid their choral song and dance just as they did previously by summoning her as the nightingale. But whereas in the first stasimon they did succeed in bringing Helen back onstage, here their *choreia* heralds the arrival of the Dioskouroi instead, thus bringing the play to a close.

Like the parodos and first stasimon, the ode begins with an arresting invocation, this time to the Sidonian ship carrying Helen to Greece, which, like the Sirens, nightingale, and Great Mother, functions in large part as a figure of musicality:[154]

Φοίνισσα Σιδωνιὰς ὦ
ταχεῖα κώπα, ῥοθίοισι Νηρέως
εἰρεσία φίλα,
χοραγὲ τῶν καλλιχόρων
δελφίνων, ὅταν αὔ- (1455)
ραν πέλαγος ἀνήνεμον ᾖ,
γλαυκὰ δὲ Πόντου θυγάτηρ

---

152. Eur. *IT* 1123–52.
153. Cf. Marshall 2014: 123.
154. On the meaning of the imperative in line 1459 (*katapetasate*), see Diggle 1994b: 430–36; Allan 2008: 321.

Γαλάνεια τάδ' εἴπηι·
κατὰ μὲν ἱστία πετάσατ', αὔ-
ρας λιπόντες εἰναλίας, (1460)
λάβετε δ' εἰλατίνας πλάτας,
ὦ ναῦται ναῦται,
πέμποντες εὐλιμένους
Περσείων οἴκων Ἑλέναν ἐπ' ἀκτάς.

O swift Phoenician ship of Sidon, oarage dear to the waves of Nereus, leader of the dolphins of beautiful choruses, whenever the sea is free from the winds' breezes, and the gray-eyed daughter of Pontus, Galaneia, says these words: "Let down the sails, leaving the sea-breezes behind, and take up your fir-wood oars, O sailors, sailors, escorting Helen to the well-harbored shores of Perseus's home." (1451–64)

As we saw in chapters 1 and 2, choral descriptions of naval travel in Euripides frequently involve highly choreographic language, indicating a correspondence between seafaring and dance in the orchestic imaginary of the tragedian and his audience. Like the chorus of *Electra*, who begin their first stasimon by addressing the Greek ships carrying Achilles to Troy as if they are chorus leaders accompanied by Nereids, surrounded by the dancing of the "*aulos*-loving dolphin" (*El.* 434–37), the chorus of *Helen* invoke the ship carrying Helen to Greece as a *chorēgos* of dolphins (1454–55).[155]

This opening strophe further resembles the *Electra* ode by drawing on the cultural nexus of dithyramb, dolphins, and maritime travel to encourage mimetic interplay between the performing chorus and the scene they describe. As Deborah Steiner has observed, the focus on the swift, dancing motion of the ship (especially its oars) and dolphins points to the chorus's own movements in the *orchēstra*.[156] Within such a metamusical passage, the appearance of the "dolphins of beautiful choruses" (1454–55) in particular evokes the dithyrambic choral imaginary—an effect that would presumably be especially powerful for the Athenian audience at the City Dionysia, who would have recently experienced dithyrambic *choreia* in the very same theater. Here the allusion to the dithyramb is significant within the play's musical arc, since it continues the focus on Dionysiac cultic revelry that first appeared in the previous stasimon. This Dionysiac element, combined with the emphasis on movement and travel, contrasts starkly with the lament that dominated the first part of the play, thereby marking the contrast in Helen's own situation as she shifts from stagnant mourning to her escape back to Greece.

---

155. The two songs are also similar in beginning with a hanging apostrophe, without a predicate.
156. Steiner 2011. She emphasizes the ode's New Musical character, arguing that Euripides uses images of archetypal *choreia* (like dancing dolphins) to archaize the song's more innovative elements. Cf. Marshall 2014: 136–37 on the mimetic effects at play here; also Padel 1974: 236–38.

Mimetic musical interplay continues in the second half of the strophe (1459–64). As the chorus quote Galaneia, the subject of the address shifts from the ship to the sailors rowing it, conveying Helen back to Greece. An affinity between the dolphins and sailors is suggested here: dolphins, the archetypal maritime escorts, surround the ship like the sailors surround Helen.[157] The emphasis on rowing throughout the stanza could also carry some choreographic associations, since we know from Athenaeus (admittedly a late source) of the dance figure of the *keleustēs*, the man who keeps rowers in time.[158] Here the metonymic address to the ship as an "oar" (1452) and "oarage" (1453), as well as Galaneia's order to the sailors to take up their oars (1461), encourages a sense of merging between dancing chorus and rowing sailors.

As we saw in chapter 1, the chorus of *Iphigenia in Tauris* produce a similar effect when they describe Iphigenia's journey back to Greece on a ship with fifty oars, accompanied by Pan's syrinx and Apollo's lyre.[159] In both songs, the chorus picture the female protagonist's escape back to Greece so vividly that they even seem to enact it—although, in an ironic twist, the first attempt by Iphigenia, Orestes, and Pylades to flee is thwarted and Athena has to intervene to save them. And in both, this is an acoustic enactment as well as a choreographic one, since for the Athenian audience rowing would be closely associated with the sound of the *aulos*, which they would hear as the chorus's accompaniment: the *aulos* was played on triremes to aid the timing of the rowers' strokes;[160] according to Athenaeus, it also accompanied the *keleustēs* dance figure. Since dolphins are regularly depicted as dancing to its tune, Steiner suggests that the sound of the *aulos* in the theater links the pleonastic focus on rowing at the start of the *Helen* ode to the image of the dancing dolphins.[161] Through their own performance to the accompaniment of the *aulos*, then, the chorus merge with multiple dancing figures, thus representing Helen's journey back to Greece and vividly anticipating her imminent restoration.[162] But their embodied enactment of her departure also seems to be an attempt to bring Helen herself back onstage as their leader, as they perform like the dancing dolphin-sailors that now surround her.

In the antistrophe the chorus then jump ahead to Helen's full reintegration within cultic celebrations back in Sparta. Now the choral imagery of the previous strophe turns into a more literal presentation of Helen herself dancing:[163]

---

157. Padel 1974: 237; Steiner 2011: 303–4.
158. Ath. 14.629f. Cf. Eur. *IT* 1133. On this dance figure, see Lawler 1944 (esp. 31–33) and 1964: 45: she links it to references in Libanius (64.14) and Pollux (4.101) to a "nautical dance" (*orchēsis nautikē*).
159. *IT* 1123–36.
160. Cf. the conflation of the *triēraulēs* with the aulete of the theater in Plut. *Alc.* 32.
161. Steiner 2011: 302–3.
162. Cf. Segal 1971: 598–99, who emphasizes the restorative function of the sea now in contrast to its association with separation and death earlier in the play.
163. This text follows Allan 2008 here, except for λάβοις (not λάβοι) in 1467.

ἦ που κόρας ἂν ποταμοῦ (1465)
παρ' οἶδμα Λευκιππίδας ἢ πρὸ ναοῦ
Παλλάδος ἂν λάβοις
χρόνωι ξυνελθοῦσα χοροῖς
ἢ κώμοις Ὑακίν-
θου νύχιον ἐς εὐφροσύναν, (1470)
ὃν ἐξαμιλλασάμενος
τροχὸν ἀτέρμονα δίσκου
ἔκανε Φοῖβος, τᾶι †δὲ† Λακαί-
ναι γᾶι βούθυτον ἀμέραν
ὁ Διὸς εἶπε σέβειν γόνος· (1475)
μόσχον θ' ἃν †λίποιτ' οἴκοις†
⟨×-×-⏑⏑-⟩
ἃς οὔπω πεῦκαι πρὸ γάμων ἔλαμψαν.

Perhaps you may find the daughters of Leukippos alongside the swell of the river or in front of the temple of Pallas, when at last you have joined the choruses or revels for Hyacinthus for nighttime joy, he whom Phoebus, after competing over the unending wheel of the discus, killed, †and† the son of Zeus told the land of Sparta to observe a day of sacrifice. And the calf that †she [you?] left at home† ... for whom wedding pines have not yet blazed. (1465–77)

In line 1467 above I have retained the reading *labois* ("you may find") found in manuscript L instead of following the common emendation to *laboi*, the third-person form.[164] With this second-person-singular verb, the invocation to the musical figure of the ship in the opening line of the ode turns into an address to Helen herself, mirroring the shift from the singing nightingale to Helen in the first stasimon. Now, like the ship, she is dancing, joining the choruses and revels (*kōmoi*, 1469) for the Leucippides and Hyacinthus. This parallel with the first strophe encourages us to picture Helen, like the ship, as a *chorēgos*—the role with which she is so strongly associated within both the play and Greek culture more broadly.[165] The theme of uniting in *mousikē* continues on from the parodos and first stasimon, with the *syn-* prefix of *xynelthousa* ("joined," 1468) recalling the language with which Helen summoned the Sirens (the chorus) and the chorus summoned the nightingale (Helen) to participate in music making.[166] Now, by joining the initiatory cults of the Leucippides and the Hyacinthia,[167] she is imagined as taking up

---

164. Dale 1967 and Kannicht 1969 likewise keep λάβοις; Diggle 1994a, Burian 2007, and Allan 2008 emend it to λάβοι.
165. Cf. Murnaghan 2013: 165–69 on Helen's reintegration as a chorus leader in Sparta.
166. σύνοχα, 173; ξυνωιδά, 174b; ξυνεργός, 1112.
167. On the initiatory role of the Leucippides, see Calame 1997: 185–91. The Hyacinthia also seems to have been a cult of adolescence but involved all Spartan citizens, not just girls (though an exclusively female ritual may have been part of it): Calame 1997: 174–85.

her choral role in transition rituals for Spartan girls, the same role in which we see her at the end of Aristophanes' *Lysistrata*.[168]

Through their own song and dance the dramatic chorus seem to perform these cultic celebrations in which they picture Helen taking part, just as they enacted the *choreia* of her journey from Egypt to Sparta.[169] The merging of the two choruses, tragic and ritual, becomes especially strong when they describe the aetiology for the Hyacinthia much as actual celebrants would (1471–75).[170] The various images throughout the play of Helen as a most musical performer now reach their culmination as this protean figure assumes her final identity in contemporary Spartan *choreia*—a role to which the previous stasimon already looked forward.[171] As in the first strophe, the chorus, though physically separate from her, continue to display their close association with their *chorēgos*, transcending the distance between them by recreating through their own *choreia* the cultic dances in which she is performing. Their performance here thus functions aetiologically, demonstrating just the sort of epiphanic effect of *mousikē* that would have been experienced in contemporary Spartan cult. The imagery of travel in the previous strophe further strengthens the connection between the women's choral activity and that of Helen back in Sparta: the journey of the dancing ship suggests an uninterrupted flow of *choreia* over the sea from Egypt to the banks of the river Eurotas.[172]

In the second strophe the chorus then shift back to a more figurative depiction of *mousikē* as they turn to their own desire to be with Helen as their chorus leader, making their way back from Egypt to Greece with her. They express this wish through avian imagery, continuing the motif of musical birds from the parodos

---

168. Marshall 2014: 137–39 argues that Ar. *Lys.* 1296–1321 directly responds to the third stasimon of Euripides' play.

169. Steiner 2011: 308–9 stresses the significance of the discus's "unending wheel" in line 1472, arguing that its circular movement could be mimetically reflected in the chorus's own dancing. She also suggests a conflation of linear and circular choreography in the combination of *choroi* and *kōmoi* that unites processional and dithyrambic styles of dance, even if the dramatic chorus itself would be performing in a circle. But such a mix of lines and circles is not as evident as she proposes: the only indications of dancing style in this stanza are the references to the discus's wheel (which need not be choreographically significant) and the *kōmoi*, which could be either circular or linear.

170. Cf. Kowalzig 2007b on the merging of tragic and ritual choruses; also Kowalzig 2007a on the reenactment of aetiological myth in choral performance and on Dionysian imagery of choral travel, bringing a cult to a place from elsewhere (especially by sea).

171. Battezzato 2013: 106–7 argues that the second stasimon anticipates this depiction of Helen's dancing, which alludes to actual Spartan rituals performed by the Dionysiades or Leukippides for Dionysus.

172. This effect is reminiscent of how the *kōmos* in some of Pindar's epinicians is imagined as accompanying the victor all the way home from the games in which he competed (esp. Pind. *Nem.* 9.1–5; *Ol.* 6.22–28).

and first stasimon by imagining themselves flying like the "birds from Libya" who journey north to Greece after wintering in northern Africa:[173]

δι' αἰθέρος εἴθε ποτανοὶ
γενοίμεθ' ὅπαι Λιβύας
οἰωνοὶ στολάδες (1480)
ὄμβρον χειμέριον λιποῦ-
  σαι νίσονται πρεσβυτάτου
σύριγγι πειθόμεναι
ποιμένος, ἄβροχά θ' ὃς
πεδία καρποφόρα τε γᾶς (1485)
ἐπιπετόμενος ἰαχεῖ.
ὦ πταναὶ δολιχαύχενες,
σύννομοι νεφέων δρόμου,
βᾶτε Πλειάδας ὑπὸ μέσας
Ὠρίωνά τ' ἐννύχιον, (1490)
καρύξατ' ἀγγελίαν
Εὐρώταν ἐφεζόμεναι,
Μενέλεως ὅτι Δαρδάνου
πόλιν ἑλὼν δόμον ἥξει.

If only we could be flying through the air, where the birds from Libya go in rows, leaving the wintry rain, obeying the syrinx of the eldest, the shepherd who cries out as he wings his way over the unwetted and crop-bearing plains of the earth. O long-necked winged creatures, partners of the clouds' racing, go beneath the Pleiades in their midcourse and Orion in the night. Announce the news as you land by the Eurotas, that Menelaus has taken the city of Dardanus and will come home. (1478-94)

This is not the first time a tragic chorus express a wish to fly: in the second stasimon of Euripides' *Hippolytus*, for example, there is a similar desire for avian transformation.[174] And, as we saw in chapter 1, birds are often associated with choral performers within the Greek choral imaginary; we even see visual expressions of this link in the appearance of birdlike choruses on archaic and classical vases.[175] But the various references to metaphors of flight in Aristophanes' comedies suggest that this motif was especially common in late fifth-century dithyramb:[176] as we saw in chapter 2, in *Birds* Cinesias, a contemporary dithyrambist, repeatedly sings

---

173. The text here follows Allan 2008. Dale 1967: 160 notes that the second half of the stanza describes the birds' reverse migration from south to north in early spring, the time of the play's performance at the City Dionysia.

174. On Eur. *Hipp.* 732-51, see Padel 1974: 228-32. Cf. Soph. *Trach.* 953-59, *OC* 1081-83. The chorus in Aeschylus's *Suppliants*, though they do not wish for an avian transformation, express a comparable desire to become smoke or "dust without wings" (κόνις ἄτερθε πτερύγων, 782).

175. See Rothwell 2007: 52-58.

176. Cf. Wilson 1999-2000: 441.

of flying up into the air; in *Clouds* Socrates calls composers of dithyrambs "astronomical quacks" who compose music about the clouds; in *Peace* Trygaeus describes the souls of dithyrambists as "winging about," collecting musical interludes of "the floating-through-midday-airy-breezes sort."[177] Euripides therefore draws on a combination of old and new trends within the Greek choral imaginary when he presents us with a chorus who vividly describe the birds they wish to become.

The strongly choreographic nature of this image, combined with the long-established link between choruses and birds, encourages the audience to see the avian transformation that the chorus so strongly desire. These "long-necked" (1487) creatures are most likely cranes,[178] and may therefore be meant to evoke the Athenian *geranos* (crane) dance that Theseus was said to have invented and that, according to Callimachus, Plutarch, and Pollux, was performed at Delos.[179] But even without such a specific cultural reference, the description of the birds as flying in rows (1480) invites a crossover with the chorus's own choreography, which could itself represent the typical V-formation in which cranes were known to fly.[180] Moreover, just as the chorus dance to the tune of the *aulos*, the birds follow their syrinx-playing leader. As in the second stasimon of *Electra*, these two instruments merge, producing an acoustic image of this crane chorus as well as a choreographic one.[181]

Given the depiction of Helen in her role as chorus leader in the previous antistrophe and her ship's journey to Greece described in the opening strophe, the syrinx-playing crane whom the chorus wish to follow to Sparta here must represent Helen, their absent *chorēgos* who has left them behind. The chorus's wish to be birds thus draws on Helen's own avian identity, perhaps aiming at the sort of

---

177. μετεωροφένακας, Ar. *Nub.* 333; ποτώμεναι, *Pax* 830; τὰς εὐδιαεριαυρινηχέτους τινάς, *Pax* 831.

178. This identification is suggested by the migration described here from northern Africa, where eastern European cranes tend to winter: Arnott 2007: 80. Aristotle identifies their wintering place as the marshlands south of Egypt, where the Nile rises (τὰ ἕλη τὰ ἄνω τῆς Αἰγύπτου, ὅθεν ὁ Νεῖλος ῥεῖ, *Hist. an.* 597a5–6). Swans are also described as δολιχαύχενες (Bacchyl. 15.6; Eur. *IA* 794) or δουλιχοδείροι (Hom. *Il.* 2.460), also fly in a similar V-formation, and can have choral associations (as in Alcm. fr. 1 *PMGF,* 100–101). Steiner 2011: 312–15 suggests that this passage in *Helen* evokes the crane dance, but the broader choral identity of these birds may be more significant than their precise species.

179. Steiner 2011: 314–15. The dance is described in Call. *Hymn* 4.310–13; Plut. *Thes.* 21; Pollux 4.101; it is also mentioned in Luc. *Orch.* 34. It may be depicted on the late sixth-century François Vase: see Muellner 1990: 93–95; Torelli 2007: 19–24; Hedreen 2011. The relevance of the name *geranos* to the nature of the dance itself has been disputed: see esp. Lawler 1946; Detienne 1983; Muellner 1990: 91; Calame 1997: 55–56. According to the literary sources, the dance represented Theseus's winding path through the Labyrinth, celebrating his triumph over the Minotaur.

180. This formation is noted in Plut. *Mor.* 967b8–c2; Ael. *NA* 3.13; Cic. *Nat. D.* 2.49.125; Philostr. *Her.* 11.4. See Arnott 2007: 80.

181. Cf. Allan 2008: 324–25; Steiner 2011: 311; Marshall 2014: 130. On the merging of the syrinx and *aulos* in Euripidean tragedy, see Weiss forthcoming a.

epiphany that their invocation of the nightingale achieved in the first stasimon, with her entrance immediately following their song. But despite the chorus's enactment of her birdlike *choreia*, now Helen is gone, and they can no longer either perform with her or produce her presence onstage.

The description of the cranes as the clouds' *synnomoi* (1488)—not merely their partners, but, as in Aristophanes' *Birds* (209), their "tune sharers"—highlights both their distance from and continued closeness to Helen by recalling their earlier language of shared *mousikē*.[182] In the parodos such language emphasized the commonality between Helen and the chorus as performers of lament and *partheneia*. In the first stasimon the chorus still addressed Helen as their musical partner, though she was no longer present to perform with them. In the second stasimon we noted the correspondence between the chorus's more detached style of song and Helen's imminent departure. Now, in their final song, the chorus cannot be these *synnomoi* of the clouds, joining the Pleiades, the archetypal star chorus;[183] the shift to the second-person apostrophe (1487) separates them from those making their dancing flight to Greece and from the *chorēgos* who leads them. Yet in their own song and dance they are simultaneously fused with Helen's own choral performance, and as a result this strophe is not just an expression of their frustration at being left behind but a celebration of her presence in and through their continued *choreia*.

The ode finishes with another vision of an aerial journey in the final antistrophe, but this time the route is reversed as the chorus summon the Dioskouroi, Helen's brothers, to travel over the sea to Egypt, the present setting of the play:

μόλοιτέ ποθ' ἵππιον οἶμον (1495)
δι' αἰθέρος ἱέμενοι,
παῖδες Τυνδαρίδαι,
λαμπρῶν ἀστέρων ὑπ' ἀέλ-
 λαις οἳ ναίετ' οὐράνιοι,
σωτῆρε τᾶς Ἑλένας, (1500)
γλαυκὸν ἐπ' οἶδμ' ἅλιον
κυανόχροά τε κυμάτων
ῥόθια πολιὰ θαλάσσας,
ναύταις εὐαεῖς ἀνέμων
πέμποντες Διόθεν πνοάς, (1505)
δύσκλειαν δ' ἀπὸ συγγόνου
βάλετε βαρβάρων λεχέων,
ἂν Ἰδαιᾶν ἐρίδων
ποιναθεῖσ' ἐκτήσατο, γᾶν

---

182. On the musical meaning of *synnomoi* here, cf. Dunbar 1995: 203–4; Steiner 2011: 316. Steiner also stresses the conflation of choral and racing activity suggested by the word *dromos* in 1488.

183. On the Pleiades as a star chorus, see Csapo 2008: 266–67.

οὐκ ἐλθοῦσά ποτ᾽ Ἰλίου (1510)
Φοιβείους ἐπὶ πύργους.

> May you come, hastening through the air on the path of horses, sons of Tyndareus, you who dwell in the heavens beneath whirlings of bright stars, saviors of Helen, over the gray-green salt swell and the dark blue-grayish surge of the sea's waves, as you send sailors fair-blowing breezes from Zeus, cast away the ill repute from your sister of a foreign marriage bed, which she obtained as punishment for the strife on Mount Ida, never having gone to Phoebus's towers in the land of Ilium. (1495–1511)

The chorus's depiction of the journey of the Dioskouroi continues the ode's choreographic imagery, particularly that of the previous stanza. Drawing on the long-established association of equine imagery with dance in choral lyric, Euripides presents the famous horse riders as flying on a "path of horses" (1495);[184] like the crane chorus, these catasterized brothers fly beneath the stars, whose "whirlings" (1498–99) suggest circular choral movement.[185] Such musical imagery has an epiphanic element here, with the chorus calling on the Dioskouroi to come (*moloite*, 1495) in the same way that they, as Sirens, were summoned by Helen in the parodos (*moloit'*, 170). The Dioskouroi really do appear just over a hundred lines later, resolving the remaining conflict by ordering Theoclymenus not to kill his sister, Theonoe, and by declaring Helen's apotheosis (1642–79). So though the chorus are no longer able to bring Helen onstage, their *choreia* still has an epiphanic effect—and one that is vital to the resolution of the play.

As we saw in chapter 1, strongly metamusical language in tragic lyric is often associated with epiphany: in Aeschylus's *Persians* and *Libation Bearers*, such *mousikē* is performed in order to bring a ghost onstage; in Sophocles' *Ajax* and *Women of Trachis*, the chorus's misguidedly exuberant performances draw on the idea—often expressed in archaic poetry—that gods and heroes can be summoned to a religious festival through the power of *choreia*.[186] The audience may expect the Dioskouroi in particular to respond to this sort of epiphanic appeal, since they were the most frequent recipients of *theoxenia* ("god-entertaining"). Their presence was also traditionally invoked by sailors at sea: in the Homeric Hymn to the Dioskouroi,

---

184. On horse choruses, see Steiner forthcoming: chapter 4. Steiner 2011: 319 suggests that *oimos* here can be understood as "path of song."

185. Cf. Steiner 2011: 320. Such vocabulary may have been traditional within hymns to the Dioskouroi: cf. *Hymn. Hom.*33.7. The word *aella* combines the more literal meaning "storm" with the metaphorical sense of whirling movement: cf. Soph. *OC* 1081–82, when the chorus wish to be an *aellaia* dove; Eur. *Bacch.* 873 (μόχθοις δ᾽ ὠκυδρόμοις ἀελ- / λᾶς θρώισκηι); also above on *Hel.* 1314.

186. On the production of divine presence through *choreia* in archaic poetry, see Mullen 1982: 70–89; Burnett 1985: 8–14; Kurke 2012 and 2013. On divine presence in Graeco-Roman images, see Platt 2011, who discusses "the continual slippage between presentation and representation that characterized Greek religious practice, and the difficulty of distinguishing between real and mediated presence" (16).

they are said to "appear suddenly on tawny wings" to storm-tossed sailors.[187] We see a similar effect in Pindar's third *Olympian* ode, when the chorus's initial invocation to the Dioskouroi is followed by a strongly self-reflexive focus on the *mousikē* of their epinician performance (1–10); the divine brothers' presence then becomes apparent in their attendance at the Olympian festival and their gift of kudos to Theron (33–41).

In this final epiphany in *Helen* we see the full presencing power of *choreia*. Since Helen began to put her escape plan into effect, the chorus has repeatedly invoked her presence as their musical leader. The appearance of Dioskouroi at the end of their final song marks the culmination of their appeals for epiphany in and by means of choral song and dance. That it is Helen's brothers who appear, not Helen herself, makes it clear that her new choral location is Sparta, even while she is simultaneously experienced as a transcendent *chorēgos* for the women in Egypt. The presence of the Dioskouroi also articulates the nature of Helen's cult in Sparta and beyond, since this was closely associated with that of her brothers—and indeed at the end of the play Castor declares that she will share in their *theoxenia* (1666–69).[188] In this respect, then, the chorus still seem to be sharing in their leader's *choreia* back in Greece even while they remain apart from her in Egypt. The third stasimon cements the continued choral relationship of Helen and the chorus at the same time as it enacts her journey away from them.

The shift in forms of *mousikē* in the play as a whole, from lament to Dionysiac celebration to the *choreia* of Spartan rituals, therefore works not only as an aetiology of the music of the theater, but as an aetiology of Helen as a divine *chorēgos* in contemporary cult. It also creates for the audience the sense that they too are (almost) now at Sparta, even while sitting and watching in Athens; the tragedy comes to a close as they, like Helen and Menelaus, are returned to Greece. By representing both the locality and transcendence of Helen's choral *mousikē*, the third stasimon achieves a sense of choral closure, anticipating the cessation of the play itself.

In looking beyond the timespan of the dramatic action to Helen's return to Sparta, the third stasimon helps to bring *Helen* to an end. The chorus's vivid enactment of her journey and resumption of her choral role in Greece also comes in sharp contrast with their shared lament at the start of the play, both in terms of the

---

187. ἐξαπίνης ἐφάνησαν / ξουθῆισι πτερύγεσσι, *Hymn. Hom.* 33.12–13. On this epiphany of the Dioskouroi, see Platt 2011: 66. On the Dioskouroi and *theoxenia*, see Parker 2011: 142–43 on Bacchyl. fr. 21 SM. According to a fragment of the early comic poet Chionides, in the *Anakeia* festival at Athens a meal was prepared for the Dioskouroi in the Prytaneion (fr. 7 KA).

188. Since there is strong evidence of Helen's inclusion in the *theoxenia* rite in Attica, these lines also work as an aetiology for the Athenian audience's own cultic experience: see esp. Parker 2005: 72, 457; Allan 2008: 15–16, 342–43; Battezzato 2013: 109 n. 85 (with bibliography). On the relationship between Helen's cult and that of the Dioskouroi in Sparta, see Calame 1997: 191–201.

type of *mousikē* described and performed in each song and in how this final ode represents the culmination of a process of separation of Helen from the chorus whom she leaves behind in Egypt. The performance and language of *mousikē* thus work in tandem with the narrative arc of the tragedy's *mythos,* complementing the transition from Helen's expressions of helplessness in the opening scenes to the formation and execution of her escape plan with Menelaus. But as in Euripides' *Electra, mousikē* also plays a more active role in pushing the drama forward and directing the audience's experience of it, moving them from pitiful lament to the ecstasy of Dionysiac celebration and finally to Helen's own cultic *choreia* back in Greece. In doing so, it enacts and anticipates crucial moments in Helen's story, both within and beyond the tragedy itself.

5

# From *Choreia* to Monody in *Iphigenia in Aulis*

The last and latest play in this study of Euripidean *mousikē* is the posthumously produced *Iphigenia in Aulis*. Like *Bacchae,* alongside which it was probably first performed in 405 B.C.E.,[1] this tragedy contains a remarkably high proportion of choral song, thus contradicting the traditional narrative that the later works of Euripides showcase increasing amounts of actors' song at the expense of the chorus. Unlike the exuberant Dionysiac performances in *Bacchae,* however, the musical element of *Iphigenia in Aulis* has been largely neglected in modern scholarship.[2] Yet this play contains many allusions to music and dance that not only interact with its actual performance but, in doing so, become intertwined with its dramatic narrative. As in Euripides' other plays in which music and dance play a prominent part, these moments of intensely self-conscious musicality draw on traditional images of *choreia* and music making just as much as they point to the tragedian's own innovative skill in adapting them for the tragic stage.

Various musical effects at play in Euripides' earlier works come together here. In *Electra, Trojan Women,* and *Helen* we have seen how *choreia* can expand the

---

1. The tetralogy also included *Alcmeon in Corinth:* see schol. Ar. *Ran.* 66–67. The transmitted text of *Iphigenia in Aulis* was probably prepared for production by Euripides Minor, the tragedian's son or nephew, and accumulated further material when it was adapted for a fourth-century revival and as a result of later interpolations. See below on possible interpolations in the play; also Page 1934: 122–216; Kovacs 2003.

2. Scholarship has instead been concerned with the play's textual difficulties (esp. Page 1934; Mellert-Hoffmann 1969; Willink 1971; Knox 1972; Bain 1977; Irigoin 1988; Kovacs 2003) or the themes of sacrifice (Foley 1982 and 1985: 65–105), sight (Zeitlin 1994: 157–71 and 1995), or changing minds (esp. Sansone 1991; Gibert 1995: 222–37).

temporal and spatial scope of the drama, transforming the performance space so that the audience can experience scenes that are either offstage or from the mythical past (or even, as in the third stasimon of *Helen,* the near future). In *Iphigenia in Aulis,* as I show in the first two sections of this chapter, the chorus through their song and dance bring onstage both the sight of the vast Greek army arrayed nearby and moments of the past that are bound up with the dramatic present—the Judgment of Paris and the wedding of Peleus and Thetis. As in *Electra,* their enactment of these scenes has an anticipatory effect, pointing toward Iphigenia's sacrifice, which the increasingly ominous presence of the army demands. This effect is especially pronounced in the third stasimon, which becomes a turning point in the play, shifting our focus from the army onto Iphigenia herself and her dramatic change of attitude as she suddenly insists upon her sacrifice. As in *Trojan Women,* in which the constant, unsettling play with the absence and presence of *choreia* underscores the breakdown of community and the unhappy fate of the protagonists, this ode, while recalling the *mousikē* performed at the wedding of Achilles' parents, ironically marks the absence of such song and dance for Iphigenia.

The interplay of choral and solo song in this tragedy also demonstrates Euripides' continued experimentation with the relationship between dramatic and musical narrative. Its musical arc is the inverse of *Helen*'s, in which a mixture of individual and antiphonal lament in the first two-thirds of the play transitions into a very strong choral presence, with all three stasima performed in the last 550 lines. In contrast, the first two-thirds of *Iphigenia in Aulis* are rich with choral song (especially so if we accept the authenticity of the extraordinarily long parodos), but in the last part of the play Iphigenia's own song takes over from that of the chorus as her character becomes vital to the tragedy's conclusion. As we saw in chapter 1, Sophocles' *Women of Trachis* has a similar musical shape, with a shift from *choreia* to monody in the closing scenes; likewise in Euripides' *Heracles* the chorus are virtually silent in the last third of the play as the focus turns to the exchange between Amphitryon, Heracles, and Theseus instead.[3] The shift to monody in *Iphigenia in Aulis* should not therefore be viewed simply in terms of the New Music, even though Iphigenia's songs bear the markings of musical complexity suited to a star actor of the late fifth century. Moreover, although this play provides evidence of the increased prominence of actor's song in later Euripidean tragedy, its chorus still play a vital dramatic role through their *choreia,* which returns at the very end in a remarkable antiphonal exchange with Iphigenia as she goes to her death.

---

3. The musical structure of *Heracles* also consists in a shift from increasingly celebratory *choreia* in the three stasima to the chorus's focus on frenzied, ill-sounding music following the entrance of Isis and Lyssa (875–905). Soon they struggle to know what to sing at all, at which point Amphitryon tells them to be silent (1042–44); they are then quiet for the rest of the play. On images of negative *mousikē* in this tragedy, see Henrichs 1996: 61–62; Wilson 1999–2000; Gurd 2016: 129–30.

## SPECTATORSHIP, ENACTMENT, AND DESIRE

All tragic choruses are in some sense spectators, observing and commenting on the events in which the actors are involved, and so directing the audience as to what they too should see.[4] In *Iphigenia in Aulis*, however, the chorus's role as spectators is especially pronounced, not only in terms of what they see onstage but also in their viewing of scenes beyond it. The parodos in particular is full of highly pictorial language and verbs of seeing, as the chorus enter singing of the vast Greek fleet, which they have just seen spread out on the shore.[5] They also, as I will argue here, reenact this sight through the interplay between the verbal and musical elements of their song, particularly at its center point, when they describe Achilles and his Myrmidons. In doing so, they position the audience in their own role as spectators. In chapter 3 we saw how the chorus of *Trojan Women* perform the destruction of Troy in the closing scene of the play, bringing this otherwise-unseen backdrop physically into the *orchēstra*. In *Iphigenia in Aulis*, the Chalcidean women provide not just a verbal description but a virtually visible scene of the Greek army, thus becoming simultaneously past spectators and present performers of *choreia*. This description of the amassed forces provides a tense visual backdrop to the whole play, in which they are a constant, intimidating presence, waiting at Aulis until Iphigenia's sacrifice enables them to depart—a moment that never quite happens within Euripides' original play.[6] It is also an audible backdrop, as the chorus temporarily assume the identity of the army while simultaneously acting as spectators of it, so that their own vocal dominance here intensifies the presence of the army itself.[7] The emphasis on the army is especially charged following the opening scene, since Agamemnon has just sent a servant with a message to Clytemnestra not to bring Iphigenia to Aulis: without her, the Trojan War cannot happen.[8] The chorus, however, feel none of this tension as they delight in the visual splendor of this incredible sight.[9]

Because of the unusual length of this song, as well as the uncommon language and grammar, and the apparently monotonous, trochaic meter of the last five stanzas, lines 231–302 have been deemed one of several inorganic additions made after

---

4. Schlegel 1846: 76–77 famously deemed the chorus to be the ideal spectator; Battezzato 2005a: 154–56 sees the chorus members more as "empirical readers/spectators."

5. Their song is reminiscent of both the Catalogue of Ships and the Teichoscopia in the *Iliad* (2.494–759, 3.161–244): see Scodel 1997 (esp. 87–91); Michelakis 2006: 27.

6. It is especially menacing when Achilles describes how the whole army, even his own Myrmidons, forced him through the threat of stoning to abandon his attempt to save Iphigenia (1345–53). On the army as an offstage character, see Michelakis 2006: 44–45.

7. Cf. 814–18, where Achilles relates in direct speech the Myrmidons' loud complaints at their delay in Aulis.

8. Hose 1990: 160–61; Zeitlin 1994: 165–66.

9. See Mastronarde 2010: 129 on the chorus's aloofness and lack of anxiety in this song.

Euripides' death either for its first performance or for a fourth-century revival.[10] The appearance of rare vocabulary at least should come as no surprise, given Euripides' predilection for many unusual compound words in his later plays, especially in his supposedly dithyrambic choral songs. The authenticity of the whole parodos has been defended on the basis of its symmetrical relationship with the equally unusual prologue, in which Agamemnon's monologue is sandwiched between two passages of anapaestic dialogue.[11] This claim is convincing if at least Agamemnon's iambics are somewhat authentic.[12] A stronger argument for the authenticity of the entire parodos, however, is that its theme—the spectacle of the great Greek army—provides such an effective backdrop to the rest of the tragedy, and that, as we shall see, the dynamics of spectatorship that this song initiates are continued throughout the drama.[13] The image of *choreia* in the view of the ships in lines 231–41 can also be likened to other Euripidean passages of choral spectatorship, as we shall see at the end of this section through a comparison with songs from *Ion* and *Hypsipyle*.[14] Ultimately, however, what is important for my argument here is that, even if the last five stanzas of the parodos were not written by Euripides himself, they were composed in his style and are consistent with the striking degree of reflexively performative choral song in the rest of the play. In what follows I will focus in particular on two stanzas of the parodos: the first epode (206–30), which is almost certainly by Euripides himself, and the second strophe (231–41), which is Euripidean in style and very possibly in authorship too.

As soon as the chorus enter, they make it clear that they have traveled from Chalcis specifically "to look upon the army of the Achaians."[15] They repeat this wish in the antistrophe, and then start to recount what they did in fact see:

... ἀσπίδος ἔρυμα καὶ κλισίας
ὁπλοφόρους Δαναῶν θέλουσ'
ἵππων τ' ὄχλον ἰδέσθαι.
κατεῖδον δὲ ...

---

10. See esp. Page 1934: 142–46. Willink 1971: 361 n. 4 suggests Cephisophon as the author of lines 231–302; Kovacs 2003: 83–84 thinks they were composed either by Euripides Minor for the play's first performance or by a fourth-century producer ("the Reviser").

11. Irigoin 1988. See also Jouan 1983: 29–30 on the unity of the parodos as a whole.

12. Knox 1972; Mellert-Hoffmann 1969: 107–30; Kovacs 2003: 80–83. Page 1934: 138 rejects 106–14 but thinks Euripides wrote the rest of the iambics.

13. See also Zeitlin 1994: 161–71 on visual imagery in the play. Wiles 1997: 110 argues for the authenticity of the whole parodos by emphasizing how its Panhellenism, which becomes clear only if the last five stanzas are allowed to stand, unites "the Homeric world of the story and the immediate here-and-now of the Peloponnesian War."

14. It is also similar to the teichoscopia in *Phoenician Women* 88–192, when Antigone and the Old Man spot from the roof the different renowned warriors amid the besiegers of Thebes: Zeitlin 1994: 173–85; Scodel 1997: 85–87.

15. Ἀχαιῶν στρατιὰν ὡς ἐσιδοίμαν, 171.

... wishing to see the bulwark of armament and the arms-bearing tents of the Danaans, and the mass of horses. And I looked down upon ... (189–92)

As Froma Zeitlin has shown, this desire to see is part of the pervasive imagery of sight and spectacle in the parodos, as the chorus describe the masses of Greek warriors in strikingly vivid—and visual—terms.[16] Zeitlin argues that this scene essentially becomes an ecphrasis, since the chorus recount the tableau of the army as if it is a pictorial representation.[17] This ecphrasis sets the temporal and spatial context of the play in a highly visual way: "The impression is one of a full *skēnographia*, a painted backdrop to frame the drama of Iphigenia as it unfolds onstage before the eyes of the spectators in the audience."[18]

But this pictorial display is not just generated verbally: it also becomes present in the *orchēstra* through the chorus's own dancing bodies. The reflexive correspondence between text and choreography is especially pronounced at the center point of the song (the first nonstrophic epode and second strophe), as the chorus focus on Achilles and his Myrmidons:

| | |
|---|---|
| τὸν ἰσάνεμόν τε ποδοῖν | [epode] |
| λαιψηροδρόμον Ἀχιλλέα, | |
| τὸν ἁ Θέτις τέκε καὶ | |
| Χείρων ἐξεπόνησεν, | |
| ἴδον αἰγιαλοῖς παρά τε κροκάλαις | (210) |
| δρόμον ἔχοντα σὺν ὅπλοις· | |
| ἅμιλλαν δ' ἐπόνει ποδοῖν | |
| πρὸς ἅρμα τέτρωρον | |
| ἑλίσσων περὶ νίκας· | (215) |
| ὁ δὲ διφρηλάτας ἐβοᾶτ' | |
| Εὔμηλος Φερητιάδας, | |
| οὗ καλλίστους ἰδόμαν | |
| χρυσοδαιδάλτοις στομίοις | |
| πώλους κέντρωι θεινομένους, | (220) |
| τοὺς μὲν μέσους ζυγίους | |
| λευκοστίκτωι τριχὶ βαλιούς, | |
| τοὺς δ' ἔξω σειροφόρους | |
| ἀντήρεις καμπαῖσι δρόμων | |
| πυρσότριχας, μονόχαλα δ' ὑπὸ σφυρὰ | (225) |
| ποικιλοδέρμονας· οἷς παρεπάλλετο | |

---

16. Zeitlin 1994: 157–66 and 1995: 180–92. Cf. Hose 1990: 160.

17. Cf. Eur. *Ion* 184–218, when the chorus describe the scenes depicted on the pediments and walls of the temple at Delphi.

18. Zeitlin 1995: 182. She suggests that the organization of the parodos in *IA* evokes the beginnings of a mnemonic system reliant on pictorial images: Zeitlin 1994: 161–65, 171, and 1995, esp. 184–87. Cf. Jouan 1983: 47.

Πηλεΐδας σὺν ὅπλοισι παρ' ἄντυγα
καὶ σύριγγας ἁρματείους. (230)

ναῶν δ' εἰς ἀριθμὸν ἤλυθον [2nd strophe]
καὶ θέαν ἀθέσφατον,
τὰν γυναικεῖον ὄψιν ὀμμάτων
ὡς πλήσαιμι †μείλινον† ἁδονάν.
καὶ κέρας μὲν ἦν (235)
δεξιὸν πλάτας ἔχων
Φθιωτίδας ὁ Μυρμιδὼν Ἄρης
πεντήκοντα ναυσὶ θουρίαις·
χρυσέαις δ' εἰκόσιν κατ' ἄκρα Νη-
ρῇδες ἕστασαν θεαί, (240)
πρύμναις σῆμ' Ἀχιλλείου στρατοῦ.

And the one equal to the wind on his feet, swift-running Achilles, whom Thetis bore and Chiron trained, I saw him by the seashore having a race in armor. And he was working on a contest on feet against a four-horsed chariot, whirling around for victory. And the driver was shouting, Eumelos, Pheres' grandson, whose beautiful steeds I saw, with bridles embellished with gold, being struck by the goad, the yoke bearers in the middle, dappled with white-flecked hair, and the trace horses on the outside, facing the bends of the course, with flaming hair, and with dappled skin beneath their single-hoofed ankles. Beside them leapt the son of Peleus in his armor, by the chariot rail and wheel hubs.

I came to count the ships and see the indescribable sight, so that I might fill the womanly vision of my eyes, a †sweet† pleasure. And the force of Myrmidons from Phthia formed the wing on the right, with fifty swift ships. And in golden likenesses the Nereid goddesses stood on the sterns, at the very ends, the emblem of Achilles' army. (206–41)

The image of Achilles racing against a four-horse chariot encourages the audience to see an interplay between the chorus's own movements and the ones that they describe. Even for this famously fast-footed hero, the emphasis placed on both speed and feet is remarkable, with the hapax compound *laipsērodromos* within the pleonastic description of "the one equal to the wind on his feet, swift-running Achilles" (206–7);[19] his race is then called a "contest on feet" (212).[20] As we saw in chapter 2 in the case of *Electra*, when the chorus sing of Achilles as "swift in the leap of his feet" (451), such descriptions of fast, running movement can point to the chorus's own dancing in the *orchēstra*. Indeed, running was presumably often part of or at

---

19. Cf. Stockert 1992: 2.249.
20. The word for "contest" here is *hamilla*, which the chorus in [Aesch.] *PV* also use to refer to their own fast movements: ἥδε τά- / ξις πτερύγων θοαῖς ἁμίλ- / λαις προσέβα ("This band of ours has come with the speedy rivalry [*hamillais*] of wings," 128–30).

least closely linked to *choreia*, as the description of the dancing youths and maidens depicted on Achilles' shield in the *Iliad* indicates:[21]

οἱ δ' ὁτὲ μὲν θρέξασκον ἐπισταμένοισι πόδεσσι
ῥεῖα μάλ', ὡς ὅτε τις τροχὸν ἄρμενον ἐν παλάμῃσιν (600)
ἑζόμενος κεραμεὺς πειρήσεται, αἴ κε θέῃσιν·
ἄλλοτε δ' αὖ θρέξασκον ἐπὶ στίχας ἀλλήλοισι.
πολλὸς δ' ἱμερόεντα χορὸν περιίσταθ' ὅμιλος
τερπόμενοι· δοιὼ δὲ κυβιστητῆρε κατ' αὐτοὺς (604–605)
μολπῆς ἐξάρχοντες ἐδίνευον κατὰ μέσσους.

And at times they would run with knowing feet very swiftly, as when a potter, sitting, tests the wheel fitted in his palms, [to see] if it will run. And at other times they would run in rows through one another. And a great crowd stood around the desirable chorus, delighting in it. And two tumblers among them, leading off the song and dance, were whirling through their midst. (Hom. *Il.* 18.599–606)

Such running/dancing could be done in rows; it could also be in the form of a circle, as the image of the potter's wheel suggests,[22] and include individual circular movements, like those of the two tumblers.

In the parodos of *Iphigenia in Aulis* the suggestive interplay between Achilles' movements and those of the chorus becomes even more powerful when he is pictured as "whirling" around the track (*helissōn*, 215). This verb is used once in Homer in a similar context to express the swift directing of a chariot around the turning posts.[23] If that use is evoked here, then the application of the verb to Achilles himself would augment the picture of him as a runner who can outmatch the speed of a chariot. But we have also repeatedly seen that in Euripides' later plays words of the *heliss-* root tend to occur in choral passages with highly metamusical language and to suggest the circular movement of the chorus in the *orchēstra* (and perhaps also the spinning of individual choreuts).[24] The verb is also very similar in sense to *dineuein*, which is used of the twirling tumblers in the Iliadic passage. We may imagine that, as in that scene, the dramatic chorus here could use a combination of group and individual movements to give the impression of Achilles' racing.

---

21. Running and dancing—as well as chariot racing—are also closely connected in Aeschylus's *Libation Bearers*, when the chorus call on Zeus to impose a "measure" (*metron*) and "rhythm" (*rhythmos*) on Orestes, whom they describe as a colt yoked to a chariot in a race (794–99). This metaphor could assume a visual form through the chorus's own dancing. On the equine imagery in this passage, see Steiner forthcoming: chapter 4.

22. Cf. Lib. 64.104 on the equation of *dromos* ("running, race") and *trochos* ("wheel, circle").

23. Hom. *Il.* 23.309: see Stockert 1992: 2.251–52.

24. Wiles 1997: 108 suggests that "the non-strophic dancing suits Achilles' linear progression to the finishing post," but the dancing itself need not have been linear rather than circular.

In the second half of the epode the chorus concentrate on the horses racing alongside the hero, although at the end they return to Achilles with another strongly choreographic verb, *parepalleto* ("was leaping alongside," 226).[25] As we saw in chapter 1, the association of horses and *choreia* (especially *partheneia*) was traditional; it is especially clear in Alcman's first *Partheneion* and Euripides' *Iphigenia in Tauris*.[26] Now, then, the audience are prompted to visualize the dancing chorus as the horses that they describe in such visual and attractive terms: their bridles are "embellished with gold" (219); the center pair have "white-flecked hair" (222); the trace horses are flame-colored with dappled skin (225–26). As the individual runner/dancer against the team of horses, Achilles stands out almost as a *chorēgos* is distinguished from the rest of a chorus. As a result of such interaction between the chorus's own dancing and the movements that they describe in their song, the audience can themselves share in the sight of this scene, not just hear about it.

In the following strophe the chorus emphatically shift back to the position of a female viewer watching an "indescribable sight" (232) before again enacting the viewed object—now the Myrmidon fleet (235–41)—and bringing it to life through their own dancing bodies.[27] On the sterns of the fifty ships are golden images of Nereids, the archetypal choreuts who often appear in highly metamusical contexts, such as the description of their dancing in Bacchylides 17 and the first stasimon of Euripides' *Electra*; later in *Iphigenia in Aulis*, as we shall see, they are pictured as "whirling in circles" in their dance.[28] The number of ships (and so also of Nereids) here is significant, since it is also the number of choreuts in the performance of a dithyramb, and so encourages us to see this ecphrastic image as choral. As in the first stasimon of *Electra*, the reference to the Nereids here has a doubling effect, making the audience see them as both the dramatic chorus and the imagined one. At this center point of the *Iphigenia in Aulis* parodos, then, the chorus again enact the object of their desirous gaze, now by representing this other chorus, the golden Nereids on the ships' sterns.

Unlike the Nereids in *Electra*, however, these are works of art. They stand in golden likenesses (240), presumably as carved figures at the tips of the sterns, like statues.[29] As we saw in chapter 1, the association between choruses and crafted

---

25. This compound is a hapax, but *pallein* can often refer to dance: Naerebout 1997: 281–82. The verb is used choreographically at Eur. *El.* 435, 477, *Tro.* 325; also Ar. *Ran.* 1317, *Lys.* 1304. It appears in a compound form (*anapallein*) at Ar. *Lys.* 1310 to describe the movement of horses and maidens.

26. See also Steiner forthcoming: chapter 4.

27. At 231 ἤλυθον ("I came"), which resumes the pattern of verbs of coming or going at the start of each stanza (cf. 164, 186), helps to reestablish the first-person perspective.

28. Bacchyl. 17.101–8; Eur. *El.* 442, *IA* 1055–57.

29. Stockert 1992: 2.259 thinks they could be either carved or painted. They could resemble statues in either case but are more likely meant to be carved, since an *eikōn*, particularly when it is described as golden, often denotes a sculpture: e.g., Hdt. 1.50.3, 7.69.2; Pl. *Phdr.* 235d9; Plut. *Mar.* 32.4,

objects—also evident in the simile of the potter's wheel used to describe the dancing youths and maidens on Achilles' shield in the *Iliad*—was part of the traditional imaginary of *choreia* in archaic and classical Greece.[30] Though the Nereids in *Electra* are not described as artifacts, we saw in the following stanzas of that first stasimon how the chorus can merge with a precious object—in that case Achilles' armor, which they describe with strongly choreographic language. Like the golden *Kēlēdones* in Pindar's eighth *Paean*, the works of art to which choruses are frequently assimilated tend to be "products of divine or uncanny crafting."[31] The chorus of *Iphigenia in Aulis* do not know the provenance of golden Nereids standing on the ships' sterns, but they clearly find them extraordinary, as part of a scene that is *athesphaton* (232)—one that not even a god could describe.[32]

As in the previous epode, viewer and viewed are simultaneously separate and fused here. The chorus wonder at these Nereids as focalizers who are explicitly female, finding delight in what they see in part because of the very alterity of this scene of great male warriors. But in performance they also become assimilated to those golden crafted objects, embodying this emblem (*sēma*, 241) of Achilles' forces and thus visually representing it to the audience.[33] This process could continue in the following stanzas, in which *sēmata* represent almost all the other groups of Greek ships, though with less explicit focus (at least in the text itself) on choreographic correspondence: the sixty Argive ships are decorated with the emblem of Pallas on a winged chariot (247–52); the fifty Theban ones show Cadmus's golden dragon (253–60); on Nestor's ships, from Pylos, is a river-bull emblem (275–76).[34]

The choreographic visualization of Achilles and his ships is thus in part a feminization through *choreia* of an otherwise alien male scene—even while, underneath their masks and costumes, the choreuts performing it are male citizens. The equine imagery in the previous stanza creates a similar effect by adding a parthenaic coloring to the depiction of his horses. As we shall see, this sort of female appropriation of a male group points forward to Iphigenia's own usurpation of both the paean (which was typically performed by men) and masculine language

---

*Alex.* 336c10, *De Pyth. Or.* 401e2; Ath. 11.505d–e; Diod. Sic. 2.15.3, 34.5. Other references to carved figures on the sterns or prows of ships in fifth-century Athenian literature include Ar. *Ran.* 933, when Aeschylus explains that "the golden horse-rooster" is an emblem carved upon ships (ἐν ταῖς ναυσὶν ... ἐνεγέγραπτο); cf. Aesch. *Myrmidons* fr. 134. See also Ar. *Ach.* 547 on the gilding of figures of Pallas (presumably for ships).

30. See Power 2011; Kurke 2012 and 2013.
31. Kurke 2012: 224. On Pind. *Pae.* 8, see chapter 1, pp. 34–35.
32. Cf. Neer 2010: 60–61 on speechlessness as an effect of seeing a wonder (*thauma*).
33. Cf. Neer 2010: 57–69 (esp. 66–68) on the doubling effect of nearness and alterity in *thauma*, particularly with respect to artwork. See also Steiner 2001: 20–22; Kurke 2012 and 2013.
34. Wiles 1997: 108–9 sees each of these as a "choreographic image" and discusses the transition from Nereids to "chthonic monsters and monstrous men."

of bravery on behalf of the community as she goes to her sacrifice at the end of the play. The mismatch of female chorality and male army, though it helps to communicate their delight in this scene, is also unsettling, reminding us of what the army's presence will mean for Iphigenia.

The merging of the chorus of spectators and the chorus of divine Nereids exemplifies what Leslie Kurke describes as the "mimetic chain of presence" whereby gods, dancers, and human spectators are fused together through *choreia* and the erotic desire that it invokes.[35] It also extends to the actual audience in the theater, since they join the Chalcidean women as spectators of *choreia*, virtually seeing as they do through the chorus's bodily assimilation to viewed objects. This twofold overlap of extradramatic and intradramatic spectators on the one hand and performing and imagined chorus on the other occurs when the delight expressed by the chorus at what they saw verges on the erotic: the sight for their female eyes is a "pleasure" (*hadonan*, 234); although the adjective *meilinon* ("sweet"), which is found in ms L, must for metrical reasons be corrupt, all proposed emendations still intensify the force of *hadonan*.[36] Froma Zeitlin has noted that their fixation on Achilles in the previous stanza also has an erotic coloring and suggests that this dramatically foreshadows Iphigenia's first view of her pretended bridegroom.[37] In the second strophe, then, this desirous focus on the individual hero expands to include his whole force of Myrmidons, and its effects are heightened through the suggestive power of *choreia*.[38] Although Iphigenia's reaction of shame at the sight of Achilles later in the play may in part suggest her attraction to him,[39] the erotic prominence of Achilles in the parodos presages a more general focus on him as an ideal bridegroom ("not to be faulted," as Clytemnestra says after hearing of his

---

35. Kurke 2013: 148. Cf. Power 2011. Peponi 2009 emphasizes that an important element of the ideal *choreia* represented in *the Homeric Hymn to Apollo* is how "the line separating the act of performing from the act of attending tends to disappear" (67); cf. Peponi 2012: 88–94 on the "aesthetics of fusion." See also Platt 2011 on epiphanic images and how the distinction between a deity and its representation can be blurred in ritual contexts.

36. Jouan 1983 and Günther 1988 both favor Wilamowitz's emendation λίχνον ἁδονάν ("greedy pleasure"). Stockert 1992: 2.258 suggests μελιχρῶν ἁδονᾶν ("honey-sweet pleasures").

37. Zeitlin 1994: 159–60 and 1995: 183. See also Foley 1985: 79–80.

38. On the theme of *erōs* in the play, see Michelini 1999–2000: 51–54.

39. Eur. *IA* 1341. Smith 1979 argues that Iphigenia's desire for Achilles motivates her change of mind as she shifts from supplication to the resolve to die. But to view her motivation as one merely of desire is to underappreciate both the complexity of her virginal character and the pattern of changing minds in this play. Her expression of shame, even if it recalls the chorus's own reddened cheeks as they look upon the army (187–88), suggests modesty and embarrassment as much as erotic feelings toward Achilles: she explains that "the unfortunate situation of our marriage brings me shame" (τὸ δυστυχὲς μοι τῶν γάμων αἰδῶ φέρει, 1342). On the issue of Iphigenia's motivation, see also Jouan 1983: 36–38; Foley 1985: 76–77; McDonald 1990; Sansone 1991; Gibert 1995: 222–37; Burgess 2004: 51–55; Michelakis 2006: 38–40; Mastronarde 2010: 238–40.

lineage).[40] It also sets up an ironic contrast between the idealization of Achilles and the reality of his character in the play: ultimately this great warrior will be too weak to resist the demands of his own army, so that Iphigenia's marriage will become her sacrifice.

The surviving Euripidean corpus includes two other examples of the choral enactment of the object of viewing. In the third stasimon of *Ion*, the chorus of Athenian maidens sing of their shame at the idea of Ion, apparently a non-Athenian, witnessing the Eleusinian Mysteries as a *theōros*:

αἰσχύνομαι τὸν πολύ-
μνον θεόν, εἰ παρὰ Καλλιχόροισι παγαῖς  (1075)
λαμπάδα θεωρὸς εἰκάδων
ἐννύχιον ἄυπνος ὄψεται,
ὅτε καὶ Διὸς ἀστερωπὸς
ἀνεχόρευσεν αἰθήρ,
χορεύει δὲ σελάνα  (1080)
καὶ πεντήκοντα κόραι
†Νηρέος αἱ κατὰ πόντον
ἀεναῶν τε ποταμῶν†
δίνας χορευόμεναι
τὰν χρυσοστέφανον κόραν  (1085)
καὶ ματέρα σεμνάν·

I feel shame before the much-hymned god, if by the Springs of Beautiful Dances ⟨he as⟩ a watcher will view, sleepless, the all-night torch procession of the twentieth day, when even the starry-faced aether of Zeus has begun dancing, and the moon dances and the fifty daughters †of Nereus, through the sea and †the eddies† of ever-flowing rivers,† dancing in honor of the golden-crowned Kore and her august mother. (1074–86)

The chorus's description of the Mysteries is dominated by Dionysiac images of cosmic and divine dance (the dancing aether, stars, and moon; the fifty Nereids),[41] and these converge with their own dance in the theater so that they appear to be performing the spectacle that Ion would see. The detail with which they imagine these performances suggests that they themselves are to be seen as Athenian *mystai*, initiated in the Mysteries and therefore both participants in and spectators of the dancing that they describe.[42] As Eric Csapo has shown, the image of cosmic *choreia* has strong associations with mystery cult in antiquity;[43] it also suggests the

---

40. οὐ μεμπτός, 712.
41. See Csapo 2008: 268. Cf. Lee 1997: 277; Csapo 2003: 73 ("if they dance on eddies, they must dance in circles"). On Dionysiac associations in *Ion*, see Zacharia 2003: 110–11. The "Springs of Beautiful Dances [*Kallichoroisi*]" refer to the Kallichoron Well at Eleusis: see Henrichs 1996: 51.
42. Most Athenians, both men and women, were initiated in the Eleusinian Mysteries: Burkert 1985: 285–86.
43. Csapo 2008.

experience of "the mimetic chain of presence" in attending the dances of mystic initiation, whereby human, divine, and even cosmic spectators and choreuts merge together. Unlike the chorus of *Iphigenia in Aulis*, however, they do not explicitly position themselves as viewers: rather, the *theōros* (Ion) is imagined as an uninitiated foreigner seeing what he should not.

More similar to the chorus's simultaneous description and choreographic enactment of the sight of the Greek army in *Iphigenia in Aulis* is the parodos of the fragmentary *Hypsipyle*, another late play by Euripides.[44] Here, in a lyric exchange with Hypsipyle, the chorus of Nemean women picture the passing army of the Seven with vivid metamusical language (fr. 752f). This description follows musical images in the previous lines, when the chorus ask Hypsipyle if she is singing of the "fifty-oared" *Argo* or if she is thinking of Lemnos, "which the wave-beating Aegean makes resound, whirling around";[45] the self-referential participle *helissōn* is combined with the adjective *kymoktypos* ("wave-beating"), in which the alliteration of the hard *k*- sound strengthens the acoustic and choreographic image of beating (or clapping).[46] The chorus then draw Hypsipyle's attention to the immediate scene of the army of the Seven in the plain, picturing it as "flashing with bronze arms".[47] These lines are fragmentary, but they seem to continue the choreographic language of the first half of the strophe with the epithet "swift-footed" used of Adrastus and the description (most likely) of horses as "single-stepping" and "raising" or "raising themselves from" the ground.[48] As in the parodos of *Iphigenia in Aulis*, then, the Nemean women here reproduce through their metamusical language and choreography the sight that they simultaneously describe, bringing it into the theater for the audience to share in as well.

But these lines take up only half a strophe, and although the chorus seem to take delight in the glittering spectacle of the army of the Seven, Hypsipyle rejects the scene that they have so vividly described. Instead she yearns for the sight of the Argonauts arriving in Lemnos (where she bore her twin sons to Jason), the very scene on which the chorus had suspected she was dwelling: "these, these my spirit

---

44. On the dating of *Hypsipyle*, see Bond 1963: 144; Cropp and Fick 1985: 80–81; Cockle 1987: 40–41; Collard and Cropp 2008b: 254.

45. τὰν Αἰγαῖος ἑλί[σ]σων / κυμο⟨κ⟩τύπος ἀχεῖ, fr. 752f.27–28.

46. Cf. Csapo 1999–2000: 419. *Ktypos* ("beat") is often used in synaesthetic images of *mousikē*: see chapter 1, p. 41, on Aesch. *Sept.* 100–103; chapter 3, p. 137, on Eur. *Tro.* 1325; cf. ποδῶν κτύπος, Luc. *Salt.* 68.7. The parody of *Hypsipyle*'s choral lyric in Aristophanes' *Frogs* suggests that the percussive element of the play's *mousikē* was especially striking: to accompany the song the character Aeschylus summons Euripides' Muse, "the one who beats with her potsherds" (ἡ τοῖς ὀστράκοις / αὕτη κροτοῦσα, 1305–6). On the reference to *krotala* here, see Griffith 2013a: 143.

47. ἀσ[τ]ράπ[τ]ει χαλκέο[ι]σ⟨ιν⟩ ὅπλο[ις, fr. 752f.30. Euripides may be influenced here by the parodos of Aeschylus's *Seven Against Thebes*, in which the chorus also enact the scene of the approaching army of the Seven that they so vividly describe: chapter 1, pp. 40–41.

48. ᾧ[κυ]πόδας (752f.33); μονοβάμονε[ς / ἀειρόμενοι χθ[ον (38–39).

desires to see, but let someone else cry of the labors of the Danaans."⁴⁹ What survives of her sung response continues the performative language of the previous strophe: we can imagine the chorus dancing as she describes Peleus leaping and the rowers keeping time to the song of Orpheus's lyre (fr. 752g3–14). In the parodos of *Hypsipyle*, then, two views are described and performed for the audience: that of the army of the Seven, which the characters onstage can actually see (or have just seen), and that of the *Argo* and its heroes, which is in the realm of memory, temporally and geographically distant, yet crucial as a backdrop for the ensuing drama, in which Hypsipyle is reunited with her sons and returns with them to Lemnos.⁵⁰

The chorus's enacted view of the army in *Iphigenia in Aulis* likewise remains a crucial backdrop for the play's action. The dynamics of viewing set up in the parodos, whereby the chorus shift between being spectators and being spectacle, continue to play an important role, resuming in the last third of the tragedy as the army and Iphigenia (rather than the chorus) alternately become the subject and the object of spectatorship. Just before Iphigenia changes her mind and submits to sacrifice, Agamemnon tells her and Clytemnestra to look at the same scene that the chorus describe (and enact) in the parodos:

ὁρᾶθ' ὅσον στράτευμα ναύφαρκτον τόδε
χαλκέων θ' ὅπλων ἄνακτες Ἑλλήνων ὅσοι.

Behold how great this army of ships here is, and how many leaders of bronze-clad Greek warriors there are. (1259–60)

Yet toward the end of the tragedy it is Iphigenia to whom the gaze of the army, chorus, and audience turns exclusively: as she changes her mind, she repositions herself as the viewed instead of the viewer, stating that "the whole of mighty Greece now looks upon *me*."⁵¹ The chorus reinforce this transition in their final song, as they direct everyone—Clytemnestra onstage, the army in the (imagined) background, and the audience—to look at Iphigenia, who through her sacrifice replaces the army as the sacker of Troy:⁵²

---

49. τ[ά]δε μοι τάδε θυμὸς ἰδεῖν ἵεται, / Δαναῶν δὲ πόνους / ἕτερος ἀναβοάτω, fr. 752g.15–17.

50. Wiles 1997: 126 argues that the forward and backward movement of the strophic dance in the parodos parallels the opposition between the positive journey of the *Argo* and the negative one of the army of the Seven.

51. εἰς ἔμ' Ἑλλὰς ἡ μεγίστη πᾶσα νῦν ἀποβλέπει, 1378. The army in *IA* is presented synecdochically as "the whole of mighty Greece"; cf. 1352, when Achilles says "all Greeks" (πάντες Ἕλληνες) threatened him. Mellert-Hoffmann 1969: 23–26 emphasizes the Panhellenic aspect of the Greek army scene in the parodos.

52. Cf. 1475–76: ἄγετέ με τὰν Ἰλίου / καὶ Φρυγῶν ἑλέπτολιν. Iphigenia thus assumes Helen's role but in more positive terms. Cf. Helen as city sacker (*heleptolis*) at Aesch. *Ag.* 689–90.

ἰὼ ἰώ.
ἴδεσθε τὰν Ἰλίου
καὶ Φρυγῶν ἑλέπτολιν
στείχουσαν.

*Iō iō!* Behold the city sacker of Ilium and the Phrygians as she goes on her way.
(1510–12)

The chorus's song is then followed by the messenger's speech, in which Iphigenia's sacrifice is described very vividly, as Zeitlin has shown.[53] Even though this speech is probably spurious, the act of viewing is again stressed, this time with a poignant echo of Iphigenia's earlier statement as Agamemnon, Menelaus, and the army avert their gaze from the girl herself: "The sons of Atreus and the whole army stood, looking to the ground."[54] This shift of visual focus toward Iphigenia and away from the army complements the transition through the play from male to female, group to individual, choral song to Iphigenia's monody that we will see at the end of this chapter.

## PAST AND PRESENT *MOUSIKĒ*

In the parodos, as we have seen, the chorus concentrate on a present scene that forms the temporally concurrent backdrop of the entire play. The following stasima, however, extend the play's temporal scope by focusing on the past and the future.[55] In the first stasimon (543–606), after gnomic speculation in the strophic pair, the chorus dwell on the recent past—Paris igniting the conflict between Troy and Greece and so causing the Greek army to be here in Aulis. In the second stasimon (751–800) the chorus describe with vivid detail the Trojan War, imagining the arrival of the Greek fleet on the river Simois, the weeping of Helen, and the lamentation of the Trojan women at their looms.[56] In the third stasimon (1036–97) their focus spans past, present, and future: initially shifting back to the more distant past (though with relevance to the present) as they dwell on the marriage of Peleus and Thetis, their song then moves toward the future with images of the destruction that Achilles will wreak at Troy; in the epode the chorus sing of the present and the immediate future (Iphigenia's death) within the *mythos* itself. In their final song (1509–31), as in the parodos, they are fixated on the present, but this time they

---

53. Zeitlin 1994: 169–70.
54. ἐς γῆν δ' Ἀτρεῖδαι πᾶς στρατός τ' ἔστη βλέπων, 1577.
55. As Barlow 1971: 24–25 notes, this temporal pattern of choral odes is common in Euripides' plays: the parodos tends to situate the audience within the immediate environment of the *mythos*; the stasima often look forward and backward.
56. It may also include a vision of Paris's bloody corpse if we accept Murray's conjecture ⟨Πάριν Ἀτρείδας⟩ for line 777.

respond to what the audience themselves also see onstage—Iphigenia being led away for sacrifice.

Both the first and third stasima contain strikingly vivid descriptions of music making that bring these scenes of past and future to life; merging with the chorus's own performance, they are enacted for the audience within the frame of the present drama. The musical images in the two songs thus intensify the significance of these scenes for the immediate *mythos*, but they are also undermined by it, offering glimpses of carefree *mousikē* that can belong only to the past.

### Playing the Syrinx in the First Stasimon

Language of *mousikē* in the first stasimon is limited to just three lines of the epode, yet it plays an important part in the movement and meaning of the ode as a whole. As if escaping from the action they were previously so keen to witness, now that Agamemnon has determined to sacrifice Iphigenia despite Menelaus's change of mind (506–42), the chorus here utter gnomic statements of moral wisdom in praise of restraint and virtue in love (543–72). They describe in the epode two specific scenes from the past that led to the impending war: the herdsman Paris arriving at the Judgment scene playing his syrinx (573–81); then Paris standing before Helen's palace, kindling the love between them (582–86).[57] The difference between the destructive love that brings the Greek army to Troy's walls and the restrained love that the chorus have just praised and wished for is emphasized by the wordplay of *eris* ("strife") and *erōs* ("love") in lines 585–87.[58] The transition from gnomic wisdom to descriptive narrative starts off with the depiction of Paris's music making, which vividly transports the audience to the setting on Mount Ida, capturing the moment of pastoral innocence before the stirrings of war (a moment on which Iphigenia later dwells at greater length in her monody, 1279–1335). These metamusical lines have a powerful affective impact, allowing the audience brief enjoyment of carefree *mousikē* before returning them to *eris* and the horrifying reality of the play.

The motif of Paris making music just before the Judgment scene was a common one: many archaic and classical vases show him playing a chelys lyre as the goddesses approach.[59] Here in *Iphigenia in Aulis*, however, he is described as piping

---

57. On the first stasimon's structure, see Stinton 1965: 25–26; Stockert 1992: 2.355–57. On the motif of the conflict's origin, see Stinton 1965: 13–29; Mastronarde 2010: 123–24. Cf. *Andr.* 274–92, *Hec.* 629–49; also *El.* 669–746 and *Or.* 807–43 on the Tantalid myth.

58. Cf. Alcaeus fr. 283 Voigt, in which an account of Helen's *erōs* is followed by a description of the resulting bloodshed at Troy. On the relevance of the *erōs* theme in the *IA* ode, see Foley 1985: 80; Sorum 1992: 533; Stockert 1992: 2.355; Mastronarde 2010: 135.

59. Stinton 1965: 28; Raab 1972: 62; Bundrick 2005: 65–66. In the *Iliad* Paris is associated with the *kithara* (3.54).

(*syrizōn*) on his syrinx—a different image, one that emphasizes the pastoral nature of the scene, representing Paris as a herdsman rather than a lyre-playing aristocrat:[60]

†ἔμολες, ὦ Πάρις, ᾗτε σύ γε†
βουκόλος ἀργενναῖς ἐτράφης
Ἰδαίαις παρὰ μόσχοις, (575)
βάρβαρα συρίζων, Φρυγίων
αὐλῶν Οὐλύμπου καλάμοις
μιμήματα †πνέων†.

†You came, Paris, to the place where† you were reared as a herdsman among the shining white heifers of Mount Ida, piping foreign tunes on the syrinx, †breathing† on the reeds imitations of the Phrygian *auloi* of Olympus. (573–78)

The participle *syrizōn* could either refer to what Paris was doing as he approached the goddesses or be part of the subordinate clause, describing his activity as he was growing up in the bucolic setting of Mount Ida. This ambiguity is surely deliberate, encapsulating his entire existence before being sent to Helen as well as the specific moment at which the Judgment took place. The description of Paris as a herdsman, made vivid through the image of his music making, indicates the rustic nature both of the geographical setting and of his own identity before meeting Helen (as it does in Iphigenia's monody toward the end of the play).[61] As we saw in the second stasimon of Euripides' *Electra*, when the chorus sing of Pan blowing on the syrinx as he brings the Golden Fleece to Argos from the mountains, this instrument is often a marker of pastoral simplicity.[62] Its rusticity may

---

60. Bundrick 2005: 65 emphasizes the class associations of the two instruments. In the Homeric poems, however, herdsmen (including Paris himself) can also be associated with kings: see Gutzwiller 1991: 26–29.

My translation follows Kovacs 2002: 223, understanding the objective genitive with *mimēmata* to be the *auloi* rather than Olympus. But the precise meaning here is unclear: Barker 1984: 92 instead translates these lines as "breathing imitations of Olympus on the reeds of Phrygian *auloi*"; we could even understand Olympus as the mountain in Phrygia rather than the musician. I argue in Weiss forthcoming a that such ambiguity is deliberate, exploiting the perceived intimacy of the *aulos* and syrinx in a clever interplay of imagined and performed *mousikē*.

61. IA 1291–93 (τὸν ἀμφὶ / βουσὶ βουκόλον τραφέντ᾽ Ἀ- / λέξανδρον). The reference to his heifers (μόσχοις, 575) may also suggest a romantic coloring to this pastoral scene, since these animals are often part of an erotic setting in Greek literature: see esp. Theoc. *Id.* 8.71–79, 9.7–12; Long. 1.15.3, 1.18.1, 2.4.3; cf. Hor. *Carm* 2.5.5–8.

62. Eur. *El.* 699–706. Cf. [Aesch.] *Prom.* 575–76; Eur. *Alc.* 568–87, *Ion* 492–502, *IA* 1085–86, *Rhes.* 551–53, *Phaethon* fr. 773.27–28; also *Hymn. Hom. Merc.* 512; *Hymn. Hom. Pan.* 16–18; Hom. *Il.* 18.526; Soph. *Phil.* 213; Plato *Rep.* 399d; Longus *Past.* 2.31. On the associations of the syrinx with Pan and pastoral settings in Euripides, see Pereira 1998: 52–58; Weiss forthcoming a. On the pastoral connections of the syrinx in general, see West 1992: 110; Landels 1999: 69; Mathiesen 1999: 222–23. Though the syrinx only occasionally appears in Attic vase painting, it tends to be in this setting: see Bundrick 2005: 42.

also be indicated by the reference to its reeds (577), which appear as a metonym for the instrument itself.[63]

The syrinx also situates the scene in the foreign setting of Troy. This environment is evoked not only by a description of the physical geography of Mount Ida (as it is later by Iphigenia in her monody) but through its soundscape.[64] The tunes piped by Paris are focalized by the Chalcidean women as foreign (*barbara*, 576);[65] the instrument itself, though said in the *Homeric Hymn* to have been invented by Hermes,[66] was also often conceptualized as foreign in origin.[67] The accompaniment of the *aulos* represents this non-Greek soundscape acoustically as well: as in the second stasimon of *Electra*, the audience would probably not see or hear the syrinx itself (though some miming might be possible), but could instead hear the tune of the *aulos* as the imagined sound of the syrinx. Paris's pipe playing may also be represented visually through the figure of the aulete playing in the *orchēstra*, whose elaborate clothing could bring to mind Paris's own reputation for Phrygian luxury (when he is not depicted as a herdsman). The description of Paris's tunes as "imitations of the Phrygian *auloi* of Olympus" (577–78) intensifies the fusion of the two instruments: the syrinx in the song is represented by the sound of the *aulos* in the theater, so that Paris seems to be playing both at once.[68]

The combination of these two instruments creates a doubly foreign soundscape, since the *aulos*, though used in many Greek settings, was often associated with Phrygia. Indeed the *auloi* mentioned here are described as "Phrygian" (576), an adjective that mostly denotes their location but could indicate a particular type of *aulos* that apparently consisted of unequal pipes (one of which ended in a horn). Unsurprisingly, these *Phrygioi auloi* were associated with Asiatic or at least non-

---

63. Cf. Eur. *IA* 1038, *El*. 702, *IT* 1125–27; also Ar. fr. 738 KA (καλαμίνην σύριγγα). The syrinx was also associated with *donakes*: Eur. *Or.* 146; Long. 2.34.2–3; Nonnus, *Dion.* 11.105–6, 19.294.

64. Cf. *IA* 1279–1335 (Iphigenia's monody), esp. 1291–99. On soundscapes, see Schafer 1977; Feld 1990 (esp. 264–66) and 2000: 183–84. Cf. Hall 1989: 129–32 on barbarian music.

65. Cf. Aesch. *Sept.* 463. On the syrinx, Paris, and Olympus as *barbaroi*, see Stockert 1992: 2.371.

66. *Hymn. Hom. Merc.* 511–12. It is possible that Hermes enters with the syrinx in Sophocles' *Inachus* as if he has just invented it: see Seidensticker 2012: 222 n. 62.

67. See Ath. 4.184a4–b2, Diod. Sic. 3.58, Poll. 4.77. Cf. Mathiesen 1999: 222–23.

68. *Kalamoi* ("reeds") were associated with the *aulos* as well as the syrinx, so the mention of them here may add to the merging of the two instruments. Cf. Theophr. *Hist. pl.* 4.6; Ar. fr. 150 KA; Theoc. *Id.* 5.6–7; Ath. 4.184a. The aulete could also make use of a syrinx device to raise the pipes' pitch, in which case these lines would be strongly metamusical, referring to both Paris's music and the technical manipulation of the *aulos*'s sound in the theater: on this device, see esp. West 1992: 86, 102–3; Hagel 2012. It is mentioned in texts from the mid-fourth century B.C.E. onward; see Aristox. *Harm.* 1.20–21; ps.-Arist. *De Aud.* 804a14; ps.-Plut. *De Mus.* 1137f4–38a6; Plut. *Mor.* 1096b. *Syrigmos* also refers to the hissing of a snake, and at the Pythian auletic contest it seems to have traditionally represented the dying serpent killed by Apollo, for which auletes tended to use the syrinx device: see Xen. *Symp.* 6.5, Strabo 9.3.10. On the close relationship between the *aulos* and syrinx, see further Weiss forthcoming a.

Greek settings.⁶⁹ The two instruments, syrinx and *aulos*, actually appear together to convey the sound of the Trojans in the *Iliad*, when Agamemnon looks out at their camps in front of the city:⁷⁰

θαύμαζεν πυρὰ πολλά, τὰ καίετο Ἰλιόθι πρό,
αὐλῶν συρίγγων τ' ἐνοπὴν ὅμαδόν τ' ἀνθρώπων.

He marveled at the many fires that were burning in front of Ilium and at the noise of *auloi* and syrinxes and the din of men. (Hom. *Il.* 10.12–13)

The *aulos* and the Phrygian *harmonia* with which it was associated were commonly thought to have been invented in Phrygia by Hyagnis, father of Marsyas, who was in turn believed to have been the teacher of Olympus.⁷¹ By the late fifth and early fourth centuries the *aulos* was conceptualized by conservative critics of New Musical trends as dangerously powerful in arousing emotions, a trait that was also linked to the Phrygian *harmonia*.⁷² Not only could the instrument's origin and possible mode be imagined as non-Greek, but by the late fifth century its professional players in Athens tended to be from outside the city (especially Boeotia and the Peloponnese),⁷³ so that it could also appear foreign visually in performance, even though its music had pervaded Athenian life for so long. The image of Paris playing the syrinx is therefore coded as doubly foreign: his *barbara* tunes on the syrinx represent those of another foreign instrument, the Phrygian *auloi*. The fact that these *auloi* are those of Olympus also augments the non-Greek soundscape, since this aulete was commonly said to have introduced instrumental music to Greece from Phrygia.⁷⁴

Throughout this book we have repeatedly seen examples of imaginative suggestion shaping the audience's reception of the sounds they hear in the theater, so that

---

69. Barker 1984: 74 n. 79. West 1992: 91–92 cites pre-Hellenistic references to the Phrygian *auloi*: Archil. fr. 269 W, Soph. frr. 450 and 644 (both in Asiatic settings), Eur. *Bacch.* 127 (Phrygian *auloi* in the Cretan cult of Rhea), Callias fr. 23 KA, Cratinus Junior fr. 3 KA (in Cyprus); cf. Paus. 5.17.9.

70. *Auloi* are played by Greeks in the *Iliad* too, appearing in the wedding scene on Achilles' shield (18.495).

71. On Hyagnis as the inventor of *auloi*, see esp. ps.-Plut. *De Mus.* 1132f, 1133f, 1135f; Ath. 14.624b. On Marsyas as the teacher of Olympus, see Pl. *Symp.* 215c2–3; Paus. 10.30.9. By the mid-fifth century B.C.E., Marsyas was represented in conservative discourse as a satyr who took up the *aulos* once it had been rejected by Athena: see Arist. *Pol.* 1341b, Ath. 14.616e–f, and Paus. 1.24; also Wilson 1999: 59–63; Martin 2003; Wallace 2003: 82–83. In Pind. *Pyth.* 12.18–25 Athena invents the "many-headed tune" of the *aulos*. Wallace 2003: 79–80 suggests this story may be an invention by Pindar himself, but it could instead indicate an alternative tradition for the origin of the *aulos* and its music existing alongside the conservative one.

72. Arist. *Pol.* 1341a21–23, 1442b3. See also Mathiesen 1999: 178; Wilson 1999: 86–93; Martin 2003: 155–57.

73. On non-Athenian auletes, see Wilson 1999: 74–75 and 2002: 46–48; Wallace 2003: 76.

74. *Sud.* O 221; ps.-Plut. *De Mus.* 5.1132e–f, 7.1133d–f (at 11.1134f–35c Olympus is also credited with the discovery of the enharmonic genus); [Pl.] *Min.* 318b.

the instrumental accompaniment becomes part of a song's narrative. Here in *Iphigenia in Aulis* we find a surprisingly direct description of this process, with the phrase "breathing imitations [*mimēmata*] of the Phrygian *auloi* of Olympus" (576–78). This is the only time in extant tragedy that music is described as *mimēmata*—a word I have translated as "imitations" even though we should not assume a sense of literal mimesis here.[75] The same word, also in the plural form, appears in a fragment of Euripides' *Aeolus* in which the title character talks about the fragile nature of age, stating, "we old men are nothing but sound [*psophos*] and shape [*schēma*], and we creep along as representations [*mimēmata*] of dreams."[76] Though this statement is not explicitly musical, it does become a self-reflexively performative reference to the actor's own voice and movement (*psophos* and *schēma*). But as we saw in chapter 1, more direct allusions to the mimetic enactment or representation of musical sound (and movement) appear in earlier, non-dramatic choral lyric, especially in Pindar, and often in connection with the *aulos*: in *Pythian* 12, for example, Athena makes the *aulos* to "represent [Euryale's] loud-sounding wail with instruments";[77] in *Partheneion* fragment 94b the chorus claim to produce (*mimēsom'*) the Sirens' sound in their song "to the accompaniment of the *lōtos* pipes."[78] Euripides applies this idea of mimetic doubling to the depiction of Paris playing his syrinx, though here, rather than producing a vocal effect, one instrument represents another.

This vivid depiction of instrumental mimesis is another example of Euripides' innovating through adapting traditional musical motifs. Such experimentation may have been widespread in the late fifth and the early fourth century; certainly it was sufficiently popular for Plato, in his conservative rhetoric against the new trend for musical genre mixing, to complain that recent poets "represented *aulos* songs with kithara songs."[79] The instrumental mimesis or overlap he decries recalls that described in *Iphigenia in Aulis*: *aulos* songs (or even tunes)[80] are apparently

---

75. Stockert 1992: 2.371 rightly sees μιμήματα †πνείων† at *IA* 578 as a lofty paraphrase for (αὐλοὺς) μιμούμενος ("wobei αὐλοί die Flötenmusik bezeichnet"), but the wording also conveys the idea of the product of piping (i.e., the sound itself) more than just the participle μιμούμενος would.

76. γέροντες οὐδέν ἐσμεν ἄλλο πλὴν ψόφος / καὶ σχῆμ', ὀνείρων δ' ἕρπομεν μιμήματα, fr. 25.2–3.

77. σὺν ἔντεσι μιμήσαιτ' ἐρικλάγκταν γόον, Pind. *Pyth.* 12.21.

78. αὐλίσκων ὑπὸ λωτίνων, Pind. fr. 94b SM, 14.

79. καὶ αὐλωιδίας δὴ ταῖς κιθαρωιδίαις μιμούμενοι, Pl. *Leg.* 700d7–8. *Mousikē* in general is characterized as mimetic in Plato's *Laws* and Aristotle's *Politics*, but this trait more often concerns character and feeling (*ēthos, tropos, pathos*) than the copying of other musical performances: see Pl. *Leg.* 655c5–656b7, 668a6–e5; Ar. *Pol.* 1340a2–b19.

80. *Aulōidia* literally means "*aulos* song": cf. Paus. 10.7.4–6 on how songs to the *aulos* came to be excluded from the Pythian festival. It may also refer to the art of playing the *aulos* itself, just as *kitharōidia* can mean not just "singing to the kithara" but its playing too (both of which the kitharode, unlike the aulete, could do himself): cf. ps.-Plut. *De Mus.* 1132f; also Pl. *Ion* 533b on *kitharōidia*. Power 2010 sees *kitharōidia* as a combination of vocal and instrumental music.

represented by another instrument—this time the kithara, presumably in the hands of musicians like Timotheus, with whom Euripides was associated in antiquity.[81] With the image of Paris breathing imitations of Olympus's *auloi*, Euripides combines these new trends with metamusical language inherited from archaic lyric and at the same time displays such instrumental mixing not just verbally but also in performance through the use of the *aulos* to represent the sound of the syrinx.[82]

Given how frequently the chorus refer to the *aulos* when describing music making in Euripides' later tragedies, its appearance here is not surprising. Nevertheless, it is an especially apt instrument for this sort of mimetic process. As we have seen, already in Pindar the *aulos* is represented as especially mimetic—hence the repeated use of the adjective *pamphōnos* ("sounding everything") to describe the instrument and its tune.[83] In Plato's *Republic* this trait causes Socrates to exclude makers and players of the *aulos* from the city, while Aristotle in *Poetics* condemns *aulos* players who represent absolutely everything.[84] Once again, then, Euripides combines new and old, as the link made between mimesis and the *aulos* in the first stasimon of *Iphigenia in Aulis* draws on its traditional imaginary and its more recent conservative conceptualizations.

Here, however, Euripides has apparently transferred such imitative ability over to the syrinx, as it is this instrument, not the *aulos*, that is said to be producing *mimēmata*. In performance the mimetic relationship between the two instruments becomes circular: while the chorus are singing of the syrinx representing the *aulos*, the audience would be hearing the sound of the *aulos* representing the syrinx. Imagined music (the syrinx) merges with performed music (the *aulos*), but what is described is the inverse of the audience's experience in the theater, where the *aulos* is the musical accompaniment. Euripides' innovation here therefore lies not simply in the mix of old and new, but in the complex mimetic layering produced by the performance of these lines. The *mimēmata* produced by Paris on his pipes come to life in the theater, so that despite the scene's distance from the immediate *mythos*, the audience can be absorbed within it: they are taken to Mount Ida not just through the description of sound but through what they actually hear as the instrumental accompaniment to the chorus's performance. The combination of imagined and performed *mousikē* thus extends the temporal and geographical scope of the play, transporting us to this bucolic, peaceful scene of the past so that we feel all the more sharply its contrast with the brutal present of the surrounding drama.

---

81. According to Satyrus's *Life of Euripides* (*POxy*. 1176, fr. 39, col. 22), they even collaborated.
82. Cf. Steiner 2011: 311 on *Hel*. 1483.
83. Pind. *Ol*. 7.12, *Pyth*. 12.19, *Isth*. 5.27.
84. Plato *Rep*. 399d3-6 (cf. *Leg*. 669c-e); Aristotle's criticism (*Poet*. 1461b30-32) focuses on the movement of "base" auletes rather than the sound of their instrument.

## *Performing the* Hymenaios *in the Third Stasimon*

The third stasimon continues the motif of the roots of the Trojan War, shifting back from the Judgment scene that is depicted so vividly in the first stasimon to the wedding where Eris first threw the apple, and then predicting the destruction that will ensue at the hands of Achilles, the offspring of the marriage.[85] Unlike the first stasimon, with its brief image of Paris's music making in the epode, this ode opens with strikingly rich and extended language of *mousikē* (instrumental, vocal, and choreographic) as the chorus describe the wedding celebrations of Peleus and Thetis. The effect of such a performative focus from the start of the ode is to transport the audience immediately into this vivid scene of the past, making them not only hear about such *mousikē* but experience it too. As a result, the song leads them to suspend their disbelief and to imagine the happy marriage of Iphigenia and Achilles—to hope that Achilles' professed confidence in his ability to dissuade Agamemnon from sacrificing Iphigenia will prove justified. But, like Cassandra's pathetic wedding song in *Trojan Women*, the third stasimon of *Iphigenia in Aulis* presents a painful contrast to the reality of the dramatic action, in which there is no possibility of such a celebration for Iphigenia and Achilles.[86] By transporting us to a scene that is so at odds with the drama itself, their song therefore undermines Achilles' hollow promises and intensifies our expectation of Iphigenia's imminent death, which we know must occur.

The ode's musical imagery and performance highlight this contrast, underscoring the lack of any such music, song, or dance for Iphigenia.[87] The opening strophe has been described as having a static, pictorial quality,[88] yet it is full of self-reflexive descriptions of sound and movement, creating a suggestive interplay with the chorus's own song and dance in the theater:

τίν' ἄρ' Ὑμέναιος διὰ λωτοῦ Λίβυος
μετά τε φιλοχόρου κιθάρας
συρίγγων θ' ὑπὸ καλαμοεσ-
σᾶν ἔστασεν ἰαχάν,

---

85. Cf. Alcaeus fr. 42 Voigt, in which the marriage of Peleus and Thetis is linked to both Helen and the destruction of Troy.

86. On the ironic contrast between the song and the dramatic reality, see Panagl 1971: 208; Walsh 1974; Foley 1982: 163–64 and 1985: 81–83; Stockert 1992: 2.496.

87. The ode's musicality has generally gone unnoticed (an exception is the brief discussion of the opening acoustic images in Panagl 1971: 209–10, 213). Kranz 1933: 240–41 notes the mimetic character of lines 1036–39, likening it to that of "der neuen Nomoi und Dithyramben."

88. Walsh 1974: 242; Foley 1982: 167–68 and 1985: 82. Pictorial images of music making need not have been static either, particularly when they interacted with music and dance performed on the occasions when they were used: depictions of music making on sympotic vessels, for example, would be brought to life by the musical entertainments at the symposium itself. See below on the depiction of musical scenes on the François Vase.

ὅτ' ἀνὰ Πήλιον αἱ καλλιπλόκαμοι (1040)
Πιερίδες †ἐν δαιτὶ θεῶν†
χρυσεοσάνδαλον ἴχνος
ἐν γᾶι κρούουσαι
Πηλέως ἐς γάμον ἦλθον,
μελωιδοῖς Θέτιν ἀχήμασι τόν τ' Αἰακίδαν (1045)
Κενταύρων ἐν ὄρεσι κλέουσαι
Πηλιάδα καθ' ὕλαν;
ὁ δὲ Δαρδανίδας, Διὸς
λέκτρων τρύφημα φίλον, (1050)
χρυσέοισιν ἄφυσσε λοι-
   βὰν ἐκ κρατήρων γυάλοις
ὁ Φρύγιος Γανυμήδης.
παρὰ δὲ λευκοφαῆ ψάμαθον
εἰλισσόμεναι κύκλια (1055)
πεντήκοντα κόραι Νηρέως
γάμους ἐχόρευσαν.

What wedding hymn was it that raised its cry amid the Libyan *lōtos* [pipe] and along with the chorus-loving kithara and to the accompaniment of the reedy syrinxes, when, along the ridge of Mount Pelion, †at the feast of the gods†, the beautiful-haired Pierians, beating their golden-sandaled feet on the earth, came to the marriage of Peleus, celebrating with melodious strains Thetis and the son of Aeacus, in the mountains of the Centaurs, down through the woods of Pelion? And the Dardanian boy, the dear darling of Zeus's bed, drew off the libation wine in the golden hollows of the mixing bowls, the Phrygian Ganymede. And along the gleaming white sand, whirling in circles, the fifty daughters of Nereus celebrated the marriage in dance. (1036–57)

This initial image of the sounds of multiple instruments accompanying the cry of the wedding song immediately establishes a correspondence between the chorus's own performance and the one they describe, since they too are raising their voices in song to instrumental accompaniment, the music of the *aulos*. As we saw in chapter 3, the phrase "Libyan *lōtos*" actually denotes the *aulos* itself. The "chorus-loving" kithara and "reedy" syrinx would probably not have been onstage—they belong to the realm of imagined *mousikē*—but for the audience they could merge with and be encompassed by the sound of the *aulos*. The long association of the *aulos* with mimetic flexibility would make it well suited to such acoustic representation.[89]

---

89. Cf. *Helen* 171a–b, where the *aulos* (also described as a "Libyan *lōtos*") is combined with the syrinx and a stringed instrument (the *phorminx* instead of the *kithara*). We see a similar combination of instruments in the description of hymenaeal *mousikē* in Sappho fr. 44 Voigt, if we accept the reading [κίθαρίς] in line 24.

Following this intensely acoustic beginning, perfectly coordinated and highly attractive choral dance takes over from the instrumental accompaniment as the song's focus: the Muses are described as beating their golden-sandaled feet on the ground in unison, as if moving just one foot (note the singular *ichnos*, 1042), while they sing in praise of Peleus and Thetis. As in many other images of divine *choreia* in archaic and classical choral lyric, these dancing goddesses are also described in very attractive terms, with a focus on their beautiful hair and their feet clad in golden sandals.[90] The attraction of the Muses' *choreia* becomes erotically charged as the focus soon shifts from them to Ganymede, Zeus's beautiful plaything, whose golden mixing bowl corresponds with the gold of their feet (1049–53).[91]

The chorus of Muses seems to have been traditionally included in representations of the marriage of Peleus and Thetis, often with an emphasis on their beauty and attractiveness: in Pindar *Nemean* 5, for example, the "most beautiful chorus" of Muses sing to the accompaniment of Apollo's lyre; in *Pythian* 3 both Peleus and Cadmus are said to have enjoyed at their weddings the "golden-crowned Muses singing in the mountains."[92] As in those songs, the chorus in Euripides' ode present an image of prototypical *choreia* through which the audience can momentarily see the choral dancing in the theater as divine, merging with that of the Muses. The chorus also focus on the Muses' song, their *hymenaios* for Peleus and Thetis, emphasizing its "melodious strains" (1045) as well as its content. The Muses' *choreia* thus fuses with that of the dramatic chorus, in song as well as dance, as both choruses, imagined and performing, sing a song in celebration of Peleus and Thetis. Through the process of imaginative suggestion all three registers of *mousikē*—instrumental accompaniment, song, and dance—can correspond with the chorus's own performance in the theater.[93]

---

90. Cf. the description of the Muses as "beautiful-haired" (καλλίκομοι) in Sappho fr. 128 Voigt and of Dawn as "golden-sandaled" (χρυσοπέδιλος) in frr. 103 and 123 Voigt. On the erotic potential of *choreia*, see Kurke 2012 and 2013.

91. Cf. Barlow 1971: 112 on the correspondence of different dazzling impressions in this scene. See also Michelini 1999–2000: 53: "These moments of glowing, ideal beauty belong to the legendary and lyrical view of the erotic." The erotic focus on Ganymede with his golden bowl may recall that on Aphrodite in Sappho fr. 2 Voigt, whom the singer bids to pour nectar into golden cups (14).

92. ὁ κάλλιστος χορός, Pind. *Nem.* 5.23; χρυσαμπύκων / μελπομενᾶν ἐν ὄρει Μοισᾶν, *Pyth.* 3.89–90. Note too the presence of the Muses in the scene of the wedding of Peleus and Thetis on the François Vase and the Sophilos Dinos, both Attic black-figure from the late sixth century B.C.E. See also Thgn. 15–17 (the Graces and Muses at Cadmus's wedding). Both Graces and Muses appear, apparently in connection with wedding song, in Sappho fr. 103 Voigt; Contiades-Tsitsoni 1990: 71–91 suggests that the mythical marriage is that of Hebe and Heracles.

93. Panagl 1971: 210 thinks the Muses are the musicians as well as the dancers: "Auf der Schilderung der Klänge folgt also der Auftritt der göttlichen Musikantinnen, die wie der Dramenchor in seinen Liedern—als Göttinnen natürlich in gleicher Person—zu den instrumentalen Tönen den von Inhalt erfüllten, konkreten Gesang treten lassen."

At the end of the strophe the spotlight shifts to dancing once again, but now a new choral group takes over from the Muses: the fifty Nereids, Thetis's sisters, are described as whirling in circles in their dance (1055–57). This is one of the most explicitly choreographic descriptions in all of Euripides, and the clearest textual stage direction for the dramatic chorus to dance with similarly circular movement, whether twirling on the spot or joining hands in concentric circles (or a mixture of both).[94] This may be an example of Euripides' New Musical or at least dithyrambic style, which as we have repeatedly seen often includes both dancing Nereids and vocabulary denoting circular dancing (especially the verb *helissein*, which is used here). But it is not just a stylistic feature, nor is it strictly new or dithyrambic. The shift from one choral—and highly choreographic—image to another, which also occurs in archaic lyric like Alcman's first *Partheneion*, encourages the audience to visualize the chorus as both dancing groups (and indeed their appearance as the fifty dancing Nereids is especially apt here, since the bride herself is one of Nereus's daughters). Through their dance the chorus also transform the performance space: the "gleaming sand" (1054) along which the Nereids dance becomes the floor of the *orchēstra*.

As we have already seen, the chorus's reenactment of the celebrations for Peleus and Thetis through their own musical performance, which merges with the described *mousikē* in their song, is similar to other lyric descriptions of this prototypical marriage ceremony. The account of the chorus of Muses in Pindar's *Nemean* 5 offers a particularly noteworthy parallel, with multiple interactions between the mythic narrative and the present choral performance: not only does the "most beautiful chorus" correspond with the choral performance of the epinician, but the figure of Apollo playing on his phorminx in the middle is like the *chorēgos* in the center of the circular chorus.[95] The audience's familiarity with such effects could make the scene described in Euripides' ode especially immersive, as they are drawn into it as a live performance, not just a recorded one.

We also have several similar visual representations of this famous marriage. The most famous and best-preserved of these is Kleitias's François Vase (ca. 570 B.C.E.), which shows on its shoulder the procession of gods and chariots to the wedding of Peleus and Thetis (fig. 3). This includes the Muses, with Calliope, standing apart from her sisters, facing out toward the viewer and playing the syrinx;[96] the Horai making coordinated gestures with their hands, which could represent dancing;

---

94. The combination of *helissein* and *kyklos* appears only in the surviving plays of Euripides: see also *Hel.* 1362–63, *IT* 1103–4. It occurs twice in actors' spoken lines but with a less obviously choreographic import: *Pho.* 1185–86 (the messenger describing Capaneus's death) and *Or.* 444 (Orestes telling Menelaus that he is surrounded by hostile Argives).

95. Mullen 1982: 149, 158–60; Power 2000: 68. On the position of the *chorēgos* in the center of a choral circle, see Calame 1997: 36; on Apollo and the Muses in Pind. *Nem.* 5, see ibid.: 50.

96. On the prominence of Calliope here, see Giuliani 2013: 123. According to Hesiod, she is the greatest of all the Muses (*Theog.* 79).

FIGURE 3. The procession of gods on the François Vase, Attic black-figure volute krater, ca. 570 B.C.E. From left to right: Calliope playing the syrinx; the Horai; Dionysus. Museo Archeologico Nazionale, Florence, inv. 4209. (Photo: courtesy of Alinari / Art Resource, NY.)

and, next to them, Dionysus dancing with bent legs and arms as he carries an amphora. A similar scene appears on two roughly contemporary vases by Sophilos: a very fragmentary dinos from the Acropolis (Akr. 587), and the huge Sophilos Dinos in the British Museum, on which one of the Muses is also playing a syrinx. If vases like these were originally intended as wedding gifts, then the images of music and dance shown on them could have visually corresponded to the hymenaeal music actually performed during the celebrations—a type of interaction comparable to that between the mythical narrative and the choral performance in *Iphigenia in Aulis*.[97]

The depiction of the musical celebrations at the wedding of Peleus and Thetis in *Iphigenia in Aulis* is similar to representations of other mythical marriages too, some of which may form parts of actual *hymenaioi*.[98] In Sappho fragment 44 the marriage of Hector and Andromache is described with a striking emphasis on music, both instrumental and vocal, building up a multilayered soundscape rather like that in Euripides' ode:[99]

---

97. On the use of the François Vase at a wedding, see Stewart 1983: 69–70; Neils 2013: 120–23. It is possible that it could have been made for the symposium instead: see Giuliani 2013: 121; Iozzo 2013: 54–61.

98. In what follows I refer to the wedding song as a *hymenaios* rather than an epithalamium, since the latter term is not used in extant pre-Hellenistic literature: see Contiades-Tsitsoni 1990: 31; Swift 2010: 242–43. *Hymenaioi* referred in particular to the songs sung at the wedding procession, like those that the Muses are said to perform for Peleus and Thetis.

99. Supplements here follow Campbell 1982.

αὖλος δ' ἀδυ[μ]έλης [κίθαρίς] τ' ὀνεμίγνυ[το
καὶ ψ[ό]φο[ς κ]ροτάλ[ων, λιγέ]ως δ' ἄρα πάρ[θενοι                    (25)
ἄειδον μέλος ἄγγ[ον, ἵκα]νε δ' ἐς αἴθ[ερα
ἄχω θεσπεσία.

And the sweet-sounding *aulos* and the kithara were combined, and the noise of *krotala*, and maidens sang shrilly a holy song, and the wondrous echo reached the sky. (Sappho fr. 44 Voigt, 24–27)

Whether or not this description of the mythical wedding is a fragment of an actual *hymenaios*, it would probably have been performed as a monody to the accompaniment of the kithara, which would then sonically represent all three instruments (the *aulos*, kithara, and *krotala*) just as the *aulos* would in the performance of Euripides' ode.[100] Greek hymenaeal songs seem to have traditionally contained mythic narrative sections describing prototypical marriages, including that of Peleus and Thetis, implicitly comparing the bride and bridegroom with these divinities and heroes.[101] The description of their wedding in this choral ode may therefore resemble the content of an actual *hymenaios*. Likewise the self-reflexive performative language, along with the chorus's own dancing, would give the audience the impression that they are witnessing the performance of a wedding song, not just the description of one, even though the ode as a whole is not a formal *hymenaios*.[102]

The chorus in *Iphigenia in Aulis* thus do not just perform (or reperform) the celebratory *mousikē* of the wedding of Peleus and Thetis by complementing their account of that event with their own song and dance: they also seem to enact the *hymenaios* of Iphigenia and Achilles themselves, bringing into the theater an event that, though anticipated at this point in the drama, cannot in the end occur.[103] Indeed the content of this song, particularly its musical focus, corresponds with

---

100. On Sappho fr. 44 Voigt as a hymenaeal fragment, see Rösler 1975; Hague 1983: 134; Lasserre 1989: 81–106; Contiades-Tsitsoni 1990: 102–9. The choice of the wedding of Hector and Andromache, however, seems a rather ominous theme for such a celebration, particularly if, as Nagy 1974: 138 suggests, the epithets used of Paean Apollo ironically allude to the Homeric Apollo, who deserts Hector just before he dies, and if the epithet "godlike" (θεοείκελος) used of Hector in line 34 refers to Achilles, his killer (cf. Hom. *Il.* 1.131, 19.155). See also Kakridis 1966 and Schrenk 1994. On fr. 44 as a monodic song, see Lasserre 1989: 81–106; Contiades-Tsitsoni 1990: 102–8; Lardinois 1996: 159.

101. Cf. Sappho frr. 103 and 144 Voigt, both of which seem to refer to a divine wedding. See Hague 1983: 133–34; Swift 2010: 247. In Aristophanes' *Birds* the chorus perform a *hymenaios* in which they describe the wedding of Zeus and Hera (1731–43). Sappho fr. 141 Voigt, which describes a divine marriage, may also be from a wedding song.

102. See Rösler 1975: 277–78; Hague 1983: 132–38, Contiades-Tsitsoni 1990; Swift 2010: 242–49 on elements of the *hymenaios*. It is impossible for us to know to what extent the melody may also have imitated that of wedding songs.

103. Cf. Wilson 2005: 189 on the "restaging" of different kinds of musical performances in tragedy.

the rites that the messenger in ignorance bids Agamemnon to set up upon Iphigenia's arrival:

ἀλλ' εἶα τἀπὶ τοισίδ' ἐξάρχου κανᾶ, (435)
στεφανοῦσθε κρᾶτα, καὶ σύ, Μενέλεως ἄναξ,
ὑμέναιον εὐτρέπιζε, καὶ κατὰ στέγας
λωτὸς βοάσθω καὶ ποδῶν ἔστω κτύπος·
φῶς γὰρ τόδ' ἥκει μακάριον τῆι παρθένωι.

But come now, given these events, set up the basket, wreathe your head, and you, lord Menelaus, make ready the *hymenaios* song, and let the *lōtos* pipe shout out through the tents and let there be the beat of feet! For this day has come, a blessed one for the maiden. (435–39)

The hymenaeal song that the audience hears in the third stasimon contains in both language and performance the cry of the *lōtos* pipe—the *aulos*—and the beat (acoustic and choreographic) of the dancing chorus's feet.[104] The messenger's description of the day as "blessed" (*makarion*, 439) for Iphigenia may also refer to the blessing (*makarismos*) within a *hymenaios*—and just such a blessing occurs in the antistrophe of the third stasimon, when the gods establish the divine marriage as *makarios* (1076–79). As we shall see, the wreathing of heads is also taken up as a motif in the third stasimon, though of course it refers to neither Menelaus nor Agamemnon: the Centaurs are garlanded in Dionysiac celebration (1058); Iphigenia, for sacrifice (1080). There is thus a complete merging of identity between the chorus and the Muses on the one hand and the chorus and the Nereids on the other: just as the chorus of Chalcidean women are (momentarily) celebrating the union of Iphigenia and Achilles by performing a *hymenaios*, so the Muses and Nereids sing and dance in honor of that of Achilles' parents. Unlike the performance context of a *hymenaios*, however, the marriage of Iphigenia and Achilles is impossible, so the enactment of their hymenaeal song paradoxically also underscores the lack of any such celebratory *mousikē* for Iphigenia.[105]

We become increasingly aware of this lack through the rest of the ode. The Dionysian imagery established by the whirling Nereids continues into the antistrophe with the entrance of the *thiasos* of Centaurs,[106] but this is an image of chaotic revelry rather than the sort of coordinated *choreia* that is described and enacted in the previous strophe:

ἅμα δ' ἐλάταισι στεφανώδει τε χλόαι
θίασος ἔμολεν ἱπποβάτας
Κενταύρων ἐπὶ δαῖτα τὰν (1060)

---

104. Cf. Walsh 1974: 243.
105. Cf. Foley 1982: 163–64, 168, on the multiple ironies of this ode's epithalamic themes.
106. See Panagl 1971: 214; Stockert 1992: 2.505.

θεῶν κρατῆρά τε Βάκχου.
μέγα δ' ἀνέκλαγον· Ὦ Νηρηὶ κόρα,
παῖδά σε Θεσσαλίαι μέγα φῶς
μάντις ὁ φοιβάδα μοῦσαν
εἰδὼς γεννάσειν
Χείρων ἐξονόμαζεν.

And with staffs of silver-fir and wreathed greenery, the horse-mounted revel-rout of Centaurs came to the feast of the gods and the mixing bowl of Bacchus. And they shouted out loudly, "O daughter of Nereus, Chiron, who knows the music of Phoebus, has declared that you will give birth to a son who will be a great light to Thessaly." (1058–66)

Given the Centaurs' attempted rape at the wedding of Perithoos and Hippodameia, their takeover from the Muses and Nereids as a performing group introduces an unsettling tone within this hymenaeal context.[107] Now, instead of melodious singing, there is loud shouting as they address Thetis and recount Chiron's prophecy regarding her son.[108] This prophecy draws the audience away from the immersive celebrations of the past toward the dramatic present and future, to Achilles as sacker of Troy:[109]

ὃς ἥξει χθόνα λογχήρεσι σὺν Μυρμιδόνων
ἀσπισταῖς Πριάμοιο κλεινὰν
γαῖαν ἐκπυρώσων, (1070)
περὶ σώματι χρυσέων
ὅπλων Ἡφαιστοπόνων
κεκορυθμένος ἐνδύτ', ἐκ
  θεᾶς ματρὸς δωρήματ' ἔχων
Θέτιδος, ἅ νιν ἔτικτεν. (1075)

"[A son] who will come to the land with the spear-wielding shield bearers of the Myrmidons, to burn the famous country of Priam to ashes, armed about his body with a covering of golden armor made by Hephaestus holding the gifts from his divine mother, Thetis, who bore him." (1068–75)

Although the song is still framed within a hymenaeal context, its mood continues to become more ominous with this shift forward, particularly as Achilles' presence

---

107. Cf. Walsh 1974: 244–45. For the wedding of Perithoos and Hippodameia, see Hom. Od. 21.295–304; Pind. fr. 166 SM.

108. Kovacs 2003: 283 rightly corrects previous translations of these lines that make Chiron the subject governing ἀνέκλαγον: Chiron himself is not present; his prophecy is embedded within the Centaurs' cry.

109. The prophecy also emphasizes Achilles' ancestry, which Agamemnon has already recounted to a quizzical Clytemnestra at 695–713; cf. 208–9, 926–27.

at Troy precludes Iphigenia's survival.[110] In these lines the visual focus of desire is also transformed, shifting from the golden-sandaled Muses and Ganymede with his golden mixing bowl to Achilles with his golden armor in the antistrophe (1071–72). This view of Achilles recalls the more extended erotic focus on him in the parodos, racing alongside the colorful horses with their golden trappings; but now, in contrast to his previous show of athleticism, he is depicted as a warrior about to burn Troy to the ground. The previously carefree eroticism is here directed at a much more destructive subject.

The theme of Achilles' future (his death as well as his warring) seems to have been common in representations of the marriage of Peleus and Thetis. The bottom section of the François Vase shows Achilles' pursuit of Troilus; on the neck are the funeral games of Patroklos; on the handles is Achilles' lifeless corpse, being carried by Ajax away from the battle. It is also possible that the amphora Dionysus carries in the procession on the central frieze is meant to represent the urn that will hold the ashes of Achilles and Patroklos.[111] Likewise in Pindar's *Isthmian* 8 the story of Thetis's marriage to Peleus is followed by the later bloody exploits of Achilles:

ὃ καὶ Μύσιον ἀμπελόεν
αἵμαξε Τηλέφου μέλα- (50)
νι ῥαίνων φόνωι πεδίον

γεφύρωσέ τ' Ἀτρεΐδαι-
σι νόστον, Ἑλέναν τ' ἐλύσατο, Τροΐας
ἶνας ἐκταμὼν δορί.

He even bloodied the vine-clad plain of Mysia, sprinkling it with Telephos's dark gore, and he bridged a return home for the sons of Atreus, and released Helen, after cutting out Troy's sinews with his spear. (Pind. *Isthm.* 8.49–52).

A similar transition from the joy of the wedding to the destruction of the Trojan War is evident in Alcaeus fragment 42: after the birth of Achilles comes the chilling reminder that "they perished for Helen's sake, both the Phrygians and their city."[112] Euripides' adaptation of this motif within the ode of his tragedy, however, is especially charged because of the surrounding dramatic context: Achilles has just assured Clytemnestra that Iphigenia will be spared—in which case there would be

---

110. Walsh 1974: 244–47; Foley 1982: 168 and 1985: 83; Sorum 1992: 535–36; Stockert 1992: 2.496, 506–7.

111. See Stewart 1983. Giuliani 2013: 121 rejects this interpretation, arguing that we should instead see Dionysus's amphora as full of wine, thus pointing to the sympotic context that he proposes for the vase itself.

112. οἱ δ' ἀπώλοντ' ἀμφ' Ἑ[λέναι Φρύγες τε / καὶ πόλις αὔτων, Alcaeus fr. 42 Voigt, 15–16, with Wilamowitz's supplements. The song of the Parcae in Catullus 64 also concentrates on both the destructive exploits of Achilles and his death (338–70).

no Trojan War.[113] The striking absence of vivid musical imagery in the antistrophe reflects this return to the more unsettling present and immediate future of the *mythos,* away from the previous celebratory scenes of *mousikē*.

It is possible that already in the strophe there was some hint of this more ominous turn through the focus on the two complementary choral groups of Muses and Nereids. One of the most memorable occasions when they appear together is at the funeral of Achilles, as described by the ghost of Agamemnon in Book 24 of the *Odyssey*:

ἀμφὶ δέ σ' ἔστησαν κοῦραι ἁλίοιο γέροντος
οἴκτρ' ὀλοφυρόμεναι, περὶ δ' ἄμβροτα εἵματα ἕσσαν.
Μοῦσαι δ' ἐννέα πᾶσαι ἀμειβόμεναι ὀπὶ καλῇ (60)
θρήνεον· ἔνθα κεν οὔ τιν' ἀδάκρυτόν γ' ἐνόησας
Ἀργείων· τοῖον γὰρ ὑπώρορε Μοῦσα λίγεια.

> And about you stood the daughters of the old man of the sea, mourning pitifully, and clothed you in immortal garments. And all nine Muses, answering one another with beautiful voice, were singing a dirge. There you would have seen not one of the Argives tearless, for such was the shrill Muse's power to move. (Hom. *Od.* 24.58–62)

The combination of the two choruses may herald the disturbing shift toward the present and future through the rest of the ode, which further stresses the impossibility of a *hymenaios* for Iphigenia and Achilles, and so also undermines its enactment. The wedding song can be present in performance, but it is uncomfortably at odds with the reality of the play.

Despite this shift away from the joyful music making with which the ode begins, there may still be some correspondence between the language of the antistrophe and the musicality of the strophe. David Wiles has argued for the "choreographic identity" of strophe and antistrophe, with the result that the same visual image can receive two meanings.[114] There is something of this sort of association between the strophe and antistrophe in third stasimon, although the choreography may not be exactly identical: it is hard, for example, to imagine the same dancing accompanying both the start of Chiron's reported prophecy (1062–66) and the Muses' performance (1040–43). But the simultaneous merging and transformation of images between the two stanzas, partly realized by the chorus's own singing and dancing, adds to the increasingly unsettling effect of the antistrophe, undoing any enjoyment

---

113. As Walsh 1974: 245–47 notes, it also suggests a disconnect between the traditional heroic image of powerful Achilles (as he is presented in the third stasimon, and also in the parodos) and Achilles as a character in this play, who will be unable to resist the sway of the army (even his own men).

114. Wiles 1997: 87–113. I am more inclined to agree with Dale 1968: 212–14 that the choreographic mirroring of strophe and antistrophe need not have been an absolute rule and instead could have allowed for some variation of gesture and movement between them according to the requirements of the dramatic action.

of the earlier hymenaeal fantasy on the part of the audience. Not only do the chorus shift from the Muses and Nereids to the Centaurs, a much more problematic performing group, but the Muses' song becomes the prophecy of Chiron, "who knows the music of Phoebus" (1064–65).[115] Instead of the quoted *hymnos* of the Muses that we hear in Pindar's *Nemean* 5, here it is Chiron's prophecy that is enframed, and without any indication of beautiful, orderly *mousikē*.[116] At the end of the antistrophe the previous image of the Nereids' joyful dancing transforms into that of the gods blessing the marriage (1076–79). If the chorus's choreography here did recall their earlier circular movements, such correspondence would underscore the ironic disconnect between past and present, divine and human: the marriage of Peleus and Thetis may be blessed, but that of Achilles and Iphigenia is impossible.

With the epode, the chorus fully transition away from the hymenaeal scene of the past and return to the horror of the immediate present before ending with gnomic speculation on the powerlessness of modesty and virtue that contrasts with the praise of such traits in the first stasimon. Now the Centaurs' address to Thetis, Peleus's bride, shifts to that of the chorus in their own person to Iphigenia, the sacrificial bride of Achilles:[117]

σὲ δ' ἐπὶ κάραι στέψουσι καλλικόμαν (1080)
πλόκαμον Ἀργεῖοι, βαλιὰν
ὥστε πετραίων
ἀπ' ἄντρων ἐλθοῦσαν ὀρέων
μόσχον ἀκήρατον, βρότειον
αἱμάσσοντες λαιμόν·
οὐ σύριγγι τραφεῖσαν οὐδ' (1085)
ἐν ῥοιβδήσεσι βουκόλων,
παρὰ δὲ ματέρι νυμφοκόμον
Ἰναχίδαις γάμον.

But you, upon your head the Argives will crown your beautiful hair, your locks, like a dappled, untouched calf that's come from rocky mountain caves, they bloodying your mortal neck: not raised with the syrinx nor among the whistlings of herdsmen, but dressed as a bride at the side of your mother, a wedding for the sons of Inachus. (1080–88)

The ode as a whole is thus an example of a characteristically Euripidean pattern that Donald Mastronarde calls "narrative followed by application," whereby a choral song opens with a mythic narrative and eventually turns to the immediate

---

115. *Mousa* can metaphorically mean "prophecy" (Stockert 1992: 2.506), but its literal meaning, "music" or "Muse," is extremely apposite here.
116. See Power 2000: 75 on the Muses' song in Pind. *Nem.* 5.
117. On the unaccompanied σὲ (1080) referring to Iphigenia, see Mastronarde 1979: 99–100.

situation in the *mythos*.[118] The use of this pattern here, with the shift from a seemingly carefree image of the past to the more ominous present, is very similar to the first stasimon of the *Electra*. There, as we saw in chapter 2, the typically celebratory figures of chorality described in the account of the Greeks' sea journey to Troy in the first strophe (choruses of Nereids and a whirling, leaping, *aulos*-loving dolphin) are later transformed into more threatening images of *mousikē*, as the chorus describe Achilles' terrifying armor with strongly choreographic language. In the epode the chorus of Argive women then address Clytemnestra directly, turning from the bloodiness of Achilles' weapons to her own murder of Agamemnon (*El.* 478–86). Through this movement back toward the present, the chorus not only apply the narrative of the ode to the immediate dramatic situation but also anticipate a pivotal point in the plot—Clytemnestra's murder at the hands of Orestes and Electra.

In the epode of the third stasimon of *Iphigenia in Aulis* musical images are similarly used for a deeply unsettling effect as the chorus allude to details of music and dance from the previous verses but transfer them from the context of marriage to one of sacrifice.[119] In doing so, the chorus here, as in *Electra*, anticipate the inevitable turning point in the plot of the play as Iphigenia submits to her sacrifice. The garlanding of her head (*stepsousi*, 1080) recalls the shouting, reveling *thiasos* of Centaurs with their "wreathed [*stephanōdei*] foliage" (1058), while the focus on her beautiful hair (*kallikoman / plokamon*, 1080–81) reminds us of the "beautiful-haired" (*kalliplokamoi*, 1040) Muses dancing and singing.[120] Through the course of the ode, then, the focus of erotic attraction has shifted from the Muses' *choreia* and Ganymede in the strophe to Achilles in the antistrophe and finally—and most disturbingly—to Iphigenia, the sacrificial bride, in the epode.

The chorus also refer to the syrinx again, which takes on a twofold meaning as a result of the instrumental sound with which the ode began.[121] On the one hand, the fact that Iphigenia was not raised to the sound of the syrinx and the whistling of herdsmen emphasizes the difference between her and the mountain calf, a more

---

118. Mastronarde 2010: 140–43, 148–49. Other examples include *Andr.* 274–308, *El.* 699–746, *Phoen.* 638–89, 1019–66, and most likely *Hel.* 1301–68 (but the corrupt lines at the end of this ode make the pattern harder to recognize); also Aesch. *Cho.* 585–662; Soph. *Ant.* 332–75, *OT* 863–910.

119. On the combination of marriage and sacrificial imagery in *IA*, see Foley 1982 and 1985: 82–83; Seaford 1987: 108–10; Michelakis 2006: 70–71. Cf. Rehm 1994 and Swift 2010: 250–55 on the conflation of marriage and funerary rituals in Greek tragedy.

120. Lines 1080–81 also foreshadow Iphigenia's song as she goes to be sacrificed: "Give me garlands to be cast about me, bring them—here are my locks to garland—and streams of lustral water" (στέφεα περίβολα δίδοτε, φέρε- / τε—πλόκαμος ὅδε καταστέφειν—/ χερνίβων τε παγάς, 1477–79).

121. ῥοιβδήσεσι, translated here as "whistlings," may also refer to both the sound and the technique of playing the syrinx: Stockert 1992: 2.509 understands 1085–86 to mean essentially "nicht beim schrillen Klang der ländlichen Syringen."

usual sacrificial animal to which the preceding simile compares her. In this respect the reference to the syrinx reminds us of the image of Paris as a herdsman piping on his syrinx at the end of the first stasimon—another image of pastoral innocence that is used to contrast with the surrounding dramatic context. The similar language here also points to the causal connection between the moment of the Judgment scene and Iphigenia's sacrifice.[122] On the other hand, the absence of a syrinx for Iphigenia here contrasts with the inclusion of the "reedy syrinxes" along with the *aulos* and kithara in the opening of the ode (1038). The syrinx therefore also functions as a representative of wedding music, just as it does in the hands of Calliope on both the François Vase and the Sophilos Dinos, so that the mention of it here highlights the absence of any such celebratory *mousikē* for Iphigenia. This absence would have been further stressed through the performance of the third stasimon as a whole if, given the lack of references to choreography here, we can assume that the chorus would dance less in the epode or even that they might be stationary, as William Mullen has suggested might happen in the epodes of Pindar's choral lyric.[123]

Like Cassandra's distorted, monodic performance of a *hymenaios* in *Trojan Women*, the third stasimon of *Iphigenia in Aulis* not only provides a contrast with the reality of the immediate *mythos* but is embedded within the dramatic fabric of the play as a whole. We saw in chapter 3 that the emphasis on the lack of a chorus in Cassandra's performance plays into the motif of absent *choreia* that runs throughout the earlier tragedy, emphasizing the complete breakdown of communal worship and civic structure in the wake of Troy's destruction. At the same time, the lack of *hymenaioi* sung by a chorus of *parthenoi* (rather than by the bride herself) points forward beyond the span of the play itself to Cassandra's death; Euripides here seems to be exploiting a traditional idea that the distortion or absence of a proper *hymenaios* signals doom for the bride. Similarly, in *Iphigenia in Aulis*, the ironic emphasis on the lack of any such celebratory *choreia* for Iphigenia—an emphasis that becomes clear through the performance of the ode, not just in its language—anticipates her sacrifice rather than her marriage.

Even while this ode transports us to a time and place beyond the scope of the play itself, then, both the language and performance of *mousikē* forge close ties with the surrounding drama. Like other odes within Euripides' oeuvre that contain vivid accounts of *mousikē*, this song's intensely musical language reveals the tragedian's experimentation with how choral performance could (and could not) relate to the surrounding drama. But the highly metamusical character of the ode, as well as its engagement with the choral imaginary within and through its performance, also derives from traditional hymenaeal choral lyric, and it is through the audience's

---

122. This image recurs with Paris as a *boukolos* in Iphigenia's lament (1291–93).
123. Mullen 1982: 90–142.

acquaintance with this long-established genre that the song achieves its devastatingly ironic impact, directing us toward Iphigenia's death rather than her marriage.

## CHOREIA AND MONODY

In addition to having this anticipatory effect, the third stasimon fits within a larger pattern of *mousikē* that runs through the whole play. The first two-thirds of the tragedy are rich with choral song, especially if we accept the authenticity of the entire parodos: over a quarter of the lines are sung by the chorus in the parodos and three stasima. The third stasimon, however, is the last intensely lyrical outburst of choral song, and in the last third of the play *choreia* is largely absent, only briefly appearing in response to Iphigenia's request that the chorus sing to Artemis. The shift of focus onto Iphigenia herself in the epode therefore heralds not just a turning point in the play as her death becomes more certain (as we know it must) but a change in terms of the tragedy's musical performance.

Following the third stasimon, the next song is performed by Iphigenia, not the chorus. At a break in the action that would naturally be marked by another choral ode, between the exit of Agamemnon and entrance of Achilles, she sings a monody that develops the motif of the Judgment of Paris, which the chorus mentioned in the first stasimon.[124] Previously she has appeared only in the exchange between her, Clytemnestra, and Agamemnon upon her arrival (631–750), but from the moment when she wishes she had Orpheus's power of speech (1211) she becomes the dominant voice of the tragedy: almost half of all the lines from this point onward are hers (over half if, as is likely, the play ended with the chorus's song at 1510–32 and did not include the following messenger speech).[125] The style of her first monody also suggests that it involved complex and impressive music of the sort that required the talents of a star actor rather than an amateur chorus.[126] The loose syntactical structure, enjambment, metrical variety (trochees, anapaests, dochmiacs, dactyls, paeons), repetitions of words, and assonant and alliterative wordplay are all indicative of the musical and verbal complexity typical of monodies in Euripides' work at the end of the fifth century.[127]

---

124. *IA* 1279–1335; 573–89. Cf. Kranz 1933: 229; Lesky 1972: 479; Kovacs 2003: 97. On the use of an actor's monody rather than choral song in an act-dividing position here, see Taplin 1984: 122. On act-dividing choral songs between exits and entrances in tragedy, see Taplin 1977, esp. 51–58; Poe 1993.

125. On the dubious authenticity of lines 1532–1629, see Page 1934: 192–204; Willink 1971: 314; West 1981: 73–76; Jouan 1983: 26–28; Stockert 1992: 1.79–87; Kovacs 2003: 98–100.

126. Cf. Csapo 1999–2000: 407; Hall 2002: 8–11.

127. Repetition: e.g., Ἰδαῖος Ἰ- / δαῖος ἐλέγετ' ἐλέγετ', 1289–90. Assonance and alliteration: e.g., ὁ δὲ τεκών με τὰν τάλαιναν, 1312. Cf. Aeschylus's parody of such monodies in Ar. *Ran.* 1331–63. On the increasing complexity of actors' song in late Euripides, see Hall 1999: 113–14; Csapo 1999–2000: 407 and 2004: 216, 222–27. On Iphigenia's monody, see Stinton 1965: 29–34.

The focus of musical performance thus shifts from chorus to individual actor in the last section of the play, just as the focus of the dramatic action turns toward her alone—and toward her crucial change of mind as she decides voluntarily to die so that the army can leave Aulis for Troy.[128] As we have seen, this narrower focal point is in sharp contrast with the chorus's Panhellenic perspective in the parodos as they report on the sight of the vast Greek army. The transition from *choreia* to monody therefore mirrors the increasing importance of Iphigenia as a character in the play over that of the collective (Greece, the army, and the chorus).

Before her second and final song, however, Iphigenia calls the chorus back to perform a paean to Artemis before preparing for her sacrifice:

ὑμεῖς δ' ἐπευφημήσατ', ὦ νεάνιδες,
παιᾶνα τἠμῆι συμφορᾶι Διὸς κόρην
Ἄρτεμιν.

But you, O maidens, sing a paean over my misfortune in praise of the daughter of Zeus, Artemis. (1467–69)

Despite her order to the chorus, it is Iphigenia herself who then begins this celebratory song:

ἄγετέ με τὰν Ἰλίου (1475)
καὶ Φρυγῶν ἑλέπτολιν.
στέφεα περίβολα δίδοτε φέρε-
τε—πλόκαμος ὅδε καταστέφειν—
χερνίβων τε παγάς.

Lead me, the city sacker of Ilium and the Phrygians. Give me garlands to be cast about me, bring them—here are my locks to garland—and streams of lustral water. (1475–79)

In this song she marks her changed resolve to be sacrificed by transforming her previous performance of lament: the repeated refrain of *iō iō* now becomes part of the paean to Artemis, in singing to whom she bids the chorus to join her ("*Iō iō* young women, sing with me in celebration of Artemis," 1491–92).[129] Her song then turns into a brief lyric iambic exchange with the chorus before she departs (1500–1509). As she makes her way offstage, the chorus take up her song, watching her as she goes to be sacrificed and celebrating Artemis at her request (1510–32).

---

128. Conacher 1967: 249–50 and Michelakis 2006: 31 divide the tragedy into three parts: the first focusing on Agamemnon and his dilemma over his daughter's sacrifice; the second on Clytemnestra and Achilles, who learn the reason for Iphigenia's presence; the third on Iphigenia and her decision to be sacrificed. On Iphigenia's change of mind and consistency (or inconsistency) of character, see esp. Siegel 1980; Luschnig 1988: 53–54; Sorum 1992. Her instructions to the chorus (1467–74) and her monody (1475–99) seem to me to be strong declarations of willing self-sacrifice, even if she does change her stance in part because of the overwhelming force of the army. (Cf. Siegel 1980: 310–11.)

129. ἰὼ ἰὼ νεάνιδες, / συνεπαείδετ' Ἄρτεμιν. The refrain *iō* previously appeared at 1283, 1333, 1491, and 1497.

This final choral song has traditionally been regarded as spurious, largely on account of the striking degree of repetition between it and Iphigenia's monody.[130] Recently David Kovacs has countered this view by arguing for the authenticity of this song and suggesting that Iphigenia's monody is interpolated instead, in which case she was originally meant to depart for her sacrifice immediately after giving her instructions to the chorus to sing to Artemis (1466–74).[131] If so, then the choral performance would in fact have been part of the exodos. It is generally agreed that the last hundred lines, containing the messenger's speech, are interpolated, perhaps added as late as the seventh century C.E., while even the alternative lines quoted in Aelian implying the appearance of Artemis ex machina contain some problematic postclassical elements.[132]

The focus on the question of authenticity, however, has neglected how both Iphigenia's monody and the chorus's final song respond musically to each other and together fit within the pattern of *choreia* and monody that runs through the play as a whole. By "respond musically" I mean not metrical responsion—the chorus's song is astrophic—but a form of antiphony in which the chorus echo Iphigenia's monody in style and diction, and follow her directions to perform in a particular way. These songs therefore need not be mutually exclusive: both of them could have been in the play at its first performance, and they respond to each other in ways that suggest that they were originally intended by Euripides, even if he himself did not write them—in which case they were probably composed by an early actor or producer trying to reproduce the tragedian's style.[133]

Given the narrowing focus on Iphigenia and her solo song over the previous four hundred lines, the reappearance of *choreia* here at the end of the play may seem surprising. Now, however, the chorus perform with Iphigenia as she exits the stage, not separately from her; and the shared nature of their performance should prompt us to question both the common view that the return of *choreia* here is interpolated and Kovacs's suggestion that Iphigenia's monody should be rejected instead. Whatever their quality, the repetitions (1475–1509 vs. 1510–31) are surely deliberate, as both Iphigenia and the chorus, following her instructions, sing together in praise of Artemis.

This joint performance is most clearly signaled by Iphigenia's unusual compound imperative *synepaeidete* ("join in celebrating/appeasing with song,"

---

130. See esp. Page 1934: 191–92; also West 1981: 74. Diggle, following Kirchhoff and England (who in his 1891 edition deems this song "a feeble and at times senseless reproduction of the language and the ideas of vv. 1475ff."), marks 1510–32 as "vix Euripidei" in his (1994a) edition of the Greek text.

131. Kovacs 2003: 98–100.

132. Ael. *NA* 7.39. On the dubious authenticity of lines 1532–1629, see Page 1934: 192–204; Willink 1971: 314; West 1981: 73–76; Jouan 1983: 26–28; Stockert 1992: 1.79–87; Kovacs 2002: 161 and 2003: 98–100

133. Early interpolations are most likely histrionic, whereas readers' interpolations are generally from a later stage in the transmission of Euripides' tragic texts: see esp. Mastronarde 1994: 39–41.

1493).¹³⁴ The chorus, following this command, start to respond to her song shortly afterward in an antiphonal exchange in which their lines complement Iphigenia's own concerning her city and glory in dying (1498–1504). They then take up her paeanic refrain *iō iō* (1510) and sing astrophic lyrics that in diction are initially so similar to her monody that the chorus really do seem to be joining her in song:

ἰὼ ἰώ.
ἴδεσθε τὰν Ἰλίου (1510)
καὶ Φρυγῶν ἐλέπτολιν
στείχουσαν, ἐπὶ κάραι στέφη
βαλουμέναν χερνίβων τε παγάς.

*Iō iō!* Behold the city sacker of Ilium and the Phrygians as she goes on her way, with garlands cast about her head and streams of lustral water. (1510–13)

Like Iphigenia, they begin with a second person plural imperative (*idesthe*, 1510; cf. *agete*, 1475) directing our attention to the same accusative object—Iphigenia as the city sacker of Ilium and the Phrygians (1510–11 = 1475–76).¹³⁵ They then with similar language refer to her sacrificial garlands and streams of lustral water (1512–13; cf. 1477–79). The chorus soon turn to celebrating Artemis, just as Iphigenia bade them to (1521–22), and continue to recall the language of her song with their invocation "O lady, ⟨lady⟩" (*Ō potnia* ⟨*potnia*⟩, 1524; cf. 1487).¹³⁶

---

134. Cf. Stockert 1992: 2.614: "Die Wiederholungen in v. 1509ff. könnten freilich ... auch als Ausdruck der Gleichstimmigkeit und des συνεπαείδειν (v. 1492) verstanden werden." Kovacs 2003: 99 argues that this verb is probably interpolated, both because of its rarity and because it takes an accusative object here. It is worth noting that, although *epaeidein* does not tend to have an accusative object, both *aeidein* and other verbs with the *synep-* prefix do (e.g., *synepainein*). Given Euripides' penchant for unusual vocabulary in the lyric passages of his later plays, the verb's rarity should not strike us as too surprising. On the combined sense of celebration and appeasement (the latter as in *epaeidein*), see Stockert 1992: 2.614: Artemis is to be appeased so that the Greeks can leave Aulis.

135. Kovacs 2003: 99 finds *agete* ("lead") in line 1475 inappropriate, as Iphigenia is apparently being accompanied by just one servant to sacrifice (cf. 1462), yet this plural imperative is addressed as much to the chorus as to any servant (or servants). He also feels it is awkward since it is combined with others that can be carried out only at Iphigenia's destination, but the same combination of real present and vividly imagined future is evident earlier in the play in reference to Iphigenia, particularly in the final stanza of the third stasimon (1080–97).

136. As Kovacs 2003: 99 points out, *potnia māter* in line 1487 is unparalleled as an address to one's own mother rather than to a goddess or mistress and therefore points to some corruption in this part of Iphigenia's song. It is possible that Iphigenia is addressing Artemis here, not Clytemnestra, particularly since the rest of her song is so focused on the goddess, whom the chorus then address as *potnia* at 1524. An invocation of Artemis as *māter* (Burges's accepted reading of an obscure set of letters in ms. L), however, would also be surprising, even if, as Stockert advises, we consider the goddess's "Doppelcharakter" (1992: 2.614). Perhaps the chorus's similar invocation should instead be understood as a transformation of Iphigenia's address rather than a precise repetition.

The similarities between the songs of Iphigenia and the chorus here thus suggest an antiphonal exchange in the style of a paean, which is the very type of song she has instructed them to perform. Although this paean has a sacrificial context, the militaristic tone with which both songs start, picturing Iphigenia as the sacker of Troy, may in particular evoke the performance of a battle paean, with the leader (here Iphigenia) beginning the song and being answered by the army (the chorus).[137] The imperative *synepaeidete* may also suggest such a battle paean. This verb appears only here and in Theophrastus, but, as Ian Rutherford has noted, the communal response in the performance of paeans in Xenophon is twice denoted by another verb with a *synep-* prefix, *synepēchein* ("join in singing").[138] The same verb is used similarly (though not in the immediate context of battle) in Thucydides,[139] and verbs with the *epi-* prefix often refer to the singing of a paean. If the performance at the end of *Iphigenia in Aulis* is meant to suggest that of a battle paean, the chorus would again appear to merge with the Greek army, just as they did through their *choreia* when describing the arrayed troops in the parodos.

This evocation of the paeanic genre inverts the gender roles it usually entails: whereas performances of paeans outside tragedy were almost exclusively male, here a female chorus answer the opening song of a female leader.[140] Their combined performance also seems to confuse this paean with Iphigenia's previous mode of song, lament, which, when not in its purely solo form, typically involves a lyric exchange between a female leader and a sympathetic female chorus.[141] Such merging of genres is intensified by the refrain *iō iō*, which is also used in lament in tragedy (as in Iphigenia's earlier song at 1283 and 1332)—and indeed this is the type of song the audience would expect to hear now, as Iphigenia is led to her sacrifice. Yet the female usurpation of the paean's male musical form complements Iphigenia's appropriation of the male language of bravery and service to community as she accepts her sacrifice. This is already evident when she explains to Clytemnestra how she is determined to die with *kleos* through her marriage to Greece (1374–1401). Her final exchange with the chorus also resembles male Panhellenic rhetoric, as she claims that Mycenae "raised me as a light for Greece" (1502).[142] By evok-

---

137. See Rutherford 2001: 42–47 on paeans before battle and after victory.
138. Theophr. *Hist. pl.* 9.10.4. See Rutherford 2001: 66 on *synepēchein* at Xen. *Cyr.* 3.3.58, 7.1.26.
139. Thuc. 6.32.2.
140. On the gender of paeanic performers, see Calame 1997: 76–79; Rutherford 2001: 58–59; Swift 2010: 64–65.
141. As at Hom. *Il.* 24.719–46, when Andromache leads the *goos* among a wider group of women who also lament as well as the bards who lead their *thrēnoi*: see Alexiou 1974: 134–38; Swift 2010: 301–2. Cf. *Tro.* 98–229, 1216–59, 1287–1330; *IT* 143–235; *Hel.* 167–251. On the mixing of paean and lament in tragedy, see Rutherford 1994–95: 121–24 and 2001: 118–20; Swift 2010: 71–72.
142. ἐθρέψαθ''Ελλάδι με φάος. For a particularly pessimistic view of Iphigenia's language here, see Siegel 1980: 311–16. (He views her rhetoric of *kleos* as completely delusional.)

ing in particular a battle paean, the chorus, though previously characterized as female non-combatants, further complement this change in Iphigenia's (self-) presentation by performing with her like an army in response to their leader.[143]

The mixing of genders and genres was well established in Athenian tragedy by the time Euripides composed *Iphigenia in Aulis*. Despite Plato's complaints about feminine tunes and styles being attached to male verses (and vice versa) and about the "unlawful" poets who "mixed dirges with hymns and paeans with dithyrambs," this was not an especially recent musical practice, and we find similarly hybrid performances in earlier tragedy:[144] in Aeschylus's *Libation Bearers*, for example, Electra instructs the chorus to sing a paean over Agamemnon's tomb (149–51); a female chorus also performs a paean in Sophocles' *Women of Trachis* (205–24).[145] For Euripides, however, such generic distortion is closely tied to the dramatic— and musical—narrative, with Iphigenia now becoming the paean-singing city sacker rather than the army with which the first song of the play was so occupied. In Aeschylus's *Agamemnon*, as we saw in chapter 1, the chorus of Argive elders picture her singing a paean in her father's banqueting halls (240–47) but in doing so keep her silent, confined to a description that is uncomfortably at odds with their own live performance. In *Iphigenia in Aulis*, Euripides presents her actually singing such a song onstage at the climax of a shift in both the focus of the drama and its style of musical performance: a shift from the army to Iphigenia, group to individual, male to female; and from *choreia* to monody to, finally, an antiphonal exchange between chorus and soloist as she acts on the community's behalf.

The response of the chorus to Iphigenia's directions to sing a paean with her may begin before they actually start singing in their antiphonal exchange. Near the beginning of her monody she bids the chorus to "whirl around" the altar of Artemis (*IA* 1480–84). We have already seen that the verb used here (*helissein*) also appears within a particularly self-referential passage of the parodos, when the chorus describe the running and leaping of Achilles, and that it often occurs in highly metamusical choral passages in Euripides' later plays. Here in Iphigenia's song the verb may also suggest some sort of simultaneous choreography, particularly as the circular movement that it implies is stressed by the repetition of the preposition *amphi* ("around"). But this is not merely a reference to the speaker's own movement: it is an imperative given as a stage direction by the actor to the chorus. Such circular dance was a common form of paeanic performance, and we can imagine

---

143. While the mixing of genders here demonstrates how the tragic paean was "freed from the gender constraints of the real world" (Swift 2010: 65), it also indicates that it relied on the audience's experience of its real-life enactment for its full dramatic effect.

144. Pl. *Leg.* 669c3–5, 700d6–7 (κεραννύντες δὲ θρήνους τε ὕμνοις καὶ παίωνας διθυράμβοις).

145. Rutherford 1994–95: 120 and 2001: 113. On genre mixing in Greek tragedy, see Weiss forthcoming b.

that the chorus may at this point in Iphigenia's song respond to her directions by moving accordingly. Certainly they are likely to have danced in this way when singing their own paean to Artemis.[146]

Although Iphigenia and the chorus respond musically to each other through their shared paeanic celebration, there is also a more unsettling undercurrent to their performance as a result of the unusual nature of their antiphony. Antiphonal *mousikē* tends to stress the solidarity of a leader and chorus, and in tragedy it does so especially in the form of lament: as we saw in chapter 4, the shared parodos of Euripides' *Helen* has this effect; so does the extended performance of non-Greek mourning sung by Xerxes and the chorus at the end of Aeschylus's *Persians*. In *Iphigenia in Aulis*, however, the chorus's response to Iphigenia's song ironically brings them together with her as their *chorēgos* just when she is exiting the stage to go to her sacrifice.[147] The emotional poignancy of this performance is comparable to that at the end of Euripides' *Trojan Women*, when, as we saw in chapter 3, the long, antiphonal lament of Hecuba and the chorus as she is about to be led away to Odysseus's ship marks the end of their *choreia*—and so too the complete breakdown of any remaining social bonds or institutions in the aftermath of Troy's fall. The metrical disjointedness of the antiphony in the later play, with both Iphigenia and the chorus singing astrophic songs, further underscores her separation from them at the same time as their joint performance highlights their communality. Such distorted antiphony reflects the paradoxical nature of Iphigenia's final action, through which she both withdraws herself from the Greek community by leaving for her sacrifice and simultaneously acts as its savior, ensuring the army's departure and subsequent victory at Troy. So though the *mousikē* of Iphigenia and the chorus here gives the impression of a celebratory antiphonal paean, this type of performance is also disturbingly flawed.

The usual categorization of Iphigenia's song at 1475–99 as a monody is therefore misleading, since it ignores how it is related to the chorus's own performance. If we take all aspects of performance into account (dance as well as song), some sort of responsive exchange between her and the chorus seems to occur even before the chorus start singing (1510). Iphigenia's instructions (1467–69) that the chorus sing a paean are not made redundant because they are not immediately followed by the chorus's own song: they *are* followed by a choral performance, as the Chalcidean women dance in accompaniment to her song, which begins the paean that they

---

146. Rutherford 2001: 65 sees such movement as belonging only to the imagined realm of *mousikē* even though the chorus could actually dance in a circle while Iphigenia sings. Cf. Calame 1997: 76–77.

147. As the text stands, Iphigenia must leave the stage after she finishes singing (1508), so that there can be an interval between her exit and the arrival of the messenger (1532) to report her death. But with the more likely ending (1531), we can imagine that Iphigenia may have left the stage gradually during the chorus's song, thereby emphasizing their separation just as they perform in response to her. The moment of Clytemnestra's exit is unclear: she could depart into the house at 1509 or stay onstage through the chorus's song until the end of the play.

then take over. When the chorus do begin to sing as well as dance, their response seems not just to complement Iphigenia's performance but also to replace it, marking the end of both her singing and her voice in the tragedy as a whole: *choreia* returns with Iphigenia's departure and death.

The performance of this paean therefore presents the final coalescing of chorus and actor as they become intimately involved in her story, carrying out her instructions to celebrate and appease Artemis in her memory just at the moment when she leaves them to be sacrificed. To deem the repetitions between the songs of Iphigenia and the chorus in the closing scene of the *Iphigenia in Aulis* as evidence for one or the other's being spurious is to miss how the merging of their singing in an antiphonal performance concludes the interplay of *choreia* and monody in the drama as a whole. It is above all through the performance of *mousikē* (music and dance) that the audience's attention is increasingly directed toward Iphigenia through the course of the tragedy, away from the Panhellenic *choreia* of the parodos. In the Chalcidean women's last song they function as both audience and chorus, beholding Iphigenia as she goes to her sacrifice and finally joining her in song, transforming her death into a paeanic celebration while also reminding us of the poignancy of her sacrifice.

Even in one of Euripides' very latest tragedies, then, and even in one in which actor's song comes to the fore, *choreia* still plays a vital dramatic role. The overall musical arc of *Iphigenia in Aulis*, transitioning from an intense amount of choral song and dance to solo song in the last third of the drama, is not in itself new: as I mentioned at the start of this chapter, both Euripides' *Heracles* and Sophocles' *Women of Trachis* exhibit a similar shift, directing our attention to the suffering of the individual protagonists. But the pattern is especially marked in *Iphigenia in Aulis,* complementing the change in dramatic focus from the collective—the Greek army—to Iphigenia herself. Paradoxically, the extraordinary return of *choreia* at the end of the play stresses this shift, through the contrast between the parodos, in which the chorus describe the sight of the army (especially Achilles), and their final song, when they focus exclusively on Iphigenia herself.

Within this overarching musical pattern, Euripides combines various dramatic uses of *mousikē* that we saw at work in his earlier plays. In the parodos the chorus expand the spatial scope of the play, bringing onstage through their own song and dance the sight of the great army, whose presence repeatedly reminds us of the inevitability of Iphigenia's sacrifice. In the first and third stasima the chorus extends its temporal-mythical bounds, bringing into the performance space scenes from the mythical past that form a painfully ironic backdrop to the present action. In the third stasimon, the irony generated through the chorus's (re)enactment of past *choreia* has an anticipatory effect, pushing us toward Iphigenia's death. And in all these songs, Euripides draws on traditional elements of the Greek choral imaginary, redeploying them within the dramatic context of tragedy.

# Conclusion

## *Euripides' Musical Innovations*

The central aim of this book has been to show that the *mousikē* of tragedy is intimately tied to its *mythos*. The four case studies examine the different ways in which, in the latter part of his career, Euripides experimented with the roles song, dance, and instrumental accompaniment could play within a drama. They demonstrate that *mousikē* continued to be an integral element of tragedy for Euripides, as it had been for previous playwrights, and also that his subtle and innovative use of traditional choral forms made a crucial difference to how an audience experienced a play.

*Mousikē*, the inseparable mix of song (words, tune, rhythm, pitch, timbre), dance, and instrumental music, works on various levels. The transition from one type of musical performance to another—or, as in *Trojan Women*, the appearance of generic consistency—shapes a tragedy as a whole and the audience's response to each stage of the plot. It intensifies feelings of relief and excitement as Helen and Menelaus effect their escape in *Helen*, or pity and shock as Iphigenia performs a paean, a maiden with her female chorus, usurping the *choreia* with which the entire Greek army came to life in the opening song of *Iphigenia in Aulis*. *Mousikē* can reflect or complement a plot; it can also demarcate and anticipate critical turning points, driving the play forward even as it offers moments of escapism. In the first and second stasima of *Electra*, for example, we saw how the combination of described and performed *mousikē* initially transports the audience away from the immediate action in Argos but brings them back into it with a terrifying jolt as the images to which the chorus's own performance corresponds become increasingly ominous. By the end of both these songs the audience are primed for the dreadful revenge they know is about to be committed.

*Mousikē* is also closely linked to character, especially in these plays with female choruses and protagonists. Certain characters are defined by a particular type of musical performance, whether or not it truly matches their situation, as we saw with the very different laments of Hecuba and Electra. Their songs can encourage the audience's empathy but also, as in Electra's case, complicate it—the contrast between her insistence on lament (or on no *choreia* at all) and the chorus's more celebratory performances reveals a distance between their outlooks and social situations that tempers both the chorus's sympathy and our own. *Trojan Women* instead demonstrates how *mousikē* can reinforce a common bond between the female protagonist and her chorus, setting them apart from male characters and creating an almost exclusively female world for the audience to inhabit—temporarily so, of course, since the actors and choreuts were all male, and also as female characters, especially elite ones like Hecuba, can produce surprisingly male rhetoric that seems to contradict their claims to helplessness. In *Helen* this close bond between women is clearly demonstrated at the start of the play, when Helen participates in the parodos, but loosens as she moves away from female mourning and back toward Menelaus and her role in Spartan cult. In *Iphigenia in Aulis* we find the inverse of this pattern: chorus and actor finally come together at the end of this play, completing a change in focus from the all-male army to the maiden whose sacrifice will allow them to depart for Troy. These plays thus demonstrate how dramatically effective the musical relationship between a female protagonist and her chorus could be. This particular gender combination, of which Euripides was so fond, also enabled him to exploit the dramatic potential of musical performances associated with women (*partheneia, hymenaioi,* lament) and at the same time play with how much the chorus's own song and dance could correspond with the extensive imaginary of female *choreia*.[1]

Throughout this book I have emphasized the interplay of performed and imagined *mousikē*—the connection between the chorus's own live performance and the images of music making that frequently appear in their songs. I have approached the "music" of tragedy in this way partly because the verbal part is (almost) all we have left but also because it is so closely bound up with the musical and kinetic elements of a performance: words were central to the ancient conception of *mousikē* more generally, and *choreia* is consistently presented as a unity of words, music, and dance. Nevertheless, the relationship between these different elements of a play's *mousikē* is complex, and sometimes there can be a deliberate mismatch between them. In both *Trojan Women* and the third stasimon of *Iphigenia in Aulis*, the disconnect between the words and performance of *choreia* is pitifully ironic. It is also deeply unsettling, as sights and sounds undermine each other, reminding

---

1. On Euripides' preference for female choruses (and female protagonists), see esp. Castellani 1989; Hose 1990: 17–20; Mastronarde 1999: 94–95 and 2010: 101–5; Foley 2001 and 2003.

the audience of a character's prior or alternative existence while simultaneously negating it. At the same time, such *mousikē* can contradict the *mythos* itself, prompting our desire for an outcome that we know is impossible.

So *mousikē* intensifies, varies, extends, and at times even challenges the *mythos*. This is the fundamental point that I have tried to show through my readings of *Electra*, *Trojan Women*, *Helen*, and *Iphigenia in Aulis*. I have also tried to position Euripides' experimentation with the dramatic potentialities of *mousikē* within the traditions both of Athenian tragedy and of choral lyric more generally in order to understand what is musically different about these plays from the last fifteen years of his career. Each study has demonstrated a certain degree of continuity between Euripides' *mousikē* and his tragic predecessors'—in the affective impact of metamusical language merging with the live performance, in the presencing power of *choreia*, in the characterization of choruses and protagonists, and in the shaping of a musical narrative in tandem with the dramatic one. But they have also revealed that the extent to which Euripides draws on traditional forms and figures of *choreia* and incorporates them within his dramas is largely unprecedented in surviving tragedy prior to the production of *Electra*, around 420 B.C.E.

## ENGAGING THE AUDIENCE WITH *MOUSIKĒ*

The musical innovation of Euripides' late work partly lies, then, in its traditionalism. We are still left, however, with the question of why he incorporates these traditional elements of *choreia* so extensively, and what his use of them may suggest about his involvement with the new musical trends of his day. In this concluding discussion, I propose that Euripides is pushing the dramatic possibilities of *mousikē* to their full extent to develop a new form of engagement with his audience and that this is closely tied to the New Music more broadly. The process is not one-sided: in adapting traditional elements of Greek choral culture for the tragic stage Euripides relies on the audience's own immersion within that culture to draw them into the dramatic narrative and make them feel more intensely the emotional force of his plays.

The choral odes of Euripides' later plays have a certain doubleness, a mix of alterity and proximity, that distinguishes them from his earlier work.[2] These songs demonstrate his fondness for narratives and scene descriptions that appear very remote from (even at odds with) the immediate *mythos*, such as the choral image

---

2. My idea of doubleness, as well as the focus on how Euripidean *choreia* engages its audience, owes much to Richard Neer's discussion of changes in Greek sculpture in the classical period: to produce wonder (*thauma*), "the statue should seem simultaneously alien and familiar, far and close, inert and alive, absent and present. The Classical style consists in part of new poses that dramatically engage the beholder: they throw things at us, rush toward us, overwhelm us with sheer scale and glitter" (2010: 4).

of Achilles going off to Troy just when the recognition scene is about to occur in *Electra* or the tale of the Great Mother's search for her daughter just as the escape plan begins in *Helen*. But while he takes his audience as far from the dramatic action as he can, exaggerating the distance between then and now, there and here, he simultaneously engages them more intensely with these mythical scenes through the immersive performance of *choreia*. It is worth now reflecting more on the nature of such engagement so that we may better understand what is "new" in these odes.

When Euripides employs traditional figures of chorality, such as Nereids, Sirens, dolphins, horses, or birds, he also exploits their metamusical character—that is, how they can interact with the live performance of *choreia*. His choruses thus become hypermimetic, assuming different identities within a single song while retaining their dramatic one. In chapter 1 we saw a similar sort of choral flexibility in Alcman's first *Partheneion*, in which Agido and Hagesichora themselves seem to be recurring roles for Spartan girls, but at the same time the chorus direct us to see them as horses, doves, and even stars. The choral images at work in this song require of its audience a particular mode of viewing and hearing *choreia*: they invite the audience to visualize the chorus in different ways, beyond what they physically see and hear.[3] Euripides likewise repeatedly prompts his audience to imaginatively link the music and dance in the theater to the scenes and figures to which the chorus refer in their songs and to hold multiple images in mind as the chorus identify with one and then the other in quick succession. This process of visualization, of experiencing one thing as another, is not passive: rather, the audience must connect the verbal and musical/choreographic components of *choreia* and swiftly move from one combination to another while also fitting it within their understanding of the dramatic narrative.[4] Sometimes, as we have seen, metamusical language also prompts the audience to notice the dissonance between the music and dance on the one hand and the words on the other.

It is also an active process in how it triggers the audience's own prior experience of *choreia* as frequent spectators of and participants in various types of choral performance both in and outside the theater.[5] *Choreia* was a regular and prominent part of Athenian life:[6] indeed, the dithyramb alone, to which Euripides frequently alludes, involved a total of a thousand choreuts each year. Several scholars of Dance Studies

---

3. Peponi 2004a; cf. Peponi 2015, esp. 214–15.

4. Cf. Peponi 2015: 214: "Far from being attached to a singular mimetic referent, the orchestic imaginary encourages a creative mental process, a model of active perceptiveness while a spectator contemplates dance."

5. Cf. Revermann 2006b on the competence of audiences of tragedy in fifth-century Athens; also Gagné and Hopman 2013b: 26; Peponi 2013a: 212–13.

6. Even female choruses seem to have been a regular occurrence in classical Athens (if not as common or well-documented as in Sparta or Argos): see Budelmann and Power 2015.

have shown how someone familiar with a particular dance genre, as a performer or spectator, tends to respond emotionally and corporeally much more deeply than someone who lacks such cultural competence.[7] This type of embodied response, often called kinesthetic contagion or empathy, can be cognitive too: a spectator can reflect upon the performance she sees in addition to responding to a particular dance with a corresponding emotion or by moving or breathing in synchrony with her perception of both the movement and the accompanying music. Sarah Olsen has demonstrated how frequently ancient Greek writers refer to such a phenomenon, indicating that it was a common experience among audiences of *choreia*.[8] The immediate somatic identification between performers and audiences is especially clear in a famous passage of the *Homeric Hymn to Apollo* in which the Delian maidens are said to represent people's voices and movements so well that "each one may think that he himself is giving voice."[9] In this ideal model of *choreia*, "the very bodies of the audience members on Delos are implicated in the performance, drawn into a powerful sense of participation and identification with the Delian maidens."[10] As these lines suggest, such contagion or empathy is not restricted to dance. Indeed, in the last book of his *Politics* Aristotle talks of music's effects on its listener in terms of *enthousiasmos* (we may loosely translate this as "excitement" or even "ecstasy") and discusses how emotional music provokes a corresponding emotion in the audience, making them *sympatheis*.[11] In *Problems* he also briefly considers music's *ethos* in terms of a movement (*kinēsis*) that moves us in turn.[12]

By so often including in his choral odes figures of chorality and scenes of music making to which his audience would be accustomed as frequent spectators and performers of *choreia*, Euripides urges on them a similar sense of embodied participation in his plays' *mousikē*.[13] These images would intensify the effect of the

---

7. See esp. Foster 2008 and 2010; Sklar 2008; Reason and Reynolds 2010. The term "cultural competence" comes from Bourdieu 1987: "A work of art has meaning and interest only for someone who possesses the cultural competence, that is, the code, into which it is encoded.... A beholder who lacks the specific code feels lost in a chaos of sounds and rhythms, colors and lines, without rhyme or reason" (2).

8. Olsen 2017.

9. φαίη δέ κεν αὐτὸς ἕκαστος / φθέγγεσθ' (*Hymn. Hom. Ap.* 163–64). On these much-discussed lines, see esp. Peponi 2009; Kurke 2012: 224–26 and 2013: 147–49.

10. Olsen 2017: 8. Cf. Peponi 2009: 67 on "a system of intense reciprocity," where "the line separating the act of performing from the act of attending tends to disappear."

11. Arist. *Pol.* 1342a7–17, 1340a8–14. There have been many studies in both musicology and neuroscience of how music can produce particular emotions in the listener, as well as bodily sensations accompanying them: see, e.g., Kivy 1989 and 1990; Patel 2008; Bicknell 2009.

12. Ps.-Arist. *Prob.* 919b27–37.

13. Cf. Meineck 2013: he draws on the concept of embodied empathy in the work of Anna Bogart and recent work on the neural mirror system to suggest a crossover of choral spectatorship and participation in the Greek theater.

accompanying tunes, rhythms, and dance movements characteristic of various nondramatic lyric genres (dithyrambs, paeans, epinicians, *hymenaioi, partheneia*) with which the audience would presumably also be familiar. So while descriptions of dolphins dancing around ships, Nereids at a wedding, or parthenaic celebrations at Troy appear to distract us from the dramatic narrative, Euripides' incorporation within tragedy of these traditional elements of Greek choral culture, combined with their enactment by the singing and dancing chorus, invites the audience to be more actively invested in and part of the drama.[14] Their embodied involvement can result in an uncomfortably mixed experience, such as when they are drawn into joyful *choreia* and simultaneously prompted to realize how inappropriate or premature such a performance is within the immediate dramatic context. Lacking such immersion in Greek choral culture, however, we have difficulty appreciating the affective force that the mix of metamusical language and live performance must have had—and have often found it easier to deem some of Euripides' odes irrelevant instead.

Euripides, then, is exploiting the ability of *choreia* to draw in his audience in a way that spoken dialogue and monodies cannot, even as he simultaneously uses it to take us beyond the geographical and temporal scope of a tragedy's *mythos*.[15] Aristotle, when discussing the structure of a tragic plot in *Poetics*, tells us that Euripides is the "most tragic" of the tragedians in his ability to produce the tragic emotions, a claim Victoria Wohl has recently addressed by showing how the formal structure of his plays can exert a psychagogic force on the audience.[16] *Mousikē* also contributed to a tragedy's powers of *psychagōgia*. In this respect too Euripides may be considered the master of *pathos*, generating a variety of responses in his audience through the immersive capacity of song, dance, and musical accompaniment.

*Mousikē* in Euripides' later plays is therefore marked both by a hypermimeticism and by a powerfully affective engagement with his audience. This conclusion provides a more nuanced interpretation of what "new music" in the case of Euripides may mean—beyond the more technical innovations that mostly lie beyond the scope of this study and are much harder to access through the bare texts that

---

14. The audience could also thus be led (at least temporarily) to identify more deeply with the status and perspective of the chorus—even a foreign, non-Greek one like that in *Trojan Women*. On the much-debated question of how much the Athenian audience might relate to or feel represented by the chorus of tragedy, see esp. Goldhill 1996; Gould 1996; Mastronarde 1998, 1999, and 2010: 89–122; Foley 2003; Visvardi 2015.

15. Of course an audience could also have a powerful emotional—even physical—response to styles of dialogue or sets of speeches (such as an *agōn* in the manner of a law court) with which they were familiar both within and outside the theater.

16. Arist. *Poet*. 1453a29–30; Wohl 2015. Visvardi 2015 explores how the tragic chorus enacts, triggers, and participates in collective emotion.

survive. Can it also inform our understanding of the so-called New Music as a cultural movement in fifth- and fourth-century Athens?

Euripides' play with multiple levels of mimesis, having his choruses flit from one musical identity to another while retaining their dramatic character, suggests that he was at the forefront of the New Music, which was known for excessive mimeticism. Conservative ancient critics of this trend complain of how visual and aural effects take over from narrative, as we can already see in the early fifth-century fragment of Pratinas, when the satyr chorus complain that the sound of the *aulos* is overwhelming their song.[17] It is also evident in a passage of Plato's *Laws* that I briefly mentioned in chapter 4, when the Athenian Stranger claims that the Muses "would never combine the cries of beasts and of humans and of instruments and all kinds of noises into the same piece as a way to represent one thing."[18] In a similar vein, Socrates in the *Republic* describes the speaker who uses so much mimesis that "all his narrative will be through imitation in voices and gestures, or else include only a little narration."[19] As this remark suggests, and as Pauline LeVen has emphasized, the reputation for mimeticism concerned the use of emotive language as much as—or combined with—the musical and choreographic aspects of a performance.[20] Euripides' later plays indicate that he was a leader in this trend, experimenting with the different ways in which the semantic content of a song could be conveyed—not merely through the words themselves but through the singing and dancing bodies of the chorus. And yet, as we saw in chapter 1, the merging of described and performed *mousikē* that his choruses encourage had a long history within nondramatic choral lyric. It is not entirely unprecedented on the tragic stage either—indeed, it is especially reminiscent of some of the metamusical effects achieved by Aeschylus's choral odes. But Euripides' work is distinct from that of both Aeschylus and Sophocles in the way his choruses frequently assimilate themselves to various (and multiple) traditional images of chorality that seem far from their own character and from the immediate *mythos*. Euripides' *mousikē* is new, but, like the New Music more generally, it did not appear suddenly within a cultural vacuum.

Euripides' use of *choreia* to involve his audience more with the dramatic narrative and emotional impact of his plays may point to a broader cultural phenomenon—though one closely linked to the trend for mimeticism—in late fifth-century Athens whereby poets were increasingly interested in using the combination of words,

---

17. *TrGF* I, 4 F 3 (Ath. 14.617). On the date of this fragment, see Griffith 2013b: 273 n. 57, with further bibliography.
18. ἔτι δὲ θηρίων φωνὰς καὶ ἀνθρώπων καὶ ὀργάνων καὶ πάντας ψόφους εἰς ταὐτὸν οὐκ ἄν ποτε συνθεῖεν, ὡς ἕν τι μιμούμεναι, Pl. *Leg.* 669c8–d2.
19. καὶ ἔσται δὴ ἡ τούτου λέξις ἅπασα διὰ μιμήσεως φωναῖς τε καὶ σχήμασιν, ἢ σμικρόν τι διηγήσεως ἔχουσα, Pl. *Rep.* 397b1–2.
20. LeVen 2014, esp. 189–93.

music, and dance to exert an ever more powerful affective force. LeVen emphasizes the verbal dimension of this trend: her close reading of Timotheus's *Persians*, for example, shows how the use of the imperfect tense has an effect of "displaced immediacy," which "immerses its audience in a scene, without mediation by an omniscient narrator or internalization, thus creating for that audience the impression that it is directly observing something."[21] The abundance of sound words in this nome also suggests a merging of verbal and musical soundscape as words, voice, and the accompanying kithara together represent the crashing of ships and various shouts, screams, and wails of the drowning Persians.[22] At the same time, the disturbing polyphony in the text goes far beyond the voice and instrument of the kitharode, transporting the audience into an acoustic landscape that is uncomfortably at odds with what they physically hear within the theater.[23] As in many of Euripides' choral odes, the audience actively participate in the materialization of this dissonant world. As LeVen writes, "the force of any momentary dramatic assimilation of performer and fictional character [and, I would add, fictional scene], by means that include gestures and sounds, is fundamentally dependent on the audience's willingness to commit to a mental displacement."[24]

For LeVen, the mental displacement required of the audience points to a changing relationship between them and the fictional world that the poet creates through narrative—a change that she sees as a major innovation of Greek lyric poetry in the late classical period. She likens this to the development of naturalism in the visual arts as characterized by Jaś Elsner: "the shift from a voice of authority making direct contact with its audience to a performative model whereby the viewer observes an imaginary world that is insulated within its own context and to which he or she must relate by identification or some form of wish-fulfillment fantasy."[25] Judging by the surviving titles and plot indications of dithyrambs and nomes, this world was often romantic, involving travel, adventure, and exotic locations—a tendency that matches Euripides' own predilection for scenes that seem to take us far from the immediate *mythos* of the play.[26]

---

21. LeVen 2014: 201. On Timotheus and the New Music, see also Csapo and Wilson 2009; Power 2010: 500–554; Budelmann and LeVen 2014.

22. On Timotheus's manipulation of the voice as a "carrier of sonic effects," see Gurd 2016: 118–23.

23. On the link between noise and disturbance in Greek poetry, see Gurd 2016. The auditory movement of this song is remarkably similar to that of the Great Mother ode in Euripides' *Helen*. As in that song, disturbing noise is finally replaced by new, pleasing *mousikē* that is more easily—and explicitly—linked to the immediate performance within the theater: after describing the Greeks' paean (fr. 791 *PMG* 196–201), Timotheus links his own music to the Paean god (Apollo), "you who exalt the new-fashioned Muse of the golden kithara" (ὦ χρυσεοκίθαριν ἀέ- / ξων Μοῦσαν νεοτευχῆ, 202–3).

24. LeVen 2014: 218.

25. Elsner 2006: 89, quoted in LeVen 2014: 193.

26. See LeVen 2014: 220–32 for a list and discussion of these titles. Her definition of "romantic" comes from Griffith 2015: 109–28.

We may understand Euripides' innovative forms of engagement with his audience as part of this shift, though his plays demonstrate that music and dance were as important as narrative and worked closely with it in producing such imaginary worlds. Yet this process did not involve just a mental displacement, for the audience were also emotionally and physically involved in a choral performance. As we have seen, Euripides uses *choreia* to bring onstage scenes that are otherwise beyond the dramatic action, so that they erupt into the theater for the audience to see, hear, and feel. He also exploits traditional elements of Greek chorality to draw his audience in as a participant, not just an observer.[27] Poets of nondramatic choral lyric like the dithyramb may involve their audiences through similar means within an "insulated" world, but Euripides does this within a play, and in doing so he creates a musical experience for his audience that is intimately connected with the surrounding drama.

## DIONYSIAC *MOUSIKĒ* IN EURIPIDES' *BACCHAE*

Conspicuously missing from my account thus far, however, is *Bacchae*, Euripides' very latest surviving play (along with *Iphigenia in Aulis*), one in which musical language and performance play a prominent and powerful role. Though it too draws on the audience's own familiarity with choral songs within and beyond the theater, this tragedy is also markedly different from his other work in terms of the pattern and consistency of its *mousikē*. Performed alongside *Iphigenia in Aulis* in Athens in 405 B.C.E., a year after Euripides' death, it presents us with a contrasting end point of his musical career.

It has long been noticed that the chorus is extraordinarily prominent in *Bacchae*, singing and dancing for almost a quarter of the lines—an amount of *choreia* unmatched in any other surviving Euripidean or Sophoclean tragedy.[28] The *choreia* is also remarkably uniform, resembling for much of the tragedy a cult song for Dionysus, especially a dithyramb.[29] Dionysus declares in his prologue that he has come to Greece "after setting everything there [in Asia] dancing in choruses and establishing my rites."[30] Then he himself summons his chorus onstage to perform his cultic *mousikē* so that the city of Thebes "may see," suggesting a close tie

---

27. Cf. Tanner 2006: 31–96 on the development of naturalism in classical Greek sculpture: like Elsner, he emphasizes the changing relationship between viewer and image but sees this in terms of a new sense of accessibility whereby art engages with the embodied beholder. See also Neer 2010 on the effects of *thauma*.

28. Cf. Winnington-Ingram 1948: 2 ("in no other extant Greek play since Aeschylus . . . is the chorus so prominent").

29. On the play's generic consistency, see Battezzato 2005a: 163–64; Weiss forthcoming b.

30. τἀκεῖ χορεύσας καὶ καταστήσας ἐμὰς / τελετάς, *Bacch.* 21–22.

between his own epiphany and the chorus's song and dance.[31] The chorus respond with their parodos, singing of Dionysus's birth and summoning him to Thebes, where soon "the whole land will dance."[32] They also include in their song an aetiology for the Dionysiac cultic *mousikē* that they are simultaneously producing onstage, focusing on the drums (*tympana*) invented by the Korybantes and mixed with the "sweet-shouting breath of Phrygian *auloi*."[33] In the second stasimon they make the connection between their own performance and the dithyramb explicit when they call upon Dionysus by his name *Dithyrambus*.[34]

The form and consistency of the play's *choreia* are tied to the identity of the chorus and their leader. Instead of a female chorus and protagonist, a combination that Euripides employs in the four tragedies I have analyzed here, in *Bacchae* a female chorus sing and dance in response to a male god. In following his lead, the chorus do not include in their songs the wide array of choral lyric that we see elsewhere in Euripides' oeuvre—in particular, there is no hint of the parthenaic, hymenaeal, or mourning songs typically associated with women. Since this play, like Aeschylus's own *Bacchae* and *Bassarids*, has a chorus of maenads, the songs they sing are consistently Dionysiac.

*Bacchae* thus lacks the sense of doubleness, the mix of alterity and proximity, evident in the *choreia* of Euripides' other late plays. The performance of *choreia* here is closely linked to the chorus's own dramatic identity, and when it takes us away from the action, as it does in the parodos, it still revolves around the god and refers directly to the form of the chorus's own performance in his honor. In this respect Euripides seems to be harking back to Aeschylean choruses, whose *mousikē*, as we noted in chapter 1, tends to be closely aligned with their dramatic characters.[35] As a result, the mimeticism at work in the play's choral lyric is less complex, involving less work on the part of the audience to see and hear in the chorus's performance the

---

31. ὡς ὁρᾶι Κάδμου πόλις, 61.
32. γᾶ πᾶσα χορεύσει, 114.
33. ἡδυβόαι Φρυγίων / αὐλῶν πνεύματι, 127–28.
34. *Bacch.* 526.
35. *Bacchae* has often been thought of as the culmination of Euripides' tendency toward archaism in his later work, perhaps as a result of his stay in Macedon: scholars have remarked upon not only the predominance of Dionysiac language in the play but the Aeschylean quality of its vocabulary, the rarity of *antilabē* (division of a line between speakers), and its use of rhythms (especially ionics) and refrains associated with traditional cultic hymns. See Dodds 1960: xxxvii–viii with reference to previous scholarship. Some of these same features have also led scholars to see the play as closely tied to contemporary musical developments—Euripides' "New Musical *pièce de résistance*" (Csapo 1999–2000: 426; cf. Zimmerman 1992: 134). Given the concentration of contemporary musicians and actors cultivated by Archelaus at Aegae, along with the king's own ambitions in creating a cultural center to rival Athens, such archaisms are indeed likely to represent another form of Euripidean innovation. Cf. D'Angour 2011: 89 on "the use of deliberate archaism to create something new in artistic and verbal contexts." On the significance of Euripides' time in Macedon, see esp. Revermann 1999–2000; Duncan 2011.

scenes and images that they describe. This is because they are a chorus of maenads, but also because, beneath their masks and costumes, they are male Athenian citizens singing and dancing for Dionysus in his theater. In this same space they would regularly perform dithyrambs too, which—though rather more sober than the *choreia* of these Lydian traveling maenads—could, as Pindar's second *Dithyramb* shows us, include similar descriptions of ecstatic and originary music making, evoking these forms of Dionysiac worship for both the performers and the audience.[36]

Athenian members of the audience not only would have been regular spectators of dithyrambs, including those performed prior to the tragic competition at the City Dionysia, but would likely have sung and danced in one of the twenty performances put on each year within the city, each one involving fifty men or boys. They would also have participated in other forms of Dionysiac *mousikē* and related cultic performances beyond the theater, such as in the Eleusinian Mysteries or Korybantic rituals.[37] (The latter are mentioned directly in the parodos.) The play's *choreia* would therefore be especially affective, able to engage with the audience's own embodied experience of this type of performance and draw them into it, even as they are aware of the distance between themselves and this foreign chorus of maenads.[38] Moreover, *mousikē* associated with Dionysus appears to have been especially exciting and mood-altering: Aristotle describes such a performance as *enthousiastikos* or orgiastic—even *pathos*-inducing (*pathētikos*).[39] Both as a result of their own familiarity with the play's *choreia* and because of the nature of such *mousikē* itself, then, the audience would be more likely to feel the ecstasy expressed by the chorus for their god, and so (virtually) become his celebrants alongside the Lydian bacchants and Theban maenads. Dionysus sets Athens dancing in the play, not just Thebes.

Through participating in the play's *choreia*, the audience also become implicated in Pentheus's bloody downfall. Like the chorus of Trojan women at the end of *Trojan Women* as they perform Troy's fall, the chorus of *Bacchae* both describe the destruction of the palace and physically enact it. Immediately following the second stasimon Dionysus's voice is heard from within the *skēnē*, calling upon his bacchants and bringing on the earthquake that will demolish the palace. The chorus tell us to see the columns falling;[40] Dionysus then gives the order to "burn up, burn up Pentheus's palace," and they respond by pointing out the fire and performing the destruction that ensues, thus merging with the god as agents of destruction:[41]

36. See chapter 1, pp. 35–36, on Pind. fr. 70b SM.
37. On the nature of Korybantic rituals, especially their music, see Griffith forthcoming.
38. On this mix of identification and distance, cf. Zeitlin 1996.
39. Esp. Arist. *Pol.* 1341a21–22, 1342b1–12. On these types of musical performance, which are linked to the *aulos* and Phrygian mode, see esp. Griffith forthcoming.
40. εἴδετε, 591.
41. σύμφλεγε σύμφλεγε δώματα Πενθέος, 595.

δίκετε πεδόσε δίκετε τρομερὰ (600)
σώματα, μαινάδες·
ὁ γὰρ ἄναξ ἄνω κάτω τιθεὶς ἔπεισι
μέλαθρα τάδε Διὸς γόνος.

Throw, throw to the ground your trembling bodies, maenads! For our lord, Zeus's son, is attacking this palace, turning it upside down. (Eur. *Bacch.* 600–603)

Here they demand worship of Dionysus in response to his destructive power and also represent it in their own movements, as the god turns their bodies upside down along with the building itself.[42] There is hardly any distinction between the action offstage and the performance of *choreia* in the *orchēstra*. This *choreia* produces the palace's fall for the audience to witness as spectators—indeed it prompts them to do so through the direction to "see."[43] But it also involves them, as participants in the Dionysiac performances that have so dominated the play. Through this crossover between audience and chorus, and the chorus's own merging with the Theban maenads, the audience become implicated in the bloody death of Pentheus—the *sparagmos*—at the latter group's hands.[44] The sustained performance of Dionysiac *mousikē* through the tragedy thus both invites the audience to participate in ecstatic worship of the god and becomes a profoundly unsettling experience, as they share in the destruction that ensues. At the end of the play, as in Sophocles' *Women of Trachis* and Euripides' *Heracles*, *choreia* recedes, and the drama focuses on the suffering of the human characters left behind. The audience are now prompted to feel intense pity for Agave as she learns that she has killed her son but also intense fear of Dionysus and the frenzied possession that he and his music can effect.[45]

*Bacchae* shows us how difficult it is to categorize Euripides' "new music" and complicates the argument I have presented here about the nature of his musical

---

42. Zarifi 2007: 236 emphasizes the high degree of resolution in the meter here: "Just as land can 'dance' at an earthquake (Callimachus *Hymns* 4.139), so an earthquake can be danced." The question of whether the ruined palace would in fact be visible onstage through some sort of transformation of the *skēnē* or appearance of smoke has been much debated. Taplin even doubts "the earthquake was conveyed in any way less effective than the choreography and the words themselves" (1978: 119). On this question, see also Goldhill 1986: 276–86, with further bibliography.

43. Cf. Gurd 2016: 138 on how the "auditory intensities" of these lines produce visions, "transfiguring the theatrical space into Dionysian fantasy." His reading is primarily concerned with described sound rather than the mix of words, music, and dance within *choreia*.

44. Cf. Wohl 2015 (esp. 39–62) on how Euripidean tragedy can implicate the audience in the suffering that they are watching. On the merging of the two choruses (Lydian and Theban) in *Bacchae*, see Bierl 2013: 217; cf. Holzhausen 2003: 235; Visvardi 2015: 213–38. They are not, however, completely identified, at least not in terms of the destruction they cause: the Lydian chorus invite and enact Dionysus's violent actions as they sing of the burning of the palace, whereas the Theban maenads are not actually singing or dancing either when they defeat the armed men (728–64) or when they kill Pentheus (1084–1149).

45. Cf. Visvardi 2015: 213–38 on the choral enactment of Dionysiac *deinon* in *Bacchae*.

innovation. This play perhaps more than any other could draw its audience in through engaging with their own embodied experience of *choreia*, and yet Euripides achieves this effect by drawing from an older, Aeschylean model of tragedy, with a Dionysiac chorus performing consistently Dionysiac *mousikē*. In doing so, he produces a tragedy in which *mousikē* is almost indistinguishable from the *mythos*, representing the worship of Dionysus performed by both his own bacchants and the Theban women led by Agave, and producing (or reproducing) the destruction of Pentheus' palace.

The contrast between *Bacchae* and *Iphigenia in Aulis*, performed alongside each other, must have been very striking for the audience. In both tragedies musical performance and dramatic narrative are closely related, but in very different ways. In *Bacchae* the chorus of maenads are closely tied to their divine leader throughout. Their one lyric interchange, with Dionysus singing directions to the chorus from within the *skēnē*, occurs a third of the way into the play and marks the climax of a crossover between *choreia* and dramatic action. In *Iphigenia in Aulis*, the chorus and Iphigenia, their potential leader, come together only in the final scene, following a shift from *choreia* to monody that complements and shapes the dramatic arc of the tragedy as a whole.

Above all, however, the tragedies differ in terms of the types of song and dance that they include, and the relationship between these and the chorus's own character. In *Bacchae*, Euripides' more traditional use of one main type of musical performance—cultic *mousikē* performed for Dionysus by a chorus of his followers—has a powerful affective impact. In *Iphigenia in Aulis*, as in the other late plays that I discuss in this book (even *Trojan Women*), Euripides achieves the same effect but as a result of the wide variety of song types that he incorporates within the one tragedy—dithyrambic, parthenaic, hymenaeal, pastoral, lament, paeanic. Each of these different musical forms engages with the audience by drawing on their own prior experience of such performances in and beyond the theater, so that they become participants in the drama, not just observers of it. At the same time, the chorus assume multiple identities in the play's hypermimetic choral odes, which take the audience beyond the immediate geographical and temporal bounds of the dramatic action. In these odes, too, the audience need not experience such scenes just as spectators but can be physically transported as well. When the chorus momentarily appear as the fifty Nereids dancing at the wedding of Peleus and Thetis, for example, this evocation of a dithyramb (likewise involving fifty choreuts) can stimulate the audience's own embodied knowledge of such a performance, so that they not only see this scene enacted but participate in it as well. In *Bacchae* the choral songs and the audience's participation in them follow the trajectory of the plot. In *Iphigenia in Aulis*, however, the audience become uncomfortably involved in a celebratory performance that they know is impossible for Iphigenia. By combining different musical forms and images in this play, as in

*Electra, Trojan Women,* and *Helen,* Euripides expands his audience's imaginative horizons even as he maintains—and occasionally complicates—the tight connection between the *mousikē* and the *mythos.*

*Iphigenia in Aulis* and *Bacchae* were produced posthumously, and so we do not know how deliberate their juxtaposition may have been on Euripides' part. But both demonstrate how, in his later plays, he was experimenting with the dramatic potential and affective force of many different types of *mousikē.* Simultaneously innovating and archaizing, he exploited an extraordinary array of musical styles, patterns, and language in order to act ever more powerfully upon his audience.

# WORKS CITED

Agawu, V. K. 2014. *Music as Discourse: Semiotic Adventures in Romantic Music.* Oxford.
Albright, D. 2006. "Golden Calves: The Role of Dance in Opera." *The Opera Quarterly* 22: 22–37.
Alexiou, M. 1974. *The Ritual Lament in Greek Tradition.* Cambridge.
Allan, W. 2004. "Religious Syncretism: The New Gods of Greek Tragedy." *HSPh* 102: 113–55.
———, ed. 2008. *Euripides: Helen.* Cambridge.
Arnott, W. G. 1973. "Euripides and the Unexpected." *G&R* 20: 49–64.
———. 1981. "Double the Vision: A Reading of Euripides' *Electra*." *G&R* 28: 179–92.
———. 1990. "Euripides' Newfangled Helen." *Antichthon* 24: 1–18.
———. 2007. *Birds in the Ancient World from A to Z.* London.
Athanassakis, A. N. 2000. "The *Pelēades* of Alcman's *Partheneion* and Modern Greek *Poulia*." *AncW* 31: 5–14.
Austin, C., and D. Olson, eds. 2004. *Aristophanes: Thesmophoriazusae.* Oxford.
Bacon, H. 1994. "The Chorus in Greek Life and Drama." *Arion* 3: 6–24.
Bain, D. 1977. "The Prologues of Euripides' *Iphigeneia in Aulis*." *CQ* 27: 10–26.
Barker, A. 1984. *Greek Musical Writings.* Volume 1, *The Musician and His Art.* Cambridge.
———. 1989. *Greek Musical Writings.* Volume 2, *Harmonic and Acoustic Theory.* Cambridge.
———. 2004. "Transforming the Nightingale: Aspects of Athenian Musical Discourse in the Late Fifth Century." In Murray and Wilson 2004: 185–204.
———. 2007. "Simbolismo musicale nell'*Elena* di Euripide." In P. Volpe Cacciatore, ed., *Musica e generi letterari nella Grecia di età classica: Atti del II. Congresso consulta universitaria greco (Fisciano, 1 dicembre 2006),* 7–22. Naples.
Barlow, S. A. 1971. *The Imagery of Euripides: A Study in the Dramatic Use of Pictorial Language.* London.
———, ed. 1986. *Euripides: Trojan Women.* Warminster.
Barringer, J. M. 1995. *Divine Escorts: Nereids in Archaic and Classical Greek Art.* Ann Arbor.

Bassi, K. 2005. "Visuality and Temporality: Reading the Tragic Script." In V. Pedrick and S. M. Oberhelman, eds., *The Soul of Tragedy: Essays on Athenian Drama*, 251–70. Chicago.

Batson, C. R. 2005. *Dance, Desire, and Anxiety in Early Twentieth-Century French Theater: Playing Identities*. Aldershot.

Battezzato, L. 2005a. "Lyric." In J. Gregory, ed., *A Companion to Greek Tragedy*, 149–66. Oxford.

———. 2005b. "The New Music of the *Trojan Women*." *Lexis* 23: 73–104.

———. 2013. "Dithyramb and Greek Tragedy." In Kowalzig and Wilson 2013: 93–110.

Bell, C. M. 1992. *Ritual Theory, Ritual Practice*. Oxford.

Bicknell, J. 2009. *Why Music Moves Us*. Basingstoke.

Biehl, W., ed. 1970. *Euripides: Troades*. Leipzig.

———, ed. 1989. *Euripides: Troades*. Heidelberg.

Bierl, A. 1991. *Dionysos und die griechische Tragödie: Politische und "metatheatralische" Aspekte im Text*. Tübingen.

———. 2009. *Ritual and Performativity: The Chorus in Old Comedy*. Trans. A. Hollmann. Cambridge, MA.

———. 2013. "Maenadism as Self-Referential Chorality in Euripides' *Bacchae*." In Gagné and Hopman 2013a: 211–26.

Boedeker, D. 2009. "No Way Out? Aging in the New (and Old) Sappho." In Greene and Skinner 2009: 71–83.

Bond, G. W., ed. 1963. *Euripides: Hypsipyle*. Oxford.

Born, G., and D. Hesmondhalgh. 2000. "Introduction: On Difference, Representation, and Appropriation in Music." In G. Born and D. Hesmondhalgh, eds., *Western Music and Its Others: Difference, Representation, and Appropriation in Music*, 1–58. Berkeley and Los Angeles.

Bothe, F. H., ed. 1845. *Aristophanis Comoediae*. Vol. 3. Leipzig.

Bourdieu, P. 1987. *Distinction: A Social Critique of the Judgement of Taste*. Trans. R. Nice. Cambridge, MA.

Bowie, E. 2011. "Alcman's First *Partheneion* and the Song the Sirens Sang." In L. Athanassaki and E. Bowie, eds., *Archaic and Classical Choral Song: Performance, Politics and Dissemination*, 33–66. Berlin.

Briginshaw, V. A. 2001. *Dance, Space, and Subjectivity*. Basingstoke.

Brown, R. 2010. *Sound: A Reader in Theatre Practice*. Basingstoke.

Budelmann, F., ed. 2009. *The Cambridge Companion to Greek Lyric*. Cambridge.

Budelmann, F., and P. LeVen. 2014. "Timotheus' Poetics of Blending: A Cognitive Approach to the Language of the New Music." *CPh* 109: 191–210.

Budelmann, F., and T. Power. 2015. "Another Look at Female Choruses in Classical Athens." *ClAnt* 34: 252–95.

Bühler, K. 1934. *Sprachtheorie: Die Darstellungsfunktion der Sprache*. Jena.

Buitron-Oliver, D., and B. Cohen. 1995. "Between Skylla and Penelope: Female Characters of the *Odyssey* in Archaic and Classical Greek Art." In Cohen 1995: 29–58. Oxford.

Bull, M., and L. Back. 2003. "Introduction: Into Sound." In M. Bull and L. Back, eds., *The Auditory Culture Reader*, 1–18. Oxford.

Bundrick, S. 2005. *Music and Image in Classical Athens*. Cambridge.

Burgess, D. L. 2004. "Lies and Convictions at Aulis." *Hermes* 132: 37–55.

Burian, P., ed. 2007. *Euripides: Helen*. Oxford.

Burkert, W. 1985. *Greek Religion.* Trans. J. Raffan. Cambridge. MA.

———. 1987. *Ancient Mystery Cults.* Cambridge. MA.

Burkhardt, H. 1906. "Die Archaismen des Euripides." Ph.D. dissertation, University of Erlangen.

Burnett, A. P. 1960. "Euripides' *Helen:* A Comedy of Ideas." *CPh* 55: 151–63.

———. 1971. *Catastrophe Survived: Euripides' Plays of Mixed Reversal.* Oxford.

———. 1985. *The Art of Bacchylides.* Cambridge, MA.

Buschor, E. 1944. *Die Musen des Jenseits.* Munich.

Buxton, R. G. A. 1994. *Imaginary Greece: The Contexts of Mythology.* Cambridge.

Calame, C. 1994–95. "From Choral Poetry to Tragic Stasimon: The Enactment of Women's Song." *Arion* 3: 136–54.

———. 1997. *Choruses of Young Women in Ancient Greece: Their Morphology, Religious Role, and Social Function.* Trans. D. Collins and J. Orion. Lanham, MD.

———. 1999. "Performative Aspects of the Choral Voice in Greek Tragedy: Civic Identity in Performance." In Goldhill and Osborne 1999: 125–53.

———. 2009. "Apollo in Delphi and in Delos: Poetic Performances between Paean and Dithyramb." In L. Athanassaki, R. P. Martin, J. F. Miller, eds., *Apolline Politics and Poetics,* 169–97. Athens.

———. 2013. "Choral Polyphony and the Ritual Functions of Tragic Songs." In Gagné and Hopman 2013a: 35–57.

Campbell, D., ed. 1982. *Greek Lyric Poetry: A Selection of Early Greek Lyric, Elegiac and Iambic Poetry.* Bristol.

Carson, A. 2001. "Screaming in Translation: The *Electra* of Sophocles." In A. Carson, trans., *Sophocles' Electra,* 41–48. Oxford.

Carter, D. M., ed. 2011. *Why Athens? A Reappraisal of Tragic Politics.* Oxford.

Castellani, V. 1989. "The Value of a Kindly Chorus: Female Choruses in Attic Tragedy." In J. Redmond, ed., *Women in Theatre,* 1–18. Cambridge.

Chong-Gossard, J. 2003. "Song and the Solitary Self: Euripidean Women Who Resist Comfort." *Phoenix* 57: 209–31.

———. 2008. *Gender and Communication in Euripides' Plays: Between Song and Silence.* Leiden.

Cockle, W. E. H., ed. 1987. *Euripides, Hypsipyle: Text and Annotation Based on a Re-examination of the Papyri.* Rome.

Cohen, B., ed. 1995. *The Distaff Side: Representing the Female in Homer's Odyssey.* Oxford.

Cole, S. L. 1985. *The Absent One: Mourning Ritual, Tragedy, and the Performance of Ambivalence.* University Park, PA.

Collard, C., and M. Cropp, eds. 2008a. *Euripides: Fragments; Aegeus–Meleager.* Cambridge, MA.

———. 2008b. *Euripides: Fragments; Oedipus–Chrysippus, Other Fragments.* Cambridge, MA.

Conacher, D. J. 1967. *Euripidean Drama: Myth, Theme and Structure.* Toronto.

Connery, M., and J. Steichen, eds. 2015. *Opera and Dance. The Opera Quarterly* 31. Oxford.

Contiades-Tsitsoni, E. 1990. *Hymenaios und Epithalamion: Das Hochzeitslied in der frühgriechischen Lyrik.* Stuttgart.

Corbel-Morana, C. 2004. "Euripide lecteur d'Aristophane: Les trilles du rossignol." *RPh* 2: 223–38.

Cousland, J. R. C., and J. R. Hume, eds. 2009. *The Play of Texts and Fragments: Essays in Honour of Martin Cropp*. Leiden.
Croally, N. T. 1994. *Euripidean Polemic: The Trojan Women and the Function of Tragedy*. Cambridge.
Cropp, M., ed. 1988. *Euripides: Electra*. Warminster.
———, ed. 2000. *Euripides: Iphigenia in Tauris*. Warminster.
Cropp, M., and G. Fick. 1985. *Resolutions and Chronology in Euripides: The Fragmentary Tragedies*. London.
Cropp, M., K. Lee, and D. Sansone, eds. 1999-2000. *Euripides and Tragic Theatre in the Late Fifth Century* (ICS 24-25). Champaign, IL.
Csapo, E. 1999-2000. "Later Euripidean Music." In Cropp, Lee, and Sansone 1999-2000: 399-426.
———. 2003. "The Dolphins of Dionysus." In E. Csapo and M. C. Miller, eds., *Poetry, Theory, Praxis: The Social Life of Myth, Word and Image in Ancient Greece; Essays in Honour of William J. Slater*, 69-98. Oxford.
———. 2004. "The Politics of the New Music." In Murray and Wilson 2004: 207-48.
———. 2008. "Star Choruses: Eleusis, Orphism, and New Musical Imagery and Dance." In M. Revermann and P. Wilson, eds., *Performance, Iconography, Reception: Studies in Honour of Oliver Taplin*, 262-90. Oxford.
———. 2009. "New Music's Gallery of Images: The 'Dithyrambic' First Stasimon of Euripides' *Electra*." In Cousland and Hume 2009: 95-109.
———. 2010. *Actors and Icons of the Ancient Theater*. Malden, MA.
Csapo, E., and W. J. Slater, eds. 1995. *The Context of Ancient Drama*. Ann Arbor.
Csapo, E., and P. Wilson. 2009. "Timotheus the New Musician." In Budelmann 2009: 277-94. Cambridge.
Cunningham, M. 1994. "Thoughts on Aeschylus: The Satyr Play *Proteus*." *LCM* 19: 67-68.
Currie, B. 2005. *Pindar and the Cult of Heroes*. Oxford.
Dale, A. M., ed. 1967. *Euripides: Helen*. Oxford.
———. 1968. *The Lyric Metres of Greek Drama*. 2nd ed. Cambridge.
———. 1969. *Collected Papers*. Ed. T. B. L. Webster and E. G. Turner. Cambridge.
D'Alessio, G. B. 1997. "Pindar's *Prosodia* and the Classification of Pindaric Papyrus Fragments." *ZPE* 118: 23-60.
———. 2004. "Past Future and Present Past: Temporal Deixis in Greek Archaic Lyric." *Arethusa* 37: 267-94.
———. 2013. "'The Name of the Dithyramb': Diachronic and Diatopic Variations." In Kowalzig and Wilson 2013: 113-32.
D'Angour, A. 1997. "How the Dithyramb Got Its Shape." *CQ* 47: 331-51.
———. 2006. "The New Music: So What's New?" In S. Goldhill and R. Osborne, eds., *Rethinking Revolutions through Ancient Greece*, 264-83. Cambridge.
———. 2007. "The Sound of *Mousikē*: Reflections on Aural Change in Ancient Greece." In R. Osborne, ed., *Debating the Athenian Cultural Revolution: Art, Literature, Philosophy, and Politics, 430-380 BC*, 288-300. Cambridge.
———. 2011. *The Greeks and the New: Novelty in Ancient Greek Imagination and Experience*. Cambridge.

———. 2015. "Sense and Sensation in Music." In P. Destrée and P. Murray, eds., *A Companion to Ancient Aesthetics*, 188–203. Malden, MA.
Davidson, J. F. 1986. "The Circle and the Tragic Chorus." *G&R* 33: 38–46.
Decharme, P. 1906. *Euripides and the Spirit of His Dramas*. Trans. J. Loeb. London.
Denniston, J. D., ed. 1939. *Euripides: Electra*. Oxford.
Derrida, J. 1976. *Of Grammatology*. Trans. G. C. Spivak. Baltimore.
Detienne, M. 1983. "La grue et le labyrinthe." *MEFRA* 95: 541–53.
Diamond, E. 1996. "Introduction." In E. Diamond, ed., *Performance and Cultural Politics*, 1–14. London.
Di Benedetto, V. 2004. "Osservazioni sul nuovo papiro di Saffo." *ZPE* 149: 5–6.
Dickson, K. M. 1993. "Nestor among the Sirens." *Oral Tradition* 8: 21–58.
Diggle, J., ed. 1970. *Euripides: Phaethon*. Cambridge.
———, ed. 1981. *Euripidis Fabulae*. Volume 2, *Supplices, Electra, Hercules, Troades, Iphigenia in Tauris, Ion*. Oxford.
———, ed. 1994a. *Euripidis Fabulae*. Volume 3, *Helena, Phoenissae, Orestes, Bacchae, Iphigenia Aulidensis, Rhesus*. 2nd ed. Oxford.
———. 1994b. *Euripidea*. Oxford.
Dillon, E. 2006. "Representing Obscene Sound." In N. McDonald, ed., *Medieval Obscenities*, 55–84. Woodbridge.
Dillon, M. 2002. *Girls and Women in Classical Greek Religion*. London and New York.
Dodds, E. R., ed. 1960. *Euripides: Bacchae*. 2nd ed. Oxford.
Doherty, L. E. 1995a. *Siren Songs: Gender, Audiences, and Narrators in the Odyssey*. Ann Arbor.
———. 1995b. "Sirens, Muses, and Female Narrators in the *Odyssey*." In Cohen 1995: 81–92.
Dover, K. J. 1972. *Aristophanic Comedy*. Berkeley and Los Angeles.
———, ed. 1993. *Aristophanes: Frogs*. Oxford.
Downing, E. 1990. "*Apatê, Agôn*, and Literary Self-Reflexivity in Euripides' *Helen*." In M. Griffith and D. J. Mastronarde, eds., *Cabinet of the Muses*, 1–16. Berkeley and Los Angeles.
Dué, C. 2006. *The Captive Woman's Lament in Greek Tragedy*. Austin.
Dunbar, N., ed. 1995. *Aristophanes: Birds*. Oxford.
Duncan, A. 2011. "Nothing to Do with Athens? Tragedians at the Courts of Tyrants." In Carter 2011: 69–84.
Dunn, F. M. 1996. *Tragedy's End: Closure and Innovation in Euripidean Drama*. Oxford.
Easterling, P. E., ed. 1982. *Sophocles: Trachiniae*. Cambridge.
———. 1997. "Form and Performance." In P. E. Easterling, ed., *The Cambridge Companion to Greek Tragedy*, 151–77. Cambridge.
———. 2005. "The Image of the Polis in Greek Tragedy." In M. Hansen, ed., *The Imaginary Polis: Symposium, January 7–10, 2004*, 49–72. Copenhagen.
Eisner, R. 1979. "Euripides' Use of Myth." *Arethusa* 12: 153–74.
Elsner, J. 2006. "Reflections on the 'Greek Revolution' in Art: From Changes in Viewing to the Transformation of Subjectivity." In S. Goldhill and R. Osborne, eds., *Rethinking Revolutions through Ancient Greece*, 68–95. Cambridge.
England, E. B., ed. 1891. *The Iphigeneia at Aulis of Euripides*. London.
Farnell, L. R. 1921. *Greek Hero Cults and Ideas of Immortality*. Oxford.
Fearn, D., ed. 2011. *Aegina: Contexts for Choral Lyric Poetry: Myth, History, and Identity in the Fifth Century BC*. Oxford.

Feld, S. 1984. "Communication, Music, and Speech about Music." *Yearbook for Traditional Music* 16: 1–18.
———. 1990. *Sound and Sentiment: Birds, Weeping, Poetics, and Song in Kaluli Expression.* 2nd ed. Philadelphia.
———. 2000. "Sound Worlds." In P. Kruth and H. Stobart, eds., *Sound,* 173–200. Cambridge.
Feld, S., et al. [Feld, S., A. A. Fox, T. Porcello, and D. Samuels.] 2004. "Vocal Anthropology: From the Music of Language to the Language of Song." In A. Duranti, ed., *A Companion to Linguistic Anthropology,* 321–45. Malden, MA.
Ferrari, G. 2008. *Alcman and the Cosmos of Sparta.* Chicago.
Finglass, P. J., ed. 2007. *Sophocles: Electra.* Cambridge.
Fitton, J. W. 1973. "Greek Dance." *CQ* 23: 254–74.
Fleming, T. 1977. "The Musical Nomos in Aeschylus' *Oresteia.*" *CJ* 72: 222–33.
Folch, M. 2015. *The City and the Stage: Performance, Genre, and Gender in Plato's* Laws. Oxford.
Foley, H. P. 1982. "Marriage and Sacrifice in Euripides' *Iphigeneia in Aulis.*" *Arethusa* 15: 159–80.
———. 1985. *Ritual Irony: Poetry and Sacrifice in Euripides.* Ithaca, NY.
———. 1992. "Anodos Dramas: Euripides' *Alcestis* and *Helen.*" In R. J. Hexter and D. L. Seldon, eds., *Innovations of Antiquity,* 133–60. New York.
———. 2001. *Female Acts in Greek Tragedy.* Princeton.
———. 2003. "Choral Identity in Greek Tragedy." *CPh* 98: 1–30.
———. 2006. Review of Wright 2005. *AJPh* 127: 465–69.
Ford, A. 1992. *Homer: The Poetry of the Past.* Ithaca, NY.
———. 2010. "'A Song to Match My Song': Lyric Doubling in Euripides' *Helen.*" In P. Mitsis and C. Tsagalis, eds., *Allusion, Authority, and Truth: Critical Perspectives on Greek Poetic and Rhetorical Praxis,* 283–302. Berlin.
Foster, S. 2008. "Movement's Contagion: The Kinesthetic Impact of Performance." In T. C. Davis, ed., *The Cambridge Companion to Performance Studies,* 46–59. Cambridge.
———. 2010. *Choreographing Empathy: Kinesthesia in Performance.* New York.
Fraenkel, E., ed. 1950. *Aeschylus: Agamemnon.* Oxford.
Franklin, J. C. 2013. "Song-Benders of Circular Choruses: Dithyramb and the Demise of Music." In Wilson and Kowalzig 2013: 213–36.
Franko, M., and A. Richards. 2000. "Actualizing Absence: The Pastness of Performance." In M. Franko and A. Richards, eds., *Acting on the Past: Historical Performance across the Disciplines,* 1–12. Hanover, NH.
Gagné, R. 2013. "Dancing Letters: The *Alphabetic Tragedy* of Kallias." In Gagné and Hopman 2013a: 297–316.
Gagné, R., and M. G. Hopman, eds. 2013a. *Choral Mediations in Greek Tragedy.* Cambridge.
Gagné, R., and M. G. Hopman. 2013b. "Introduction: The Chorus in the Middle." In Gagné and Hopman 2013a: 1–34.
Garvie, A. F. 1969. *Aeschylus: Supplices; Play and Trilogy.* Cambridge.
Gellie, G. 1981. "Tragedy and Euripides' *Electra.*" *BICS* 28: 1–12.
Gibert, J. 1995. *Change of Mind in Greek Tragedy.* Göttingen.
Gilpin, H. 1996. "Lifelessness in Movement; or, How Do the Dead Move? Tracing Displacement and Disappearance for Movement Performance." In S. L. Foster, ed., *Corporealities: Dancing Knowledge, Culture, Power,* 109–32. London.

Giuliani, L. 2013. *Image and Myth: A History of Pictorial Narration in Greek Art.* Trans. J. O'Donnell. Chicago.
Goff, B. 2009. *Euripides: Trojan Women.* London.
Golann, C. P. 1945. "The Third Stasimon of Euripides' *Helena.*" *TAPhA* 76: 31–46.
Goldhill, S. 1986. *Reading Greek Tragedy.* Cambridge.
———. 1996. "Collectivity and Otherness: The Authority of the Tragic Chorus; Response to Gould." In M. S. Silk, ed., *Tragedy and the Tragic: Greek Theatre and Beyond,* 244–55. Oxford.
———. 2012. *Sophocles and the Language of Tragedy.* Oxford.
———. 2013. "Choreography: The Lyric Voice of Sophoclean Tragedy." In Gagné and Hopman 2013a: 100–129.
Goldhill, S. and R. Osborne, eds. 1999. *Performance Culture and Athenian Democracy.* Cambridge.
Gordon, R. L. 1979. "The Real and the Imaginary: Production and Religion in the Graeco-Roman World." *Art History* 2: 5–34.
Gould, J. 1996. "Tragedy and Collective Experience." In M. S. Silk, ed., *Tragedy and the Tragic: Greek Theatre and Beyond,* 217–43. Oxford.
Green, J. R. 1985. "A Representation of the *Birds* of Aristophanes." *Greek Vases in the J. Paul Getty Museum* 2: 95–118.
———. 1994. *Theatre in Ancient Greek Society.* London.
Greene, E., and M. Skinner, eds. 2009. *The New Sappho on Old Age: Textual and Philosophical Issues.* Washington, D.C.
Gregory, J. 1991. *Euripides and the Instruction of the Athenians.* Ann Arbor.
———. 2006. Review of Wright 2005. *Hermathena* 181: 230–33.
Griffith, M. 2011. "Extended Families, Marriage, and Inter-City Relations in (Later) Athenian Tragedy: Dynasts II." In Carter 2011: 175–208. Oxford.
———. 2013a. *Aristophanes' Frogs.* Oxford.
———. 2013b. "Satyr-Play, Dithyramb, and the Geo-politics of Dionysian Style in Fifth-Century Athens." In Kowalzig and Wilson 2013: 257–81.
———. 2015. *Greek Satyr Play: Five Studies.* Berkeley and Los Angeles.
———. Forthcoming. "Is Korybantic Performance a (Lyric) Genre?" In L. Kurke, M. Foster, and N. Weiss, eds., *The Genres of Archaic and Classical Greek Poetry: Theories and Models.* Leiden.
Gronewald, M., and W. R. Daniel. 2004. "Ein neuer Sappho-Papyrus." *ZPE* 147: 1–8.
Guépin, J. P. 1968. *The Tragic Paradox: Myth and Ritual in Greek Tragedy.* Amsterdam.
Günther, H. C., ed. 1988. *Euripides: Iphigenia Aulidensis.* Leipzig.
Gurd, S. A. 2005. *Iphigenias at Aulis: Textual Multiplicity, Radical Philology.* Ithaca, NY.
———. 2016. *Dissonance: Auditory Aesthetics in Ancient Greece.* New York.
Gutzwiller, K. J. 1991. *Theocritus' Pastoral Analogies: The Formation of a Genre.* Madison.
Hagel, S. 2005. "Twenty-Four in *Auloi*: Aristotle, *Met.* 1093b, the Harmony of the Spheres, and the Formation of the Perfect System." In S. Hagel and C. Harrauer, eds., *Ancient Greek Music in Performance: Symposion Wien 29. Sept.–1. Okt. 2003,* 51–91. Vienna.
———. 2012 "The Aulos Syrinx." In D. Castaldo, F. Giannachi, and A. Manieri, eds., *Poesia, musica e agoni nella Grecia antica: Atti del IV. Convegno internazionale di ΜΟΙΣΑ, Lecce, 28–30 Ottobre 2010,* 489–518. Galatina.

Hague, R. H. 1983. "Ancient Greek Wedding Songs: The Tradition of Praise." *Journal of Folklore Research* 20: 131–43.
Haldane, J. A. 1965. "Musical Themes and Imagery in Aeschylus." *JHS* 85: 33–41.
———. 1966. "Musical Instruments in Greek Worship." *G&R* 13: 98–107.
Hall, E. 1989. *Inventing the Barbarian: Greek Self-Definition through Tragedy.* Oxford.
———. 1999. "Actor's Song in Tragedy." In Goldhill and Osborne 1999: 96–124.
———. 2002. "The Singing Actors of Antiquity." In In P. Easterling and E. Hall, eds., *Greek and Roman Actors: Aspects of an Ancient Profession,* 3–38. Cambridge.
———. 2007. "Greek Tragedy 430–380 BC." In R. Osborne, ed., *Debating the Athenian Cultural Revolution: Art, Literature, Philosophy, and Politics, 430–380 BC,* 264–87. Cambridge.
———. 2010. "Towards a Theory of Performance Reception." In E. Hall and S. Harrop, eds., *Theorising Performance: Greek Drama, Cultural History and Critical Practice,* 10–28. London.
Halleran, M. 1985. *Stagecraft in Euripides.* Totowa, NJ.
Halliwell, S. 1986. *Aristotle: Poetics.* Chapel Hill.
———. 1987. *The Poetics of Aristotle: Translation and Commentary.* London.
———, ed. 1988. *Plato: Republic 10.* Warminster.
———. 2002. *The Aesthetics of Mimesis: Ancient Texts and Modern Problems.* Princeton.
Halporn, J. W. 1983. "The Skeptical Electra." *HSPh* 87: 101–18.
Handel, S. 1989. *Listening: An Introduction to the Perception of Auditory Events.* Cambridge, MA.
Hansen, M. H., ed. 2005. *The Imaginary Polis: Symposium, January 7–10, 2004.* Copenhagen.
Hardie, P. R. 1985. "*Imago Mundi:* Cosmological and Ideological Aspects of the Shield of Achilles." *JHS* 105: 11–31.
Hart, M. L., ed. 2010. *The Art of Ancient Greek Theater.* Los Angeles.
Hedreen, G. 2007. "Myths of Ritual in Athenian Vase-Paintings of Silens." In E. Csapo, and M. C. Miller, eds., *The Origins of Theater in Ancient Greece and Beyond: From Ritual to Drama,* 150–95. Cambridge.
———. 2011. "*Bild,* Mythos, and Ritual: Choral Dance in Theseus's Cretan Adventure on the François Vase." *Hesperia* 80: 491–510.
———. 2013. "The Semantics of Processional Dithyramb: Pindar's Second Dithyramb and the Archaic Athenian Vase-Painting." In Kowalzig and Wilson 2013: 171–97.
Heikkilä, K. 1991. "'Now I Have the Mind to Dance': The References of the Chorus to Their Own Dancing in Sophocles' Tragedies." *Arctos* 25: 51–68.
Helg, W. 1950. "Das Chorlied der griechischen Tragödie in seinem Verhältnis zur Handlung." Ph.D. dissertation, University of Zurich.
Henderson, J., ed. 2000. *Aristophanes.* Volume 3, *Birds, Lysistrata, Women at the Thesmophoria.* Cambridge. MA.
Henrichs, A. 1994–95. "'Why Should I Dance?': Choral Self-Referentiality in Greek Tragedy." *Arion* 3: 56–111.
———. 1996. "Dancing in Athens, Dancing on Delos: Some Patterns of Choral Projection in Euripides." *Philologus* 140: 48–62.
Herington, C. J. 1985. *Poetry into Drama: Early Tragedy and the Greek Poetic Tradition.* Berkeley and Los Angeles.
Hoff, F. 1976. "Dance to Song in Japan." *Dance Research Journal* 9: 1–15.

Holford-Strevens, L. 2006. "Sirens in Antiquity and the Middle Ages." In L. P. Austern and I. Naroditskaya, eds., *Music of the Sirens,* 16–51. Bloomington.
Holst-Warhaft, G. 1992. *Dangerous Voices: Women's Laments and Greek Literature.* London.
Holzhausen, J. 2003. *Euripides Politikos: Recht und Rache in 'Orestes' und 'Bakchen.'* Munich.
Hordern, J. H., ed. 2002. *The Fragments of Timotheus of Miletus.* Oxford.
Hose, M. 1990. *Studien zum Chor bei Euripides.* Vol. 1. Stuttgart.
———. 1991. *Studien zum Chor bei Euripides.* Vol. 2. Stuttgart.
———. 1995. *Drama und Gesellschaft: Studien zur dramatischen Produktion in Athen am Ende des 5. Jahrhunderts.* Stuttgart.
Hourmouziades, N. 1965. *Production and Imagination in Euripides: Form and Function of the Scenic Space.* Greek Society for Humanistic Studies 5. Athens.
Hoxby, B. 2005. "The Doleful Airs of Euripides: The Origins of Opera and the Spirit of Tragedy Reconsidered." *Cambridge Opera Journal* 17: 253–69.
Hutchinson, G. O. 2001. *Greek Lyric Poetry: A Commentary on Selected Larger Pieces.* Oxford.
Ihde, D. 2003. "Auditory Imagination." In M. Bull and L. Back, eds., *The Auditory Culture Reader,* 61–66. Oxford.
Iozzo, M. 2013. "The François Vase: Notes on Technical Aspects and Function." In H. A. Shapiro, M. Iozzo, and A. Lezzi-Hafter, eds., *The François Vase: New Perspectives,* 53–66. Zurich.
Irigoin, J. 1988. "Le prologue et la parodos d'*Iphigénie à Aulis*." *REG* 101: 240–52.
Issacharoff, M. 1981. "Space and Reference in Drama." *Poetics Today* 2: 211–24.
Jackson, L. Forthcoming. *The Chorus of Drama in the Fourth Century BCE.* Oxford.
Jens, W., ed. 1971. *Die Bauformen der griechischen Tragödie.* Munich.
Johnson, B. 2005. "*Hamlet*: Voice, Music, Sound." *Popular Music* 24: 257–67.
Jouan, F. 1983. *Euripide.* Tome 7, *Iphigénie à Aulis.* Paris.
Kakridis, J. 1966. "Zur Sappho 44 LP." *WS* 79: 21–26.
Kannicht, R. 1969. *Euripides: Helena.* Heidelberg.
———, ed. 2004. *Tragicorum Graecorum Fragmenta.* Vol. 5. Göttingen.
Kenner, H. 1941. "Zur Achilleis des Aischylos." *Wiener Jahreshefte* 33: 1–24.
Keuls, E. C. 1978. *Plato and Greek Painting.* Leiden.
King, K. C. 1980. "The Force of Tradition: The Achilles Ode in Euripides' *Electra*." *TAPhA* 110: 195–212.
Kip, A. M. van Erp Taalman. 1987. "Euripides and Melos." *Mnemosyne* 40: 414–19.
Kitto, H. D. F. 1939. *Greek Tragedy: A Literary Study.* London.
Kivy, P. 1989. *Sound Sentiment: An Essay on the Musical Emotions.* Philadelphia.
———. 1990. *Music Alone: Philosophical Reflections on the Purely Musical Experience.* Ithaca, NY.
Kloetzel, M., and C. Pavlik, eds. 2009. *Site Dance: Choreographers and the Lure of Alternative Spaces.* Gainesville.
Knox, B. M. W. 1972. "Euripides' *Iphigenia in Aulide* 1–163 (in That Order)." *YClS* 22: 239–61.
Koller, H. 1954. *Die Mimesis in der Antike: Nachahmung, Darstellung, Ausdruck.* Bern.
Koniaris, G. L. 1973. "*Alexander, Palamedes, Troades, Sisyphus*: A Connected Tetralogy? A Connected Trilogy?" *HSPh* 77: 85–124.
Kovacs, D. 1997. "Gods and Men in Euripides' Trojan Trilogy." *ColbyQ* 33: 162–76.

———, ed. 2002. *Euripides*. Volume 6, *Bacchae, Iphigenia at Aulis, Rhesus*. Cambridge, MA.

———. 2003. "Toward a Reconstruction of 'Iphigenia Aulidensis.'" *JHS* 123: 77–103.

Kowalzig, B. 2004. "Changing Choral Worlds: Song-Dance and Society in Athens and Beyond." In Murray and Wilson 2004: 39–65.

———. 2007a. "'And Now All the World Shall Dance!' (Eur. *Bacch*. 114): Dionysus' *Choroi* between Drama and Ritual." In E. Csapo, and M. C. Miller, eds., *The Origins of Theater in Ancient Greece and Beyond: From Ritual to Drama*, 221–53. Cambridge.

———. 2007b. *Singing for the Gods: Performances of Myth and Ritual in Archaic and Classical Greece*. Oxford.

———. 2013. "Dancing Dolphins on the Wine-Dark Sea: Dithyramb and Social Change in the Archaic Mediterranean." In Kowalzig and Wilson: 31–58.

Kowalzig, B., and P. Wilson, eds. 2013. *Dithyramb in Context*. Oxford.

Kramer, L. 2002. *Musical Meaning: Toward a Critical History*. Berkeley and Los Angeles.

Kranz, W. 1933. *Stasimon: Untersuchungen zu Form und Gehalt der griechischen Tragödie*. Berlin.

Kraut, R., trans. 1997. *Aristotle: Politics, Books VII and VIII*. Oxford.

Kruth, P., and H. Stobart, eds. 2000. *Sound*. Cambridge.

Kubo, M. 1967. "The Norm of Myth: Euripides' *Electra*." *HSPh* 71: 15–31.

Kurke, L. 2007. "Visualizing the Choral: Epichoric Poetry, Ritual, and Elite Negotiation in Fifth-Century Thebes." In C. Kraus et al., eds., *Visualizing the Tragic: Drama, Myth, and Ritual in Greek Art and Literature: Essays in Honour of Froma Zeitlin*, 63–104. Oxford.

———. 2012. "The Value of Chorality in Ancient Greece." In J. K. Papadopoulos and G. Urton, eds., *The Construction of Value in the Ancient World*, 218–35. Los Angeles.

———. 2013. "Imagining Chorality: Wonder, Plato's Puppets, and Moving Statues." In A.-E. Peponi, ed., *Performance and Culture in Plato's Laws*, 123–70. Cambridge.

Kyriakou, P. 2006. *A Commentary on Euripides' Iphigenia in Tauris*. Berlin.

Lämmle, R. 2013. *Poetik des Satyrspiels*. Heidelberg.

Landels, J. G. 1999. *Music in Ancient Greece and Rome*. London.

Lardinois, A. 1996. "Who Sang Sappho's Songs?" In E. Greene, ed., *Reading Sappho: Contemporary Approaches*, 150–72. Berkeley and Los Angeles.

———. 2009. "The New Sappho Poem (*P.Köln* 21351 and 21376): Key to the Old Fragments." In Greene and Skinner 2009: 41–57.

Larson, J. 1995. *Greek Heroine Cults*. Madison.

———. 2001. *Greek Nymphs: Myth, Cult, Lore*. Oxford.

Lasserre, F. 1989. *Sappho: Une autre lecture*. Padua.

Lawler, L. B. 1944. "The Dance of the Ancient Mariners." *TAPhA* 75: 20–33.

———. 1946. "The Geranos Dance: A New Interpretation." *TAPhA* 77: 112–30.

———. 1948a. "A Necklace for Eileithyia." *The Classical Weekly* 42: 2–6.

———. 1948b. "Orchēsis Kallinikos." *TAPhA* 79: 254–67.

———. 1950. "A Figure of the Tragic Dance." *CB* 27: 3–4.

———. 1964. *The Dance of the Ancient Greek Theatre*. Iowa City.

Leach, E. E. 2007. *Sung Birds: Music, Nature, and Poetry in the Later Middle Ages*. Ithaca, NY.

Lech, M. L. 2009. "Marching Choruses? Choral Performance in Athens." *GRBS* 49: 343–61.
Lee, K. H., ed. 1976. *Euripides: Troades.* Basingstoke.
———, ed. 1997. *Euripides: Ion.* Warminster.
Lehnus, L. 1984. "Pindaro: Il dafneforico per Agasicle." *BICS* 31: 61–92.
Lepecki, A. 2004. "Introduction: Presence and Body in Dance and Performance Theory." In A. Lepecki, ed., *Of the Presence of the Body: Essays on Dance and Performance Theory,* 1–12. Middletown, CT.
Lesky, A. 1971. *Geschichte der griechischen Literatur.* 3rd ed. Bern.
———. 1972. *Die tragische Dichtung der Hellenen.* 3rd ed. Göttingen.
LeVen, P. 2011. "Timotheus' Eleven Strings: A New Approach (*PMG* 791.229–36)." *CPh* 106: 245–54.
———. 2014. *The Many-Headed Muse: Tradition and Innovation in Late Classical Greek Lyric Poetry.* Cambridge.
Ley, G. 2007. *The Theatricality of Greek Tragedy: Playing Space and Chorus.* Chicago.
Lidov, J. 2009. "Acceptance or Assertion? Sappho's New Poem in Its Books." In Greene and Skinner 2009: 84–102.
Lloyd, M. 1986. "Realism and Character in Euripides' *Electra.*" *Phoenix* 40: 1–19.
———. 1992. *The Agon in Euripides.* Oxford.
Lloyd-Jones, H. 1964. "The *Supplices* of Aeschylus: The New Date and Old Problems." *AC* 33: 356–74.
———, ed. 1996. *Sophocles: Fragments.* Cambridge, MA.
Lonsdale, S. 1993. *Dance and Ritual Play in Greek Religion.* Baltimore.
Loraux, N. 1986. *The Invention of Athens: The Funeral Oration in the Classical City.* Trans. A. Sheridan. Cambridge, MA.
———. 1998. *Mothers in Mourning.* Trans. C. Pache. Ithaca, NY.
———. 2002. *The Mourning Voice: An Essay on Greek Tragedy.* Trans. E. Trapnell Rawlings. Ithaca, NY.
Luschnig, C. A. E. 1988. *Tragic Aporia: A Study of Euripides' Iphigenia at Aulis.* Berwick, Victoria.
Maas, M., and J. M. Snyder. 1989. *Stringed Instruments of Ancient Greece.* New Haven.
Marinis, M. 1987. "Dramaturgy of the Spectator." *TDR: The Journal of Performance Studies* 31: 100–114.
Marshall, C. W. 1995. "Idol Speculation: The Protean Stage of Euripides' *Helen.*" *Text and Presentation* 16: 74–79.
———. 2000. "*Alcestis* and the Problem of Prosatyric Drama." *CJ* 95: 229–38.
———. 2009. "Sophocles' *Chryses* and the Date of *Iphigenia in Tauris.*" In Cousland and Hume: 141–56.
———. 2014. *The Structure and Performance of Euripides'* Helen. Cambridge.
Martin, R. 2003. "The Pipes Are Brawling: Conceptualizing Musical Performance in Athens." In C. Dougherty and L. Kurke, eds., *The Cultures within Ancient Greek Culture: Contact, Conflict, Collaboration,* 153–80. Cambridge.
———. 2008. "Keens from the Absent Chorus: Troy to Ulster." In A. Suter, ed., *Lament: Studies in the Ancient Mediterranean and Beyond,* 118–38. Oxford.
Mastronarde, D. J. 1979. *Contact and Discontinuity: Some Conventions of Speech and Action on the Greek Tragic Stage.* Berkeley and Los Angeles.

———, ed. 1994. *Euripides: Phoenissae*. Cambridge.
———. 1998. "Il coro euripideo: Autorità e integrazione." *QUCC* 60: 55–80.
———. 1999. "Knowledge and Authority in the Choral Voice of Euripidean Tragedy." *SyllClass* 10: 87–104.
———, ed. 2002. *Euripides: Medea*. Cambridge.
———. 2010. *The Art of Euripides: Dramatic Technique and Social Context*. Cambridge.
Matheson, S. B. 1995. *Polygnotos and Vase Painting in Classical Athens*. Madison.
Mathiesen, T. J. 1999. *Apollo's Lyre: Greek Music and Music Theory in Antiquity and the Middle Ages*. Lincoln, NE.
———. 2007. Review of S. Hagel and C. Harrauer, eds., *Ancient Greek Music in Performance: Symposion Wien 29. Sept.–1. Okt. 2003* (2005). *Music and Letters* 88: 316–22.
McClure, L. 1999. *Spoken like a Woman: Speech and Gender in Athenian Drama*. Princeton.
McDonald, M. 1990. "Iphigenia's *Philia*: Motivation in Euripides *Iphigenia at Aulis*." *QUCC* 34: 69–84.
Meineck, P. 2013. "'The Thorniest Problem and the Greatest Opportunity': Directors on Directing the Greek Chorus." In Gagné and Hopman 2013a: 352–83.
Mellert-Hoffmann, G. 1969. *Untersuchungen zur Iphigenie in Aulis des Euripides*. Heidelberg.
Michelakis, P. 2002. *Achilles in Greek Tragedy*. Cambridge.
———. 2006. *Euripides: Iphigenia at Aulis*. London.
Michelini, A. N. 1987. *Euripides and the Tragic Tradition*. Madison.
———. 1999–2000. "The Expansion of Myth in Late Euripides: *Iphigeneia at Aulis*. In Cropp, Lee, and Sansone 1999–2000: 41–57.
Miller, M. C. 2004. "In Strange Company: Persians in Early Attic Theatre Imagery." *MedArch* 17: 165–72.
Miller, S. G. 1986. "Eros and the Arms of Achilles." *AJA* 90: 159–70.
Morwood, J. 1981. "The Pattern of Euripides' *Electra*." *AJPh* 102: 362–70.
Muecke, F. 1982. "A Portrait of the Artist as a Young Woman." *CQ* 32: 41–55.
Muellner, L. 1990. "The Simile of the Cranes and Pygmies: A Study of Homeric Metaphor." *HSPh* 93: 59–101.
Mullen, W. 1982. *Choreia: Pindar and Dance*. Princeton.
Mulryne, J. R. 1977. "Poetic Structures in the *Electra* of Euripides." *LCM* 2: 31–50.
Murnaghan, S. 2005. "Women in Groups: Aeschylus' *Suppliants* and the Female Choruses of Greek Tragedy." In V. Pedrick and S. M. Oberhelman, eds., *The Soul of Tragedy: Essays on Athenian Drama*, 183–98. Chicago.
———. 2011. "*Choroi Achoroi*: The Athenian Politics of Tragic Choral Identity." In Carter 2011: 245–68. Oxford.
———. 2013. "The Choral Plot of Euripides' *Helen*." In Gagné and Hopman 2013a: 155–77.
Murray, P., and P. Wilson, eds. 2004. *Music and the Muses: The Culture of "Mousikē" in the Classical Athenian City*.
Naerebout, F. G. 1997. *Attractive Performances: Ancient Greek Dance; Three Preliminary Studies*. Amsterdam.
Nagler, M. N. 1974. *Spontaneity and Tradition: A Study in the Oral Art of Homer*. Berkeley and Los Angeles.
Nagy, G. 1974. *Comparative Studies in Greek and Indic Meter*. Cambridge, MA.

———. 1990. *Pindar's Homer: The Lyric Possession of an Epic Past.* Baltimore.
———. 1994–95. "Transformations of Choral Lyric Traditions in the Context of Athenian State Theater." *Arion* 3: 41–55.
———. 1996. *Poetry as Performance: Homer and Beyond.* Cambridge.
Neer, R. T. 2010. *The Emergence of the Classical Style in Greek Sculpture.* Chicago.
Neils, J. 1995. "*Les Femmes Fatales:* Skylla and the Sirens in Greek Art." In Cohen 1995: 175–84.
———. 2013. "Contextualizing the François Vase." In H. A. Shapiro, M. Iozzo, and A. Lezzi-Hafter, eds., *The François Vase: New Perspectives,* 119–30. Zurich.
Neitzel, H. 1967. "Die dramatische Funktion der Chorlieder in den Tragödien des Euripides." Ph.D. dissertation, University of Hamburg.
Nikolaidou-Arabatzi, S. 2015. "Choral Projections and *Embolima* in Euripides' Tragedies." *G&R* 62: 25–47.
Nooter, S. 2012. *When Heroes Sing: Sophocles and the Shifting Soundscape of Tragedy.* Cambridge.
O'Brien, M. J. 1964. "Orestes and the Gorgon: Euripides' *Electra.*" *AJPh* 85: 13–39.
Olsen, S. 2017. "Kinesthetic Choreia: Empathy, Memory, and Dance in Ancient Greece." *CPh* 112: 1–22.
Padel, R. 1974. "'Imagery of the Elsewhere': Two Choral Odes of Euripides." *CQ* 24: 227–41.
———. 1990. "Making Space Speak." In Winkler and Zeitlin 1990: 336–65.
Page, D. L. 1934. *Actors' Interpolations in Greek Tragedy: Studied with Special Reference to Euripides' Iphigeneia in Aulis.* Oxford.
———. 1973. *Folktales in Homer's Odyssey.* Cambridge, MA.
Panagl, O. 1971. *Die "dithyrambischen Stasima" des Euripides: Untersuchungen zur Komposition und Erzähltechnik.* Vienna.
Papadimitropoulos, L. 2008. "Causality and Innovation in Euripides' *Electra.*" *RhM* 151: 113–26.
Papadopoulou, T. 2000. "Cassandra's Radiant Vigour and the Ironic Optimism of Euripides' *Troades.*" *Mnemosyne* 53: 513–27.
Papastamati-von Moock, C. 2015. "The Wooden Theatre of Dionysos Eleuthereus in Athens: Old Issues, New Research." In R. Frederiksen, E. R. Gebhard, and A. Sokolicek, eds., *The Architecture of the Ancient Greek Theatre,* 39–80. Aarhus.
Parker, R. 1996. *Athenian Religion: A History.* Oxford.
———. 2005. *Polytheism and Society at Athens.* Oxford.
———. 2011. *On Greek Religion.* Ithaca, NY.
Parry, H. 1965. "The Second Stasimon of Euripides' *Heracles* (637–700)." *AJPh* 86: 363–74.
Patel, A. H. 2008. *Music, Language, and the Brain.* Oxford.
Pearson, A. C., ed. 1903. *The Helena of Euripides.* Cambridge.
Peponi, A.-E. 2004a. "Initiating the Viewer: Deixis and Visual Perception in Alcman's Lyric Drama." *Arethusa* 37: 295–316.
———. 2004b. "Χωρογραφία θεάτρου· Ομηρικός ύμνος εις Απόλλωνα 146–206." In D. I. Jakob and H. Papazoglou, eds., *Θυμέλη: Festschrift in Honor of N. Chourmouziades,* 303–22. Heraklion.
———. 2007. "Sparta's Prima Ballerina: *Choreia* in Alcman's Second *Partheneion* (3 *PMGF*)." *CQ* 57: 351–62.

———. 2009. "Choreia and Aesthetics in the *Homeric Hymn to Apollo:* The Performance of the Delian Maidens (Lines 156–64)." *ClAnt* 28: 39–70.

———. 2012. *Frontiers of Pleasure: Models of Aesthetic Response in Archaic and Classical Greek Thought.* Oxford.

———. 2013a. "Choral Anti-Aesthetics." In A.-E. Peponi, ed., *Performance and Culture in Plato's Laws,* 212–39. Cambridge.

———. 2013b. "Theorizing the Chorus in Greece." In J. Billings, F. Budelmann, and F. Macintosh, eds., *Choruses, Ancient and Modern,* 15–34. Oxford.

———. 2015. "Dance and Aesthetic Perception." In P. Destrée and P. Murray, eds., *A Companion to Ancient Aesthetics,* 204–17. Malden, MA.

Pereira, A. R. 1998. "Problemas organológicos relativos à Syrinx." *Humanitas (Coimbra)* 50: 49–59.

Phelan, P. 1993. *Unmarked: The Politics of Performance.* London.

Phillips, T. 2013. "Epinician Variations: Music and Text in Pindar, *Pythians* 2 and 12." *CQ* 63: 37–56.

Pickard-Cambridge, A. 1968. *The Dramatic Festivals of Athens.* 2nd ed. Oxford.

Pintacuda, M. 1978. *La musica nella tragedia greca.* Cefalù.

Platnauer, M., ed. 1938. *Euripides: Iphigenia in Tauris.* Oxford.

Platt, V. 2011. *Facing the Gods: Epiphany and Representation in Graeco-Roman Art, Literature and Religion.* Cambridge.

Podlecki, A. J. 1970. "The Basic Seriousness of Euripides' *Helen.*" *TAPhA* 101: 401–18.

Poe, J. P. 1993. "The Determination of Episodes in Greek Tragedy." *AJPh* 114: 343–96.

Pohlenz, M. 1954. *Die griechische Tragödie.* 2nd ed. Göttingen.

Pöhlmann, E., and M. L. West. 2001. *Documents of Ancient Greek Music: The Extant Melodies and Fragments.* Oxford.

Poole, A. 1976. "Total Disaster: Euripides' *The Trojan Women.*" *Arion* 3: 257–87.

Porter, J. 2013. "Why Are There Nine Muses?" In S. Butler and A. Purves, eds., *Synaesthesia and the Ancient Senses,* 9–26. Durham.

Power, T. 2000. "The *Parthenoi* of Bacchylides 13." *HSPh* 100: 67–81.

———. 2010. *The Culture of* Kitharôidia. Washington, D.C.

———. 2011. "Cyberchorus: Pindar's Κηληδόνες and the Aura of the Artificial." In L. Athanassaki and E. Bowie, eds., *Archaic and Classical Choral Song: Performance, Politics and Dissemination,* 67–113. Berlin.

———. 2012. "Sophocles and Music." In A. Markantonatos, ed., *Brill's Companion to Sophocles,* 283–304. Leiden.

———. 2018. "New Music in Sophocles' *Ichneutai.*" In R. Andújar, T. Coward, and T. Hadjimichael, eds., *Paths of Song: The Lyric Dimension of Greek Tragedy,* 341–63. Berlin.

Prauscello, L. 2012. "Epinician Sounds: Pindar and Musical Innovation." In P. Agócs, C. Carey, and R. Rawles, *Reading the Victory Ode,* 58–82. Cambridge.

———. 2013. "Demeter and Dionysos in the Sixth-Century Argolid: Lasos of Hermione, the Cult of Demeter Chthonia, and the Origins of Dithyramb." In Kowalzig and Wilson 2013: 76–92.

———. 2014. *Performing Citizenship in Plato's Laws.* Cambridge.

Prins, Y. 1991. "The Power of the Speech Act: Aeschylus' Furies and Their Binding Song." *Arethusa* 24: 177–95.

Prudhommeau, G. 1965. *La danse grecque antique*. Paris.
Pucci, P. 1979. "The Song of the Sirens." *Arethusa* 12: 121–32.
———. 1987. *Odysseus Polutropos: Intertextual Readings in the Odyssey and the Iliad*. Ithaca, NY.
———. 1997. "The *Helen* and Euripides' Comic Art." *ColbyQ* 33: 42–75.
———. 1998. *The Song of the Sirens: Essays on Homer*. Lanham, MD.
Quijada, M. 2006. "'Por Ilión, ¡Oh Musa! Cántame entre lágrimas un canto de duelo, un himno nuevo' (Eurípides, *Troyanas* 511 Ss.)." In E. Calderón, A. Morales, and M. Valverde, eds., *Koinòs Lógos: Homenaje al Profesor José García López*, vol. 2: 841–53. Murcia.
Raab, I. 1972. *Zu den Darstellungen des Parisurteils in der griechischen Kunst*. Frankfurt.
Raeburn, D. 2000. "The Significance of Stage Properties in Euripides' *Electra*." *G&R* 47: 149–68.
Reason, M., and D. Reynolds. 2010. "Kinesthesia, Empathy, and Related Pleasures: An Inquiry into Audience Experiences of Watching Dance." *Dance Research Journal* 42: 49–75.
Rehm, R. 1994. *Marriage to Death: The Conflation of Wedding and Funeral Rituals in Greek Tragedy*. Princeton.
———. 1996. "Performing the Chorus: Choral Action, Interaction, and Absence in Euripides." *Arion* 4: 45–60.
Revermann, M. 1999–2000. "Euripides, Tragedy and Macedon: Some Conditions of Reception." In Cropp, Lee, and Sansone 1999–2000: 451–67.
———. 2006a. *Comic Business: Theatricality, Dramatic Technique, and Performance Contexts of Aristophanic Comedy*. Oxford.
———. 2006b. "The Competence of Theatre Audiences in Fifth- and Fourth-Century Athens." *JHS* 126: 99–124.
Richardson, N. J., ed. 2010. *Three Homeric Hymns: To Apollo, Hermes, and Aphrodite, Hymns 3, 4, and 5*. Cambridge.
Richter, G. M. A. 1936. *Red-Figured Athenian Vases in the Metropolitan Museum of Art*. New Haven.
Rizzo, G. I. 2002. *Inquieti commerci tra uomini e dei: Timpanisti, Fineo A e B di Sofocle*. Rome.
Roach, J. R. 1996. *Cities of the Dead: Circum-Atlantic Performance*. New York.
Robinson, D. B. 1979. "Helen and Persephone, Sparta and Demeter. The 'Demeter Ode' in Euripides' *Helen*." In G. W. Bowerstock, W. Burkert, and M. C. J. Putnam, eds., *Arktouros: Hellenic Studies Presented to Bernard M. W. Knox on the Occasion of His 65th Birthday*, 162–72. Berlin.
Rode, J. 1971. "Das Chorlied." In W. Jens, ed., *Die Bauformen der griechischen Tragödie*, 85–115. Munich.
Roller, L. E. 1996. "Reflections of the Mother of the Gods in Attic Tragedy." In E. Lane, ed., *Cybele, Attis and Related Cults: Essays in Memory of M. J. Vermaseren*, 305–22. Leiden.
———. 1999. *In Search of God the Mother: The Cult of Anatolian Cybele*. Berkeley and Los Angeles.
Romer, F. E. 1983. "When Is a Bird Not a Bird?" *TAPhA* 113: 135–42.
Rosen, R. M. 1999. "Comedy and Confusion in Callias' *Letter Tragedy*." *CPh* 94: 147–67.
Rösler, W. 1975. "Ein Gedicht und sein Publikum: Überlegungen zu Sappho Fr. 44 Lobel-Page." *Hermes* 103: 275–85.

Rothwell, K. 2007. *Nature, Culture, and the Origins of Greek Comedy: A Study of Animal Choruses.* Cambridge.

Rusten, J. 2006. "Who 'Invented' Comedy? The Ancient Candidates for the Origins of Comedy and the Visual Evidence." *AJPh* 127: 37–66.

Rutherford, I. 1994–95. "Apollo in Ivy: The Tragic Paean." *Arion* 3: 112–35.

———. 1995. "The Nightingale's Refrain: P. Oxy. 2625 = SLG 460." *ZPE* 107: 39–43.

———. 2001. *Pindar's Paeans: A Reading of the Fragments with a Survey of the Genre.* Oxford.

Sadie, S., ed. 2001. *The New Grove Dictionary of Music and Musicians.* 2nd ed. Oxford.

Sansone, D. 1991. "Iphigeneia Changes Her Mind." *ICS* 16: 161–72.

———. 2009. "Euripides' New Song: The First Stasimon of the *Trojan Women.*" In Cousland and Hume 2009: 193–203.

Savage, R. 2010. "Precursors, Precedents, Pretexts: The Institutions of Greco-Roman Theatre and the Development of European Opera." In P. Brown and S. Ograjenšek, eds., *Ancient Drama in Music for the Modern Stage,* 1–31. Oxford.

Schafer, R. M. 1977. *The Tuning of the World.* New York.

Schlegel, A. W. von. 1846. *Vorlesungen über dramatische Kunst und Literatur.* Vol. 1. Schlegel, *Sämtliche Werke,* ed. E. Böcking. Leipzig.

Schmidt, D. A. 1990. "Bacchylides 17: Paean or Dithyramb?" *Hermes* 118: 18–31.

Schmidt, M. 1967. "Dionysien." *AK* 10: 70–81.

Schrenk, L. P. 1994. "Sappho Frag. 44 and the 'Iliad.'" *Hermes* 122: 144–50.

Schubart, W., and U. von Wilamowitz-Moellendorff, eds. 1907. *Griechische Dichterfragmente.* Volume 5, *Lyrische und dramatische Fragmente.* Berlin.

Scodel, R. 1980. *The Trojan Trilogy of Euripides.* Göttingen.

———. 1997. "Teichoscopia, Catalogue, and the Female Spectator in Euripides." *ColbyQ* 33: 76–93.

———. 2007. "Lycurgus and the State Text of Tragedy." In C. Cooper, ed., *Politics of Orality,* 129–54. Leiden.

Scott, W. C. 1984. *Musical Design in Aeschylean Theater.* Hanover, NH.

———. 1996a. *Musical Design in Sophoclean Theater.* Hanover, NH.

———. 1996b. "Musical Design in Sophocles' *Oedipus Tyrannus.*" *Arion* 4: 33–44.

Seaford, R. 1987. "The Tragic Wedding." *JHS* 107: 106–30.

———. 1994. *Reciprocity and Ritual: Homer and Tragedy in the Developing City-State.* Oxford.

———. 2009. "Aetiologies of Cult in Euripides: A Response to Scott Scullion." In Cousland and Hume 2009: 221–34.

Segal, C. 1971. "The Two Worlds of Euripides' *Helen.*" *TAPhA* 102: 553–614.

———. 1983. "Sirius and the Pleiades in Alcman's Louvre *Partheneion.*" *Mnemosyne* 36: 260–75.

———. 1993. *Euripides and the Poetics of Sorrow: Art, Gender, and Commemoration in Alcestis, Hippolytus, and Hecuba.* Durham, NC.

Seidensticker, B. 2010. "Dance in Satyr-Play." In O. Taplin and R. Wyles, eds., *The Pronomos Vase and Its Context,* 213–30. Oxford.

———. 2012. "The Satyr Plays of Sophocles." In A. Markantonatos, ed., *Brill's Companion to Sophocles,* 211–42. Leiden.

Seremetakis, C. N. 1990. "The Ethics of Antiphony: The Social Construction of Pain, Gender, and Power in the Southern Peloponnese." *Ethos* 18: 481–512.
Shaw, C. A. 2014. *Satyric Play: The Evolution of Greek Comedy and Satyr Drama*. Oxford.
Siegel, H. 1980. "Self-Delusion and the 'Volte-Face' of Iphigenia in Euripides' *Iphigenia at Aulis*." *Hermes* 108: 300–321.
Sifakis, G. M. 1967. "Singing Dolphin Riders." *BICS* 14: 36–37.
———. 1971. *Parabasis and Animal Choruses: A Contribution to the History of Attic Comedy*. London.
———. 2001. *Aristotle on the Function of Tragic Poetry*. Heraklion.
Silk, M. S., ed. 1996. *Tragedy and the Tragic: Greek Theatre and Beyond*. Oxford.
Sklar, D. 2008. "Remembering Kinesthesia: An Inquiry into Embodied Cultural Knowledge." In C. Noland and S. A. Ness, eds., *Migrations of Gesture*, 85–111. Minneapolis.
Slater, N. W. 2005. "Nothing to Do with Satyrs? *Alcestis* and the Concept of Prosatyric Drama." In G. W. M. Harrison, ed., *Satyr Drama: Tragedy at Play*, 83–101. Swansea.
Smith, B. R. 1999. *The Acoustic World of Early Modern England: Attending to the O-Factor*. Chicago.
Smith, W. 1979. "Iphigenia in Love." In G. W. Bowerstock, W. Burkert, and M. C. J. Putnam, eds., *Arktouros: Hellenic Studies Presented to Bernard M. W. Knox on the Occasion of His 65th Birthday*, 173–80. Berlin.
Snell, B. 1971. *Szenen aus griechischen Dramen*. Berlin.
Snyder, J. M. 1979. "Aulos and Kithara on the Greek Stage." In T. E. Gregory and A. J. Podlecki, eds., *Panathenaia: Studies in Athenian Life and Thought in the Classical Age*, 75–95. Lawrence, KS.
Solmsen, F. 1934. "*Onoma* and *Pragma* in Euripides' *Helen*." *CR* 48: 119–21.
Sommerstein, A. H., ed. 2000. *Aristophanes*. Volume 3, *Birds, Lysistrata, Women at the Thesmophoria*. Cambridge, MA.
———, ed. 2008a. *Aeschylus*. Volume 1, *Persians, Seven Against Thebes, Suppliants, Prometheus Bound*. Cambridge, MA.
———, ed. 2008b. *Aeschylus*. Volume 3, *Fragments*. Cambridge, MA.
———. 2010. *Aeschylean Tragedy*. 2nd ed. London.
Sorum, C. E. 1992. "Myth, Choice, and Meaning in Euripides' *Iphigenia at Aulis*." *AJPh* 113: 527–42.
Stanford, W. B. 1983. *Greek Tragedy and the Emotions*. London.
Stehle, E. 1997. *Performance and Gender in Ancient Greece: Nondramatic Poetry in Its Setting*. Princeton.
Steiner, D. 2001. *Images in Mind: Statues in Archaic and Classical Greek Literature and Thought*. Princeton.
———. 2011. "Dancing with the Stars: Choreia in the Third Stasimon of Euripides' *Helen*." *CPh* 106: 299–323.
———. 2013. "The Gorgons' Lament: Auletics, Poetics, and Chorality in Pindar's *Pythian* 12." *AJPh* 134: 173–208.
———. Forthcoming. *Choral Constructions: The Chorus in Archaic and Early Classical Greek Art, Texts, Social Practices and Technology*. Cambridge.
Stewart, A. 1983. "Stesichoros and the François Vase." In W. G. Moon, ed., *Ancient Greek Art and Iconography*, 53–74. Madison.

Stinton, T. C. W. 1965. *Euripides and the Judgement of Paris*. London.
Stockert, W. 1992. *Euripides: Iphigenie in Aulis*. 2 Volumes. Vienna.
Suksi, A. 2001. "The Poet at Colonus: Nightingales in Sophocles." *Mnemosyne* 54: 646–58.
Summers, K. 1996. "Lucretius' Roman Cybele." In E. Lane, ed., *Cybele, Attis and Related Cults: Essays in Memory of M. J. Vermaseren*, 337–66. Leiden.
Suter, A. 2003. "Lament in Euripides' *Trojan Women*." *Mnemosyne* 56: 1–28.
———. 2008. "Male Lament in Greek Tragedy." In A. Suter, ed., *Lament: Studies in the Ancient Mediterranean and Beyond*, 156–80. Oxford.
Swift, L. A. 2009a. "How to Make a Goddess Angry: Making Sense of the Demeter Ode in Euripides' *Helen*." *CPh* 104: 418–38.
———. 2009b. "The Symbolism of Space in Euripidean Choral Fantasy (*Hipp.* 732–75, *Med.* 824–65, *Bacch.* 370–433)." *CQ* 59: 364–82.
———. 2010. *The Hidden Chorus: Echoes of Genre in Tragic Lyric*. Oxford.
Tanner, J. 2006. *The Invention of Art History in Ancient Greece: Religion, Society and Artistic Rationalism*. Cambridge.
Taplin, O. 1977. *The Stagecraft of Aeschylus: The Dramatic Use of Exits and Entrances in Greek Tragedy*. Oxford.
———. 1978. *Greek Tragedy in Action*. Berkeley and Los Angeles.
———. 1984. "Lyric Dialogue and Dramatic Construction in Later Sophocles." *Dioniso* 55: 115–22.
———. 2007. *Pots and Plays: Interactions between Tragedy and Greek Vase-Painting of the Fourth Century B.C.* Los Angeles.
Thomas, O. Forthcoming. "Music in Euripides' *Medea*." In A. D'Angour and T. Phillips, eds., *Music, Texts, and Culture in Ancient Greece*. Oxford.
Thompson, D. W. 1936. *A Glossary of Greek Birds*. 2nd ed. Oxford.
Torelli, Mario. 2007. *Le strategie di Kleitias: Composizione e programma figurativo del Vaso François*. Milan.
Torrance, I. 2013. *Metapoetry in Euripides*. Oxford.
Tsagalis, C. C. 2009. "Blurring the Boundaries: Dionysus, Apollo and Bacchylides 17." In L. Athanassaki, R. P. Martin, and J. F. Miller, eds., *Apolline Politics and Poetics*, 199–215. Athens.
Tsiafakis, D. 2001. "Life and Death at the Hands of a Siren." In M. True and M. L. Hart, eds., *Studia Varia from the J. Paul Getty Museum*, vol. 2: 7–24. Los Angeles.
Vidali, S. 1997. *Archaische Delphindarstellungen*. Wurzburg.
Visvardi, E. 2015. *Emotion in Action: Thucydides and the Tragic Chorus*. Leiden.
Wallace, R. W. 2003. "An Early Fifth-Century Athenian Revolution in Aulos Music." *HSPh* 101: 73–92.
Walsh, G. B. 1974. "Iphigenia in Aulis: Third Stasimon." *CPh* 69: 241–48.
———. 1977. "The First Stasimon of Euripides' *Electra*." *YClS* 25: 277–89.
Watson, S. 2015. "*Mousikē* and Mysteries: A Nietzschean Reading of Aeschylus' *Bassarides*." *CQ* 65: 455–75.
Weicker, G. 1902. *Der Seelenvogel in der alten Literatur und Kunst: Ein mythologisch-archaeologische Untersuchung*. Leipzig.
Weiss, N. 2014. "The Antiphonal Ending of Euripides' *Iphigenia in Aulis* (1475–1532)." *CPh* 109: 119–29.
———. 2016. "The Choral Architecture of Pindar's Eighth Paean." *TAPhA* 146: 237–55.

———. 2017. "Noise, Music, Speech: The Representation of Lament in Greek Tragedy." *AJP* 138: 243–66.

———. Forthcoming a. "Hearing the Syrinx in Euripidean Tragedy." In A. D'Angour and T. Phillips, eds., *Music, Texts, and Culture in Ancient Greece*. Oxford.

———. Forthcoming b. "Generic Hybridity in Athenian Tragedy." In L. Kurke, M. Foster, and N. Weiss, eds., *The Genres of Archaic and Classical Greek Poetry: Theories and Models*. Leiden.

Wellenbach, M. C. 2015. "The Iconography of Dionysiac *Choroi*: Dithyramb, Tragedy, and the Basel Krater." *GRBS* 55: 72–103.

West, M. L. 1981. "Tragica V." *BICS* 28: 61–78.

———. 1990. *Studies in Aeschylus*. Stuttgart.

———. 1992. *Ancient Greek Music*. Oxford.

———. 2005. "The New Sappho." *ZPE* 151: 1–9.

Whitman, C. H. 1974. *Euripides and the Full Circle of Myth*. Cambridge, MA.

Wilamowitz-Moellendorff, U. von, ed. 1895. *Euripides: Herakles*. Berlin.

———. 1921. *Griechische Verskunst*. Berlin.

Wiles, D. 1997. *Tragedy in Athens: Performance Space and Theatrical Meaning*. Cambridge.

———. 2000. *Greek Theatre Performance: An Introduction*. Cambridge.

———. 2010. "Greek and Shakespearean Plays in Performance." In E. Hall and S. Harrop, eds., *Theorising Performance: Greek Drama, Cultural History and Critical Practice*, 29–42. London.

Willink, C. W. 1971. "The Prologue of *Iphigenia at Aulis*." *CQ* 21: 343–64.

———. 1990. "The Parodos of Euripides' *Helen* (164–90)." *CQ* 40: 77–99.

———. 1999. Review of J. Chadwick, *Lexicographica Graeca: Contributions to the Lexicography of Ancient Greek* (1996). *JHS* 119: 175.

———. 2009. "Euripides, *Electra* 432–486 and *Iphigenia in Tauris* 827–899." In Cousland and Hume 2009: 205–17.

Wilson, P. 1999. "The *Aulos* in Athens." In Goldhill and Osborne 1999: 58–95.

———. 1999–2000. "Euripides' Tragic Muse." In Cropp, Lee, and Sansone: 427–49.

———. 2000. *The Athenian Institution of the Khoregia: The Chorus, the City, and the Stage*. Cambridge.

———. 2002. "The Musicians among the Actors." In P. Easterling and E. Hall, eds., *Greek and Roman Actors: Aspects of an Ancient Profession*, 39–68. Cambridge.

———. 2003. "The Politics of Dance: Dithyrambic Contest and Social Order in Ancient Greece." In D. J. Phillips and D. Pritchard, eds., *Sport and Festival in the Ancient Greek World*, 163–94. Swansea.

———. 2004. "Athenian Strings." In Murray and Wilson 2004: 269–306.

———. 2005. "Music." In J. Gregory, ed., *A Companion to Greek Tragedy*, 183–93. Malden, MA.

———. 2009. "Thamyris the Thracian: The Archetypal Wandering Poet?" In R. Hunter and I. Rutherford, eds., *Wandering Poets in Ancient Greek Culture*, 46–79. Cambridge.

Wilson, P., and O. Taplin. 1993. "The 'Aetiology' of Tragedy in the *Oresteia*." *PCPhS* 39: 169–80.

Winkler, J. J. 1990. "The Ephebes' Song: *Tragoidia* and *Polis*." In Winkler and Zeitlin 1990: 20–62.

Winkler, J. J., and F. I. Zeitlin, eds. 1990. *Nothing to Do with Dionysos? Athenian Drama in Its Social Context*. Princeton.

Winnington-Ingram, R. P. 1948. *Euripides and Dionysus: An Interpretation of the Bacchae*. Cambridge.
Wohl, V. 2015. *Euripides and the Politics of Form*. Princeton.
Wolff, C. 1973. "On Euripides' *Helen*." *HSPh* 77: 61–84.
———. 1992. "Euripides' *Iphigenia among the Taurians*: Aetiology, Ritual, and Myth." *ClAnt* 11: 308–34.
Wright, M. 2005. *Euripides' Escape-Tragedies: A Study of Helen, Andromeda, and Iphigenia among the Taurians*. Oxford.
———. 2010. "The Tragedian as Critic: Euripides and Early Greek Poetics." *JHS* 130: 165–84.
Young, D. C. 1968. *Three Odes of Pindar: A Literary Study of Pythian 11, Pythian 3, and Olympian 7*. Leiden.
Zacharia, K. 2003. *Converging Truths: Euripides' Ion and the Athenian Quest for Self-Definition*. Leiden.
Zarifi, Y. 2007. "Chorus and Dance in the Ancient World." In M. McDonald and J. M. Walton, eds., *The Cambridge Companion to Greek and Roman Theatre*, 227–46. Cambridge.
Zeitlin, F. I. 1970. "The Argive Festival of Hera and Euripides' *Electra*." *TAPhA* 101: 645–69.
———. 1990. "Playing the Other: Theater, Theatricality and the Feminine in Greek Drama." In Winkler and Zeitlin 1990: 63–96.
———. 1994. "The Artful Eye: Vision, Ecphrasis and Spectacle in Euripidean Theatre." In S. Goldhill and R. Osborne, eds., *Art and Text in Ancient Greek Culture*, 138–96. Cambridge.
———. 1995. "Art, Memory and *Kleos* in Euripides' *Iphigenia in Aulis*." In B. E. Goff, ed., *History, Tragedy, Theory: Dialogues on Athenian Drama*, 174–201. Austin.
———. 1996. *Playing the Other: Gender and Society in Classical Greek Literature*. Chicago.
———. 2010. "The Lady Vanishes: Helen and Her Phantom in Euripidean Drama." In P. Mitsis and C. Tsagalis, eds., *Allusion, Authority, and Truth: Critical Perspectives on Greek Poetic and Rhetorical Praxis*, 263–82. Berlin.
Zimmermann, B. 1992. *Dithyrambos: Geschichte einer Gattung*. Göttingen.
Zinar, R. 1971. "The Use of Greek Tragedy in the History of Opera." *Current Musicology* 12: 80–95.
Zuntz, G. 1960. "On Euripides' *Helena*: Theology and Irony." In J. C. Kamerbeek et al., *Euripide: Sept exposés et discussions*, 199–241. Geneva.
Zweig, B. 1999a. "Euripides' *Helen* and Female Rites of Passage." In M. W. Padilla, ed., *Rites of Passage in Ancient Greece: Literature, Religion, Society*, 158–82. Lewisburg, PA.
———. 1999b. "Introduction to Euripides' *Helen*." In R. Blondell et al., eds., *Women on the Edge: Four Plays by Euripides*, 219–36. New York.

# GENERAL INDEX

absence: embodied, 107n32; performed, 106–7, 121–23, 137–38; visual, 131n101
Achilles: armor of, 77–78, 80, 84, 85–90, 98, 197, 199, 219, 222; birth of, 219; death of, 219, 220; on François Vase, 219; in *Iphigenia in Aulis*, 200–201, 211; running, 196–98, 199; at Troy, 219–20
actor's song, 1, 11, 192, 224
Aegae, musical culture of, 242n35
Aelius Aristides, on Alcman, 32
Aeschylus: *Achilleis* trilogy, 80n72; *Bacchae*, 242; *Bassarids*, 44, 242; choral character in, 42–44, 57, 73, 242; choral transitions in, 38–39, 143; dominance of *choreia* in, 36; *Edonians*, 44; experimentation by, 45; *Eumenides*, 15, 38, 42–43, 47, 73; in *Frogs*, 2–3, 12–14, 44–45, 78; imaginative suggestion in, 39–42; *Libation Bearers*, 38, 39, 41, 42, 60, 73, 74, 135, 188, 229; metamusicality in, 38–46, 57; musical imagery in, 38; *Nereids*, 43–44, 45, 46, 79, 80; *Oresteia* trilogy, 38, 57; *Persians*, 12, 14, 39, 42, 48, 62–63, 102, 110–11, 135, 188, 230; *Prometheus Bound*, 61n6, 93, 196n20; proportion of lyric in, 7; *Proteus*, 143n15; ritual performance in, 42–44, 52; *Seven against Thebes*, 40–42, 99, 202n47; *Suppliants*, 7, 39, 42, 50, 160–61, 185n174
Agathon (tragic poet), 126–28
Alcaeus: Helen's *erōs* in, 205n58; marriage of Peleus and Thetis in, 211n85, 219

Alcman fr. 1 *PMGF* (first *Partheneion*): birds in, 28, 29, 112–13; chorus leaders of, 28–29, 67; horses in, 87, 198; imaginative suggestion in, 27–29, 236; metallic radiance in, 34, 67; *Pelēades* in, 28, 30, 51; *Pleiades* in, 28, 88n94; Sirens in, 32, 150, 153n56, 154
Alcman fr. 3 *PMGF*, sexual maturation in, 70n43
Allan, William, 157, 178
Amphion, founding of Thebes, 106n28
*Anakeia* festival, 189n187
animals, in *choreia*, 29–31, 55, 143. See also dolphins
Anthesteria festival, tragic performance at, 1n1
Archelaus, 242n35
Arion, founding of dithyramb, 79
Aristophanes: *Birds*, 30, 37, 67, 144, 160n81, 163, 164, 165–67, 185–86, 187, 216n101; *Clouds*, 124n88, 175n134, 176n136, 186; dance in, 14; dithyrambists in, 66, 185–86; on Euripides, 2–3, 8, 12, 13–14, 45, 78, 81, 202n46, 128; flight imagery of, 66, 185–86; *Frogs*, 2–3, 7, 12–13, 14, 37, 44–45, 78, 81, 199n29, 202n46, 224n127; on *Helen*, 143; *Lysistrata*, 37, 69, 141, 179, 184; metamusicality of, 37; nightingale in, 144, 160n81, 163, 164, 165–67; *Peace*, 186; *Wasps*, 14; *Women at the Thesmophoria*, 37, 143, 126–28
Aristotle: on auletes, 210; on cranes, 186n178; on *embolima*, 6, 58, 76; on *enthousiasmos*, 237,

267

268  GENERAL INDEX

Aristotle *(continued)*
    243; on *mousikē*, 5, 6, 13, 209n79, 237; on the nightingale, 159n76, 160n77; on *pathos*, 21, 243; on tragedy, 3–6
Athena, as inventor of *aulos*, 208n71
Athens, *passim;* auletes in, 208; burial rites in, 102n14; choral trends in, 126; female choruses at, 236n6; New Music in, 8–9, 96, 239; song culture of, 2; Telamon and, 130; tragedy in, 1–2, 3, 176n138; warning to, 101
Athenaeus: on Callias, 53n109; on *hyporchēmatikē*, 26n10; on *krotala*, 171n117; on *keleustēs* dance, 182
Attica: performance of tragedy in, 1n1; *theoxenia* rite in, 189n188; worship of Helen in, 179
audience: competence of, 80, 236n5, 237; embodied response of, 24n1, 237–38, 241, 243; engagement with Euripidean *mousikē*, 235–41; experience as performers, 2, 36, 236, 243; identification with chorus, 238n14; mental displacement of, 240; merging with chorus, 200; modes of viewing, 24, 26–29, 35, 81, 236; perception of images, 28; reception of sound, 16–17, 32–24; response to tragedy, 2, 5
aulete, 1; Aristotle on, 210; non-Athenian, 208; Plato on, 210; use of syrinx device, 207n68. *See also aulos*
*aulōidia*, 209n80
*aulos* (double-reed pipe), 1; accompanying actor's anapaests, 110n41; associated with maritime travel, 110, 181, 182; cheek straps of, 46n85; in *Electra*, 72, 73, 80, 92–93, 94, 207; in *Helen*, 155, 166–67, 168–69, 171, 174–76, 182, 186; invention of, 208; in *Iphigenia in Aulis*, 209–10, 212, 216, 223; *lōtos* pipe as, 120, 155, 212, 217; merging with syrinx, 17, 42, 55–56, 92–94, 130, 186, 206n60, 207n68, 208, 210, 212n89; mimeticism of, 120, 175–76, 209, 210, 212; nightingale and, 164n97, 166–67; Phrygian, 120, 207–8, 209; soundscape of, 207; as timing for rowers, 182; in *Trojan Women*, 110, 120, 122; vase paintings of, 12–13

Bacchylides: dithyramb of, 31–32, 35, 79; fawn imagery in, 71; imaginative suggestion in, 18, 31–32; Nereids in, 31–32, 67, 79, 198; on the nightingale, 160
Barker, Andrew, 159, 178
Barlow, S. A., 133n107
Batson, Charles, 121–22
Battezzato, Luigi, 109n37, 110n42, 122, 125, 130n99, 135, 176n139, 179n148, 184n171, 193n4

Biehl, W., 134n110
Bierl, Anton, 18
Bogart, Anna, 237n13
Bothe, F. H., 127n95
Bourdieu, Pierre, 237n7
Bühler, K., 131n101
Bundrick, S., 206n60
Burian, Peter, 157n68

Callias, *Alphabetic Tragedy*, 53n109
Catullus, Song of the Parcae, 219n112
Cephisophon, additions to *Iphigenia in Aulis*, 194n10
Chimaera, in *Electra*, 77, 89
Chionides (comic poet), 189n187
Chong-Gossard, Kim, 65
choral imaginary, 3, 17, 20, 23, 24, 29, 30, 36, 37, 42, 45, 52, 58, 59, 67, 68, 83–84, 117, 143, 146, 185–86, 199, 231
choral lyric, archaic: adaptation to tragedy, 24, 36–37; Aeschylus' use of, 45–46; avian imagery in, 29–30, 67n31, 87; divine *choreia* in, 67, 213; dolphins in, 30–31, 80; equine imagery in, 27–30, 87, 188; Euripides' use of, 10, 11, 17–18, 19, 24, 58, 144, 209–10, 235–39, 241; imaginative suggestion in, 23–36, 42, 214; metallic imagery in, 34–35; metamusical effects of, 10, 23, 23–36, 209, 210; mimetic enactment in, 209; nightingale in, 144; Sirens in, 31, 32–33, 144, 160; Sophocles' use of, 51; star imagery in, 27–30
choral odes, *passim;* joy-before-disaster, 19, 47–48, 49, 51, 57; strophe/antistrophe symmetry of, 84n84
choral odes, Euripidean, *passim;* dithyrambic character of, 9–10; doubleness in, 235–36; escapist, 76, 90, 91, 98, 117n67, 233; self-contained (*embolima*), 6, 9, 58, 76, 168; temporal patterns of, 204n55. *See also* choral odes; *choreia;* chorus, tragic; Euripides; *mousikē*
*choreia* (choral song and dance), *passim;* absent, 74, 100–116, 121–22, 128, 129, 137–38, 139, 146, 223; archetypes of, 67, 178, 213, 237; associational processes of, 23, 26–29, 33, 39; in Athenian life, 236; audience engagement with, 25, 29, 235–41; birds and, 29–30, 67, 185–86; characterization and, 60; civic function of, 3, 101, 105–6, 138; cosmic, 88, 153, 201–2; dolphins and, 17, 30–31, 79, 80–84, 90, 181–82, 236; epiphanic effect of, 12, 48, 99, 184, 188–89; generative power of, 54, 90–98; horses and, 29–30, 87–88, 170n113, 188, 198,

236; imaginative suggestion of, 17–18, 20, 23–36, 37, 39, 42, 46, 52, 55, 56, 60–61, 80, 81, 87, 88, 117, 138, 213; kinesthetic empathy in, 237; mystery cult and, 201–2; nightingale's initiation of, 167; Plato on, 3, 8, 25, 88–89, 105; precious objects and, 34–35, 198–99, 203; presencing effect of, 20, 48, 99, 104, 138, 189, 235; running and, 47, 196–97; social cohesion through, 105–6; social demarcation through, 60; spectators of, 200–203, 236–37, 244; stars and, 27–30, 51, 87, 88–89, 90, 95, 162, 201; as subset of *mousikē*, 25; traditional, 10, 18, 58, 191, 235, 236, 238, 241; transition to monody, 50–51, 192, 204, 224–31, 245; unity of song and dance in, 14–15, 23, 25–27, 234. *See also* choral lyric, archaic; choral odes, Euripidean; chorus, tragic; *mousikē*

*choreia*, Spartan: Athenian conceptualization of, 141

choreography. *See* dance

chorus, tragic, *passim*; act-dividing, 224; Aristotle on, 5–6; audience identification with, 238n14; dance formations of, 13; decline in importance, 6–8; female, 20, 60, 65–66, 69–70, 99, 102, 111–13, 116–30, 228, 234, 242; female protagonists and, 20, 60, 61–75, 99, 112–13, 135, 140–90, 228, 230, 234; fourth-century, 8n35; gender of, 6n29; hypermimetic, 236, 245; self-referential, 15, 16, 18, 19, 25; size of, 1n2; vase images of, 12–13. *See also* choral odes; choral odes, Euripidean; *choreia*; *mousikē*

Cinesias (dithyrambist), 8

City Dionysia, 1; ritual context of, 9, 19, 52, 54n112, 176, 181, 243

Conacher, D. J., 225n128

Croally, N. T., 113n52

Cropp, M., 94n114, 142n8

Csapo, Eric, 8, 9, 59, 77, 81n76, 84n83, 86n85, 87, 94, 117, 201

Cybele. *See* Great Mother

Dale, A. M., 185n173, 220n114

dance, *passim*; in Aristophanes, 14; circular, 9, 80, 86–87, 88, 89, 95, 153, 170, 177–78, 184n169, 188, 197, 201n41, 214, 221, 229–30; crane, 186; in Dionysiac ritual, 48; dolphins', 14, 20, 30, 42, 79, 80–84, 87, 89, 181–82; ecphrasis and, 85–87; fifth-century tragic, 11; formations in tragedy, 13; *hormos* (chain), 68; kinesthetic empathy in, 14n66, 24n1, 237; Nereids' association with, 9, 31, 79–80, 198, 201, 214; in opera, 2n5; relationship to song, 14–15, 26–29; in satyr play, 12, 37n48; *sikinnis*, 37n48; whirling (*hēlissein*), 9, 68, 80, 81, 108, 115, 170n113, 177, 188, 197, 198–99, 202, 214, 229. *See also choreia*; *mousikē*

Dance Studies, 236–37

D'Angour, A., 12n52, 25n6, 53n109

Dante, sound in, 172n120

Delos, crane dance at, 186

Delphi: auletic contest at, 33; temple of Apollo at, 34–35, 106n28, 195n17

Demeter: search for daughter, 168; syncretism with Great Mother, 168, 169, 174n131, 176; worship at Mysteries, 177n140. *See also* Great Mother

Diggle, J., 226n130

Dillon, E., 172n120

Dionysiac cult: in *Bacchae*, 242; cries in, 114, 174n128; in *Helen*, 141, 177–79, 181, 189, 190; *mousikē* of, 18, 35–36, 44, 168–69, 171, 175–79, 181, 241–46; star choruses of, 88

Dionysus: Bromios, 171, 175n134, 176, 177; destructive power of, 243, 244; *Dithyrambus*, 242; on François Vase, 215; in *Frogs*, 2, 3; Iacchus song to, 133; syncretism with Great Mother, 168n108, 169, 171, 178

Dioskouroi: in *Helen*, 179, 180, 187–89; hymns to, 188n185; in Pindar, 189; *theoxenia* festival of, 189

dithyramb: animal choruses and, 30n23; Arion's founding of, 79; circular formation of, 86–87, 178; dolphins' association with, 30, 80, 81–84, 86n85, 181; Euripides' use of, 9–10, 45, 76, 87, 89, 116, 124, 125, 168, 181, 194, 198, 241–42; flight imagery in, 67, 185; imaginary of, 79, 80, 81, 83, 181; narrative perspective of, 117n66; Nereids' association with, 9, 32, 36, 45, 79, 86n85, 198, 245; New Music and, 9, 76, 117, 214; sea travel and, 79, 84, 181; social order and, 105

dolphins: *choreia* and, 17, 30–31, 79, 80–84, 90, 181–82, 236; dancing, 14, 20, 30, 42, 79, 80–84, 87, 89, 181–82; dithyramb and, 30, 80, 81–84, 86n85, 181; in *Electra*, 79, 80, 81–82, 84, 87, 89, 90, 138; in *Helen*, 14, 20, 30, 42, 79, 181–82; human hybrids of, 81; with riders, 30, 43, 82–85; in vase paintings, 30, 79, 80, 81–82

ecphrasis: in *Electra*, 75–91; in *Iliad*, 88; in *Ion*, 195n17; in *Iphigenia in Aulis*, 195, 198; performed, 75–91

Eleusinian Mysteries, 88, 201, 243; star choruses of, 88; syncretism in, 176
Elsner, Jás, 240
*embolima*, 6; Aristotle on, 6, 58, 76; of *Helen*, 168. *See also* choral odes
epinician, 10; choreography of epode, 90; in *Electra*, 71; generic mixing of, 18, 124, 126; in *Heracles*, 126n92; imaginative suggestion in, 35; *kōmos* in, 184; in *Trojan Women*, 124, 130, 131n102
Euripides: adaptation of traditional forms, *passim*, esp. 10, 18, 58, 191, 235, 236, 238, 241; *Aeolus*, 209; *Alcestis*, 38, 55–56, 57; *Alcmeon in Corinth*, 191n1; *Alexander*, 104, 105n23, 122, 123; *Andromache*, 61; *Andromeda*, 61, 66, 142, 143n8, 145, 152–53; *Antiope*, 61n6, 106n28; archaizing by, 24, 58, 181n156, 242, 246; Aristotle on, 5, 6; *Bacchae*, 6, 7, 9, 42, 120, 175n134, 191, 241–46; *Children of Heracles*, 53, 54, 57; chronology of, 21; *Cresphontes*, 144n17, 161–62; death of, 194; *Electra*, 11, 14, 19, 20, 37, 54, 57, 59–99, 109, 110, 113, 117, 141, 181, 186, 190, 192, 196, 198, 199, 206, 207, 222, 233, 235, 236; female chorus in, 20, 60, 65–66, 69–70, 99, 102, 111–13, 116–30, 228, 234, 242; female protagonists of, *passim*, esp. 20, 61–75, 234; in *Frogs*, 2–3, 12–14, 44–45, 78; genre mixing by, *passim*, esp. 10, 13, 56, 124–26, 155, 228–29; *Hecuba*, 7, 57n117, 61, 119–20; *Helen*, 11, 17, 20, 34, 56, 61, 63, 65, 70, 75, 87–88, 99, 101, 106, 110, 112, 113, 123, 140–90, 191–92, 212n89, 230, 233, 234, 236, 240n23; *Heracles*, 9n41, 17, 19, 64n20, 72n47, 102n13, 117, 125–26, 133, 192, 231, 244; *Hippolytus*, 56–57, 185; *Hypsipyle*, 14, 61n6, 61n6, 194, 202–3; interpolations in, 226n133; *Ion*, 61n6, 62, 88, 194, 195n17, 201–2; *Iphigenia in Aulis*, 6, 7, 12, 18, 19, 20, 21, 29, 40n59, 67, 80, 92, 99, 114, 138, 191–232, 234, 241, 245–46; *Iphigenia in Tauris*, 29–30, 42, 65, 78, 88, 101, 113, 141, 146n21, 180, 182, 198; in Macedon, 7, 242n35; *Medea*, 53–54, 57, 61n6; musical innovations of, *passim*, esp. 10, 23, 35, 58, 233–46; New Music and, 8, 9–10, 58, 103, 116–30, 172, 214, 235–41; *Oedipus*, 167n106; *Orestes*, 12–13, 102n13; *Palamedes*, 104–5, 122–23; *Phaethon*, 161, 162–63; *Phoenician Women*, 73n50, 163n96, 194n14; proportion of lyric in, 7; *Sisyphus*, 139; *Suppliants*, 154n62; *Trojan Women*, 8n40, 16, 19–20, 41, 60, 61, 63, 73, 74, 75, 100–139, 141, 146, 148, 155, 192, 193, 211, 223, 230, 233, 234, 238n14, 243. *See also* choral odes, Euripidean
Euripides minor, 191n1

Ford, A., 147n25, 164n98
François Vase (Kleitias): Achilles on, 219; Calliope on, 214, 223; marriage of Peleus and Thetis on, 213n92, 214; procession of gods on, 214–15; sympotic context of, 219n111; use at wedding, 215n97

Gagné, R., 93n111, 95n118
Gellie, George, 76
Glück, Christoph Willibald: *Iphigénie en Tauride*, 2n5
*goos*. *See* lament
Gorgon: *aulos* and, 33; cry of, 33, 153; in *Electra*, 86, 90
Great Mother (Cybele): cultic *mousikē* of, 36, 169, 171, 172, 174–76; cult in Greece, 179; in *Helen*, 165, 168–79, 236, 240n23; instruments associated with, 168–69; as *mater dolorosa*, 168; reconciliation to loss, 173–75; search for Kore, 169–70; syncretism with Demeter, 168, 169, 174n131, 176; syncretism with Dionysus, 168n108, 169, 171, 178
Gregory, J., 112n47
Griffith, M., 37n48
Gurd, S. A., 16n73

Haigood, Joanna: *Ghost Architecture*, 35n43
Haldane, J. A., 40
*harmonia*: Aristotle on, 13; Phrygian, 120n72, 208; Plato on, 89, 153
Harpies, 151n41
Hector: death of, 89–90, 112; marriage of, 34, 215–16
Helen: birth of, 142, 143n13, 144, 164; as *chorēgos*, *passim*, esp. 141; in *Helen*, *passim*, esp. 140–90; in *Iliad*, 112, 125n90, 140; in *Lysistrata*, 69, 141, 184; as parthenaic figure, 70, 150–52, 155, 165, 167n107, 178; as protean figure, *passim*, esp. 142–44; in Spartan cult, 141, 179, 182, 183–84, 189, 234; Stesichorus on, 143n15; Theocritus's epithalamium for, 141; in *Thesmophoriazusae*, 143; in *Trojan Women*, 101, 103
Henrichs, Albert, 15, 18, 25, 50, 47–48, 54n112
Heraia festival: in *Electra*, 65, 66, 67, 69, 70, 71; ritual celebrations at, 69n41, 98
Hesiod, on Muses, 132, 214n96
*Homeric Hymn to Apollo*, 68, 140, 237
*Homeric Hymn to Demeter*, 175n131
*Homeric Hymn to Dionysus*, 79, 81n76
*Homeric Hymn to Hermes*, 207
*Homeric Hymn to the Dioskouroi*, 188–89

*Homeric Hymn to the Mother of the Gods:* 172, 175
Hopman, M. G., 93n111, 95n118
Horace, 127n95
Hyacinthia festival, 183; aetiology for, 184
Hyagnis, 208
*hymenaios* (wedding song), 10, 215n98; in *Agamemnon*, 129; in *Birds*, 216n101; in *Iphigenia in Aulis*, 18, 19, 20, 114, 211–24; in Sappho, 215–16; in *Trojan Women*, 103, 113–16, 129, 130, 211, 223
*hyporchēmata*, imaginative suggestion in, 26–27

Iamblichus, on cosmic harmony, 153
*Iliad*: Achilles' shield in, 88, 89, 197, 199; Andromache in, 114n56, 228n141; Catalogue of Ships, 193n; Hector's death in, 112; Helen in, 125, 140; lament in, 63, 112, 124, 140, 228n141; Paris in, 123, 205n59; Sirens and, 154; sonic effects of, 132; syrinx and *aulos* in, 208; Teichoscopia in, 193n5
imaginative suggestion: *passim*, esp. 17–18, 20, 23–36, 37, 39, 42, 46, 52, 55, 56, 60–61, 80, 81, 87, 88, 117, 138, 213. *See also choreia*
instrumentation: auditory reception of, *passim*, esp. 16; foreign, 120, 175, 207, 208; of Great Mother, 168–69, 175–78; imaginative suggestion of, *passim*, esp. 33–34; mimetic, 92–93, 171, 209–10, 212, 216; mixed, 172–73; Sirens and, 154–55. *See also* names of instruments

Kabuki, imaginative suggestion in, 26n12
*kallinikos* song, 72
Kannicht, R., 147n25, 171n117, 178
kithara: in *Alcestis*, 55; combined with *aulos*, 125, 126, 209; in *Iphigenia in Aulis*, 212, 223; Paris and, 123, 205n59; in Sappho, 34, 216; Sirens and, 154; Sophocles' playing of, 46n82; suggested by *aulos*, 55–56, 212; suggesting other instruments, 34, 209–10, 216; in *Thamyras*, 47; in Timotheus, 240; in *Women at the Thesmophoria*, 128
kitharodic song: in *Clouds*; in *Helen*, 147; musical innovation in, 8, 35n44, 96, 123, 240; in *Thamyras*, 47; in *Trojan Women*, 124, 125
*kitharōidia*, 209n80
Kleitias. *See* François Vase
Korybantes: in *Bacchae*, 242; ritual of, 243
Kovacs, David, 218n108, 226, 227n135, 227n136
Kowalzig, Barbara, 81, 84
Kranz, Walter, 8n40, 9, 24n4, 59, 116, 117n63, 168

*krotala* (castanets): associated with Great Mother, 168, 169, 172, 175; in *Frogs*, 3, 202n46; linked to elemental sound, 170; suggested by *aulos*, 34, 171; suggested by kithara, 216; suggested by meter, 171
Kurke, Leslie, 34–35, 200

lament: antiphonal, 42, 62–63, 65n23, 73, 74, 101, 112–13, 134–35, 146, 148, 230; association with foreigners, 42, 102; association with swans, 64; in Athenian culture, 102; for cities, 106n29; in Euripides' *Electra*, 61–64, 66, 69, 73, 74, 75, 97; false, 159; female characters', 102–3; gestures of, 41, 42, 135n112, 137, 156; *goos*, 61, 62, 63, 147, 228n141; in *Helen*, 61, 65n23, 101, 141, 144–67, 187, 189, 234; in *Iliad*, 63, 112, 124, 140, 228n141; in *Iphigenia in Aulis*, 192, 228, 230; in *Iphigenia in Tauris*, 65n23, 142; in *Libation Bearers*, 38, 39, 41, 42, 65, 73, 74, 135; male, 102n13; nightingales' association with, 161–62; percussive element of, 41, 137; in *Persians*, 62–63, 102, 135; Procne's, 161; repetitive language in, 132n103; ritual, 42, 135; Solon's regulations on, 102n14; in Sophocles' *Electra*, 61; in *Suppliants* (Euripides), 154n62; *thrēnos*, 63, 147n27, 228n141; in *Trojan Women*, 61, 63, 101–3, 106–13, 116, 128–29, 131–37, 234
Lawler, Lillian, 68, 182n158
Lehnus, L., 155n65
Leucippides, cult of, 183, 184n171
Le Ven, P., 240
Loraux, N., 133n109
*lōtos* pipe. *See aulos.*
Lucian, on *hormos* (chain) dance, 68

Macedon, Euripides in, 7, 242n35
marriage, conflation with funerary ritual, 222n119. *See also* Hector; *hymenaios;* Peleus and Thetis, marriage of
Marshall, C. W., 87n87, 142, 157n69, 164n100
Marsyas: father of Olympus, 208; satyr with *aulos*, 208n71
Mastronarde, Donald J., 56n115, 221
Meineck, P., 237n13
Melanippides (dithyrambist), 8, 10
melisma: acoustic effect of, 81; Euripides' use of, 12, 14
Mellert-Hoffmann, G., 203n51
*melopoiia* (musical part of tragedy), Aristotle on, 4–6
Melos: Athenian atrocities at, 101, 139

metamusicality, *passim*, esp. 8, 15, 25; in Aeschylus, 38–46; in archaic lyric, 25–36; in Aristophanes, 37; in early Euripides, 52–58; in later Euripides, *passim*; in satyr play, 37, 56; Sophoclean, 46–52. *See also choreia*; imaginative suggestion; *mousikē*
Michelakis, P., 225n128
Michelini, A. N., 213n91
mimesis, 16, 209; Aristotle on, 209n79; choral roles as, 29; in *hyporchēmata*, 26; instrumental, 209–10; Plato on, 16, 172–73, 209n79; tragedy as, 4; *See also* mimeticism
mimeticism: of *aulos*, 120, 209, 210, 212; of *Bacchae*, 242; of Helen, 143n14; in *Helen*, 172–73, 182; hypermimetic, 236, 245; instrumental, 209; in *Iphigenia in Aulis*, 20, 209–10; of New Music, 239; Plato on, 172–73, 239; in *Trojan Women*, 136. *See also* imaginative suggestion; metamusicality; mimesis.
monody: in *Andromeda*, 61; in *Antigone*, 231; *choreia* and, 50–51, 192, 204, 224–31, 245; in *Electra*, 61–64, 99, 110; in *Helen*, 145, 150, 156; in *Heracles*, 231; in *Hypsipyle*, 61n6; in *Ion*, 62; in *Iphigenia in Aulis*, 20, 204, 206, 207, 224–30; in *Medea*, 61n6; transition to *choreia*, 192, 231; in *Trojan Women*, 74, 106–13; in *Women of Trachis*, 192, 231
mourning. *See* lament
*mousikē* (music, song, dance), *passim*; affective impact of, 4, 13, 19, 21, 235–41, 243, 245; Aristotle on, 4, 13, 243; choral character and, 42–44, 102, 242; continuity in, 57; cultural inclusiveness of, 2n6; described/imagined and performed, *passim*, esp. 15–16, 18, 23, 24, 35, 37, 46, 53, 56, 57, 61, 88, 93, 117, 121, 136, 143, 179, 190, 203, 210, 212, 233, 234–35, 239; different registers of, 16; Dionysiac, 18, 35–36, 44, 168–69, 171, 175–79, 181, 241–46; dramatic narrative and, *passim*, esp. 6–9, 20, 38–39, 44, 47, 54, 57–58, 59, 98, 101–2, 141–42, 168, 179, 189–90, 231, 233, 235–38, 241, 245; dramatic role of, *passim*, esp. 6–9, 18–21, 37, 38–39, 57–58, 233, 235–38, 240–41; engagement with audience, 235–41; examination through text, 14–18; experimentation in, *passim*, esp. 8, 19, 21, 23, 36, 37, 54, 59–60, 143, 146, 233, 235; in founding of cities, 106n29; hypermimeticism of, 236, 238, 245; innovation in, *passim*, esp. 8–10, 123–30, 239; *katharsis* through, 5n23; mimetic, 209n79; mixing genres of, 10, 125–26; and musical imaginary, 11, 231; *mythos* and, *passim*, esp. 6–11, 20, 98, 223,

235, 246; *pathos* and, 21; presencing effect of, 138; terminology of, 11n49; as totality, 11, 23, 25; in tragedy, *passim*, esp. 2–21. *See also choreia*; metamusicality; New Music; names of individual tragedians
Mullen, William, 223
Murnaghan, S., 107n32
Muses: as archetypal chorus, 31; beautiful-haired, 213; on François Vase, 214–15; golden-sandaled, 67; in Hesiod, 132; in *Iphigenia in Aulis*, 213, 217, 220, 222; in Pindar, 31, 213, 214; in Sappho, 213n90; in *Trojan Women*, 123–24, 128
music, *passim*; Aristotle on, 4; ethical characterization in, 4n21; kinetic response to, 47; and mimesis, 16, 172–73, 209; production of emotion, 237n11; semiotics of, 14n66. *See also choreia*; *mousikē*
musical culture, Greek, 2n6; of Aegae, 242n35; audience immersion in, 235, 238; experimentation in, 23. *See also choreia*; *mousikē*
musical notation, survival of, 12
*mythos* (plot structure): Aristotle on, 4, 5; audience anticipation of, 19; choral self-referentiality and, 19; *choreia* and, *passim*; *mousikē* and, *passim*, esp. 6–11, 20, 168, 190, 205, 220, 223, 233–35, 246.

Nagy, Gregory, 29, 161
Nausicaa, 70; as *chorēgos*, 69
Neer, Richard, 235n2
Neitzel, H., 6n27
Nereids: association with dance, 9, 31, 79–80, 198, 201, 214; association with dithyramb, 9, 32, 36, 45, 79, 86n85, 198, 245; in Bacchylides, 31–32, 67, 79, 198; in *Electra*, 77–81, 84–87, 89, 90, 138, 198, 199; in *Iphigenia in Aulis*, 198–99, 214, 217–18, 220, 222, 245; in New Music, 79; riding dolphins, 43–44, 82, 83n; in *Trojan Women*, 107, 108; in vase painting, 43
New Music: as cultural movement, 8, 239; dithyramb and, 9, 76, 117, 214; drama's participation in, 9; in *Electra*, 59; engagement with audience, 235, 240; Euripides' involvement in, 8, 9–10, 58, 103, 116–30, 172, 214, 239; hanging apostrophe in, 78; of *Helen*, 167–79, 181n156; innovation prior to, 10, 24; mimeticism of, 239; mixing of genres in, 125; modern scholarship on, 45; modulatory style of, 162n89; Nereids in, 79; old/new combinations in, 10n47; Plato on, 13, 125, 172; self-referentiality

GENERAL INDEX    273

in, 76; Sophocles and, 46–47; Timotheus and, 240; in *Trojan Women*, 103, 116–30

nightingale: in *Agamemnon*, 160; in *Ajax*, 160; as aulete, 166n105; in *Birds*, 144, 160n81, 163, 164, 165–67; in *Cresphontes*, 161–62; in Greek lyric, 160; in *Helen*, 144, 158–67, 183; as initiator of *choreia*, 167; lament and, 161–62; musicality of, 163; in *Phaethon*, 161–63; Pliny on, 159n76, 160n77, 167n106; in *Suppliants* (Aeschylus), 160–61; as symbol of composition, 161; in *Tereus*, 160n82, 165

Noh: imaginative suggestion in, 26n12

*Odyssey*: environmental sound in, 132; Helen in, 140; Nausicaa in, 69, 150; nightingale in, 159n76, 160n77; Sirens in, 150, 153, 154n60, 155

Old Comedy: choral self-referentiality in, 18

Olsen, Sarah, 132n106, 237

Oltos Psykter, 30, 82–83

Olympus (musician), 208; *auloi* of, 207; as *barbaros*, 207n65

opera: libretto in, 2n5; parallel to tragedy, 2

*opsis* (spectacle): Aristotle on, 4

*orchēstra* (performance space), 1; aulete in, 207; dance in, *passim*, esp. 61, 81, 121, 177, 195, 196, 197, 214; shape of, 1n3

Orestes, epinician imagery and, 71n46

paean: in *Agamemnon*, 39–40, 229; to Artemis, 225–31, 233; battle, 110–11, 228, 229; circular dance of, 229; city building and, 106; to the dead, 147–48; dithyramb and, 32n29; female performance of, 39–40, 199, 228–29; generic mixing of, 18, 49; in *Helen*, 147–48; imaginative suggestion in, 34–35; in *Iphigenia in Aulis*, 225–31; joy-before-disaster odes and, 19, 47–48; lament and, 38, 147–48; in *Libation Bearers*, 229; marker of Greekness, 110–11; in *Trojan Women*, 110–11; in *Women of Trachis*, 229; in Xenophon, 228

Pan: association with paean, 48n94; as chorus leader, 48

Panagl, O., 213n93

Paris: as *barbaros*, 207n65, 208; kithara and, 123, 205n59; music of, 205–8, 210

*partheneia* (maidens' songs), 10; communality in, 60, 99; in *Electra*, 65–66, 99; equine imagery in, 30, 87–88, 199; generic mixing of, 18, 49; in *Helen*, 143–44, 145, 148, 150–52, 155, 165, 170, 178, 187, 199; imaginative suggestion of, 35; in *Iphigenia in Aulis*, 199; lament and, 150, 152–53; marriage and, 70, 121, 144; Sirens and, 150–53, 154, 165; in *Trojan Women*, 121, 127

*pathos*, 21, 237, 243

*Peleades* (doves), 28; linked to *Pleiades*, 28, 30

Peleus and Thetis, marriage of: in Alcaeus, 211n85, 219; on François Vase, 213n92, 214–15; in *Iphigenia in Aulis*, 192, 204, 211–21, 245; in Pindar, 213, 214, 219

Peponi, Anastasia-Erasmia, 3, 5, 26n11, 27, 32, 200n, 236n35

Performance Studies, 121

Perithoos and Hippodameia, wedding of, 218

Persians, Greek conceptualization of, 42, 102

Pherecrates, 8, 10, 96

Philodamus of Scarpheia, 106n28

phorminx: Apollo's, 167; in *Helen*, 149n34, 155n64, 212n89

Phrynis (kitharode), 8

Pindar: absent *hymenaios* in, 114–15; on Achilles at Troy, 219; on *aulos*, 33, 209, 210; *choreia* linked to physical environment, 106n28; chorus as precious objects in, 34–35, 199; Dionysiac *mousikē* in, 35–36, 243; Dioskouroi in, 189; dithyramb of, 35–36, 243; dolphins in, 30–31; fall of Troy in, 131; *hyporchēmata* of, 26–27; imaginative suggestion in, 18, 26–27, 30–31, 33, 34, 35–36; *kōmos* in, 184; on marriage of Peleus and Thetis, 219; Muses in, 18, 31, 213, 214, 221; Sirens in, 33, 150–51, 154

Plato: on *aulos*, 210; on *choreia*, 3, 8, 25, 88–89, 105; on cosmic harmony, 88, 89, 153; on genre mixing, 209, 229; on mimeticism, 172–73, 209n79, 239; on *mousikē*, 25; on New Music, 13, 125, 172, 239; on tragedy, 3, 7–8

*Pleiades* (star cluster), 28; as chorus, 28, 87, 88, 162, 187

Pliny the Elder, on nightingales, 159n76, 160n77, 167n106

Plutarch, on words and dance, 25–26

Podlecki, A. J., 178n144

Porter, J., 41n64

Power, Timothy, 46–47, 93

Pratinas, 37–38, 239

Prins, Yopie, 43

Procne: in *Birds*, 165–66; lament of, 161n85; transformation into nightingale, 160. *See also* nightingale

projection, choral, 15, 16, 17, 24, 117; ritual and, 18

protagonists, female, 20, 99; link to *mousikē*, 234; monodies of, 145; relationship with chorus,

protagonists *(continued)*
  20, 60, 61–75, 99, 112–13, 135, 140–90, 228, 230, 234
Pucci, Pietro, 164, 178n146

*Relâche* (ballet), 121
Robinson, D. B., 178n144
Rode, J., 76n59
Rural Dionysia, 1n1
Rutherford, Ian, 19, 48, 148n28, 228, 230n146

Sansone, David, 124, 125n91
Sappho: Aphrodite in, 213n9; hymenaeal *mousikē* in, 212n89, 215–16; on inability to dance, 108; instrumental layering in, 34, 212n89, 216; Muses in, 213n90; on the nightingale, 160; wedding songs of, 114, 216n100
satyr play: dance in, 12; experimentation in, 56; musicality of, 37, 56; pastoral elements of, 56n114
Scott, William, 38n56, 50
sculpture, Greek: Euripidean *choreia* and, 235n2; naturalism in, 241n27
Segal, C., 182n162
self-referentiality, choral, *passim*, esp. 15, 16, 18, 25; avian imagery and, 87; equine imagery and, 87; New Music and, 76; ritual aspect of, 18–19, 43
Shakespeare, William: polyphony in, 16
Sicilian Expedition, Athenian, 101
Sifakis, G. M., 4n21, 82n79
Sirens: in Alcman, 32, 153n54, 154; in *Andromeda*, 152–53; in Hesiodic *Catalogue of Women*, 151; chthonic aspects of, 152; on funerary monuments, 155; in *Helen*, 144–56, 159, 163–66, 183; imaginative suggestion and, 32–33; instruments of, 154–55; mother of, 153; as mourners, 152n49; Muses and, 154; musical skill of, 153; in *Odyssey*, 150, 153, 154n60, 155; parthenaic, 150–53, 154, 165; Persephone and, 151–52; in Pindar, 33, 150, 154; vase depictions of, 151n44, 154
Skaggs, Sarah: *9/11 Dance*, 100, 138
*skēnē*, of tragic theater, 1
Smith, Bruce, 16
Smith, W., 200n39
Sophilos Dinos, 213n92, 215, 223
Sophocles: actor's song in, 7n30; *Ajax*, 47–49, 160; *Antigone*, 51–52, 54, 88; Aristotle on, 5, 6; choral imagery in, 51–52; chorus's integration in, 5, 6, 52; *Electra*, 61, 64, 65; *Ichneutae*, 37, 56, 58; *Inachus*, 37; metamusicality in, 46–52, 57; musical transitions in, 49–50, 143, 192; *Mysians*, 46; New Music and, 46–47; *Oedipus Tyrannus*, 106n27; performative language of, 46; proportion of lyric in, 7; reputation as musician, 46; use of *mousikē*, 46–52; satyr plays, 52; *Tereus*, 160n82, 165, 166; *Thamyras*, 46n82, 47, 52, 58; *Tympanistae*, 46; *Women of Trachis*, 49–50, 52n106, 53–54, 188, 192, 229, 231.
sound, *passim*; imaginative suggestion of, 32–34; registers of, 16
soundscape: foreign, 207, 208; multilayered, 215; of Timotheus's *Persians*, 240
Sound Studies, 16
spectatorship, choral, 193–94; in *Iphigenia in Aulis*, 193–204; audience participation and, 237n13.
Sphinx, in *Electra*, 86, 89
stage directions, 16n72
star shields, Greek tradition of, 88
Stehle, E., 33n35
Steiner, Deborah: 153n58, 181, 184n169; 186n178, 188
Stesichorus, on Helen, 143n15
Stockert, W., 198n29, 209n75, 227n134
Suter, Ann, 131–32
Swift, Laura, 10, 121, 178
syrinx: association with reeds (*donakes, kalamoi*), 93, 207n68; association with wedding music, 223; Calliope and, 223; in *Electra*, 92–93, 94, 206; in *Helen*, 149, 154, 155n, 186, 212n64; in *Homeric Hymn to Hermes*, 207; in *Inachus*, 37; imitation of snake, 207n68; in *Iphigenia in Aulis*, 205–10, 222–23; merging with *aulos*, 42n, 55–56, 92–94, 130, 186n, 208, 210, 212n; Pan and, 92, 206n62; pastoral, 92, 206–7, 223; in *Prometheus Bound*, 93; soundscape of, 207; in *Trojan Women*, 130; in vase painting, 206n62, 223

Tanner, J., 241n27
Taplin, O., 38n55, 176n138, 244n42
television drama, musical, 2
Tereus, in *Birds*, 163, 164n97, 166–67
Theater of Dionysus, 1; musical experience in, 176
Thebes, mythic construction of, 106n28
Theocritus, epithalamium for Helen, 141
Theophrastus, 228
Thomas, O., 53n109

*thrēnos. See* lament

Thucydides: on Athenian burial rites, 102n14; on paeans, 228

Timotheus (kitharode), 8; associated with Euripides, 210; mimeticism of, 240; New Music and, 8, 35n44, 123, 240; *Persians*, 35n44, 111, 240

Torrance, I., 124n84

tragedy, *passim;* Aristotle on, 3–6; audience expectations of, 146–47; audience response to, 2; civic importance of, 3; Dionysiac context of, 18; metamusical language in, *passim,* esp. 8, 10, 15, 36–58, 235–36; mixing of genres in, 18, 125–26, 229; musical performance in, *passim,* esp. 1–6, 11–14; negated song in, 106; Plato on, 3; pleasure in, 4, 101n5; quantitative elements of, 5n24; revival in opera, 2n5; structure of, 1; as type of *mousikē,* 11n49; visual perception in, 131n101

Troy: past *choreia* in, 118–30; performed fall of, 130–38

vase painting: avian choruses on, 185; dolphins on, 30, 79, 81–83; hoplites on, 82–83; marriage of Peleus and Thetis on, 213n92, 214–15; Muses on, 214–15; musical images in context, 211n88; tragic *mousikē* on, 12–13; Nereids on, 43; Sirens on, 151n, 154; syrinx on, 206n62

Wallace, R. W., 208n71
Walsh, G. B., 91n103, 220n113
West, M. L., 208n69
Wiles, D., 84n84, 194n13, 197n24, 199n34, 203n50, 220
Willamowitz-Moellendorff, U. von, 117n63, 124
Willink, C. W., 79n70, 84n82, 194n10
Wilson, Peter, 9n41, 38n55, 46n82, 106n30, 176n138, 216n103
Wohl, Victoria, 101n6, 238
Wright, M., 142n8

Xenophon, paeans in, 228

Young, David, 114–15

Zarifi, Y., 244n42
Zeitlin, Froma, 195, 200, 204

# INDEX LOCORUM

| | | | | | |
|---|---|---|---|---|---|
| Aeschylus | | | 623–80 | | 12 |
| *Agamemnon* | | | 918–1076 | | 132n103 |
| 228–30 | | 40 | 1046 | | 42 |
| 240–47 | | 39, 229 | 1046–58 | | 62–63 |
| 688–98 | | 39 | 1048–49 | | 135 |
| 699–716 | | 129–30 | *Seven Against Thebes* | | |
| 1142 | | 38 | 83–89 | | 40 |
| 1142–45 | | 160, 163 | 100–103 | | 41 |
| 1130–77 | | 116 | 151 | | 40 |
| 1178–330 | | 116 | 158 | | 40 |
| *Bassarids* | | | 854–56 | | 41 |
| fr. 23a | | 44 | *Suppliants* | | |
| *Edonians* | | | 58–71 | | 50, 160–61 |
| fr. 57 | | 44 | 392–95 | | 161 |
| *Eumenides* | | | 540–79 | | 39 |
| 307 | | 43 | 779–83 | | 161 |
| 368–76 | | 43 | 782 | | 185n174 |
| 1047 | | 38n55 | 792–99 | | 161 |
| *Libation Bearers* | | | [Aeschylus] | | |
| 149–51 | | 229 | *Prometheus Bound* | | |
| 306–478 | | 65, 73 | 88–127 | | 61n6 |
| 423–28 | | 42, 135 | 128–30 | | 196n20 |
| 427–28 | | 41 | 574–75 | | 93 |
| 794–99 | | 197n21 | | | |
| *Nereids* | | | Alcaeus | | |
| fr. 150 | | 43, 79–80 | fr. 42 Voigt | | |
| *Persians* | | | 15–16 | | 211n85, 219 |
| 388–94 | | 110–11 | fr. 283 Voigt | | |
| 619–21 | | 39 | | | 205n58 |

277

278    INDEX LOCORUM

Alcman
fr. 1 *PMGF*
   40–43    67
   45–63    27–29, 34, 236
   51–54    67
   58–59    87–88
   60–63    88
   85–87    112–13
   64–69    67
   96–99    32
fr. 30 *PMGF*    32, 153n56

Apollonius Rhodius
*Argonautica*
   4.898    151

Aristophanes
*Birds*
   209    163–64, 187
   209–14    165–67
   217–22    167
   676–84    166–67
   1388–90    67
*Clouds*
   311–13    176n136
   313    175n134
   333    186
   595    124n88
*Frogs*
   933    199n29
   1028–29    14
   1301–3    13–14
   1305–6    3, 202n46
   1309–19    78
   1309–23    14
   1313–19    81
   1314    12
   1329–33    14
   1419    3
   1435–36    3
   1526–27    3
*Lysistrata*
   1295    37
   1296–321    179, 184
   1315    69, 141
*Peace*
   830    186
   831    186
*Wasps*
   1512–37    14

*Women at the Thesmophoria*
   101–29    126–28
   850    143

Aristotle
*History of Animals*
   632b24    159n76
*Poetics*
   1449a33–34    21
   1449b24–26    4
   1449b28    4
   1450a8–b20    4–5
   1452a2–1454a15    21
   1452b13–24    5n24
   1453a29–30    238
   1453b3–6    4
   1456a25–31    5, 6, 52
   1461b30–32    210
   1462a15–16    4n22
*Politics*
   1339a11–1342b35    4
   1340a8–14    237
   1340a23    13
   1341a21–22    243
   1341b40    5n23
   1342a7–17    237
   1342b1–12    243

[Aristotle]
*Problems*
   919b27–37    237
   922b26    5

Athenaeus
*Deipnosophistae*
   10.453d–e    53n109
   14.631c5    26n10
   14.629f    182

Bacchylides
   3.98    160
   13.84–90    71
   17.101–8    31–32, 67, 198

Catullus
   64.338–70    219n112

Euripides
*Aeolus*
   fr. 25.2–3    209
*Alcestis*
   569–87    55–56

INDEX LOCORUM 279

Euripides *(continued)*
*Alexander*
  frr. 41a–62i                        104
*Andromache*
  103–16                               61
*Andromeda*
  frr. 114–22                          61
  frr. 116–17                     152–53
  frr. 117–120                    66n24
  fr. 122                             66n24
*Antiope*
  fr. 182a                           61n6
  fr. 223.90–95                 106n28
*Bacchae*
  21–22                              241
  61                                 241–42
  114                                242
  127–28                             242
  160                                120
  526                                242
  591                                243
  595                                243
  600–603                        243–44
*Children of Heracles*
  777–83                              54
  892–93                              54
*Cresphontes*
  fr. 448a.82–86           144n17, 162
*Electra*
  43–44                                69
  98–99                                69
  112–13 (=127–28)               62
  115–19                           63–64
  125                                64
  125–26                             62
  150                                62
  151–56                             64
  167–73                             65
  173–74                             69
  175–89                          66–69
  178                                68
  179                                69
  180                                68
  195–96                             69
  432–41                             110
  432–51                           77–85
  432–86             10–11, 75–91
  434–37                    79–84, 181
  438                                84
  439                                84
  442                                198
  451                         84, 196
  452–86                     85–91
  455                             87
  458                             87
  464–68                  87–89, 95
  469                           89, 90
  471–74                            89
  477                           89–90
  478–86                           222
  480–81                            90
  485–86                            90
  585–95                            70
  699–726                      91–94
  699–746          75–77, 91–96
  702                             93
  703                             93
  712                             93
  716–17                            93
  720                             94
  727–36                         94–95
  737–46                         95–97
  745–46                         90, 96
  747–60                            97
  824–25                          71n46
  854–55                          71n46
  860–65                         70, 71
  866–72                     70, 71–72
  874–78                     70, 72–73
  1147–64                  75, 97–98
  1151–54                            97
  1163                            86
  1165–67                            97
  1168–70                            97
  1177–237                          73
  1198–200                     69–70
  1204–5                        73, 74
  1221–23                           86
  1226                            74
  1233–37                            75
  1249                            70
  1292–356                           75
  1325–26                           75
*Hecuba*
  59–89                             61
  444–83                         57n117
  916–17                          119–20
*Helen*
  19–21                             142
  164–66                       63, 146–47
  165                             154
  167–78            144–45, 147–56

280  INDEX LOCORUM

| | | | |
|---|---|---|---|
| 167–251 | 61, 65 | 1452–53 | 182 |
| 168 | 152 | 1454–55 | 17, 78–79, 181–82 |
| 170 | 188 | 1461 | 182 |
| 171a–b | 154–55, 212n89 | 1465–77 | 159, 182–84 |
| 172 | 166 | 1467–69 | 183–84 |
| 172–73 | 159 | 1471–75 | 184 |
| 173 | 148 | 1478–94 | 56, 87–88, 161, 184–87 |
| 174a | 163 | 1487–88 | 186–87 |
| 174a–b | 159 | 1495 | 188 |
| 174b | 166 | 1495–511 | 187–89 |
| 174b–78 | 147–48 | 1498–99 | 188 |
| 179–90 | 148–50 | 1516 | 144 |
| 184–85 | 106 | 1589–610 | 151 |
| 185 | 149 | 1642–79 | 188 |
| 191–228 | 148 | 1666–69 | 179, 189 |
| 195 | 149–50 | *Heracles* | |
| 211 | 149 | 636–700 | 19 |
| 245–49 | 150 | 673–86 | 72n47 |
| 262–63 | 179 | 680–94 | 126 |
| 375–85 | 144 | 692–94 | 64n20 |
| 541–42 | 150 | 781–97 | 17 |
| 618 | 144 | 875–905 | 192n3 |
| 633 | 144 | 1042–44 | 192n3 |
| 1107–21 | 17, 158–67 | *Hippolytus* | |
| 1107–64 | 144–45 | 732–51 | 56, 185 |
| 1108–9 | 163–64 | 752–63 | 56–57 |
| 1109a–10 | 112 | *Hypsipyle* | |
| 1110 | 163 | fr. 752f | 61n6, 202 |
| 1111 | 163, 165–67 | fr. 752g | 202–3 |
| 1112 | 159, 163–64, 165–66 | fr. 752h | 61n6 |
| 1114–15 | 164 | *Ion* | |
| 1231–35 | 151 | 82–183 | 61n6, 62 |
| 1301–2 | 170 | 184–218 | 195n17 |
| 1301–18 | 169–73 | 1074–86 | 201–2 |
| 1301–68 | 11, 34, 167–79 | 1078–79 | 88 |
| 1304–5 | 170, 175 | *Iphigenia in Aulis* | |
| 1308–9 | 170–72 | 171 | 194 |
| 1312–14 | 152 | 189–92 | 194–95 |
| 1314 | 170 | 206–7 | 196–97 |
| 1319–37 | 173 | 206–41 | 195–201 |
| 1338–52 | 173–76 | 212 | 196–97 |
| 1340–41 | 174 | 215 | 197 |
| 1346–47 | 174–75 | 216–30 | 198 |
| 1350–52 | 175–76 | 231–41 | 198–201 |
| 1353–68 | 176–79 | 232 | 198–99 |
| 1359–61 | 177 | 234 | 200–201 |
| 1362–63 | 177–78 | 239–41 | 67, 198–99 |
| 1364 | 177 | 247–60 | 199 |
| 1365 | 171 | 275–76 | 199 |
| 1368 | 178–79 | 435–39 | 216–17 |
| 1451–64 | 110, 144, 180–82 | 543–606 | 204–10 |
| 1451–511 | 179–90 | 573–78 | 205–10 |

Euripides, *Iphigenia in Aulis (continued)*

| | | | |
|---|---|---|---|
| 573–81 | 17 | 393–466 | 78–79 |
| 575 | 206n61 | 1123–52 | 180 |
| 576 | 207–8 | 1123–36 | 42, 182 |
| 576–78 | 92 | 1137–46 | 29–30 |
| 577–78 | 207–10 | 1138–52 | 88 |
| 585–87 | 205 | *Medea* | |
| 712 | 200–201 | 96–167 | 6n6 |
| 751–800 | 204 | 195–97 | 53 |
| 814 | 193n7 | 410–28 | 53 |
| 1036–57 | 211–17 | *Palamedes* | |
| 1036–97 | 18, 19, 204–5, 211–24 | frr. 578–89 | 104–5 |
| 1038 | 223 | fr. 580 | 104n22 |
| 1040 | 222 | fr. 586 | 122–23 |
| 1042 | 213 | fr. 588 | 104–5 |
| 1045 | 213 | *Phaethon* | |
| 1049–53 | 213 | fr. 773 | 162–63 |
| 1054 | 214 | *Phoenician Women* | |
| 1055–57 | 80, 198, 214 | 88–192 | 194n14 |
| 1058 | 222 | 203 | 73n50 |
| 1058–66 | 217–21 | 234–36 | 73n50 |
| 1064–65 | 221 | 1514 | 163n96 |
| 1068–75 | 218–21 | *Suppliants* | |
| 1076–79 | 217, 221 | 71–72 | 154n62 |
| 1080–81 | 222 | *Trojan Women* | |
| 1080–88 | 221–23 | 2–3 | 107 |
| 1211 | 224 | 25–27 | 105 |
| 1259–60 | 203 | 28–29 | 107 |
| 1279–335 | 205, 224 | 98–234 | 61 |
| 1291–93 | 206, 223 | 115–21 | 107–8 |
| 1341 | 200 | 121 | 107–8, 141 |
| 1345–53 | 193n6 | 122–37 | 109–11 |
| 1352 | 203n51 | 126–27 | 110–11 |
| 1374–401 | 228 | 143 | 121 |
| 1378 | 203 | 143–52 | 111–13 |
| 1467–69 | 225 | 144 | 121n76 |
| 1467–531 | 225–31 | 146 | 112–13 |
| 1475–76 | 203n52 | 146–52 | 73 |
| 1475–79 | 225 | 151–52 | 120 |
| 1475–509 | 226–31 | 167–73 | 114 |
| 1477–79 | 222n120 | 176–234 | 113 |
| 1480–84 | 229–30 | 279–80 | 135n112 |
| 1491–92 | 225 | 307 | 114 |
| 1493 | 226–27 | 308–41 | 113–16 |
| 1498–504 | 227 | 341–42 | 115–16 |
| 1509–31 | 204–5 | 342 | 114 |
| 1510–12 | 203–4 | 353–443 | 116 |
| 1510–13 | 227 | 370–74 | 156 |
| 1510–32 | 225–31 | 444–61 | 116 |
| 1577 | 204 | 466–510 | 116 |
| *Iphigenia in Tauris* | | 511–67 | 116–30 |
| | | 512 | 8, 60, 102, 103, 123–30 |
| 179 | 65n23 | 512–14 | 123–30 |

## 282    INDEX LOCORUM

| | | | |
|---|---|---|---|
| 515 | 129 | 24.761 | 63 |
| 544–45 | 120, 122 | 24.761–76 | 140 |
| 546–47 | 121, 122 | *Odyssey* | |
| 551–55 | 121 | 4.277–79 | 140 |
| 555–56 | 122 | 4.280–89 | 140 |
| 565–66 | 124 | 6.85–109 | 150 |
| 577–606 | 128 | 6.99–109 | 69 |
| 625–97 | 157 | 9.395 | 132 |
| 778–79 | 121 | 12.39–54 | 153 |
| 782–89 | 103 | 12.165–200 | 153 |
| 799–808 | 130–31 | 12.191 | 150–51 |
| 814–19 | 131–32 | 19.521 | 159n76, 160n77 |
| 826–32 | 132–33 | 24.58–62 | 220 |
| 841 | 131 | | |
| 886 | 105 | *Homeric Hymns* | |
| 1060–80 | 133 | *Hymn to Apollo* (3) | |
| 1071–72 | 104, 105 | 103–4 | 68 |
| 1089–92 | 102, 133–34 | 161–62 | 140 |
| 1089–99 | 102 | 163–64 | 237 |
| 1215–38 | 134 | *Hymn to Demeter* (2) | |
| 1226–37 | 63, 134–35 | 202–5 | 175n131 |
| 1230 | 133 | *Hymn to Dionysus* (7) | |
| 1242–45 | 125 | 48–53 | 79 |
| 1251–59 | 135 | *Hymn to the Dioskouroi* (17) | |
| 1287–301 | 135 | 12–13 | 188–89 |
| 1287–332 | 63 | *Homeric Hymn to Hermes* (4) | |
| 1301–10 | 135–36 | 511–12 | 207 |
| 1306 | 41 | *Homeric Hymn to the Mother of* | |
| 1325–32 | 136–37 | *the Gods* (14) | |
| | | 1–5 | 172 |
| Herodotus | | | |
| 1.23–24 | 79 | Horace | |
| | | *Odes* | |
| Hesiod | | 37.1–2 | 127n95 |
| *Theogony* | | | |
| 42 | 132 | Iamblichus | |
| 69–70 | 132 | *Life of Pythagoras* | |
| | | 82 | 153 |
| Homer | | *Life of Sophocles* | |
| *Iliad* | | 5 | 46n82 |
| 3.54 | 123 | | |
| 6.357–58 | 125n90 | Lucian | |
| 10.12–13 | 208 | *On the Dance* | |
| 18.483–89 | 88 | 12 | 68 |
| 18.490–606 | 89 | | |
| 18.599–606 | 197 | Pherecrates | |
| 21.9–10 | 132 | fr. 155 *PCG* | 8, 10, 96 |
| 22.468–72 | 114n56 | | |
| 23.309 | 197 | Pindar | |
| 24.719–46 | 228n141 | *Isthmian Odes* | |
| 24.723 | 63 | 5.27 | 210 |
| 24.747 | 63, 112 | 8.49–52 | 219 |

INDEX LOCORUM 283

Pindar *(continued)*
*Nemean Odes*
| 5.22–26 | 18 |
| 5.23 | 31, 213 |

*Olympian Odes*
| 3.1–10 | 189 |
| 3. 33–41 | 189 |
| 7.12 | 210 |
| 8.30–46 | 131n100 |
| 9.1–4 | 72n47 |

*Paean* B2.102–8 Rutherford = 8.65–71 SM   34–35

*Pythian Odes*
| 1.1–4 | 18 |
| 3.16–19 | 114–15 |
| 3.89–90 | 213 |
| 12.19 | 210 |
| 12.21 | 33, 209 |
| 12.24 | 33 |

fr. 70b SM
| 8–14 | 35–36 |

fr. 94b SM
| 8–17 | 33, 150–51, 209 |
| 34–35 | 151 |

fr. 140 SM
| 11–17 | 30–31 |

fr. 107a SM   26

Plato
*Alcibiades*
| 108c7–8 | 25 |

*Laws*
| 654b3–4 | 25 |
| 669c3–5 | 229 |
| 669c3–670a3 | 13 |
| 669c8–d2 | 172, 239 |
| 700d3–9 | 125, 209, 229 |
| 795e1–2 | 25n8 |
| 816a5 | 25 |
| 817b2–5 | 3 |

*Republic*
| 397a3–7 | 172–73 |
| 397b1–2 | 239 |
| 399d3–6 | 210 |
| 616c4–17d1 | 88–89 |
| 617b4–7 | 153 |

*Timaeus*
| 40b4–d1 | 88–89 |

Pliny
*Natural History*
| 10.81 | 159–60n76, 160n77 |
| 10.82 | 167n106 |

Plutarch
*Solon*
| 21.4–5 | 102 |

*Moralia*
| 748a3–10 | 25–26 |

Pratinas
| *TrGF* I, 4 F 3 | 37–38, 239 |

Sappho
fr. 2 Voigt
| 14 | 213n91 |

fr. 44 Voigt
| 24–27 | 34, 212n89, 215–16 |

fr. 58 Voigt (with *P.Köln*
| 21351, 21376) | 108 |
| fr. 103 Voigt | 213n90 |
| fr. 123 Voigt | 213n90 |
| fr. 128 Voigt | 213n90 |
| fr. 136 Voigt | 160 |

Scholia to Aristophanes, *Clouds* 595   124n88

Scholia to Homer, *Odyssey* 12.168   151n40

Shakespeare
*Coriolanus*
| 5.4.49–52 | 16 |

Sophocles
*Ajax*
| 622–34 | 160 |
| 693–718 | 47–48 |
| 693–705 | 48–49 |

*Antigone*
| 1146–48 | 88 |
| 1146–52 | 51–52 |

*Electra*
| 86–250 | 61 |
| 88 | 61 |
| 103–4 | 64 |

*Inachus*
| fr. 269c | 37 |

*Mysians*
| fr. 412 | 46 |

*Oedipus Tyrannus*
| 896 | 106 |

*Thamyras*
| fr. 238 | 47 |
| frr. 240–41 | 47 |
| frr. 244–45 | 47 |

*Women of Trachis*
| | |
|---|---|
| 205–24 | 49–50, 229 |
| 498–530 | 52n106 |
| 640–42 | 50 |
| 963 | 50 |
| 967–68 | 50 |
| fr. 768 | 46 |
| fr. 861 | 152n49 |

Stesichorus
| | |
|---|---|
| fr. 192 *PMGF* | 143n15 |

Theocritus
*Idyll* 18
| | |
|---|---|
| 35–37 | 141 |

Thucydides
| | |
|---|---|
| 2.34 | 102n14 |
| 5.84 | 101n6 |
| 5.114–16 | 101n6 |
| 6.32 | 228 |

Timotheus
| | |
|---|---|
| fr. 791 *PMG* | 240 |
| 196–201 | 111, 240n23 |
| 202–3 | 240n23 |
| 205 | 111 |
| fr. 796 *PMG* | 123 |

www.ingramcontent.com/pod-product-compliance
Lightning Source LLC
Chambersburg PA
CBHW030526230426
43665CB00010B/785